ENVIRONMENTAL RISKS

• • • • • • • • • • • • • • • • • • • •

IN REAL ESTATE

• • • • • • • • • • • • • • • • • •

TRANSACTIONS

• • • • • • • • • • • • • • • • • • •

A Practical Guide

• • • • • • • • • • • • • • • • • •

Second Edition

Donald C. Nanney
of Baker & Hostetler, McCutchen Black

McGraw-Hill, Inc.
New York St. Louis San Francisco Auckland Bogotá
Caracas Lisbon London Madrid Mexico Milan
Montreal New Delhi Paris San Juan São Paulo
Singapore Sydney Tokyo Toronto

Executive Enterprises Publications Co., Inc.,
New York, New York

1 2 3 4 5 6 7 8 9 0   DOC/DOC   9 8 7 6 5 4 3 2

ISBN   0-07-046000-0

The sponsoring editor for this book was Gail F. Nalven, and the production supervisor was Thomas G. Kowalczyk.

Printed and bound by R. R. Donnelley & Sons Company.

PREFACE

Newspapers report almost daily on threats to human health and the environment from hazardous wastes polluting the water, land and air. Those wastes have accumulated during decades of ignorance or disregard of health consequences. Our continued production of pollution far exceeds our ability to dispose of it in safe ways. This problem has become international in scope, as acid rain falls across borders and chlorofluorocarbons (CFCs) attack the protective ozone layer high above the earth.

Along with the increase in media coverage and growing public consciousness of environmental concerns, the federal, state and local governments have enacted numerous environmental laws and regulations, particularly since 1976. Environmental law has emerged as a specialty area in order to cope with the volume and complexity of environmental regulation. Real estate professionals such as developers, landlords, lenders, brokers and lawyers, should appreciate the important impact of environmental laws in connection with real property purchase, sale, leasing and lending transactions, and in the development of real property. This book is written to introduce real estate professionals to this growing area of the law and the potential for liability, with primary focus on hazardous waste issues (Part I); the impact of such environmental laws on the various participants to a real estate transaction (Part II); and the practical methods which have been developed so far to deal with environmental risks in real estate transactions (Part III).

This book is intended to provide an overview of the field from the practical perspective of real estate professionals who must deal with these issues in actual situations. It is not a comprehensive legal treatise on environmental law. While citations to relevant laws and authorities are included to enhance the usefulness of the materials, more detailed books or legal articles are available for any given issue. Thus, this book is a practical reference guide for use by real estate professionals.

With respect to the coverage of state laws in this book, there is an unavoidable bias in favor of references to California law in some sections as the author practices in California and is most familiar with its laws.

iii

However, a significant effort has been made to survey the laws of a number of other states as well. The potential environmental liabilities are similar in many states, and the federal environmental laws are uniform. Thus, those laws should have much the same impact, and the methods discussed in this book for investigating and allocating environmental risks should be relevant everywhere across the country. Nevertheless, it is prudent in all cases for real estate professionals to obtain the advice of qualified counsel and experts in the state where a property is located.

While the legal references in this book are believed to be accurate at the time of writing, it is necessary in any transaction to obtain the up-to-date advice of counsel and consultants. There are almost daily developments and changes in environmental laws and regulations, and there is an explosion in litigation and court interpretations of such matters.

This book must of necessity speak in general terms, out of the context of any particular transaction. Thus, this book does not purport to state how any transaction or kind of transaction should be handled. Rather, it provides the general principles, the building blocks, which are used in approaching environmental issues. The use of the building blocks in any particular case will require the exercise of judgment under the specific facts and the applicable law, as affected by the relative bargaining power and business motivations of the parties. It is the author's hope that the reader will gain an appreciation for the complexity and rapidly developing nature of the field, and will seek the assistance of expert environmental consultants and legal counsel when appropriate so that mistakes in judgment can be avoided.

Donald C. Nanney
October 1989

The rapid development of environmental law has continued, and enforcement efforts by governmental agencies have increased, since this book was originally written. Significant portions of the book have been revised to reflect such developments.

Donald C. Nanney
March 1992

iv

ABOUT THE AUTHORS

DONALD C. NANNEY is a partner of the Los Angeles, California, office of the national law firm of BAKER & HOSTETLER, McCUTCHEN BLACK, practicing in the areas of real property, business and environmental law. Mr. Nanney has an A.B. degree, with distinction, from Stanford University (1971), and a Juris Doctor degree from U.C. Davis School of Law (1974). Before entering private practice in 1979, Mr. Nanney served as a Captain in the Office of The Judge Advocate General, Department of the Army, Pentagon, Washington, D.C.

Mr. Nanney has appeared frequently as a speaker for the California Continuing Education of the Bar, the Los Angeles County Bar Association, and other professional groups on the subject of real property law and the impact of environmental laws on real property transactions and ownership. Mr. Nanney is a coauthor of the *California Environmental Law Handbook*, Government Institutes, Inc. (3d Ed., 1989, through 6th Ed., 1992). He is also the author of numerous articles, including "Hazardous Waste Issues in Real Property Transactions," Course Materials, California Continuing Education of the Bar (1988 through 1991), which provides the basis for some of the materials in this book.

Mr. Nanney would like to give special thanks to **Ronald D. Miller** who contributed Chapter 16, "Environmental Assessments and Audits." Mr. Miller currently serves as Vice-President of VISTA ENVIRONMENTAL INFORMATION, INC., located in San Diego, California. VISTA is an information service bureau that produces reports compiled from government lists of toxic waste sites, landfills, leaking underground tanks, and the like, in a computer generated map format as well as "on-line."

Previously, Mr. Miller practiced environmental and real estate law in Detroit, Michigan. He has consulted with real estate trade groups, lenders and the U.S. Department of Justice in the development of environmental due diligence policies and speaks regularly for groups of attorneys, environmental consultants and lenders. He is an instructor for environmental courses at the University of California, the National Water Well Association, the American Bankers Association, and currently chairs two committees for the American Society of Testing and Materials (ASTM) Site Assessment standardization process. Further, Mr. Miller is on the board of contributing editors for Shepard's California Environmental Law and Regulation Reporter. Mr. Miller has also served as a legislative intern to the U.S. Senate and the British House of Commons. He is a graduate of Michigan State University and the University of Detroit School of Law.

Mr. Miller has numerous previous publications including: "Tracking Environmental Risk," *New York Times* (April 28, 1991); "Excavating the File Cabinets -- Digging Through Government Records Can Unearth a Wealth of Information," *Soils Magazine* (Sept. and Oct. 1991); "In Defense of 'Innocent' Lenders and Buyers," *HAZMAT World* (March 1991); "Due Diligence Techniques for the Innocent Purchaser/Lender," *Toxics Law Reporter* (Aug. 31, 1988); "Environmental Risk in Real Estate Transactions: Due Diligence in the Secondary Market," *BNA's Banking Report* (Nov. 17, 1988); and many others. **Eileen Jarvis** and **Stacy Harper** assisted Mr. Miller in the preparation of Chapter 16.

Special thanks are also due to **Paul A. Quintiliani**, MAI, who contributed Chapter 15, "Appraisal and Valuation of Environmentally Impaired Real Estate." Mr. Quintiliani is a partner in the Southern California appraisal company COHEN, KERHART, QUINTILIANI. He has a Bachelor of Arts from University of California, San Diego, and graduated with high honors (1984). More recently, Mr. Quintiliani was awarded membership to the Appraisal Institute and holds the designation MAI.

Mr. Quintiliani has performed numerous commercial and industrial appraisals related to litigation, asset sales, asset evaluation, collateralization, and assessment district formations. In recent years, Mr. Quintiliani has conducted a number of appraisals on environmentally impaired properties, as well as consulting assignments on such special use properties as high level nuclear waste disposal facilities. Mr. Quintiliani has experience analyzing the financial implications of environmental contamination and has conducted extensive research into the value implications of contaminated properties after remediation. Mr. Quintiliani is an active member of the Appraisal Institute and currently serves on the Finance Committee of the national organization. He is also a member of the Southern California Appraisal Institute's Government Relations committee.

Chapter 23 "Bankruptcy" was originally written by **Janet S. Hoffman**, a partner with Baker & Hostetler, McCutchen Black, Los Angeles, California. Chapter 23 has been updated by **Dean G. Rallis, Jr.** who is a partner with Baker & Hostetler, McCutchen Black and leads the bankruptcy practice group in the Los Angeles office of that firm.

Mr. Nanney would, in addition, like to acknowledge the assistance of the following persons in the research and preparation of materials for the original writing of this book (including name and association at that time): **Mary L. Chapman** (associate attorney, Baker & Hostetler, McCutchen Black, Houston, Texas); **Megan Sheridan** (associate attorney, Baker & Hostetler, McCutchen Black, Los Angeles, California); **Barry Bookbinder** (law student, Loyola Law School, Los Angeles, California); **Mary T. Ellmann** (law student, Boalt Hall School of Law, Berkeley, California); **Charles I. Karlin** (law student, Southwestern University School of Law, Los Angeles, California); **Martin J. McTigue, Jr.** (law student, Southwestern University School of Law, Los Angeles, California); **Brooke K. Robertson** (law student, Boston University School of Law, Boston, Massachusetts); and **Fay Marie Playsted** (legal assistant, Baker & Hostetler, McCutchen Black, Los Angeles, California);

Mr. Nanney also wishes to thank those who assisted him in the preparation of the original version of "Hazardous Waste Issues in Real Property Transactions," and thereby indirectly assisted in the preparation of this book: **Bret V. Hannifin** (associate attorney, Riordan & McKinzie, Los Angeles, California); **Lori A. Hochman** (Director of Studio Legal Affairs, Universal City Studios, Inc., Universal City, California).

Finally, wife **Barbara** and stepdaughter **Samantha** constantly encouraged Mr. Nanney to finish writing this book instead of watching sporting events.

Note: Any views expressed in this book are the personal views of the author writing the same and are not necessarily the views of the law firm or company with whom that author is associated.

SUMMARY OF CONTENTS

TABLE OF CONTENTS

PART I   ENVIRONMENTAL LAWS AFFECTING REAL ESTATE TRANSACTIONS

Chapter One   Federal and State Superfund Laws

GLOSSARY OF SELECTED ENVIRONMENTAL ACRONYMS

ACRONYM	REFERENCE
ACM	Asbestos-Containing Material.
AHERA	Asbestos Hazard Emergency Response Act of 1986, 15 U.S.C. §§ 2643 *et seq.* (A part of TSCA, AHERA imposes controls and reporting requirements respecting the generation, handling and disposal of asbestos, and regulates asbestos in schools.)
CAA	Clean Air Act, 42 U.S.C. §§ 7401 *et seq.* (Controls the release of hazardous air pollutions, such as asbestos, from both stationary and mobile sources.)
CAL. SUPERFUND	Carpenter-Presley-Tanner Hazardous Substance Account Act, California Health & Safety Code §§ 25300 *et seq.* (California counterpart to CERCLA, California Superfund authorizes cleanup and cleanup cost recovery for sites contaminated by hazardous wastes.)
CERCLA	Comprehensive Environmental Response, Compensation and Liability Act of 1980, 42 U.S.C. §§ 9601 *et seq.* (Authorizes cleanup and cleanup cost recovery for sites contaminated by hazardous wastes.)
CERCLA LIEN	A response and cleanup cost recovery lien under CERCLA which has regular lien priority (not a superlien).
CERCLIS	The EPA's Comprehensive Environmental Response Compensation and Liability Information System of properties considered for the NPL.

CEQA	**California Environmental Quality Act**, Public Resources Code §§ 21000 *et seq.* (California counterpart to NEPA, CEQA authorizes environmental impact review of development projects proposed to be carried out or approved by public agencies.)
CGL	**Comprehensive General Liability Insurance.**
CWA	**Clean Water Act**, 33 U.S.C. §§ 1251 *et seq.* (Controls the discharge or threatened discharge of pollutants into navigable waters of the United States.)
ECRA	**Environmental Cleanup Responsibility Act**, N.J. Rev. Stat. §§ 13:1K-6 *et seq.* (New Jersey's transaction-triggered law for the assessment and cleanup of contaminated industrial real property.)
EIL	**Environmental Impairment Liability Insurance.**
EPA	**U.S. Environmental Protection Agency**, the federal agency which administers CERCLA and other federal environmental laws.
FIFRA	**Federal Insecticide, Fungicide and Rodenticide Act**, 7 U.S.C. §§ 136 *et seq.* (Provides for the registration of pesticides and regulates their use, importation, transportation and disposal.)
HWCL	**Hazardous Waste Control Law**, California Health & Safety Code §§ 25100 *et seq.* (California counterpart to RCRA, HWCL provides "cradle to grave" system for controlling hazardous wastes.)
HRS	**Hazard Rating System** for ranking the relative cleanup priority of properties on the CERCLIS list and the NPL.
NCP	**National Contingency Plan** (Provides guidelines for all aspects of site

investigation, evaluation and remediation, including priorities for allocating federal Superfund resources).

NEPA   **National Environmental Policy Act**, 42 U.S.C. §§ 4321 *et seq.* (Authorizes environmental impact review of federal, state, local and federally authorized development projects.)

NPL   The **National Priorities List** includes federal Superfund sites identified as high priority for cleanup pursuant to the Hazard Rating System.

OSHA   **Occupational Safety and Health Act**, 29 U.S.C. §§ 651 *et seq.* (Provides controls for occupational exposure to hazardous substances, such as asbestos.)

PCBs   **Polychlorinated byphenyls.**

PORTER-COLOGNE ACT   **Porter-Cologne Water Quality Control Act**, California Water Code §§ 13000 *et seq.* (California counterpart to CWA, the Porter-Cologne Act controls the discharge or threatened discharge of pollutants which could potentially affect water quality.)

PRP   **"Potentially Responsible Party,"** i.e. one of the categories of persons identified in CERCLA or state Superfund laws as potentially liable for cleanup costs.

PROPOSITION 65   **Safe Drinking Water and Toxic Enforcement Act of 1986**, California Health & Safety Code §§ 25249.5 *et seq.* (Prohibits discharge of certain chemicals into potential sources of drinking water, and requires warnings to be given when exposure to such chemicals is anticipated.)

RCRA   **Resource Conservation and Recovery Act of 1976**, 42 U.S.C. §§ 6901 *et seq.* (Establishes a generation to disposal, "cradle to grave," system for controlling hazardous wastes.)

SARA   **Superfund Amendments and Reauthorization Act of 1986**, Pub.L. 99-499, 100 Stat. 1617 (October 17, 1986). (Amended and reauthorized CERCLA, 42 U.S.C. §§ 9601 *et seq.*)

SUPERFUND   The federal **Hazardous Substance Superfund** established pursuant to CERCLA, and similar funds under state laws. Also the common name for CERCLA and state analogues.

SUPERLIEN   A response and cleanup cost recovery lien which, under the laws of some states, gains priority over some or all preexisting liens of other creditors.

TSCA   **Toxic Substances Control Act**, 15 U.S.C. §§ 2601 *et seq.* (Provides for federal control of testing, manufacture, processing and distribution of certain chemical substances, such as asbestos.)

UFLRA   **Uniform Federal Lien Registration Act** (Adopted by many states, UFLRA designates the place for filing of federal liens, including CERCLA Liens).

UST   **Underground storage tank.**

PART I

ENVIRONMENTAL LAWS AFFECTING
REAL ESTATE TRANSACTIONS

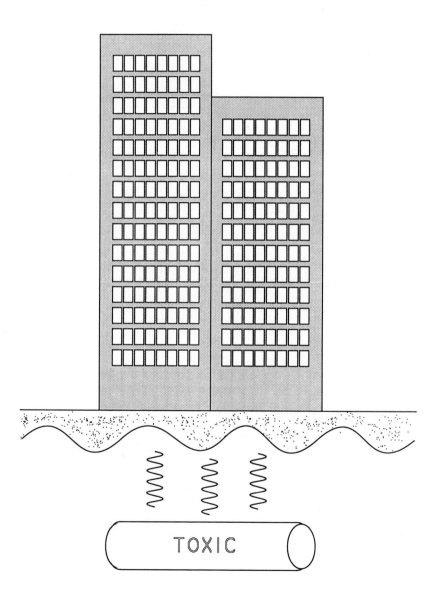

CHAPTER ONE

FEDERAL AND STATE SUPERFUND LAWS

1.1   Introduction

Part I highlights the environmental laws which have been enacted in recent years, as an essential background for the discussions to follow. Part II summarizes the impact of these new laws on real estate transactions and the value of contaminated real estate. The possibility of turning environmental problems into profit opportunities in some cases is also mentioned. Part III sets forth the techniques available to gain some extent of protection against environmental liabilities.

Chapter 1 covers the federal and state Superfund laws which have revolutionized the risks associated with the ownership and operation of real estate. It is chiefly the Superfund laws which have made environmental matters a key issue for negotiation in real estate transactions today. Even though the federal Superfund law was enacted in 1980, it took several years for the impact to be felt by real estate professionals handling day-to-day real estate transactions. A number of court rulings interpreting and applying the Superfund laws have raised the level of appreciation for the significant liabilities awaiting the unwary and even the innocent. The potential for liability on the part of persons completely innocent of causing pollution is perhaps the most astonishing aspect of the Superfund laws. It is therefore appropriate to start our discussion with those laws.

The following summary of the Superfund laws will focus on selected issues of most relevance to the parties to real estate transactions. Those issues include: (i) the nature of the liability posed by the Superfund laws, (ii) who the potentially liable parties are, (iii) what the standard of liability is, (iv) what defenses are available, and (v) what right of action exists against other responsible parties. Chapter 2 discusses the cleanup cost recovery liens which can be imposed under the Superfund laws. We will leave the rest of the technical aspects of the Superfund laws to the environmental professionals.

1.2   Federal Superfund Law

The federal *Superfund* law is the Comprehensive Environmental Response, Compensation and Liability Act of 1980 (CERCLA), as amended by the Superfund Amendments and Reauthorization Act of 1986 (SARA).[1]

---

[1]   42 U.S.C. § 9601 et seq.

4

1.2.1   Funding for Cleanups; Cost Recovery

CERCLA authorizes the federal government to respond to the release or threatened release of hazardous substances[2] and establishes the Hazardous Substance Superfund to finance the government's response activities.[3] CERCLA originally authorized $1.6 billion during the law's first five years. SARA reauthorized funding in the amount of $8.5 billion for a five year period,[4] which has been extended. Another reauthorization will be required in the future.

The federal government may order "potentially responsible parties" (PRPs) to remedy a hazardous waste problem, or if those persons refuse or have not been identified, the government may take remedial action and sue the PRPs for reimbursement. Those recoveries are used to replenish the Superfund.

The scope of liability imposed on PRPs under CERCLA is quite broad. PRPs are liable for all response or remedial action costs (with interest) incurred by the United States government, a state, or any other person (which can run into many millions of dollars), *plus* damages of up to $50,000,000 for injury to natural resources.[5] PRPs who refuse to take remedial actions ordered by the government are also liable for punitive damages of up to three times the actual costs incurred by the government[6] Compounding the extent of liability under CERCLA, civil penalties of up to $25,000 per violation may be assessed for designated violations, including failure or refusal to comply with abatement orders, and some of those penalties may be assessed for each day during which the violation continues.[7] Thus, the scope of liability under CERCLA can be staggering.

CERCLA also enables the government to record a lien upon the real property which is "subject to or affected by a removal or remedial action," and the lien is for the amount of "all costs and damages for

---

2   *Id.*, § 9604.

3   26 U.S.C. § 9507(a); 42 U.S.C.A. § 9611.

4   42 U.S.C. § 9611(a).

5   *Id.*, §§ 9607(a)(4) and (c)(1)(D).

6   *Id.*, § 9607(c)(3).

7   *Id.*, §§ 9606(b)(1) and 9609(a) and (b).

which a person is liable to the United States."[8]   Cost recovery liens under CERCLA are discussed in Chapter 2.

Despite the government's authority to pay for the cleanup and then pursue cost recovery, the available funding is woefully inadequate to cover the anticipated cost of necessary cleanup of hazardous waste sites throughout the country. A recent research report from the University of Tennessee Waste Management Research and Education Institute estimated that it will cost $752 billion under current standards to clean up known hazardous waste sites in the United States, although that amount could range from $484 billion to $1.177 trillion if cleanup standards are relaxed or made more stringent. Given that range of estimated cost, at the present rate of actual federal Superfund expenditures (i.e., $10 billion appropriated by Congress so far; $7.5 billion authorized by EPA for expenditure; but only $4.8 billion actually spent in the 12 years since 1980), it would take from 1,210 to 2,940 years to clean up the known sites. The picture is not improved very much when scarce state resources are also thrown into the equation. In all likelihood. the dimensions of the problem will mushroom and the costs will increase. In an age of budgetary constraints, sufficient governmental financing is not available for the task, and the time frame involved at available levels of funding is unacceptable.

As a result, the government must shift the cleanup cost burden to private parties. CERCLA does that in the first instance by identifying several categories of PRPs, including parties innocent of participation in the disposal of hazardous waste (see § 1.2.3), and by providing the government with both injunctive and cost recovery powers. The question then becomes one of enforcement strategy. Until recently, the federal Environmental Protection Agency (EPA), which administers CERCLA, was willing to undertake cleanup activities and then to pursue cost recovery. The EPA has in the past rarely enforced cleanup orders. That approach has proven to be slow and ineffective, and, as indicated, the Superfund is insufficient.   Accordingly, in June 1989, the Administrator of the EPA announced a change in enforcement strategy. The emphasis under that strategy is on the issuance of enforcement orders requiring cleanup action by PRPs at their own expense. In that

---

[8]   *Id.*, § 9607(l)(1).

vein, the EPA has demanded that 31 companies located in the vicinity of Burbank, California, provide over $70 million for the construction of a water treatment system to clean up chemical solvent contamination in the groundwater underlying a vast region of the eastern end of the San Fernando Valley, and several of those parties have entered into settlements providing for the implementation of that project at private party expense.

Superfund resources may be expended if no PRP is responsive or if emergency conditions require it. But in general the EPA will be pursuing PRPs with greater intensity to undertake the cleanup before the EPA will resort to the Superfund. The threat of punitive damages of three times the Superfund expenditure, and civil penalties of up to $25,000 per day, should motivate compliance with EPA cleanup orders.

CERCLA allows a person who has been ordered to abate a site to recover reimbursement from the Superfund for the reasonable costs of the required response *if* that person proves that he is not a responsible party under the statute or that the government's selection of the response action ordered was arbitrary or capricious.[9] In view of this provision, it is unclear from CERCLA whether a person who is not responsible but has been served with a cleanup order may defend against the erroneous order or must comply with the order and then seek cost recovery from the Superfund. In either case a person who receives a cleanup order from the EPA faces great expense and coercion

Even the threat of a cleanup order can have coercive effect. In the Burbank case, *only one* of the 31 companies has yet been confirmed as having actually caused or contributed to the groundwater contamination, but the EPA has made its demands nonetheless. The threat of formal cleanup orders, which might follow the demand, has resulted in several companies entering into settlements with the EPA, including the one bona fide PRP and others without any established connection with the contamination. This raises disturbing implications about the power of the EPA to issue demands and to threaten cleanup orders against

---

9   *Id.*, § 9606(b)(2) This provision does not apply if the cleanup order was given prior to the enactment of that section as a part of SARA on October 17, 1986, even if the cleanup process was completed after that date. *Wagner Seed Co. v Bush*, 946 F.2d 918 (D.C. Cir. 1991).

persons whose connection with the contamination is weak or nonexistent in order to induce settlements and avoid Superfund expenditures. As the pressure increases on the EPA to make progress on its mission and yet to preserve the Superfund, the risk of abuse of power also increases.

1.2.2 Cleanup of Hazardous Substance Releases

The applicability of CERCLA is triggered by the release or threatened release of any hazardous substance. It is therefore important to have at least a basic understanding of what substances are "hazardous" and what constitutes a "release." It is also useful to have an appreciation for the possible parameters of a cleanup process.

1.2.2-1 *Hazardous Substance*

CERCLA defines the term *hazardous substance* as meaning those substances, wastes or pollutants designated or listed under a number of other laws, including the Federal Water Pollution Control Act (i.e., the Clean Water Act), the Solid Waste Disposal Act (i.e., the Resource Conservation and Recovery Act or RCRA), the Clean Air Act, and the Toxic Substances Control Act.[10] In addition, the Administrator of the EPA has authority to designate as hazardous any "elements, compounds, mixtures, solutions, and substances which, when released into the environment may present substantial danger to the public health or welfare or the environment . . . "[11] These laws and implementing regulations provide very broad definitions or hazard criteria. Essentially, a material or substance will probably be treated as hazardous if it is, or in sufficient quantities or concentrations may be, harmful to human health or the environment due to flammability, toxicity, reactivity or corrosiveness. Some substances can be inert under certain conditions and harmful in other situations. Any hazardous substance can become a hazardous waste when, for example, it has leaked from its container or no further use is intended for it and it has been, or is to be, discarded.

The agencies administering the federal environmental laws (as well as numerous state agencies under state laws) have published lists of

---

[10]   *Id.*, § 9607(14).

[11]   *Id.*, § 9607(a).

8

substances which have been identified as hazardous.[12] Hundreds of materials and mixtures are included, many of which are contained in ordinary products. The lists are growing as additional substances are identified as meeting applicable standards or hazard criteria. These lists may be of limited utility to most real estate professionals who do not have sufficient technical backgrounds. The expert assistance of environmental consultants may be required in order to identify substances as hazardous. Such assistance is usually essential in order to determine what substances are present on or under a property, and whether any of those substances are among those already identified and listed as hazardous or may qualify as hazardous even though not yet listed.

CERCLA excludes petroleum from the definition of hazardous substance. Also excluded are natural gas, natural gas liquids, liquified natural gas, or synthetic gas usable for fuel.[13] However, these CERCLA exempted substances are or may be regulated under other environmental laws. Petroleum is regulated by the Clean Water Act and by RCRA. It is therefore often necessary to determine exactly what laws, regulations and potential liabilities are applicable to a particular substance.

For purposes of our discussion, the reader should appreciate that hazardous substances are all around us every day in many forms, and that they are often ordinary and useful materials when appropriately controlled. Thus, there is widespread risk of hazardous substance contamination when those substances are not controlled and are released into the environment. For decades since the beginning of the Industrial Revolution, proper controls have not been applied, and the accumulation of hazardous wastes and pollutants has become a worldwide problem.

1.2.2-2 *Release*

Even when a hazardous substance is present, CERCLA does not apply unless there is an actual or threatened *release*. That term includes any "spilling, leaking, pumping, pouring, emitting, emptying, discharging,

---

[12]   *See* 40 C.F.R. 302.4 for the listing of CERCLA hazardous substances and reportable quantities.

[13]   42 U.S.C. § 9601(14).

injecting, escaping, leaching, dumping, or disposing into the environment (including the abandonment or discarding of barrels, containers, and other closed receptacles containing any hazardous substance or pollutant or contaminant)."[14] However, CERCLA excludes from the definition (i) workplace exposures of employees, with respect to their claims against the employer, (ii) motor vehicle exhaust emissions, (iii) nuclear incidents subject to the requirements of the Nuclear Regulatory Commission, and (iv) the normal application of fertilizer.[15]

In addition to the statutory exclusions, it appears that the incorporation of hazardous materials into a building upon construction is not a release. It has been held that the sale of asbestos, a useful (although dangerous) product, for intended use as a construction material does not constitute a disposal or a release. Thus, the manufacturer of the asbestos was not a generator or disposer and hence not a PRP under CERCLA. A claim therefore could not be stated under CERCLA against the asbestos manufacturer. It made no difference that the asbestos later deteriorated by flaking off and posed an actual health risk.[16] Nor may a claim be stated under CERCLA against other PRPs for asbestos abatement costs; the use of asbestos in building construction is not a "disposal," and the "environment" includes the external atmosphere, not indoor air, so that entrainment of asbestos fibers into the indoor air is not a "release" (Congress did not intend to allocate liability for asbestos abatement under the CERCLA scheme).[17] But the sale of a building with knowledge that it is going to be demolished may be viewed as disposal of the asbestos in the building, so that the seller, as the owner at the time of disposal, may be liable under CERCLA for abatement costs when the asbestos is released into the outdoor environment during demolition.[18]

---

[14]   *Id.,* § 9601(22).

[15]   *Id.*

[16]   *Prudential Insurance Co. v. United States Gypsum Co.,* 711 F.Supp. 1244 (D.N.J. 1989).

[17]   *3550 Stevens Creek Associates v. Barclays Bank of California,* 915 F.2d 1355 (9th Cir. 1990), *cert. den.,* 111 S.Ct. 2014 (1991).

[18]   *CP Holdings v. Goldberg-Zoino & Associates,* 769 F. Supp. 432 (D.N.H. 1991).

The authority of the EPA to undertake response action with regard to releases from products which are part of the structure of a building and result in exposure within the building is limited to emergency situations.[19]

With those limited exceptions, the definition of release is very broad. An EPA report of releases of more than 300 carcinogenic and other hazardous substances shows that in the year 1987 alone, approximately 7 billion pounds of toxic chemicals were released into the air, land and water by manufacturing and industrial facilities in the United States, and that the figures for 1988 and 1989 were 4.5 billion and 5.7 billion pounds, respectively.[20] That data was derived from annual disclosure forms filed with the EPA under the reporting provisions of SARA Title III (the Emergency Planning and Community Right-To-Know Act of 1986) during the first three years of that program. The figures compiled through that process are a startling revelation of the scope of the ongoing problem, particularly in view of the fact that the figures are underestimates. The EPA report does not cover all hazardous substances and does not include the emissions of smaller companies which are below the "reportable quantity" thresholds established by the EPA. There are many other sources of pollution as well. At least there appears to be a downward trend in the reported numbers, hopefully reflecting beneficial results of environmental controls.

When viewed from the perspective of more than a century of industrialization, the total quantity of pollutants and toxic materials released to date is so vast that it can hardly be imagined. It is therefore clear that the jurisdictional sweep of CERCLA is considerable, and that governmental activity under CERCLA is really limited only by fiscal constraints and priorities.

1.2.2-3 The Cleanup Process

The cleanup process includes several stages, from preliminary inspection and assessment of a site, through development and implementation of a remedial action plan, and monitoring after the cleanup is completed. The time involved varies widely with the

---

[19]   42 U.S.C. §§ 9604(a)(3) and (4).

[20]   *The Toxics Release Inventory*, EPA (May 1991).

circumstances. The phases and normal time ranges are generally as follows:

	Step	Time
1.	Preliminary assessment/ site inspection (with interim measures if required)	2 months
2.	Remedial investigation re. scope of the problem	4-6 months (or years in some cases)
3.	Feasibility study re. abatement approaches, and selection of an approach	4-18 months
4.	Remedial action plan	4-6 months
5.	Remedial design phase	5-10 months
6.	Action phase (clean up until abated)	10 months to 2 years (or more in some cases)
7.	Subsequent monitoring	up to 20 years (or more in some cases).

Thus, it can take from 16 months to eight years or more to clean up and close a site, depending upon the situation. Cases of groundwater contamination are the most time consuming to clean up, often requiring many years. These phases and time ranges are according to the California Department of Health Services (now Cal-EPA), but should be fairly typical throughout the nation. The federal Superfund sites, of course, are generally the more serious ones taking the longest to remediate. The lesser sites are left to the states to handle. The potential cost of this process can be immense.

Activities under CERCLA are guided by the National Contingency Plan (NCP), which covers all aspects of site investigation, evaluation and remediation, including the establishment of priorities for allocation of Superfund resources.[21] As a part of the NCP, there is a National

---

[21]   42 U.S.C. § 9605(a); 40 C.F.R. § 300.1 *et seq.*

Priorities List (NPL) of federal Superfund sites which includes a hazard ranking system.[22] There are approximately 1,200 sites in the top priority category of the NPL out of many more thousands of sites identified under the Superfund program. Only a small fraction of those top priority sites have been completely remediated. The EPA expects the top priority category to reach 2,100, although the Congressional Office of Technology Assessment places that figure closer to 10,200. Thousands more sites are handled by state agencies. Federal resources are generally allocated on a "worst first" basis according to the procedures and priorities established by the NCP and NPL, and the states have their own procedures.

A critical issue in any cleanup is when is it completed (the "how clean is clean" question). Different parties, including any governmental agencies involved, may have diverse attitudes on that issue. Ultimately, cleanups must satisfy the regulators who have enforcement powers. But, for lack of resources, those regulators often decline involvement in private party cleanups, so that the parties and their consultants must exercise their best judgment and hope that no enforcement orders will be received in the future. Even when a governmental agency is involved with a cleanup, it is often very difficult to obtain the blessing of the agency that the cleanup is accomplished.

In sum, the cleanup process is technical, time consuming and costly, with great potential for adverse impact on real estate transactions.

1.2.3 Potentially Responsible Parties

CERCLA identifies five classes of PRPs: (1) the current owners and operators of a contaminated property, (2) the previous owners or operators at the time the hazardous substances were disposed of, (3) any intervening owners who obtained actual knowledge of the presence of the hazardous waste and failed to disclose that information upon transferring ownership of the property, (4) hazardous waste generators who arranged for the disposal of hazardous substances at the property, and (5) persons who accepted hazardous substances for transport to

---

[22]   *Id.*, § 9605(c).

facilities they selected and from which there was subsequently a release or threatened release.[23]

The list of PRPs reflects public policy that the cost of cleanup should be borne by those with a present or past connection with the contaminated property or the activity resulting in the contamination. Those PRPs are liable for the cleanup of a release from the disposal site even if the disposal was lawful at the time. The latter two categories include persons who actually were involved in the disposal of hazardous substances, and liability can be expected to follow their actual participation in the disposal. But the other categories of PRPs include persons who may have been completely innocent of any involvement in the disposal.

The first three categories of PRPs include property owners or operators who were or will be parties to real estate transactions. Moreover, others will surely succeed to their status as owners or operators (and, hence, will become PRPs) as a result of future transactions. Those persons are classified as PRPs entirely without regard to any fault or participation in the events resulting in the hazardous substance disposal or release. Their only connection is a present or past ownership or possessory interest in the contaminated land, and, in the case of intervening owners, a failure to disclose. It is the potential for liability on the part of innocent parties which gives rise to the concerns expressed in this book.

State or local governmental units have no immunity and are subject to liability under CERCLA, just like any other person, where the unit qualifies as a PRP. This issue has been decided by the United States Supreme Court.[24] The federal government may itself have liability under CERCLA. In a case arising out of the actions of the War Powers Board during World War II, *FMC Corp. v. U.S. Department of*

---

[23] The liability section of CERCLA directly identifies four categories of PRPs. 42 U.S.C. § 9607(a). However, SARA indirectly added a fifth category, listed as (3) above, in the 1986 amendment of the CERCLA definition of "contractual relationship." 42 U.S.C. § 9601(35)(C). Intervening owners were not previously identified as PRPs, and now they are PRPs only in the event of nondisclosure.

[24] *Pennsylvania v. Union Gas Company*, 109 S.Ct. 2273, 105 L.Ed.2d 1 (1989).

Commerce,[25] the former owner of a 440 acre rayon manufacturing plant increased its production of high tenacity rayon tire cord from approximately 15 million pounds to over 82 million pounds per year during the period 1942-1945. FMC Corp. contended that hazardous substance contamination occurred during that period, that the War Powers Board totally dominated the rayon production market, effectively exercising "micro-management" over the facility, and that the government was therefore liable as an operator. The court denied a motion to dismiss brought by the government,[26] and subsequently granted judgment in favor of the plaintiff, ruling that the government was liable both as an "operator" of the site when hazardous waste was disposed of, as well as an "arranger" of hazardous waste disposal at the site.[27]

CERCLA does, however, provide for limited exemptions from liability. There is a qualified immunity for persons who would otherwise be liable as a result of actions or omissions in the course of rendering care, assistance or advice in connection with a response action; however, only strict liability is avoided, as the person remains liable for negligence. The immunity of a state or local government is slightly broader in such cases, as negligence is also exempted; but the state or local government will be liable for gross negligence or intentional misconduct in connection with a response action. Of course, the qualified immunity does not affect the liability of a person or governmental unit which is a PRP in its own right.[28]

A state or local governmental unit is exempted from the definition of "owner or operator" when it acquires ownership or control of a property "through bankruptcy, tax delinquency, abandonment, or other circumstances in which the government involuntarily acquires title by virtue of its function as sovereign," and in such cases the PRP is "any person who owned, operated, or otherwise controlled activities at such

---

25 No. 90-1761, 31 ERC 1959, 1990 U.S. Dist. LEXIS 8902, 1990 WL 102941 (E.D.Pa. July 18, 1990).

26 *Id.*

27 *Id.*, 1992 U.S. Dist. LEXIS 2355 (E.D.Pa. Feb. 20, 1992).

28 42 U.S.C. § 9607(d).

facility immediately beforehand."[29]   But this does not exempt a governmental unit "which has caused or contributed to the release or threatened release of a hazardous substance from the facility."[30]

Also exempted is each person who "without participating in the management of a . . . facility, holds indicia of ownership primarily to protect his security interest in the . . . facility."[31]   The secured party exemption and lender liability are discussed in Chapter 10.

Liability under CERCLA is excluded for response costs or damages resulting from the application of pesticide products which have been registered under the Federal Insecticide, Fungicide, and Rodenticide Act (FIFRA), or from releases pursuant to permits issued under designated federal laws including the Clean Air Act, the Clean Water Act, RCRA and others.   In such cases, liability may be established under other federal or state laws, including common law, but not under CERCLA.[32]

1.2.4 Strict, Retroactive and Unending Liability

CERCLA has been interpreted to impose strict liability on PRPs, subject only to limited available defenses (which will be discussed in section 1.2.6).[33] Thus, an absentee owner of leased property may be exposed to strict liability under CERCLA as a result of activities of tenants.[34]

---

[29]   *Id.*, §§ 9601(20)(A) and (D).

[30]   *Id.*, § 9601(20)(D).

[31]   *Id.*, 9601(20)(A).

[32]   *Id.*, §§ 9607(i) and (j).

[33]   *See, e.g., Tanglewood East Homeowners v. Charles-Thomas, Inc.*, 849 F.2d 1568 (5th Cir. 1988); *State of New York v. Shore Realty Corp.*, 759 F.2d 1032 (2d Cir. 1985); *Versatile Metals, Inc. v. Union Corp.*, 693 F.Supp 1563 (E.D.Pa. 1988); *City of Philadelphia v. Stepan Chemical Co.*, 18 ELR 20133 (E.D.Pa. 1987).

[34]   *See, e.g., U.S. v. Monsanto Co.*, 858 F.2d 160 (4th Cir. 1988), *cert. den.*, 109 S.Ct. 3156 (1989).

CERCLA liability is retroactive.[35] It makes no difference *when* the property was contaminated, even if long before the current owner or operator acquired the property or long before CERCLA was enacted. It also makes no difference that a PRP sold the property or terminated its operations and was not an owner or operator when CERCLA became effective, as long as the person owned or operated the property at the time hazardous substances were disposed of there. The same is true for an intervening landowner who obtained actual knowledge of the contamination and did not disclose it upon selling the property, even if the transfer occurred long before CERCLA was enacted. All those potential defendants have become subject to strict liability under CERCLA. This can come as quite a shock to a former owner or operator who receives that knock on the door and a huge cleanup bill many years after having vacated a property. The shock is even more intense for a former owner or operator who was innocent of the disposal but is a PRP nonetheless.

Liability is also potentially unending under CERCLA, as long as any hazardous substance release is lurking beneath the surface awaiting discovery and cleanup action. Various periods for limitation of actions do begin to run once the contamination is discovered and response costs have been incurred. For instance, an action for recovery under CERCLA for costs incurred for a "remedial action" must be commenced within six years after the initiation of physical on-site remedial action.[36] Such action might not be initiated until long after the discovery of the contamination and after study and development of a remedial action plan. Thus, the exposure to liability under CERCLA can extend for many years into the future, long after most people would ordinarily expect that their involvement with a particular property was ancient history. In its effort to allocate the cleanup cost to the designated

---

[35] *See, e.g., U.S. v. Northeastern Pharmaceutical & Chemical Co.*, 810 F.2d 726 (8th Cir. 1986). The retroactive effect of CERCLA is not unconstitutional. *U.S. v. R.W. Meyer, Inc.*, 889 F.2d 1497, 1506 (6th Cir. 1989), *cert. den.*, 110 S.Ct. 1527 (1990).

[36] 42 U.S.C. § 9613(g)(2)(B). Other limitation periods apply under other circumstances; the applicable statute of limitations must be determined under the facts of each case.

categories of PRPs, CERCLA has opened the door to many old stories and transactions.

1.2.5 Joint and Several or Apportioned Liability

Liability under CERCLA has been interpreted to be joint and several unless a defendant establishes that the harm is divisible and should be apportioned among the responsible persons.[37] It is difficult in many cases to sustain that burden of proof and to demonstrate a reasonable basis for allocating responsibility among PRPs. Any effort along these lines will be extremely fact dependent.

Congress originally considered adopting an apportionment provision as a part of CERCLA. H.R. 7020, as passed by the House of Representatives on September 23, 1980, included such a provision and a list of factors to be considered by the courts in allocating liability among otherwise jointly and severally liable parties. Those factors were:

(i) the ability of the parties to demonstrate that their contribution to a discharge, release, or disposal of a hazardous waste can be distinguished;

(ii) the amount of hazardous waste involved;

(iii) the degree of toxicity of the hazardous waste involved;

(iv) the degree of involvement by the parties in the generation, transportation, treatment, storage, or disposal of the hazardous waste;

(v) the degree of care exercised by the parties with respect to the hazardous waste concerned, taking into account the characteristics of such hazardous waste; and

(vi) the degree of cooperation by the parties with Federal, State, or local officials to prevent any harm to the public health or the environment.[38]

---

[37]   *See, e.g., U.S. v. Monsanto Co.*, 858 F.2d 160, 171-73 (4th Cir. 1988), *cert. den.*, 109 S.Ct. 3156 (1989); *U.S. v. Wade*, 577 F.Supp. 1326 (E.D.Pa. 1983).

[38]   126 Cong. Rec. at 26781 (1980).

Such a provision ultimately was not enacted by Congress. The courts nevertheless determined that the deletion of express provisions for apportionment of liability from the law as finally enacted did not constitute a rejection by Congress of that concept. Rather, Congress "intended issues of liability, including joint and several liability and contribution, to be determined under traditional and evolving principles of federal common law" administered by the courts.[39] This position was ratified by Congress when it adopted SARA in 1986. At that time, CERCLA was amended to make express reference to contribution actions among PRPs and to provide that in "resolving contribution claims, the court may allocate response costs among liable parties using such equitable factors as the court determines are appropriate."[40]

Thus, the factors originally considered by Congress remain relevant. Factors such as those have been adopted under the Superfund laws of a number of states,[41] and those factors can be used to guide the courts in apportioning CERCLA liability as a matter of common law.[42] The application of those criteria, and any others which a court may wish to consider, will depend on the particular facts and circumstances of each case.

Another way to achieve apportionment of liability is to enter into a settlement with the EPA. CERCLA contemplates that the government may expeditiously resolve some cases by utilizing "*de minimis* settlement" procedures. The EPA is authorized to enter into a prompt and final settlement with a PRP if the settlement "involves only a minor portion of the response costs at the facility concerned" and either (i) the amount and toxicity of the hazardous substances contributed by that party are "minimal in comparison to other hazardous substances at the facility," or (ii) the PRP is the present or former owner of the facility and neither contributed to the release or threatened release nor

---

[39] *State of Colorado v. ASARCO, Inc.*, 608 F.Supp. 1484, 1489 (D.Colo. 1985).

[40] 42 U.S.C. § 9613(f)(1).

[41] *See, e.g.*, 35 Pa. Cons. Stat. Ann. §§ 6020.705(a) and (b); Cal. Health & Safety Code § 25356.3(c).

[42] *See, e.g.*, *U.S. v. A & F Materials Co.*, 578 F.Supp. 1249, 1256 (S.D.Ill. 1984).

permitted "the generation, transportation, storage, treatment or disposal of hazardous substances at the facility."[43] However, the latter provision relating to owners does not apply if the PRP "purchased the real property with actual or constructive knowledge that the property was used for the generation, transportation, storage, treatment, or disposal of any hazardous substance."[44]

De minimis settlements have the effect of precluding contribution actions by other PRPs with respect to matters addressed in the settlement. Unless the settlement agreement provides otherwise, the remaining PRPs continue to be liable under CERCLA, but their liability is reduced by the amount of the settlement.[45] This procedure appears, in effect, to contemplate apportionment of liability.

An EPA Policy Memorandum has set forth guidelines for *de minimis* settlements.[46] Those guidelines represent an effort by the EPA to emphasize such settlements as a means of resolving liability cases quickly with the less significant parties, allowing the EPA to "focus its resources on negotiations or litigation with the major parties."[47] The guidelines require the PRP who desires such a settlement to come forward with the information establishing his eligibility. In that regard, the EPA has interpreted the "constructive knowledge" provision in the statute as placing on the PRP a due diligence obligation, much like that under the innocent landowner defense (see section 1.2.6-1), so that the PRP must persuade the EPA that the property was acquired "without knowledge or reason to know" of the disposal of hazardous substances and after having conducted "all appropriate inquiry."[48] Additionally, if the property was contaminated by someone outside the chain of title to the property (e.g., a "midnight dumper"), the third party defense might

---

[43]   42 U.S.C. § 9622(g)(1).

[44]   *Id.*

[45]   *Id.*, §§ 9613(f)(2) and 9622(g)(5).

[46]   EPA Policy Memorandum, *Guidance on Landowner Liability under Section 107(a)(1) of CERCLA, De Minimis Settlements under Section 122(g)(1)(B), etc.*, June 6, 1989.

[47]   *Id.*, at 16.

[48]   *Id.*, at 10-13.

apply and the PRP might be eligible for a *de minimis* settlement if the PRP shows that due care was exercised under the circumstances.[49]

Once eligibility for the settlement is established, a PRP who is a landowner must provide access to the property and assurances of due care with respect to the hazardous substances. In some cases, especially where eligibility for the settlement may be weak, the PRP will be required to pay cash consideration for the settlement. The PRP is usually required to waive any claims against the government arising out of the response activities on the property. The EPA also requires that the PRP "file in the local land records a notice acceptable to EPA, stating that hazardous substances were disposed of on the site and that EPA makes no representation as to the appropriate use of the property."[50] Other requirements apply to the form and content of the settlement agreement. In return, the PRP gains protection against contribution claims by other PRPs, as noted above.

One wonders whether the EPA's new policy on *de minimis* settlements will achieve its stated objective. The due diligence requirement (which the EPA magically engrafts from the innocent landowner defense) may narrow considerably those PRPs eligible for such settlements. Also, the requirement that a notice be filed in the land records might be unacceptable to many parties who would prefer not to have such a notice in the permanent chain of title to the property in view of the stigma which would attach without regard to the current condition of the property. That requirement imposed by the EPA appears to be gratuitous and self-defeating.[51]

---

[49] *Id.*, at 15-16.

[50] *Id.*, at 20-21.

[51] On the other hand, the recordation of such a notice might already be required under other laws, including RCRA or state analogues applicable to regulated hazardous waste storage, treatment or disposal facilities. See the summary of those laws in § 3.3.3 of Chapter 3. Nevertheless, the EPA requirement for *de minimis* settlements may extend the application of the recordation concept to situations which are not covered by those other laws.

The EPA also has inherent settlement authority with respect to any PRPs, wholly aside from the *de minimis* settlement provisions.[52] The effect of any such settlement is to preclude contribution claims by other PRPs and to reduce the potential liability of other PRPs by the amount of the settlement.[53] Thus, apportionment of liability can be achieved.

When one or more PRPs enter into settlement discussions with the EPA, the remaining PRPs are subjected to pressure to participate and avoid potential liability, as nonsettling defendants, for all past cleanup costs not covered by the settlement as well as all future cleanup costs.[54]

While contribution actions or settlements with the EPA may be theoretically possible in order to apportion liability, in reality many PRPs will not be found or will be unavailable (e.g., due to death, dissolution or bankruptcy) or will otherwise be lacking in assets. Those unlucky PRPs who are located and have assets may well end up being held liable on a joint and several basis without practical recourse. Thus, it may be difficult for a PRP to obtain apportionment of liability, but the effort may be worthwhile in many cases.

1.2.6 Defenses

CERCLA provides for limited defenses against cost recovery actions. A PRP will not be liable if it can be shown "by a preponderance of the evidence" that the contamination was caused "solely by (1) an act of God, (2) an act of war, or (3) an act or omission of a third party other than an employee or agent of the defendant, or than one whose act or omission occurs in connection with a contractual relationship, existing directly or indirectly with the defendant. . . ."[55] Any combination of those three defenses will also be a defense. In order to claim the third party defense, a PRP must show that due care was exercised with respect to the hazardous substance concerned and that precautions were taken "against foreseeable acts or omissions of any such third party and the

---

[52]   EPA Policy Memorandum, *Guidance on Landowner Liability under Section 107(a)(1) of CERCLA, etc.,* at 1, June 6, 1989.

[53]   42 U.S.C. § 9613(f)(2).

[54]   *See, e.g., O'Neil v. Picillo,* 883 F.2d 176 (1st Cir. 1989).

[55]   42 U.S.C. § 9607(b).

consequences that could foreseeably result from such acts or omissions."[56]

The third party defense has been narrowly construed to apply only when there was *no* relationship, including any contractual relationship, between the PRP and the third party (and when the PRP exercised due care and took appropriate precautions).[57] The "contractual relationship" exception significantly limits the availability of the defense. For example, there is a contractual relationship between any seller and buyer which would preclude the application of the third party defense by the buyer in connection with any hazardous substance condition caused by the seller, even when the buyer was completely innocent and unknowing of the preexisting contamination.[58] The same is true between a lessor and lessee; when one causes the contamination, the other cannot rely on the third party defense because of the contractual relationship between them.[59] Moreover, the exception applies to indirect as well as to direct contractual relationships. CERCLA provides no definition of an "indirect" contractual relationship. It might be that such a relationship exists between anyone in the chain of title to real property; each conveyance is a contractual relationship which depends upon and hence is indirectly related to the previous conveyance. This would limit the third party defense to the actions or omissions of total strangers to the property, such as other landowners in the area or midnight dumpers. The EPA indeed has always taken the view that the "contractual relationship" exception to the third party defense as

---

56   *Id.*, § 9607(b)(3).

57   *U.S. v. Monsanto Co.*, 858 F.2d 160 (4th Cir. 1988), *cert. den.*, 109 S.Ct. 3156 (1989).

58   *State of New York v. Shore Realty Corp.*, 759 F.2d 1032, 1048 n.23 (2d Cir. 1985). However, in one case, the seller has been permitted to pursue the third party defense against a buyer's claim, on the theory that the hazardous waste was properly contained at the time of sale and the subsequent disturbance of the waste by the buyer during construction was not "in connection with" the contractual relationship, in essence an "innocent seller" defense. *Westwood Pharmaceuticals v. National Fuel Gas Distribution Corp.*, 767 F. Supp. 456 (W.D.N.Y. 1991) and 737 F. Supp. 1271 (W.D.N.Y. 1990).

59   *U.S. v. South Carolina Recycling & Disposal*, 653 F.Supp. 984 (D.S.C. 1984).

originally enacted eliminated "the availability of the third party defense for a landowner in the chain of title with the party who had caused or contributed to the release."[60]

The strict construction given to the third party defense by the EPA and the courts gave rise to pressure for an amendment to the statute, resulting in the so-called *innocent landowner defense* adopted in 1986 by SARA.

1.2.6-1   Innocent Landowner Defense

In order to expand the third party defense, Congress added a definition of the term "contractual relationship" for purposes of the defense. Congress first clarified that "land contracts, deeds or other instruments transferring title or possession" are indeed contractual relationships which would preclude the third party defense.[61] Congress went on to ease the restrictiveness of the defense by *excluding* from the definition of "contractual relationship," and hence *allowing* the third party defense to apply to, those situations where the defendant proves that the property was acquired *after* the disposal of the hazardous substance which is the subject of a release or threatened release *and* that one of the following circumstances applies:

(i) At the time the defendant acquired the facility the defendant did not know and had no reason to know that any hazardous substance which is the subject of the release or threatened release was disposed of on, in or at the facility.

(ii) The defendant is a governmental entity which acquired the facility by escheat, or through any other involuntary transfer or acquisition, or through the exercise

---

60   EPA Policy Memorandum, *Guidance on Landowner Liability etc.*, pp. 5, 15 (June 6, 1989). The EPA cites *U.S. v. Hooker Chemicals & Plastics Corp.*, 680 F.Supp. 546 (W.D.N.Y. 1988) as upholding the EPA position. *Id.*, at 5.

61   42 U.S.C. § 9601(35)(A). The EPA interprets this as Congressional confirmation of the EPA's strict construction of the third party defense as noted above. EPA Policy Memorandum, *Guidance on Landowner Liability, etc.*, p. 5 (June 6, 1989).

of eminent domain authority by purchase or condemnation.

(iii) The defendant acquired the facility by inheritance or bequest.[62]

Aside from governmental entities, the broadest protection is for those who inherit contaminated real property, as the statute contains no knowledge or inquiry requirement with respect to such PRPs.[63] Purchasers in normal transactions will have to qualify under item (i) by showing that they had no knowledge of, nor any reason to know of, the condition. In order to do so, CERCLA provides that a defendant

> must have undertaken, at the time of acquisition, all appropriate inquiry into the previous ownership and uses of the property consistent with good commercial or customary practice in an effort to minimize liability.[64]

Congress then set forth several criteria to be applied by courts when considering the expanded defense. The courts

> shall take into account any specialized knowledge or experience on the part of the defendant, the relationship of the purchase price to the value of the property if uncontaminated, commonly known or reasonably ascertainable information about the property, the obviousness of the presence or likely presence of

---

62 *Id.*

63 However, based on references in the legislative history, the EPA takes the position that a knowledge and inquiry requirement does apply to those who inherit property, but that the standard of inquiry is less than in commercial or private party transactions generally. EPA Policy Memorandum, *Guidance on Landowner Liability, etc.*, pp. 14-15 (June 6, 1989). *But see U.S. v. Pacific Hide & Fur Depot, Inc.*, 716 F.Supp. 1341 (D. Idaho 1989) (innocent landowner defense applied to defendants who inherited property interest without any knowledge or inquiry, but issues remained as to whether contamination continued to occur after the defendants became the owners).

64 42 U.S.C. § 9601(35)(B).

contamination at the property, and the ability to detect such contamination by appropriate inspection.[65]

These provisions clearly establish a due diligence requirement. The legislative history indicates that Congress intended to establish a significant scope of inquiry, especially in commercial transactions.[66] A consulting industry has arisen in order to provide the necessary expertise to perform environmental assessments. Most purchasers of commercial real estate now routinely consider environmental issues and often undertake assessments in order to determine the scope of any risk or, if none appears, to gain the benefit of the innocent landowner defense. The subject of environmental assessments and audits is discussed in Chapter 16.

As a practical matter, the innocent landowner defense has not yet resulted in much expansion of the third party defense. A sufficient environmental assessment must have been conducted, and it is easy for the government to take the position that a sufficient assessment would have revealed the condition. The defendant is faced with the burden of proof on an issue which necessarily involves a shortcoming of some kind in the investigation because it failed to discover contamination which was present. Thus, there has been no deluge of court rulings dismissing CERCLA actions due to the innocent landowner defense. There has not even been a trickle of such rulings. To the contrary, most of the few rulings to date have rejected the defense for one reason or another.[67]

---

[65]   *Id.*

[66]   H.R. Rep. No. 962, 99th Cong., 2d Sess. (1986), reprinted in 4 U.S. Code Cong. & Ad. News 2835, 99th Cong., 2d Sess. (1986).

[67]   In one case, the court upheld the viability of the defense, but only in response to the government's motion for summary judgment on liability. The matter still had to go to trial. *U.S. v. Serafini*, 706 F.Supp. 346 (M.D.Pa. 1988). The defense was upheld in *U.S. v. Pacific Fur Depot, Inc.*, 716 F.Supp. 1341 (D. Idaho 1989) (but perhaps lost as a result of continued contamination). The defense was successfully asserted at trial in *International Clinical Laboratories v. Stevens*, 30 ERC 2066 (E.D.N.Y. 1990) (but the usefulness of this case as authority is weakened because public records revealing the problem were not reviewed by the buyer and alternative grounds existed for the decision, including equitable appornment of liability among PRPs and the failure of the other PRPs to file any counterclaim, waiving any right of contribution).

Nevertheless, environmental assessments are becoming common practice in hopes that the sufficiency of an assessment and the applicability of the innocent landowner defense might be proven. In addition, the desire to know the true condition of a property and the associated risks is reason enough to conduct an investigation. If the results are that the property is contaminated, precluding the availability of the innocent landowner defense, that does not mean that the effort has been wasted. The prospective purchaser has gained important information which can be used to protect its interests. The purchaser may be able to terminate the transaction and avoid the risk altogether if appropriate conditions have been included in the purchase agreement. Alternatively, various contractual protections might be negotiated in order to shift or minimize the risk. Agreements can also be reached regarding cleanup of the discovered contamination. If the property can be cleaned up before closing, the buyer might have no knowledge or reason to know of any further contamination at the time of acquisition and therefore can become an innocent landowner. Another factor motivating assessments is that lenders frequently require environmental assessments as a condition of financing real estate transactions. (These subjects are discussed in Parts II and III of this book.) Accordingly, environmental assessments are here to stay, whether or not the innocent landowner defense will ultimately prove to be meritorious in connection with any particular transaction. In view of the potential liabilities under environmental laws, the cost of a reasonable assessment will almost always be money well spent.

The practical effect of the innocent landowner defense is to increase the pressure on private parties to conduct investigations and, as hazardous waste contamination is discovered, to undertake remedial activities in connection with real estate transactions. The parties should not ignore what they have found. Thus, a law which ostensibly provides a defense against liability actually operates to encourage private party expenditures, reducing the need for governmental action and preserving the Superfund.

How Much Diligence Is Due? One serious concern is the vagueness of the due diligence requirement as set forth in the statute. No one really knows *how much* due diligence is necessary. Until contamination is actually found, the due diligence effort is potentially endless as the parties go about trying to *prove a negative.* At some point there has to be a stop to the time and expenses which are required. The criteria provided in the statute do not help a purchaser or a lender very much. There is great confusion over what is "all appropriate inquiry" and "good commercial or customary practice."[68] Considerable attention has been given to this issue, and practices have developed in recent years regarding the scope of environmental assessments (see Chapter 16). But it is still uncertain whether in any given case the EPA or a court will concur that "all appropriate inquiry" has been accomplished. The lending industry is particularly affected, as transaction costs and delays increase. There is a great desire on the part of that industry to obtain clarification of exactly what steps are required in order to gain the benefit of the innocent landowner defense. Lenders want more certainty about the scope of the environmental risks undertaken by their borrowers and by themselves. Lenders desire an innocent landowner defense which will provide meaningful protection as long as due diligence of a reasonable and clear scope is undertaken and no hazardous substance contamination is discovered. Without clear standards and protection, many parties and lenders are unwilling to consider environmentally risky transactions. Killing deals does not advance the interests of CERCLA or society generally.

As a result, legislation has been proposed which would clarify what specific steps must be undertaken in order to accomplish a sufficient environmental assessment.[69] That legislation would, in effect, codify the environmental due diligence practices which have been developed by the lending industry by identifying information sources and steps to be followed, without awaiting the vagaries of EPA posturing or court judgments. The bill would shift the burden of proof to the government by creating a rebuttable presumption that an assessment is sufficient where the requirements are followed. While this would be a significant improvement, a number of difficulties would remain. For example, the

---

[68] The recently published EPA Policy Memorandum, *Guidance on Landowner Liability etc.* (June 6, 1989) provides no helpful guidance on this issue. The Memorandum simply refers back to the statutory criteria and says that determinations are to be "made on a case-by-case basis." *Id.*, at 10-12.

[69] H.R. 1643 (Rep. Owens, R-Utah). See Appendix C to this book.

bill refers to investigation of "reasonably obtainable" public records. Thus, the defendant would still have to prove the reasonableness of the search before the burden of proof would shift, which is not much different than existing law. Lenders would still have difficulty satisfying the required steps before a foreclosure when the debtor might not allow access to the property. Also, litigation and evidentiary hearings would still be required in order to determine whether the defendant's assessment was sufficient to give rise to the presumption, and then to see if the government can rebut the presumption. As the reintroduced version of an earlier bill (H.R. 2787, Rep. Weldon, R-Pa.), it is obvious that this proposed legislation is languishing. In any case, legislation along these lines would be very beneficial, especially if further clarifications are made.

Are Operators Covered by the Defense? An important open question is whether the innocent landowner defense applies only to purchasers who become *owners*, or also to lessees or others who become *operators* of real property. The answer to this question would be of great significance to lessees as well as to leasehold mortgage lenders, as lessees too would be comforted by the availability of the defense. The fact that the defense is commonly referred to as the innocent *landowner* defense exhibits a widespread perception that the defense applies only to *owners*. An examination of the statutory language reveals some support for limiting the meaning of the defense in that way. One of the factors which a court must consider is "the relationship of the purchase price to the value of the property if uncontaminated." That factor naturally would apply only to sales transactions, not leases. Another indication is that Congress concurrently adopted as a new category of PRP intervening *owners* who discovered preexisting contamination and failed to disclose it upon transferring ownership of the property. Such intervening owners are "treated as liable" without any third party defense.[70] Had Congress intended the innocent landowner defense to apply to operators, the PRP category for intervening owners would have covered operators as well.

On the other hand, the fact that one of a number of factors listed by Congress in the statute as finally enacted (i.e., the purchase price)

---

[70] 42 U.S.C. § 9601(35)(C).

happens to apply only to owners does not necessarily show that Congress intended to exclude lessees from the defense. Moreover, the explicit reference only to landowners is not included in the law as adopted, and the statute contains language which is consistent with a broader interpretation. As noted above, the term "contractual relationship" includes "instruments transferring title *or possession*," which would include leases. Other references to the condition of the property and the knowledge of the defendant at the time the site was "acquired" by him are consistent with a broader interpretation, as both buyers and lessees "acquire" their respective interests in real property (fee title and leasehold estates).

Thus, the language in the statute is at best ambiguous on the point, and the legislative history is not necessarily dispositive. In such a situation, courts normally like to use a fair and reasonable interpretation. It can be argued that the exclusion of lessees from the defense would be unfair and unreasonable. Assume, for example, that a contaminated commercial property is sold and concurrently leased to a new lessee. Both the new owner and lessee conducted environmental assessments and neither of them knew or had reason to know of the contamination at the time they acquired their respective interests. The innocent landowner defense certainly protects the new owner, so that when the contamination is later discovered and cleanup costs are incurred, the owner will have no obligation to reimburse the Superfund. This means that the property would be cleaned up, and its value enhanced, without cost on the owner's part. If the defense is not available to the lessee, then the lessee (as the "operator" of the property and hence a PRP) could be called upon to reimburse the Superfund for the expenditures. In this way, the owner would benefit at the expense of the lessee, even though both are equally innocent and exercised the same due diligence. In view of the fact that the owner clearly has the defense, the courts should avoid the unfair result by interpreting the defense to apply to the lessee as well. Whether the courts will do so is unknown. It is possible that the courts will instead interpret the defense narrowly on the grounds that (i) it is more important from a public policy standpoint that the Superfund be reimbursed by someone, and (ii) if Congress had intended to extend the innocent landowner defense to operators of property as well as owners, it would have done so more clearly. This issue will ultimately have to be resolved by litigation or by further legislative amendment.

1.2.7 Private Right of Action for Cleanup Cost Recovery

As noted above, contribution actions among PRPs are specifically authorized by CERCLA,[71] and the courts have determined that a defendant held jointly and severally liable for cleanup costs may seek contribution from other PRPs under federal common law principles as well.[72] Moreover, it is not necessary for a PRP to await governmental enforcement action. A PRP may undertake cleanup and, as long as the cleanup was necessary and conducted consistently with the NCP, seek cost recovery from other PRPs without any prior approval of any federal, state or local governmental agency.[73] Attorneys fees incurred in connection with the cleanup may also be recovered by a private party in addition to the cost of the cleanup itself, although there are divergent court decisions on this point.[74]

---

[71] *Id.*, §§ 9607(a)(4)(B) and 9613(f); *Wickland Oil Terminals v. ASARCO, Inc.*, 792 F.2d 887, 890 (9th Cir. 1986).

[72] *See, e.g., Walls v. Waste Resource Corp.*, 761 F.2d 311 (6th Cir. 1985); *Colorado v. ASARCO, Inc.*, 608 F.Supp 1484, 1489-92 (D.Colo. 1985).

[73] *Cadillac Fairview/California, Inc. v. Dow Chemical Co.*, 840 F.2d 691 (9th Cir. 1988). This case also ruled that a PRP cannot force another PRP to participate in the cleanup. CERCLA's injunctive powers can be exercised only by the government. Cost recovery is the only private right of action authorized by CERCLA.

[74] *See, e.g.,* attorneys fees recoverable: *General Electric Co. v. Litton Industrial Automation Systems*, 920 F.2d 1415 (8th Cir. 1990); *Pease & Curren Ref., Inc. v. Spectrolab, Inc.*, 744 F. Supp. 945 (C.D. Cal. 1990); *Shapiro v. Alexanderson*, 741 F. Supp. 472 (S.D.N.Y. 1990); *Bolin v. Cessna Aircraft Co.*, 759 F. Supp. 692, 710 (D. Kan. 1991); *Gopher Oil Co., Inc. v. Union Oil Co. of Calif.*, 757 F. Supp. 998 (D.Minn. 1991), *affirmed in part, remanded in part*, 1992 U.S. App. LEXIS 1076 (8th Cir. 1992); *FMC Corp. v. U.S.*, 1992 U.S. Dist. LEXIS 2355 (E.D.Pa. Feb. 20, 1992). Attorneys fees not recoverable: *Abbott Laboratories v. Thermo Chem, Inc.*, No. 1:89-CV-994, 1991 U.S. Dist. LEXIS 11789 (W.D. Mich. Aug. 20, 1991); *In re Hemingway Transport, Inc.*, 126 Bankr. 656 (D.Mass. 1991); *Fallowfield v. Strunk*, No. 89 Civ. 8644, 1990 WL 52745 (E.D.Pa. Apr. 23, 1990); *Mesiti v. Microdot*, 739 F. Supp. 57 (D.N.H. 1990); *U.S. v. Hardage*, 750 F. Supp. 1460, 1511 (W.D. Okla. 1990);

The elements of a private right of action are that (1) the defendant is a PRP, (2) there has been a release or threatened release of a hazardous substance (as defined by CERCLA), (3) the plaintiff has incurred abatement costs as a result, and (4) the response action was necessary and consistent with the NCP.[75]

It appears that the release of *any* quantity or concentration of a hazardous substance, however small, is sufficient to confer jurisdiction under CERCLA for the recovery of response costs.[76] However, the quantity or concentration of the released hazardous substances may be relevant to whether the response was "necessary" and "consistent" with the NCP. The EPA has published regulations regarding what private parties must do so that their cleanup activities will be "consistent" with the NCP. Those regulations are extensive and technical. They should be followed by any private party undertaking cleanup efforts in order to preserve cost recovery rights under CERCLA.

There are several advantages to a plaintiff in a private party action under CERCLA which might not be available under a number of other possible theories of recovery. Federal question jurisdiction exists under CERCLA so that the action can be brought in federal court. Other causes of action under state law can be included in the federal court case under the doctrine of pendent jurisdiction, unless those claims substantially broaden the action beyond the issues which would necessarily be posed in the CERCLA action itself (such as personal injury claims in addition to cleanup cost recovery).[77] Just as when the

---

[75]   *Prudential Insurance Co. v. United States Gypsum Co.*, 711 F.Supp. 1244 (D.N.J. 1989). *See also Versatile Metals, Inc. v. Union Corp.*, 693 F. Supp. 1563 (E.D.Pa. 1988) (CERCLA claim failed because the cleanup costs incurred were not consistent with the NCP for lack of the necessary remedial investigation/feasibility study with consideration of alternative remedial actions showing the cost-effectiveness or necessity of the costs incurred).

[76]   *U.S. v. Wade*, 577 F.Supp. 1326 (E.D.Pa. 1983).

[77]   *See, e.g., Piccolini v. Simon's Wrecking*, 686 F.Supp. 1063 (M.D.Pa. 1988); *Lykins v. Westinghouse Electric Corp.*, 27 ERC 1590 (E.D.Ky. 1988). However, as a result of the narrowing of pendent party jurisdiction by the United States Supreme Court in *Finley v. U.S.*, 490 U.S. 545 (1989), pendent party jurisdiction is not available under CERCLA as to a party

government sues under CERCLA, the private party plaintiff's case is enhanced by the strict and joint and several liability features of CERCLA, as well as the broad categories of potential defendants.

On the other hand, private plaintiffs are apparently not in the same position as the government when it comes to defenses. A defendant may assert equitable defenses (such as estoppel, waiver or laches) in addition to the defenses set forth in the statute.[78] Contractual defenses are also available between private parties if there has been an agreed allocation of environmental responsibilities (such as an indemnification or release agreement) which is inconsistent with the asserted claim. Contractual allocations are discussed in Chapter 18. In addition, a private contribution action might be precluded if the defendant has already entered into a settlement of its liability with the EPA which has that effect.[79]

The petroleum exclusion from the definition of CERCLA "hazardous substances" has an important impact on private actions. Leakage of petroleum products from underground storage tanks is a common source of cleanup problems. In view of the exclusion, a private right of action might not exist under CERCLA in connection with the cleanup of such releases, and other theories of liability would have to be used (e.g., common law, contract language, state law or RCRA for a cleanup order). The scope of the petroleum exclusion has been the subject of confusion and litigation due to the ambiguous wording of the statute.[80]

The exclusion covers "petroleum, including crude oil and any fraction thereof not specifically listed as a hazardous substance."[81] That

---

against which only state law claims were brought. *McGraw-Edison Co. v. Speed Queen Co.*, 768 F. Supp. 684 (E.D. Wis. 1991).

[78] *See, e.g., Pinole Point Properties, Inc. v. Bethlehem Steel Co.*, 596 F.Supp. 283 (N.D.Cal. 1984).

[79] 42 U.S.C. § 9613(f)(2).

[80] *See, e.g., Wilshire Westwood Associates v. Atlantic Richfield Corp.*, 27 ERC 2146 (C.D.Cal. Jan. 25, 1988); *Washington v. Time Oil Co.*, 687 F.Supp. 529 (W.D.Wash. 1988); *The Marmon Group, Inc. v. Rexnord, Inc.*, 822 F.2d 31 (7th Cir. 1987).

[81] 42 U.S.C. § 9601(14).

wording suggests that there might be an exception to the exclusion, namely where components of the petroleum product or additives are themselves listed as hazardous substances. Indigenous components of petroleum, refined or unrefined, include benzene, toluene, xylene, ethylbenzene and lead, all of which have been specifically listed as hazardous substances. Thus, if the exception language is given effect, then there can be no petroleum exclusion at all. If the exclusion is upheld, then the exception language is meaningless.

The EPA has taken the position that the exclusion covers crude oil and petroleum products in unrefined or refined form (including such products as leaded gasoline), but does not include waste oil or petroleum products which have been contaminated during use with other hazardous substances.[82]

The federal Court of Appeals for the Ninth Circuit has upheld part of the EPA's position. The court opted to avoid construing the petroleum exclusion as a nullity and found that the exclusion covers unrefined or refined petroleum including all of its components and additives. Accordingly, the court affirmed the dismissal of a private CERCLA action arising from the leakage of leaded gasoline out of an underground storage tank causing soil contamination.[83] The Ninth Circuit did not, however, reach the other part of the EPA's position, namely that petroleum which has been adulterated or contaminated from use is not excluded from CERCLA. Thus, there remains a possibility that CERCLA liability might apply to petroleum leakage, at least where the petroleum has been used or otherwise contaminated so that it is not in its original unrefined or refined form. Indeed, subsequent court decisions have indicated that the petroleum exclusion does not apply to sludge from petroleum tanks[84] or to waste oil.[85]

---

82   *See, e.g.,* the EPA General Counsel's Memorandum, dated July 31, 1987.

83   *Wilshire Westwood Assoc. v. Atlantic Richfield Co.,* 881 F.2d 801 (9th Cir. 1989).

84   *U.S. v. Western Processing Co., Inc.,* 761 F. Supp. 713 (W.D.Wash. 1991).

85   *Mid Valley Bank v. North Valley Bank,* 764 F. Supp. 1377 (E.D. Cal. 1991).

It is the object of the private right of action to encourage private party cleanup. This objective may be achieved particularly when a party is motivated to clean up a site in connection with a desired real estate transaction. The encouragement is enhanced, of course, where other responsible parties are creditworthy.

1.3   State Superfund Laws

Most states have followed the lead of Congress by enacting a Superfund law that parallels CERCLA. The state Superfund laws are similarly designed to provide state agencies with the authority to respond to local hazardous waste incidents and to provide the funds necessary for taking response actions. The laws of the following states have been surveyed for purposes of this discussion: **Arizona, Arkansas, California, Connecticut, Florida, Illinois, Louisiana, Maine, Maryland, Massachusetts, Michigan, Nevada, New Hampshire, New Jersey, New York, Oregon, Pennsylvania, Rhode Island, Tennessee, Texas, Vermont** and **Virginia.**

The discussion of the Superfund laws of these states will be limited to the same kinds of features highlighted above with respect to CERCLA. There are a myriad of other details and nuances regarding the various state Superfund laws which are beyond the scope of this book. In any transaction, an up-to-date review of the applicable laws and regulations should be undertaken by counsel qualified to practice in the state where the property is located. Other states not included in this survey may also have similar laws, and CERCLA applies, of course, throughout the nation. Thus, the impact of CERCLA and state analogues should be considered in all real estate transactions, wherever the property is located.

1.3.1   Funding for Cleanups; Cost Recovery

All of the states surveyed have enacted a hazardous waste response law authorizing a state agency or officer to take remedial actions when a hazardous substance release has occurred or is threatened. The laws create a fund, either as part of the general fund or as a special fund, solely for the purpose of providing money for responding to hazardous waste incidents and, in some cases, for monitoring and investigative activities or for educational purposes. For example, the **Connecticut** statute provides for the establishment of the Emergency Spill Response

Fund for the purpose of providing money for containment, removal, or mitigation of a discharge or spill, or other designated purposes including education of the public.[86] A similar fund is created in the other states surveyed.

The state Superfund laws generally provide that the funds are available for taking necessary response actions when the parties responsible for the hazardous waste incident have failed to do so or have not yet been identified; and, like CERCLA, the laws provide a mechanism for the state to recover its expenditures. All of the state Superfund laws surveyed authorize the state to institute an action against the responsible persons for all costs incurred, plus interest and, in most cases, punitive damages of up to three times the actual costs when the PRP fails to take remedial actions ordered by the state.

As is the case on the federal level, state sources of Superfund financing are limited, and we are, in general, likely to see more enforcement orders in the future before state agencies will resort to Superfund expenditures.

1.3.2   Potentially Responsible Parties

The majority of the state Superfund laws name as potential defendants the same parties named under CERCLA. For example, the **California** Superfund law defines PRPs as "those persons described in Section 107(a) of the federal act (42 U.S.C. 9607(a))."[87] Although **California** appears to be the only state that directly incorporates the definition from CERCLA by reference, most of the states adopt essentially the same language used in the federal act.

Not every state so clearly identifies those who are potential defendants, however. The **Nevada** statute provides only that "any person who possessed or had in his care any hazardous material involved in a spill or accident requiring the cleaning and decontamination of the affected area is responsible for that cleaning and decontamination."[88] At least one state goes further than CERCLA by including more classes of potential defendants in its statute. The **Oregon** Superfund law not

---

[86]   Conn. Gen. Stat. Ann. § 22a-451(d).

[87]   Cal. Health & Safety Code § 25323.5(a).

[88]   Nev. Rev. Stat. § 459.750.

only provides that owners and operators of a facility where a release has occurred are liable parties, but also includes as potential defendants any owner *or operator* who knew of a release and subsequently transferred the facility to another person without disclosing such knowledge.[89] The **Oregon** statute also includes as responsible any person who "contributed to or exacerbated the release" and "any person who unlawfully hinders or delays entry to, investigation of or removal or remedial action at a facility."[90] The PRPs named in each of the state Superfund laws surveyed will be discussed in section 1.4 below.

One open issue is whether federal governmental agencies may be held liable under state environmental laws. This question is especially important to those states in which federal weapons plants are located. The U.S. Department of Energy has identified 155 weapons plant polluted sites and has estimated that more than $80 billion will be required for cleanup over a period of 20 or more years. There are even higher cost estimates. The issue concerns whether cleanup of each site will be governed by the standards of the state in which it is located or whether federal standards alone will apply.

In late 1988, the U.S. Department of Energy entered into two settlements with the State of Ohio pursuant to which the federal agency will be responsible for the cleanup of hazardous wastes at federally owned uranium enrichment plants near Fernald and Piketon, Ohio. Those plants have generated wastes such as polychlorinated byphenyls (PCBs), solvents, metals and radioactive wastes. The cleanup will be under the supervision of the Ohio Environmental Protection Agency and subject to Ohio's environmental laws. Whether federal agencies will voluntarily submit to state environmental laws in other cases remains to be seen. Rep. Dennis E. Eckart (D-Ohio) has proposed legislation which would ensure that the states could enforce their environmental laws against federal agencies, by lifting the federal government's

---

[89] Or. Rev. Stat. § 466.567(1)(c). CERCLA, on the other hand, reaches intervening *owners* who obtain actual knowledge of contamination and fail to disclose to a buyer; the CERCLA provision apparently does not apply to intervening *operators*. 42 U.S.C. § 9601(35)(C). The **Pennsylvania** statute has a provision similar to **Oregon's** in this respect. 35 Pa. Cons. Stat. Ann. § 6020.701(b)(1)(iv).

[90] Or. Rev. Stat. § 466.567(1)(d) and (e).

sovereign immunity for that purpose.[91] Critics of that approach point out that it would threaten the "worst first" cleanup policy, as state officials would not have a national perspective on the problem.

1.3.3 Defenses

The majority of the state Superfund laws also provide for defenses similar to those set forth in CERCLA. For example, the **California** statute provides that the available defenses are those specified in the federal act.[92] Most of the state statutes adopt the same or similar language as that used in CERCLA. Many of the state laws also provide a limited immunity for those participating in cleanup efforts.

A number of state statutes do not parallel the CERCLA defenses, however. The **Connecticut** statute only provides that a "mortgagee who acquires title to real estate by virtue of a foreclosure or tender of a deed in lieu of foreclosure, shall not be liable for any assessment, fine or other costs imposed by the state for any spill upon such real estate beyond the value of such real estate, provided such spill occurred prior to the date of acquisition of title to such real estate by such mortgagee."[93] Similarly, the Maryland statute only exempts from liability those PRPs who purchased "a site containing a controlled hazardous substance without knowledge of the existence of the controlled hazardous substance at the site," or a holder of a mortgage or deed of trust who acquired title "through foreclosure to a site containing a controlled hazardous substance."[94]

New Jersey's provision on defenses also differs from CERCLA. It provides that an "act or omission caused solely by war, sabotage, or God, or a combination thereof, shall be the only defenses which may be raised by any owner or operator of a major facility or vessel responsible for a

---

[91] H.R. 1056 (Federal Facilities).

[92] Cal. Health & Safety Code § 25323.5(b).

[93] Conn. Gen. Stat. Ann. § 22a-452b. On the other hand, the categories of PRPs are more limited under the **Connecticut** law, including only persons who caused the pollution or persons who own hazardous wastes deemed to be a potential threat to human health or the environment. Conn. Gen. Stat Ann. § 22a-451(a).

[94] Md. Code Ann. § 7-201(x)(2)(i) and (ii).

discharge in any action arising under the provisions of this act."[95]   The defense for acts of "sabotage" is apparently in lieu of the CERCLA defense for acts or omissions by unrelated third parties.   Whether those defenses will be construed similarly is unknown.

A number of states have no provision for defenses in their Superfund laws, including Nevada, New York, Rhode Island, Tennessee and Virginia.   But the categories of responsible parties are also more limited under those laws.

1.3.3-1   Innocent Landowner Defense

Only some state Superfund laws have followed the lead of CERCLA by including a provision for the innocent landowner defense.[96]   For example, the **Oregon** statute expressly exempts from liability "any owner or operator who became an owner or operator after the time of the acts or omissions that resulted in the release, and who did not know and reasonably should not have known of the release when the person first became the owner or operator."[97]   Under the Oregon statute, like CERCLA, a person must show that he undertook sufficient inquiry into the previous uses of the property before he may invoke the innocent landowner defense.

As with all defenses, the burden of proof with respect to the innocent landowner defense is ordinarily on the defendant (the purchaser).   **California** has a unique provision, however, reversing the burden of proof in certain residential cases.   Owners who occupy a single-family residence on real property of five acres or less and which is the site of a hazardous substance release are presumed to have no liability under the **California** Superfund law, unless the state Department of Health Services rebuts that presumption by proving either that the release occurred after the owner acquired the property or that the owner knew or had reason to know of the release at the time of acquisition.

---

[95]   N.J. Stat. Ann. § 58:10-23.11g(d).

[96]   The **Illinois, Oregon, Pennsylvania, Texas** and **Vermont** statutes expressly include the "innocent landowner defense" as a defense to Superfund liability.   The **California** Superfund law incorporates the CERCLA defenses by reference, including the "innocent landowner defense."

[97]   Or. Rev. Stat. § 466.567(6).

The Department must make a certification to that effect prior to bringing an action against such an owner.[98]

A few states have third party defenses which are broader than the CERCLA third party defense so that an innocent landowner defense is neither included nor required. For example, both the **Maine** and **New Hampshire** statutes provide a defense for acts or omissions of third parties unless the third party is an employee, agent, or independent contractor of the defendant. No exclusion for acts or omissions of third persons with whom the defendant has had a contractual relationship is mentioned.[99] This may be interpreted as providing a defense for persons who purchase contaminated property in those states without knowledge of that condition, even without conducting the kind of due diligence investigation required under CERCLA.

1.3.4   Strict Liability

As for the type of liability imposed by the state Superfund laws, ten of the states surveyed expressly provide that liability is strict.[100] For example, the **Massachusetts** statute provides the named responsible persons "shall be liable, without regard to fault."[101] The other states surveyed do not expressly provide that liability is strict, but may be interpreted, as CERCLA has, to impose strict liability.

However, some states have a definition of responsible parties apparently limited to those who had some causal connection with the contamination or who own the hazardous waste, which is essentially a fault standard or close to it. For example, the PRPs under the **Connecticut** law include only those who caused the pollution or who own dangerous hazardous wastes.[102] **Michigan** also limits responsible persons to those "whose action or negligence caused a condition

---

[98]   Cal. Health & Safety Code § 25360.2.

[99]   Me. Rev. Stat. Ann. Tit. 38 § 1367 and N.H. Rev. Stat. Ann. § 147-B:10-a.

[100]   The **Arizona, California, Louisiana, Maine, Massachusetts, New Hampshire, New Jersey, Oregon, Pennsylvania** and **Vermont** statutes expressly provide that liability is strict.

[101]   Mass. Gen. Laws Ann. Ch. 21E § 5(a).

[102]   Conn. Gen. Stat. Ann. § 22a-451(a).

requiring expenditure of money pursuant to" the **Michigan** Environmental Response Act.[103] Liability is similarly limited under **Nevada** law to persons who possessed or had in their care hazardous material involved in a spill or accident requiring cleanup.[104] The vast majority of states, however, probably hold defendants to a standard of strict liability.

Theoretically, the standard of Superfund liability in most states (and under CERCLA) is really a form of "absolute" liability based on the mere status of a defendant as "owner" or "operator." The concept of strict liability is most commonly associated with products liability cases where the potential defendants include the manufacturers and distributors of defective products. Those defendants have a close connection with the defective product, either making or selling it and profiting from it. In the environmental area, however, completely innocent parties without any connection other than ownership or operation of the contaminated land can be held liable. This really goes beyond previous notions of strict liability and is more akin to a form of absolute liability based purely on status. The **Rhode Island** Environmental Response Fund Law tells it like it is and expressly refers to the liability as "absolute."[105]

1.3.5   Joint and Several or Apportioned Liability

The state Superfund laws are not homogeneous with respect to the issue of joint and several or apportioned liability. The **Connecticut** and **Tennessee** statutes provide that liability will be apportioned; **Florida**, **Maine** and **New Jersey** provide that liability shall be joint and several; and **Arizona**, **California**, **Louisiana**, **Maryland**, **Massachusetts**, **Pennsylvania**, **Texas** and **Vermont** provide that liability will be apportioned if there is a reasonable basis for apportionment, otherwise liability is joint and several. The remainder of the states surveyed do not specify what type of liability is imposed under the statute. If they are construed as CERCLA has been, however, a standard of joint and several liability will be read into these statutes.

---

[103]   Mich. Gen. Stat. Ann. § 299.608.

[104]   Nev. Rev. Stat. § 459.750.

[105]   R.I. Gen. Laws § 23-19.1-22.

Even where a state law provides for apportionment, however, the practical reality in many cases is that the "deep pocket" PRP will end up footing the bill without meaningful recourse. The state governments can be expected to oppose any attempt on the part of a deep pocket PRP to establish a basis for apportionment. The burden of proof is normally on the PRP in this regard.

1.3.6   Private Right of Action for Cleanup Cost Recovery

The majority of the state Superfund laws surveyed are silent on the question of whether a private right of action may be brought pursuant to the provisions of the Superfund law by a private party (who voluntarily or under order cleans up a property) to seek reimbursement or contribution from other PRPs. A number of state statutes do address this question, however. For example, the **Louisiana** statute provides that parties who clean up "the pollution source. . . may sue and recover from any other nonparticipating party who shall be liable for twice their portion of the remedial costs."[106] The **Massachusetts** statute expressly provides for a private right of action for "reimbursement from any other person liable for such release or threat of release for the reasonable costs of such assessment, containment and removal."[107] The **California** statute also authorizes contribution or indemnity actions among PRPs, except where the liability of a PRP has been formally apportioned and discharged (in which case that PRP has no further liability) or a PRP is actively participating in a pending apportionment proceeding.[108] In contrast, a private right of action cannot be stated under the **New Jersey** Superfund law.[109]

1.3.7   Hazardous Substances or Waste

The definitions of "hazardous substance" or "hazardous waste" vary from state to state. Some, like CERCLA, have a petroleum exclusion,[110]

---

[106]   La. Rev. Stat. Ann. § 30:2276.G.

[107]   Mass. Gen. Laws Ann. Ch. 21E § 4.

[108]   Cal. Health & Safety Code § 25363(e).

[109]   *Jersey City Redevelopment Authority v. PPG Industries*, 655 F. Supp. 1257, 1262-63 (D.N.J. 1987).

[110]   *See, e.g.*, Cal. Health & Safety Code § 25317(a).

but others include petroleum for purposes of their Superfund laws.[111] It is necessary to determine in each case whether a given substance is hazardous under applicable laws and regulations, including the Superfund laws as well as other environmental laws. See section 1.2.2-1 above.

1.3.8   Liens

A number of the states provide for the recordation of a lien on the property of the responsible person for the amount of the debt to the state. These liens take various forms and will be discussed in Chapter 2.

1.4 Synopsis of Selected State Superfund Laws

The following summaries of the Superfund laws of selected states cover only the highlights. Other states may have similar laws. The parties to any transaction should obtain advice regarding the latest statutory language and court interpretations in the applicable state on the kinds of issues discussed here.

It should be noted that many jurisdictions have more than one law and fund relating to environmental pollution. At the federal level, for example, the Resource Conservation and Recovery Act of 1976 (RCRA)[112] establishes a system for regulating hazardous wastes and includes authority for the federal government to order remedial action or to undertake such action and recover the cost. In some respects, therefore, the policies of RCRA overlap those of CERCLA. **California** also has both kinds of laws, including the Hazardous Waste Control Law[113] as a RCRA analogue, and the **California** Superfund law which will be discussed below. Many other states also have multiple laws and funds, and it is sometimes difficult to distinguish which is the Superfund law as opposed to the RCRA analogue or similar provisions. Some states, including **Texas**, even appear to merge the two kinds of laws together. During the survey, an effort was made to identify the Superfund law of the selected states for purposes of this discussion. While it is believed that the laws discussed below qualify as Superfund laws, that characterization is sometimes a close question.

---

[111]   *See, e.g.,* Conn. Gen. Stat. Ann § 229-451.

[112]   42 U.S.C. §§ 6901 et seq.

[113]   Cal. Health & Safety Code §§ 25100 et seq.

Arizona

The Arizona Superfund statute provides for liable persons and defenses similar to those specified in CERCLA.[114] However, the liability of an owner of real property is limited to particular circumstances. An owner will be liable only if that owner: (1) was engaged in the business of handling or disposing the hazardous substances or waste on the property or knowingly permitted others to engage in such business; (2) permitted the use of the property for disposal of a hazardous substance; (3) knew or should have known of the presence of the hazardous substance upon acquiring the property *and* "associated himself with the release"; or (4) contributed to the release after the owner knew or should have known of the presence of the hazardous substance.[115]

With respect to item (3), a written warranty or representation of the seller in a recorded instrument for the conveyance constitutes admissible evidence of whether the buyer knew or should have known of the presence of the hazardous substance.[116]

This appears to be a less stringent standard of owner liability than exists under CERCLA. There is no "innocent landowner defense" in the Arizona statute, and such a defense appears not to be necessary given the limited standard of liability in the first instance.

When applicable, liability is strict and joint and several, unless the defendant can establish that liability should be apportioned based on several criteria set forth in the law.[117] A private right of action for contribution is authorized.[118]

Arkansas

The Arkansas Superfund statute provides for much the same liable persons and defenses as CERCLA.[119] The third party defense appears

---

114 Ariz. Rev. Stat. Ann. § 49-283.A. and D.

115 *Id.*, § 49-283.B.

116 *Id.*

117 *Id.*, § 49-285.

118 *Id.*, § 49-285.B.

119 Ark. Code Ann. §§ 8-7-403, 8-7-416 and 8-7-512.

to be unqualified, however. Thus, there is no CERCLA-type innocent landowner defense and no need for one.[120] Liability is apportioned.[121] The statute does not expressly state whether a private right of action exists for indemnity or contribution. The statute is also silent on whether liability is strict, but it would probably be construed consistently with CERCLA in this respect.

California

The California Carpenter-Presley-Tanner Hazardous Substance Account Act ("California Superfund") adopts by reference the CERCLA standards for liable persons and defenses, including the innocent landowner defense.[122] However, with respect to owner-occupied, single-family residential properties of five acres or less, the statute reverses the usual burden of proof and presumes that the owner is not liable unless the state Department of Health Services certifies and then proves that the "hazardous substance release occurred after the owner acquired the property," *or* that the "hazardous substance release occurred before the owner acquired the property and at the time of acquisition the owner knew or had reason to know of the hazardous substance release."[123]

Liability under California Superfund is strict and, if a defendant can establish that only a portion of the costs are attributable to that party's actions, liability is apportioned.[124] Indemnity or contribution actions among PRPs are expressly authorized unless a PRP has already had its liability apportioned and discharged or is actively participating in an apportionment proceeding.[125]

Effective January 1, 1994, an immunity from liability under California Superfund and other state and local laws will be accorded to community redevelopment agencies that undertake and properly complete action to remove or remedy hazardous substance releases from property within a redevelopment project, and this immunity will extend

---

[120]   *Id.,* § 8-7-416(b).

[121]   *Id.,* § 8-7-414.

[122]   Cal. Health & Safety Code § 25323.5.

[123]   *Id.,* § 25360.2.

[124]   *Id.,* § 25363(a) and (d).

[125]   *Id.,* § 25363(e).

to protect agents or employees of the agency as well as persons who purchase property from such an agency for redevelopment and lenders on such projects.[126]

Connecticut

The Connecticut statute does not follow the language of CERCLA with respect to PRPs. It provides that any "person, firm, or corporation which directly or indirectly causes pollution and contamination of any land or waters of the state or causes an emergency through a discharge, spillage . . . or which owns any hazardous wastes deemed by the commissioner to be a potential threat to human health or the environment and removed by the commissioner shall be liable for all costs. . ."[127] If the pollution was caused negligently, the liability is for one and one-half times the cleanup cost, and, if willfully caused, the liability is doubled.[128]

With respect to defenses, the statute differs from CERCLA because it only provides that "a mortgagee who acquires title to real estate by virtue of a foreclosure or tender of a deed in lieu of foreclosure, shall not be liable for any assessment, fine or other costs imposed by the state for any spill upon such real estate beyond the value of such real estate, provided such spill occurred prior to the date of acquisition of title to such real estate by such mortgagee."[129] Of course, the need for defenses is diminished due to the limited definition of responsible parties.

Liability is apportioned among jointly responsible persons, and private parties who clean up a hazardous waste spill are entitled to reimbursement from other responsible persons whose negligence or other actions resulted in the pollution.[130]

---

[126]   Cal. Health & Safety Code § 33459.2 (operative Jan. 1, 1994), added by Stats. 1990, c.1113 (A.B. 3193).

[127]   Conn. Gen. Stat. Ann. § 22a-451(a).

[128]   *Id.*

[129]   *Id.,* § 22a-452b.

[130]   *Id.,* § 22a-452.

Florida

The Florida statute provides for the same liable persons as CERCLA, except that intervening landowners apparently have no statutory liability.[131] The statute also includes the same defenses as CERCLA, except that no innocent landowner defense is provided. The statute adds as a defense an "act of government, either state, federal, or local, unless the person claiming the defense is a governmental body, in which case this defense is available only by acts of other governmental bodies."[132]

Liability is probably joint and several,[133] and the statute is silent on whether liability is strict.

Illinois

The Illinois Environmental Protection Act parallels CERCLA and provides for substantially the same liable persons and defenses, including the innocent landowner defense.[134] Another defense is added, however, exempting from liability those releases which were permitted by state or federal law.[135]

There is no provision in the Illinois law as to whether liability is strict or joint and several, but the statute would probably be construed consistently with CERCLA.

Louisiana

The Louisiana Liability for Hazardous Substance Remedial Action Law provides for much the same liable persons and defenses as CERCLA,[136] but appears not to include the innocent landowner defense. Liability is strict and can be apportioned if there is a reasonable basis for apportionment, and parties who clean up hazardous

---

[131] Fla. Stat. Ann. Tit. 29 § 403.727(4).

[132] *Id.*, § 403.727(5).

[133] *Id.*, § 376.307(5).

[134] Ill. Ann. Stat. Ch. 111 1/2 paras. 1022.2(f) and (j).

[135] *Id.*, para. 1022.2(j)(2).

[136] La. Rev. Stat. Ann. §§ 30:2276 and 30:2277.

wastes may sue nonparticipating liable parties for "twice their portion of the remedial costs."[137]

Maine

The Maine Uncontrolled Hazardous Substance Site Law provides for liable persons and defenses similar to those set forth in CERCLA.[138] However, it appears that the state is required to show a causal relationship between the health or safety threat of the site and the acts or omissions of the PRP.[139] If so, this is a significant limitation on the potential for innocent party liability as compared to CERCLA and the laws of many other states. Moreover, the statute provides a defense for acts or omissions of third parties unless the third party is an agent or employee of the defendant, without excepting from the defense, as CERCLA does, acts or omissions by third parties with whom the defendant has or had a contractual relationship.[140] This appears to provide a broader third party defense, avoiding any need for an innocent landowner defense.

Liability is strict (as long as there is a causal relationship, even though without negligence) and joint and several.[141]

Maryland

The Maryland statute provides for much the same liable persons as CERCLA,[142] but excepts from the definition of responsible person: "(i) A person who purchases a site containing a controlled hazardous substance without knowledge of the existence of the controlled hazardous substance at the site; or (ii) A holder of a mortgage or deed of trust who acquires title through foreclosure to a site containing a controlled hazardous substance."[143]

---

137   *Id.*, § 30:2276.

138   Me. Rev. Stat. Ann. Tit. 38 §§ 1362 and 1367.

139   *Id.*, § 1367.

140   *Id.*

141   *Id.*

142   Md. Health-Envtl. Code Ann. § 7-201(1).

143   *Id.*, § 7-201(x)(2).

These are significant limitations on liability as compared to CERCLA and other states. The Maryland statute does not appear to require any due diligence on the part of a purchaser as a foundation for lack of knowledge. The broad exemption for purchasers without knowledge avoids the strictures of the "innocent landowner defense." Lenders who foreclose on contaminated property are exempted, which is also more favorable treatment than is accorded under CERCLA and the laws of many other states. On the other hand, the Maryland statute does not provide for the other CERCLA-type defenses.

Liability is apportioned if there is a reasonable basis for apportionment,[144] and the statute is silent on whether liability is strict.

Massachusetts

The Massachusetts Oil and Hazardous Material Release Prevention and Response Act defines liable persons in much the same way as CERCLA, but adds to the list "any person who otherwise caused or is legally responsible for a release or threat of release."[145] The statute allows the same defenses as CERCLA, except that the innocent landowner defense is apparently not available.[146]

Owners of contaminated property who can prove entitlement to one of the defenses (e.g., the third party defense) do not avoid liability altogether. Rather, their liability is limited to "the value of the property following the department's assessment, containment and removal actions."[147] At least any greater liability is avoided.

Liability is strict and joint and several unless the person can show it should be apportioned.[148] Parties who clean up a hazardous waste area are entitled to reimbursement from other responsible persons.[149]

---

144   *Id.*, § 7-221.

145   Mass. Gen. Laws Ann. Ch. 21E § 5(a).

146   *Id.*, § 5(c).

147   *Id.*, § 5(d).

148   *Id.*, § 5(a), (b) and (e).

149   *Id.*, § 4.

Michigan

The Michigan Environmental Response Act is quite different from CERCLA and other Superfund laws. Apparently the only liable persons are those "whose action or negligence caused a condition requiring expenditure of money pursuant to this act," and there are no defenses mentioned in the act.[150] Thus, it appears that fault, or at least some active participation in the creation of the condition, is required for liability under the Michigan law. The statute is silent on whether liability is joint and several or apportioned when more than one party is at fault.

Nevada

The Nevada statute does not follow CERCLA's provisions on liable persons or defenses. It provides only that any "person who possessed or had in his care any hazardous material involved in a spill or accident requiring the cleaning and decontamination of the affected area is responsible for that cleaning and decontamination."[151] There does not appear to be a provision for defenses or for the type of liability imposed.

New Hampshire

The New Hampshire statute provides for much the same liable persons and defenses as CERCLA,[152] but does not appear to provide an innocent landowner defense. However, the statute does provide a defense for acts or omissions by third parties unless the third party was an agent or employee of the defendant, without including the exception from the defense for acts or omissions by third parties with whom the defendant has or had a contractual relationship.[153] This may be construed as providing a defense for acts or omissions of third parties with whom the defendant did have a contractual relationship, so long as the defendant "exercised due care with respect to the hazardous substance concerned" and "took precautions against foreseeable acts or omissions of any such third party" as required by the statute. Thus, the New Hampshire third party defense appears to be broader than the

---

[150]   Mich. Gen. Stats. Ann. § 299.608.

[151]   Nev. Rev. Stat. § 459.750.

[152]   N.H. Rev. Stat. Ann. §§ 147-B:10 and 147-B:10a.

[153]   *Id.*, § 147-B:10a.

CERCLA third party defense, so that an innocent landowner defense is not required.

Liability is strict,[154] and the statute is silent on whether liability is joint and several or apportioned. The statute authorizes parties who clean up a hazardous waste release to sue other responsible parties for reimbursement.[155]

New Jersey

The New Jersey Spill Compensation and Control Act does not follow CERCLA's provisions on liable persons. The statute provides that any "person who has discharged a hazardous substance or is in any way responsible for any hazardous substance which the department has removed or is removing pursuant to [this act] shall be strictly liable, jointly and severally, without regard to fault, for all cleanup and removal costs."[156] However, the phrase "in any way responsible" has been given a broad interpretation so that it includes owners or controllers of a site at the time of the hazardous waste discharge, even if the property was leased and the lessee was the discharger.[157]

The defenses provided in the statute are also different from those provided in CERCLA. The only available defenses are an "act or omission caused solely by war, sabotage, or God."[158]

Liability is strict and joint and several.[159] While private cleanup is permissible "provided such persons coordinate and obtain approval for such actions with on going state or federal operations,"[160] the New Jersey law, unlike most other Superfund laws, contains no authority for indemnity or contribution actions by responsible parties. Indeed, it has

---

[154]   *Id.*, § 147-B:10.

[155]   *Id.*, § 147-B:10(III)(b).

[156]   N.J. Stat. Ann. § 58:10-23.11g.c.

[157]   *State, Dept. of Environ. Protect. v. Ventron Corp.*, 94 N.J. 473, 502, 468 A.2d 150 (1983); *Tree Realty, Inc. v. Department of Treasury*, 205 N.J. Super. 346, 500 A.2d 1075 (A.D. 1985).

[158]   N.J. Stat. Ann. § 58:10-23.11g.d.

[159]   *Id.*, § 58:10-23.11g.c.

[160]   *Id.*, § 58:10-23.11f.a.

been held by a court that a property owner could not state a claim under the Spill Compensation and Control Act against other parties who actually caused the disposal of hazardous wastes.[161] Thus, other theories of private party action must be utilized in New Jersey.

New York

The New York Environmental Conservation Law authorizes the state to order (i) the owner or operator of any inactive hazardous waste disposal site or (ii) any person responsible for the disposal of hazardous wastes at such a site, to develop and implement a remedial program.[162] The statute creates a fund and authorizes the state to use the money to develop and implement the remedial program for the site when the responsible person who has been ordered to clean up the site fails to do so.[163] The ordered person is liable to the state for the cost of the remedial action developed and taken by the state, along with any money damages and penalties.[164]

The statue is silent on the standard of liability, on whether liability is joint and several or apportioned and on whether any defenses are available.

Oregon

The Oregon statute provides for slightly different classes of "responsible persons" than does CERCLA, including:

> (a) Any owner or operator at or during the time of the acts or omissions that resulted in the release.

> (b) Any owner or operator who became the owner or operator after the time of the acts or omissions that resulted in the release, and who knew or reasonably should have known of the release when the person first became the owner or operator.

---

161   *Jersey City Redevelopment Authority v. PPG Industries*, 655 F Supp. 1257, 1262-63 (D.N.J. 1987) (distinguishing the New Jersey provisions from the private right of action accorded by CERCLA).

162   N.Y. ECL §§ 27-1313.3.a. and 27-1313.5.f.

163   *Id.*, § 27-1313.5.a.

164   *Id.*, §§ 27-1313.5.a. and 27-1313.5.f.

(c) Any owner or operator who obtained actual knowledge of the release at the facility at the time the person was owner or operator of the facility and then subsequently transferred ownership or operation of the facility to another person without disclosing such knowledge.

(d) Any person who, by acts or omissions, caused, contributed to or exacerbated the release, unless the acts or omissions were in material compliance with applicable laws, standards, regulations, licenses or permits.

(e) Any person who unlawfully hinders or delays entry to, investigation of or removal or remedial action at a facility.[165]

The Oregon statute contains all of the defenses provided in CERCLA, including the innocent landowner defense for persons who have undertaken an appropriate level of inquiry into the past ownership and uses of the property. An additional defense is provided, to the effect that there is no liability for any owner or operator "if the facility was contaminated by the migration of a hazardous substance from real property not owned or operated by the person."[166] However, the defenses can be lost if, among other things, the person obtains actual knowledge of the release and fails to notify the state promptly and fails to exercise due care with respect to the hazardous substance concerned.[167]

Liability is strict and a private right of action for reimbursement against PRPs is authorized.[168]

Pennsylvania

The Pennsylvania Hazardous Sites Cleanup Act provides for substantially the same liable persons and defenses as CERCLA,

---

[165] Or. Rev. Stat. § 466.567(1).

[166] *Id.*, §§ 466.567(2) and (6).

[167] *Id.*, § 466.567(4).

[168] *Id.*, § 466.567(1).

including the innocent landowner defense.[169] However, a foreclosing financial institution is exempted from liability if the only basis of liability is ownership of the land.[170] In addition, the statute provides that there is no liability for "an owner of real property if the real property is exclusively used as single- or multi-family housing of four units or less or for private noncommercial recreational purposes, and the owner did not place the hazardous substance on the property, or the owner did not know and had no reason to know that a hazardous substance which is the subject of the release or threatened release was disposed on, in or at the site."[171] Liability is strict,[172] but contribution actions between responsible persons are authorized and liability can be allocated if a party can prove how liability should be allocated based on a number of factual and equitable factors.[173]

Rhode Island

The Rhode Island Environmental Response Fund uses different language to define liable persons. It provides that any person who violates "the provisions of this chapter through transportation, storage, or disposal of hazardous wastes in a manner or location not authorized by this chapter. . . or who shall have caused such unauthorized transportation, storage, or disposal of hazardous wastes shall be absolutely liable for the costs of containment, cleanup, restoration and removal of the hazardous wastes, and for all damages, losses or injuries, including environmental, which result directly or indirectly from such discharge."[174] There does not appear to be a provision for defenses. Liability is strict (actually "absolute")[175] and there does not appear to be a provision on whether liability is joint and several or apportioned.

---

[169] 35 Pa. Cons. Stat. Ann. §§ 6020.701 and 6020.703.

[170] *Id.*, § 6020.701(b)(1)(vi)(D).

[171] *Id.*, § 6020.701(b)(2).

[172] *Id.*, § 6020.702(a).

[173] *Id.*, §§ 6020.705(a) and (b).

[174] R.I. Gen. Laws § 23-19.1-22.

[175] *Id.*, § 23-19.1-22(a).

Tennessee

The Tennessee statute provides for nearly the same responsible persons as CERCLA.[176] There does not appear to be a provision for defenses (other than the qualified immunity for those assisting cleanup).[177] Liability is apportioned,[178] but the statute appears to be silent on whether liability is strict.

Texas

The Texas Solid Waste Disposal Act provides for substantially the same responsible persons and defenses as CERCLA, including the innocent landowner defense, at least with respect to solid waste facilities.[179] Liability is apportioned if the release is proved to be divisible; otherwise persons are jointly and severally liable.[180] The statute is silent on whether liability is strict. Private parties who take remedial actions are allowed to seek cost recovery from other liable parties.[181]

Vermont

The Vermont statute provides for substantially the same responsible persons and defenses as does CERCLA.[182] Interestingly, the innocent landowner defense is made equally applicable to operators who conducted a due diligence investigation and had no knowledge or reason to know of the contamination upon becoming the operator of the property.[183] This appears to be an expansion or clarification of the CERCLA defense which is quite reasonable. Under CERCLA and the laws of many other states, a purchaser of land, but apparently not a lessee who becomes a mere operator, can by exercising due diligence gain the benefit of the innocent landowner defense. This distinction

---

176   Tenn. Code Ann. § 68-46-202.

177   *Id.*, § 68-46-207(d).

178   *Id.*, § 68-46-207(b).

179   Tex. Rev. Civ. Stat. Ann. Art. 4477-7 §§ 8(g)(2), (3), and (6)(A) and (B).

180   *Id.*, §§ 8(g)(4) and 11.

181   *Id.*, § 11.

182   Vt. Stat. Ann. Tit. 10 §§ 6615(a), (d), and (e).

183   *Id.*, § 6615(e).

means that lessees have greater risks than purchasers under CERCLA, a difference which can apparently be avoided under the Vermont law. (However, see section 1.2.6-1 for an argument that CERCLA's innocent landowner defense can and should be interpreted to apply to operators as well as owners.)

Liability is strict and joint and several, unless the defendant can establish that he is responsible for only a portion of the costs.[184]

Virginia

The Virginia laws differ from CERCLA in defining liable persons. The state must "promptly seek reimbursement from any party causing or contributing to an accident or incident involving hazardous materials for all sums disbursed from the Virginia Disaster Response Fund for the protection, relief, and recovery from loss or damage caused by such party."[185] Similarly, parties who have mismanaged a site are liable for cleanup costs expended from the Virginia Solid and Hazardous Waste Contingency Fund.[186] These laws appear to require fault as a basis for liability to the state. There are no provisions for CERCLA-type defenses, consistent with the limited standard of liability in the first instance.

---

[184]   *Id.*, § 6615(c).

[185]   Va. Code Ann. § 44-146.37(B). See also § 44-146.18:1.

[186]   *Id.*, § 10.1-1406.C.

CHAPTER TWO

SUPERFUND COST RECOVERY LIENS AND SUPERLIENS

2.1   Introduction

Whenever real estate is encumbered by any lien, the owner's equity in the property is reduced in an amount equal to the outstanding balance of the indebtedness secured by the lien. Most liens are voluntary, such as a mortgage or a deed of trust as security for a loan, and there is nothing remarkable about the process. However, an owner's equity is also at risk of involuntary liens which are authorized by law under some circumstances. This can threaten the value of a property to the owner. Involuntary liens, as well as previous voluntary liens, also diminish the value of the property as collateral for a new loan which might be desired by the owner. Thus, the existence of liens are important both to the owner and lenders.

CERCLA and the Superfund laws of many states expressly authorize the applicable governmental agency to impose an involuntary lien on property for repayment of hazardous substance response or cleanup costs. Those costs, and hence the amount of such a lien, can in many cases exceed the value of the property, leaving no value for the owner or other lienholders (except those with lien priority). The nature and special features of the federal and state Superfund lien laws are the subject of this chapter.

The Superfund lien laws were adopted chiefly for the purpose of providing a means of recovery even if a PRP files for bankruptcy protection. As will be discussed in Part III, the Bankruptcy Code provides for the discharge of indebtedness in general, and some courts have found that this applies to hazardous waste cleanup costs just like any other debt. Thus, the policies of the Bankruptcy Code and the Superfund laws are in conflict. That conflict was resolved to the extent possible by the adoption of the Superfund lien laws allowing for the imposition of liens on property for indebtedness to the Superfund. As a secured creditor in a bankruptcy proceeding, the government will be able to recover the amounts owed to it, at least up to the value of the property subject to the lien, in line with any other secured creditors who might have lien priority. The government may or may not recover the full amount of the cleanup costs, depending upon the value of the property, the amount of the government's lien and the amount of any senior liens. But at least the government will not be in the position of an unsecured creditor who could only share in the remainder, if any, of the debtor's estate after secured creditors and administrative claims have been paid.[1]

2.2 Federal Lien Provisions

CERCLA provides for a federal lien for the recovery of all costs and damages for which a PRP is liable to the United States in connection with the response to a release or threatened release of a hazardous substance.[2] The lien affects the real property belonging to the PRP which is the subject of a removal or remedial action.[3]

The U.S. EPA's imposition of a CERCLA lien has been challenged in several court cases. The first few court opinions rejected those challenges on the ground that the EPA had not yet sought to enforce the lien by pursuing cost recovery, and pre-enforcement judicial review of the government's removal or remedial actions is expressly barred by 42

---

[1]   This purpose for the adoption of the Superfund lien laws (both federal and state), and related legislative history, is detailed in Wagner, *Liability for Hazardous Waste Cleanup: An Examination of New Jersey's Approach*, 13 Harvard Environ. L.Rev. 245 (1989).

[2]   42 U.S.C. § 9607(l)(1).

[3]   *Id.*

U.S.C. § 9613(b) and (h).[4] However, another court has held that CERCLA does not bar judicial review of a constitutional challenge to the validity of a CERCLA lien. That court went on to hold that the CERCLA lien provisions violate the Fifth Amendment due process clause, in that a lien could be in place for years without any opportunity for a hearing, thereby depriving persons of property without adequate procedural safeguards. The court found that due process would include notice and an opportunity for a pre-deprivation hearing of a claim that the lien is not valid or is subject to a defense.[5] It remains to be seen whether this ruling will be upheld as the law in other federal circuits.

Subject to any procedural changes which may be adopted to cure any due process deficiency, as between the United States and the PRP who owns the property, the lien arises and is in effect when response costs are first incurred *or* when the PRP has been provided with formal written notice of potential liability, whichever is later.[6] The lien continues until the liability (or a judgment arising out of that liability) is satisfied or becomes unenforceable due to the running out of the statute of limitations under CERCLA.[7] The United States may foreclose the lien through an action in the federal district court; and the United States has the right, unaffected by its lien right, to pursue the PRP personally on the debt.[8]

With respect to third parties, the federal lien is perfected and gains priority as of the time when notice of the lien is filed or recorded in the proper place.[9] Thus, the federal lien is a regular priority lien, without the special precedence asserted under several state superlien laws which

---

[4] *See, e.g., Barmet Aluminum Corp. v. Reilly*, 927 F.2d 289, 293 (6th Cir. 1991); *South Macomb Disposal Authority v. U.S.E.P.A.*, 681 F.Supp. 1244, 1249-51 (E.D. Mich. 1988); *Apache Powder Co. v. U.S.*, No. 89-375-TUC-WUB (D. Ariz. Apr. 26, 1990).

[5] *See Reardon v. U.S.*, 947 F.2d 1509 (1st Cir. 1991). A dissenting judge would have been satisfied with a prompt post-deprivation hearing at the instance of a landowner claiming not to be liable.

[6] 42 U.S.C. § 9607(l)(2).

[7] *Id.*

[8] 42 U.S.C. § 9607(l)(4).

[9] 42 U.S.C. § 9607(l)(3)

will be discussed below. It is important to determine, however, what is the proper place for the filing or recordation of the federal lien, as it varies from state to state. If the government has not properly filed or recorded the lien, another lienholder who properly perfects its lien without knowledge of the federal response costs would appear to gain priority over the federal lien.

CERCLA provides that the proper place for filing the federal response cost lien is "in the appropriate office within the State (or county or other governmental subdivision), as designated by State law, in which the real property subject to the lien is located" or "[i]f the State has not by law designated one office for the receipt of such notices of liens, the notice shall be filed in the office of the clerk of the United States district court for the district where the real property is located."[10] Thus, the proper place for filing is as designated by state law or, failing that, with the United States district court. Accordingly, it is necessary to determine whether each state has by law designated the place for filing of a CERCLA lien.

California, for example, has adopted the Uniform Federal Lien Registration Act (UFLRA) which applies to federal tax liens and "other federal liens notices of which under any Act of Congress or any regulation adopted pursuant thereto are required or permitted to be filed in the same manner as notices of federal tax liens."[11] Although there are no cases addressing the issue of whether a CERCLA lien is one which is required or permitted to be filed in the same manner as notices of federal tax liens, a comparison of the filing requirements for both federal tax liens and CERCLA liens shows a substantial similarity, both in effect and in the language used.

Under federal law, notice of a federal tax lien on real property must be filed in "one office within the State (or the county, or other governmental subdivision), as designated by the laws of such State, in which the property subject to the lien is situated," *or* "[i]n the office of the clerk of the United States district court for the judicial district in which the property subject to the lien is situated, whenever the State has not by law designated one office which meets the [foregoing filing

---

[10]   *Id.*

[11]   Cal. Code Civ. Proc. § 2100.

requirement]."[12] This appears to be very similar to the CERCLA lien provision quoted above. Thus, the logical conclusion is that CERCLA liens are required or permitted to be filed in the same manner as notices of federal tax liens, and, hence, that **California's** UFLRA governs the proper place for filing of CERCLA liens in **California**.

Under **California's** UFLRA, the proper place for filing the notice of a lien in favor of the United States on real property is in the office of the recorder of the county in which the real property subject to the lien is located.[13] Thus, it appears that CERCLA liens in **California** must be recorded with the county recorder, and that if the United States instead files a CERCLA lien affecting **California** real estate with the clerk of the United States district court, the lien would not appear to be properly filed and would risk loss of priority to other, subsequent lienholders who properly perfect their liens first.

Notwithstanding the foregoing analysis, the government might file a CERCLA lien in **California** with the clerk of the United States district court. An attorney with the EPA Superfund Enforcement Branch (San Francisco) has informally advised that the EPA considers it optional in **California** whether to file a CERCLA lien with the county recorder or with the United States district court. The general practice is to record such liens with the county recorder, and in such cases the EPA has referred to UFLRA as the law authorizing the recordation of the lien. On the other hand, the lien might be filed instead with the United States district court, particularly if the EPA is also commencing a cost recovery action in the court.

This informal view of at least one EPA attorney appears to be erroneous. As pointed out above, CERCLA provides for filing of the lien in the United States district court "*if*" (presumably meaning *only if*) the state has not designated the place for filing within that state. Where a state, through adoption of UFLRA or otherwise, has designated that place, there would appear to be no option open to the EPA. Which interpretation is correct may ultimately become the subject of litigation in a case where another creditor believes that its lien has priority over a CERCLA lien because the EPA filed in the wrong place and therefore

---

[12]   26 U.S.C. §§ 6323(f)(1)(A)(i) and 6323(f)(1)(B).

[13]   Cal. Code Civ. Proc. § 2101(b).

did not properly perfect the CERCLA lien. There are no court decisions yet discussing this issue.

Many states in addition to **California** have adopted UFLRA or variations thereof, and many have not. In either case, most states have provided for a local government office to accept notices of federal liens. Of the states surveyed, however, four (**Arizona, Delaware, New Jersey** and **Pennsylvania**) have not designated any office; therefore, it appears that the proper place for filing notices of CERCLA liens in those states is with the clerk of the United States district court for the district in which the property subject to the lien is located.

Table 2-1 sets forth the proper place for the filing of notices of CERCLA liens in the states included in the table, based on the view that the EPA does not have an option where the state has designated the place for filing of such a federal lien. Naturally, as with all the legal references in this book, the reader should use this table as only the first step in research and should confirm that the information is correct and up-to-date in any particular situation.

TABLE 2-1

PLACE FOR FILING OF CERCLA LIENS

State	Filing Office[a]	Statutory Citation	Adopted UFLRA[b]
Arizona	U.S. District Court Clerk[c]	No Statute for Non-Tax Federal Liens	No
California	County Recorder	Calif. Code Civ. Pro. §§ 2100-01	Yes
Connecticut	Town Clerk	Conn. Gen. Stats. § 49-32a	Yes
Delaware	U.S. District Court Clerk	No Statute for Non-Tax Federal Liens	No
Illinois	County Recorder	Ill. Ann. Stats. ch. 82, para. 66 § 1	No
Indiana	County Recorder	Indiana Code § 36-2-11-25	No
Maine	Registry of Deeds	Maine Rev. Stats. Ann. Tit. 33 § 1803(2)	Yes
Maryland	Circuit Court Clerk	Md. Real Prop. Code Ann. §§ 3-401(a)	Yes

Superfund Cost Recovery Liens and Superliens

State	Filing Office[a]	Statutory Citation	Adopted UFLRA[b]
Massachusetts	Register of Deeds	Mass. Gen. Laws Ann. ch. 36 § 24	No
Michigan	Register of Deeds	Mich. Comp. Laws Ann. § 211.663(2)	Yes
Minnesota	County Recorder	Minn. Stats. Ann. § 272.481(b)	Yes
Missouri	Recorder of Deeds	Missouri Ann. Stats. § 14.010(2)	No
Nevada	County Recorder	Nev. Rev. Stats. Ann. § 108.827(2)	Yes
New Hampshire	Registry of Deed	N.H. Rev. Stats. Ann. § 454-B:2 II	Yes
New Jersey	U.S. District Court Clerk	No Statute for Non-Tax Federal Liens	No
New York	County Clerk[d]	N.Y. Lien Law § 240(1)	No
Ohio	County Recorder	Ohio Rev. Code Ann. § 317.09(A)	No

State	Filing Office[a]	Statutory Citation	Adopted UFLRA[b]
Oregon	Recorder of Conveyances or County Clerk	Or. Rev. Stats. § 87.806(2)	Yes
Pennsylvania	U.S. District Court Clerk	No Statute for Non-Tax Federal Liens	No
Rhode Island	Recorder of Deeds, or City or Town Clerk	R.I. Gen. Laws § 34-34-1	No
Vermont	Town Clerk	Vt. Stats. Ann. Tit. 9 § 2051	No
Virginia	Circuit Court Clerk	Va. Code Ann. § 55-142.1(B)	Yes
Wisconsin	Register of Deeds	Wisc. Stats. Ann. § 779.97(2)(b)	Yes

Notes to Table 2-1:

(a)   All offices refer to the office in the district, county, city or town in which the property is located.

(b)   Uniform Federal Lien Registration Act.

(c)   Where no state law specifies the place of filing, the lien must be filed with the U. S. District Court Clerk.

(d)   Liens on real property located in the counties of Kings, Queens, New York, or Bronx must be filed with the City Register of the City of New York in such county.

2.3   State Lien and Superlien Provisions

A number of states have followed the lead of CERCLA by enacting their own laws authorizing the state or local governments to record cleanup cost recovery liens on real property. These laws, like the lien provision in CERCLA, provide a means for the states to recoup money expended from their Superfunds, even if the debtor files for bankruptcy protection. Of the states surveyed for this section, sixteen have such lien provisions in their environmental laws, as set forth in **Table 2-2** and summarized below.

The state Superfund lien laws are not uniform. For example, **Arkansas, California, Connecticut, Louisiana, Michigan, Ohio, Tennessee, Texas** and **Virginia** have lien laws only allowing a lien to be recorded against the contaminated property or property where remedial activities were carried out. On the other hand, **Maine, Maryland, Massachusetts, New Hampshire, New Jersey** and **Oregon** have enacted lien laws allowing the state to record liens against *all* real estate of the responsible person(s).

The lien generally is for the amount of the state expenditures, and at least in some states, including **Maine, Maryland, Massachusetts** and **Oregon**, the lien includes interest and penalties. The **Arkansas** statute provides that the lien amount shall include any increase in the value of the property due to the cleanup measures, at least where the owner was at fault in causing the hazardous substance release.[14]

Several states provide for so-called *superliens*. **Connecticut, Maine, Massachusetts, New Hampshire** and **New Jersey**[15] have enacted "superlien" statutes which give the lien precedence over some or all previously recorded liens or encumbrances. While the **Texas** statute is not a superlien law, it provides that a lien will have priority over a previously recorded encumbrance if the party knew or reasonably should have known that the property was subject to cleanup action. In contrast, the cleanup cost recovery liens of other states, which are not

---

[14]   Ark. Code Ann. § 8-7-516.

[15]   The **New Jersey** superlien law has been upheld upon constitutional challenge, *Kessler v. Tarrat*s, 194 N.J. Super. 136, 476 A.2d 326 (App. Div. 1984).

accorded superlien status, operate like other, regular liens which have priority based on the time of filing or recordation.

All the superlien statutes provide for a superlien on the contaminated property of the responsible person(s). In addition, the **Maine, Massachusetts, New Hampshire** and **New Jersey** statutes provide for a regular priority lien against *other* property of the responsible person(s). These are commonly referred to as "spreading liens." The **Connecticut, Massachusetts** and **New Jersey** statutes provide that the lien is a regular priority lien with respect to residential real estate. One state, **Maine**, provides that no lien may be filed against real estate used for single or multi-family unit housing or against property owned by a municipality.[16] The superlien statutes of **New Hampshire** and **New Jersey** expressly provide that a lien may be recorded against the business revenues as well as all real and personal property of the responsible person(s). The **New Hampshire** statute also provides that the lien is a superlien with respect to business revenues generated from the contaminated facility.[17]

A significant concern is the actual extent to which a superlien "primes" other liens. The **Connecticut** statute grants priority to a superlien covering contaminated property as of June 3, 1985, the effective date of that superlien law. Other encumbrances recorded before that date would retain their priority, and only those encumbrances recorded after that date (but before the actual filing of the superlien) would lose priority.[18] **Maine** has a similar provision based on when its superlien law was enacted in 1987.[19] In contrast, the **New Hampshire** superlien is a first priority lien which primes all other liens and encumbrances, whenever recorded as to the contaminated property and business revenues generated therefrom and personal property located there; but it is a regular priority lien, as of the time of recordation as to all other assets of the debtor.[20] Thus, in each case, the

---

16   Me. Rev. Stat. Ann. Tit. 38 § 1371.5.

17   N.H. Rev. Stat. Ann. § 147-B:10-b.

18   Conn. Gen. Stat. Ann. § 22a-452a.

19   Me. Rev. Stat. Ann. Tit. 38 § 1371.2.A.

20   N.H. Rev. Stat. Ann. § 147-B:10b.III.

specific provisions of the superlien law must be analyzed and applied in order to determine the exact scope of the priority accorded as against another lien or encumbrance and as to what kind of property.

The superlien laws ensure that the state Superfund involved will be reimbursed ahead of some or all other previously secured creditors. This is naturally a controversial subject with financial institutions which do not want the priority of their mortgages to be disturbed. The lender lobby has succeeded in avoiding the enactment of superlien laws in a number of states where such laws were considered. Moreover, **Arkansas** and **Tennessee**, which formerly had superlien laws, amended their laws to provide for regular-priority liens instead. Thus, the trend toward adoption of superlien laws appears to have stalled, and time will tell whether the actions of **Arkansas** and **Tennessee** will mark the beginning of a reversal of that trend.

Although this chapter focuses on Superfund liens, there may be other environmental laws which contain lien provisions. The **California** Water Code, for example, provides for cost recovery liens on properties which have been the subject of abatement action.[21] Such state laws should not be overlooked.

2.3.1 Local Lien Laws

County or city ordinances may authorize a lien or assessment to be recorded as a means of recouping the costs of hazardous waste cleanup. In this regard, a number of local laws in **California** authorize a lien or assessment to be recorded against property that is the subject of certain remedial activities. For instance, in the city of **Los Angeles**, if a public nuisance caused by flammable or hazardous materials is abated by the fire department or any other city department, the costs of abatement will constitute a special assessment against the parcel of land upon which the nuisance was maintained, and will upon recordation be a lien upon that property.[22] In the city of **Santa Ana**, if the enforcement officer determines that a public nuisance exists, the city council may order that the cost of any abatement by the city shall be assessed against the

---

[21]   Cal. Water Code § 13305(f).

[22]   Los Angeles Municipal Code § 57.01.19.

premises.[23] The city of **San Francisco** has similar authority to record assessment liens against property where nuisances or hazards are abated by the city.[24]

While these city code provisions were not necessarily written with a view toward cleaning up contaminated real estate and recovering the cost, the language used in each of the codes is broad enough to permit that result, at least where the condition has become a public nuisance and the municipality is the governmental entity which responds to it. This kind of authority on the part of local governments is probably typical throughout the nation, consistent with the exercise of police powers for the protection of public health and safety. Under the laws of some states, local governments may obtain funding from the state Superfund for cleanup costs (unless the local government is itself the responsible party). Thus, in this indirect way, it might be possible in many states for Superfund resources to pay for a cleanup by local agencies and for an assessment lien to be imposed against the property under local law even though the state Superfund law is silent on the subject of liens.

The relative priority of local assessment liens would have to be determined by reference to the applicable laws. For example, **California** law allows public agencies, counties and cities to assess liens on real property for the cost of abatement of nuisances, with the same priority, and collected in the same manner as, a tax lien for annual property taxes.[25] Tax and assessment liens generally have priority over voluntary liens and encumbrances such as mortgages and deeds of trust. However, the operation of these laws is complex and subject to exceptions. Thus, a determination whether a particular mortgage or deed of trust would lose priority to a special assessment lien for the abatement of a nuisance can only be made in the context of actual facts and circumstances under the

---

23   Santa Ana Municipal Code § 17-24.

24   San Francisco Bldg. & Mech. Code § 203(k). In addition to the special assessment lien, the obligation to repay the city is "the personal obligation of the property owner and his heirs, successors and assigns." S.F. Bldg. & Mech. Code § 203(r).

25   Cal. Govt. Code §§ 25845 and 38773.1. *See also* Cal. Health & Safety Code §§ 6978 and 6979.

applicable laws. But at least under some circumstances, it may be possible for a local assessment lien for cleanup costs to achieve super-priority over prior recorded encumbrances.

2.3.2 Judgment Liens

Even where a lien is not specifically authorized by a state or local environmental or police power law, the general civil laws for enforcement of judgments should provide a means for imposing a lien on any property of the judgment debtor for which a method of levy is set forth in the law. For example, in **California**, when a money judgment is obtained, an abstract of that judgment may be recorded in any county, whereupon a judgment lien will apply against any and all real property owned by the judgment debtor in that county. A judgment lien has regular lien priority determined by the time of recordation.[26] This procedure should be available whenever a cleanup cost recovery judgment is obtained by a state or local governmental agency. The procedure should also apply to an indemnity or contribution judgment obtained by one PRP against another. Similar enforcement procedures probably exist in all states. Of course, this would be the least desirable form of lien for the government, because it cannot be asserted until after a judgment is obtained and other creditors might have gained priority in the meantime. This would appear, however, to be the only method open to a private party with a cost recovery claim because the statutory cost recovery lien provisions generally authorize only the government to file notices of liens, not private parties.

---

[26]   Cal. Code of Civil Procedure §§ 697.310 et seq.

TABLE 2-2

STATE CLEANUP COST RECOVERY LIEN LAWS

Type of Lien	States[a]
Regular priority lien on property where release occurred or where remedial activities took place.	**Arkansas,**[b] **California,**[c] **Louisiana,**[d] **Ohio,**[e] **Tennessee,**[f] **Texas,**[g] **Virginia**[h]
Regular priority lien against any property, both real and personal, of the responsible person(s).	**Maryland,**[i] **Oregon,**[j] **Pennsylvania**[k]
Superlien on contaminated property only; but **regular priority lien** if property is residential.	**Connecticut**[l]
Superlien on contaminated property and **regular priority lien** against other property of the responsible person(s).	**Maine,**[m] **Massachusetts,**[n] **New Hampshire,**[o] **New Jersey**[p]

Notes to Table 2-2:

(a)   Table 2-2 includes selected state cleanup cost recovery lien laws. Other states may also have similar lien laws.

(b)   The **Arkansas** statute also provides that the lien normally will be for the amount of state expenditures, but "if the expenditure results in an increase in the value of the property, the lien shall also be for the increase in value," at least where the owner was at fault in connection with the release. Ark. Code Ann. §§ 8-7-417 and 8-7-516.

(c)   Effective January 1, 1992, **California's** Superfund law was amended to allow the imposition of a lien on real property which is the subject of a removal or remedial action for costs or damages incurred and payable from Cal-Superfund, but the lien has the priority of a judgment lien upon recordation. Cal. Health and Safety Code § 25365.6. Another new law, also effective January 1, 1992, allows a lien on real property from which a discharge originated and which is owned by the discharger for civil penalties resulting from violation of sanitation laws (industrial wastes and sewer systems). This lien also has the priority of a judgment lien upon recordation. Cal. Government Code § 54740.5. See also Cal. Health and Safety Code § 25863 relating to a similar lien for the costs of impounding radioactive materials.

(d)   The **Louisiana** statute is unique in that a "declaration of abandonment" must be recorded in the mortgage records prior to the recordation of the lien. A site may be declared an "abandoned site" if the secretary finds that the site now contains hazardous wastes, that the site was not properly closed, that the site "may constitute a danger or potential danger to the public health and the environment," or that the site has no financially responsible party or that person has failed to take remedial actions ordered by the secretary. La. Rev. Stat. Ann. § 30:2225.

(e)   Ohio Rev. Code Ann. §§ 3734.12.2(d), 3734.20(B) and 3734.22.

(f)   Tenn. Code Ann. § 68-46-209. The amount of the lien "shall not exceed the amount determined by the appraisal to be the increase in the market value of the property as a result of the clean up work." Tenn. Code Ann. § 68-46-209(b).

(g)   The **Texas** statute provides that the lien is invalid if a party acquired the "real property or an interest therein" before the lien was recorded *unless* that person knew or should have known that the real property was subject to cleanup action or that the state had incurred cleanup costs. Thus, the lien will have priority over a previously recorded lien if that person knew or reasonably should have known that the property was subject to cleanup action. Tex. Rev. Civ. Stat. Ann. Art. 4477-7 § 13(g)(7).

(h)   Va. Code Ann. § 10.1-1406.

(i)   The **Maryland** statute provides that violators of the state's hazardous waste law can be liable for penalties, and a lien can be recorded against "any property, real or personal," of the person liable to pay the penalties. Md. Code Ann. § 7-266(b)(5).

(j)   Or. Rev. Stat. § 466.583.

(k)   35 Pa. Cons. Stat. Ann. § 6020.509.

(l)   The **Connecticut** statute provides that the lien is a superlien on the contaminated property as of June 3, 1985; however, if the lien affects residential real estate, the lien does not have super priority. Conn. Gen. Stat. Ann. § 22a-452a.

(m)   The **Maine** statute also provides that no lien may be filed against real estate used for single or multi-family housing or against property owned by a municipality. Me. Rev. Stat. Ann. Tit. 38 § 1371.5.   This statute is unique in that it is the only superlien statute that does not permit a regular priority cleanup cost recovery lien to be filed against real estate used for single or multi-family housing.

(n)   The **Massachusetts** statute provides that a lien on property primarily devoted to single or multi-family housing shall not have super priority.   Mass. Gen. Laws Ann. Ch. 21E § 13.   The **Massachusetts** lien has been found to cover both past and future cleanup costs.   *Acme Laundry Company, Inc. v. Sec. of Environmental Affairs*, 575 N.E.2d 1086 (Supreme Judicial Court of Mass., 1991).

(o)   The **New Hampshire** statute provides that a lien may be recorded "upon the business revenues and all real and personal property of any person subject to liability," but the lien is only a superlien with respect to "real property on which the hazardous wastes or hazardous material is located" and as to "business revenues generated from the facility on which hazardous waste or hazardous material is located and personal property located there." N.H. Rev. Stat. Ann. § 147-B:10-b.

(p)   The **New Jersey** statute provides that a lien may be recorded against "revenues and all real and personal property of the discharger," but the lien is a regular priority lien with respect to property of six or less dwelling units used exclusively for residential purposes and as to property other than the contaminated property. N.J. Stat. Ann. § 58:10-23.11f.f.

CHAPTER THREE

TRANSFER-TRIGGERED CLEANUP, DISCLOSURE AND REPORTING LAWS

3.1   Introduction

Chapter 1 shows how the Superfund laws have increased the pressure on prospective purchasers, lessees or lenders to perform environmental due diligence. When contamination is discovered, the prospective transferee might be in a position to insist that the owner clean up the problem before completing the transfer, or the parties might otherwise provide for management or allocation of the risk. CERCLA was designed to encourage private party remedial actions so that Superfund resources need not be expended. That encouragement is perhaps the greatest at the time of a desired real estate transaction. In that indirect way, the Superfund laws can be viewed as transfer-triggered cleanup laws.

Similarly under CERCLA, an intervening landowner who wishes to sell land which was already contaminated upon acquisition must disclose that condition at the time of resale in order to avoid being a PRP afterwards. The practical effect is the establishment of a transfer-triggered disclosure law.

However, cleanup and disclosure are not mandated at the time of a transaction by the liability provisions of CERCLA. No civil or criminal penalties apply at that time. A purchaser need not undertake due diligence and a seller need not disclose or clean up known contamination as far as those provisions are concerned. Exposure to Superfund cleanup liability simply is not avoided in that case, and the government will have additional PRPs with potential cleanup responsibility.

There are other provisions of law which go farther and impose an affirmative obligation on a transferor to clean up contaminated property, or to give warnings or to make prescribed disclosures or reports. For example, CERCLA contains a provision which applies to the sale or other transfer of real property "owned by the United States and on which any hazardous substance was stored for one year or more, known to have been released, or disposed of," and which requires the federal agency involved to disclose in the contract the type and quantity of such hazardous substance and when the storage, release or disposal occurred. The federal agency must also include such information in the deed along with a description of any remedial action taken and a warranty that "all remedial action necessary to protect human health and the environment . . . has been taken before the date of such transfer," and that any further remedial action found necessary after that date "shall be conducted by the United States."[1] In January 1992, Pentagon officials stated that this law should be amended because the part requiring cleanup prior to sale is inhibiting the sale of closed military installations. Those officials believe that the law should allow such property to be sold and put to productive economic use with cleanup to occur in due course after the sale, avoiding either the delay now required while contamination is being remediated or the extra cost of accelerated

---

[1]   42 U.S.C. § 9620(h), adopted as a part of SARA. This law was implemented by regulations effective October 17, 1990. *See* 40 C.F.R. Part 373, 55 Federal Register 14208-14212 (April 16, 1990), which establishes reportable quantity thresholds with regard to hazardous substance storage or release (but not disposal).

cleanup in order to permit a sale to occur on a timely basis under the existing law.

A number of states have adopted cleanup or disclosure laws. Some of the statutes provide for civil penalties and other remedies in cases where the requirements are violated. Common law principles also provide for disclosure in real estate transactions. Those *transfer-triggered* laws are the subject of this chapter.[2]

Our discussion will begin with common law disclosure duties as the common law provides the backdrop for the significant developments in state statutes on this subject in the 1980s.

3.2 Common Law--The Demise of *Caveat Emptor*

For centuries, sellers of real estate were protected by the doctrine of "*caveat emptor*," or "let the buyer beware." Under this ancient rule, a seller of land was not liable to the buyer or any other person for a dangerous condition which existed at the time of transfer or for any other aspect of the property. This rule achieved unjust results in many cases, and it was gradually modified.

Common Law Fraud. It has come to be widely accepted under the common law that sellers of real estate have a disclosure duty in those situations where the seller knows or should know of a condition existing on the property which involves an unreasonable risk of harm to persons entering the property. The seller must disclose that information if the buyer does not know or have reason to know of the condition or the risk involved and the seller has reason to believe that the buyer will not discover or appreciate the condition or the risk. If the seller fails to disclose the condition, he will be liable for physical harm caused by the condition after the buyer takes possession. That liability will continue until the buyer has had reasonable opportunity to discover and remedy the condition, or in cases of active concealment, until the buyer actually discovers the condition and has had reasonable opportunity to correct

---

[2]   This chapter focuses on the transfer of real estate. Other disclosure obligations are triggered under the securities laws upon the sale of stock of companies which own or operate contaminated property. *See* Chapter 4, § 4.2.6 for a discussion of those disclosure rules.

it.[3] This disclosure duty has been adopted by the courts in many states, and some have expanded on the rule.

Under **California** common law, for example, a seller has an affirmative duty to disclose material facts affecting the *value or desirability* of the real property which are known or accessible only to the seller and are not known to or apparent to the buyer, and the failure to disclose will constitute actual fraud.[4] Such a material fact may or may not relate to a dangerous condition or even a defect in the property. For instance, it has been held in a residential transaction that a cause of action could be stated against a seller and broker for nondisclosure of a multiple murder which took place in the home ten years before, because that fact could be material to a buyer and could affect the value or desirability of the home.[5] Hazardous substance contamination present at a property would appear to have an even greater impact on its value

---

[3]   This rule is stated in Restatement (Second) of Torts § 353 (1965). The general rule of *caveat emptor* with the Restatement disclosure exception was affirmed by the California Supreme Court in *Preston v. Goldman*, 42 Cal.3d 108, 227 Cal.Rptr. 817, 720 P.2d 476 (1986).

[4]   *Snelson v. Ondulando Highlands Corp.*, 5 Cal.App.3d 243, 84 Cal.Rptr. 800 (1970) (filled ground); *Lingsch v. Savage*, 213 Cal.App.2d 729, 735-736, 29 Cal.Rptr. 201 (1963).

[5]   *Reed v. King*, 145 Cal.App.3d 261, 193 Cal.Rptr. 130 (1983). That case was later modified by a statute providing that no claim exists for nondisclosure of a death which occurred at the property more than three years before the offer to purchase or lease, or that an occupant had or died from AIDS. However, liability will apply to an intentional misrepresentation in response to an inquiry concerning deaths on the real property. Cal. Civil Code § 1710.2. *Reed v. King* has not been persuasive in New York, where *caveat emptor* apparently still applies, *Stambovsky v. Ackley*, N.Y. Sup.Ct., No. 23241/89 (Mar. 14, 1990) (seller's nondisclosure of ghosts was not actionable). Georgia has adopted a law protecting sellers against claims for nondisclosure of facts of psychological importance, but sellers must truthfully respond to inquiries, 1989 Ga. Laws 1633.

or desirability, and nondisclosure of such a condition can be expected to expose the seller to liability for common law fraud.[6]

Partial Disclosures. Even if the seller does not have a duty to speak initially, the seller becomes obligated to make full disclosure of all pertinent facts where a partial disclosure has been made. Although the partial disclosure may be literally true, there will be actionable fraud if other pertinent facts are not disclosed which would modify or condition what was disclosed, or where the partial truth is used to create a substantially false impression. In other words, once the seller speaks, the whole truth on the subject must be disclosed, even if there was otherwise no disclosure obligation under the circumstances.[7] This rule frequently comes into play because it is often hard for a seller to say nothing about property he wishes to sell. There is a natural desire on the part of sellers to say something nice about the property, even if not the whole truth.

The **California** courts have also ruled that integration clauses or exculpatory ("AS IS") clauses in a sales contract will not relieve the seller of his duties of disclosure.[8] Where a breach of a disclosure duty exists, a purchaser might have a right to recover "damages for fraud and deceit or for breach of contract or of warranty, express or implied, or . . . to rescind the contract or to defend in the vendor's suit for specific performance."[9]

The typical kind of case which gave rise to common law disclosure duties involved such matters as landfills, termite infestations, leaking

---

[6]   *See, e.g., Roth v. Leach,* No. 30639 (Wayne County Sup.Ct. N.Y. Oct. 4. 1990) (buyer was entitled to rescind his purchase, obtain return of the purchase price, and to recover incidental and punitive damages due to the sellers fraudulent nondisclosure of the existence of buried hazardous substances at the property).

[7]   *Jacobs v. Freeman,* 104 Cal.App.3d 177, 163 Cal.Rptr. 680 (1980); *Hale v. Wolfsen,* 276 Cal.App.2d 285, 81 Cal.Rptr. 23 (1969); *Macco Construction Co. v. Fickertt,* 76 Cal.App.2d 295, 172 P.2d 951 (1946).

[8]   *Orlando v. Berkeley,* 220 Cal.App.2d 224, 33 Cal.Rptr. 860 (1963); Miller & Starr, *Current Law of California Real Estate,* Vol. 1, § 1:93, pp. 141-142 (1st. Ed.).

[9]   Annotation, *Duty of Vendor of Real Estate to Give Purchaser Information as to Termite Infestation,* 22 A.L.R. 3d 972 § 1 (1968).

roofs, essentially any latent defect or condition which was known to the seller but not readily apparent to a buyer.[10] Nondisclosure or failure to warn of hazardous waste contamination can be expected to become another common example as litigation in this area increases. In fact, such rulings have already begun to be handed down by the courts.[11]

Buyer's Duty of Care. On the other hand, while the doctrine of *caveat emptor* is comatose, it is not dead. The common law still requires prospective transferees of real estate to exercise due care for the protection of their own interests. Except where the defect is latent, a transferee normally will be charged with the knowledge which would have been learned upon reasonable inspection.[12] What inspection will be deemed "reasonable" and what knowledge a prospective buyer will be charged with depends on the facts of each case. In some cases the existence of hazardous waste contamination might be quite apparent even upon a casual inspection. In other cases, such an inspection might reveal sufficiently recognizable signs of the existence of the condition to put the buyer upon "inquiry notice" of it. In those cases, the doctrine of *caveat emptor* might still be available as a defense against various

---

10   *See, e.g., Quashnock v. Frost,* Pa. Super., 445 A.2d 121, 128 (1982) (in a residence, termite infestation is "manifestly a serious and dangerous condition and where . . . its existence is not readily observable upon reasonable inspection" justice requires the seller to disclose even if the buyer fails to inquire); *Easton v. Strassburger,* 152 Cal.App.3d 90, 199 Cal.Rptr. 383 (1984) (seller liable for nondisclosure of landfill and soil problems); *Perkins v. Marsh,* 179 Wash. 362, 365, 37 P.2d 689, 690 (1934) (lessor failed to disclose that basement flooded during the rainy season rendering the premises unfit for use).

11   *See, e.g., State Dept. of Environ. Protect. v. Ventron Corp.,* 94 N.J. 473, 486, 468 A.2d 150 (1983) (prior owner was strictly liable under common law principles for "abnormally dangerous" activity and for the subsequent abatement of the resulting nuisance where the prior owner had knowledge of mercury contamination which was not readily observable and intentionally failed to disclose this to purchasers). *See also Roth v. Leach,* footnote 6 above.

12   *Maser v. Lind,* 181 Neb. 365, 148 N.W.2d 831, 834 (1967) (fraud is not actionable if ordinary prudence would have prevented deception except where defects are latent); *Davey v. Brownson,* 3 Wash. App. 820, 825, 478 P.2d 258 (1970) (a buyer is bound by the facts which would normally be disclosed by a reasonable investigation).

common law theories of action. In many cases involving hazardous waste, however, the condition probably will be viewed as concealed or latent and not observable by a buyer upon reasonable inspection. The common law does not require a prospective buyer to undertake intrusive testing of the kind which would be necessary to discover concealed hazardous waste contamination.[13] Thus, *caveat emptor* should not be a meritorious defense in many hazardous waste cases.

The doctrine of *caveat emptor* retains more vitality in some jurisdictions. For example, in **Arizona**, a seller of real estate has no duty of disclosure unless there is a special, confidential relationship with the buyer or the buyer makes an inquiry about a particular attribute of the property. In a recent case, the buyer of an office building and retail store complex in Arizona sued the seller for nondisclosure of the presence of asbestos and the related health risks. The seller's motion for summary judgment was granted and the case was dismissed because the buyer was sophisticated, the transaction was "arms-length," the buyer actually had the property inspected by a contractor, the property was sold "as is" (suggesting the possibility of defects), the spray-on asbestos fireproofing was visible in the unfinished areas and was actually seen by the buyer during inspection, the buyer knew of the use of asbestos in buildings, the buyer knew that exposure to asbestos could be harmful, and, to top it off, the buyer admitted that the purchase would have been completed even if the presence of asbestos had been disclosed by the seller at the time of the transaction in 1980.[14]

Even in jurisdictions where the *caveat emptor* doctrine has been eroded, it is becoming increasingly common for buyers to undertake environmental risk assessments prior to purchase. Under the new environmental laws, buyers of real estate, particularly in commercial

---

[13]   *Barnhouse v. City of Pinole*, 133 Cal.App.3d 171, 183 Cal.Rptr. 881, 892 (1982) (buyer had no duty to hire experts to inspect property and will not be charged with knowledge where expert advice would have been necessary in order to discover the defective condition of the property). *See also Avner v. Longridge Estates*, 272 Cal.App.3d 171 (1982) (buyer had no duty to investigate subsurface soil conditions).

[14]   *La Placita Partners v. Northwestern Mutual Life Ins. Co.*, 766 F.Supp. 1454 (N.D. Ohio 1990), affirmed 935 F.R.2d 270 (6th Cir. 1991) (applying Arizona law).

transactions, are being held to a higher standard of inquiry as the federal and state governments search for responsible parties to share the high cost of cleanup. It remains to be seen whether the broader environmental due diligence standards contemplated by those laws, and the developing custom and practice in this regard, will come to be adopted by the courts in cases arising under common law theories, in effect reviving the *caveat emptor* doctrine from its deep sleep in some jurisdictions. At this point, however, there are no authoritative indications that those higher standards apply to anything other than the determination whether the innocent landowner defense is available under CERCLA or similar state Superfund laws.

Caveat Emptor--No Defense to Superfund Liability. The federal Court of Appeals for the Third Circuit has ruled that the *caveat emptor* doctrine is not available as a defense against Superfund liability. In that case, the seller did not conceal the existence of piles of hazardous waste (containing asbestos) on the property, the buyer was a sophisticated company and inspected the property and in fact knew of the waste, and the purchase price reflected a discount for environmental risks. Later, at the instance of the EPA, the buyer cleaned up the property at a cost of approximately $218,000 and then sued the former owner for contribution under CERCLA. The former owner argued that the buyer had known of the condition and that its claim was barred by the doctrine of *caveat emptor*. The court ruled, however, that "under CERCLA the doctrine of caveat emptor is not a defense to liability for contribution but may only be considered in mitigation of [the] amount due."[15] In order to avoid a "double recovery" by the buyer, the court could consider the amount of the price discount, the cost of cleanup and other equitable matters, but the doctrine of *caveat emptor* was not otherwise a factor.[16]

---

[15]   *Smith Land & Improvement Corp. v. Celotex Corp.*, 851 F.2d 86, 90 (3d Cir. 1988).

[16]   In the *Smith Land* case, the hazardous waste apparently had been deposited on the property during the period of ownership of the former owner so that "intervening landowner" status was not available and the former owner could not avoid PRP status simply by making a disclosure. Also, the purchase agreement apparently did not contain any waiver or release of possible CERCLA claims by the buyer.

Thus, the doctrine of *caveat emptor* has been narrowed over the years in some jurisdictions. What remains of that doctrine for common law purposes in those jurisdictions is a minimal due care requirement on the part of buyers. That remaining requirement, and even actual knowledge on the part of a buyer, has been made irrelevant to the potential liability of a seller under the Superfund laws. In addition, the doctrine has been largely supplanted by recent statutory enactments in many states which compel sellers of contaminated real estate to take various actions, including cleanup, disclosure to the buyer and/or reporting to the state. These statutes will be discussed in § 3.3 below. Further comment is necessary, however, with respect to the common law disclosure duties of landlords and brokers.

3.2.1 Disclosure Duty of Landlords

Landlords have the common law duty, upon leasing real estate, to inspect for latent defects involving an unreasonable risk of harm and to repair or warn of them.

Residential Transactions--Strict Liability. In the case of residential leases, the **California** Supreme Court has ruled that landlords have a duty to inspect and will be "strictly liable in tort for injuries resulting from a latent defect in the premises when the defect existed at the time the premises were let to the tenant."[17] This places a stringent transfer-triggered obligation upon landlords to inspect premises and correct latent defects when leasing residential properties. This rule doubtless would apply when the latent defect is a hazardous waste condition, and the rule would require some remedial action to avoid injuries which might arise from such a condition.

Commercial Transactions--Negligence. The strict liability standard has not been adopted in the context of commercial leases.[18] However, similar duties have been found under the law of negligence, at least where the building is leased for a purpose involving the admission of the

---

[17] *Becker v. IRM Corp.*, 38 Cal.3d 454, 464, 468-69, 213 Cal.Rptr. 213, 698 P.2d 116 (1985).

[18] *Muro v. Superior Court*, 184 Cal.App.3d 1089, 229 Cal.Rptr. 383 (1986) (declining to extend the strict liability standard enunciated in *Becker v. IRM Corp.* to commercial leases).

public (which is the case for many commercial enterprises). The **California** Supreme Court has ruled as follows:

> A lessor who leases property for a purpose involving the admission of the public is under a duty to see that it is safe for the purposes intended and to exercise reasonable care to inspect and repair the property before possession is transferred so as to prevent any unreasonable risk of harm to the public who may enter.[19]

This principle has been applied in a variety of contexts,[20] and has been widely adopted throughout the United States. The rationale for the rule is that each commercial landlord has a

> responsibility to the public, which he is not free to shift to the lessee in any case where he has reason to expect that the lessee will admit the public before the land is put in reasonably safe condition for their reception.[21]

This is a transfer-triggered rule which would require remedial action before a commercial property may be leased without exposure to liability for negligence. Any hazardous waste condition likely to cause injury to members of the public entering the property would probably have to be cleaned up by a landlord under this rule.

Another common law duty requires a landlord, upon leasing a property, to disclose concealed dangerous conditions of which the landlord is aware or had reason to know. Common areas retained under the landlord's control remain its responsibility.[22] Thus, even if a repair duty does not apply, there may be a common law disclosure duty.

---

[19]   *Goodman v. Harris*, 40 Cal.2d 254, 261, 253 P.2d 447 (1953).

[20]   *See, e.g., Obrien v. Fong Wan*, 185 Cal. App.2d 112, 8 Cal. Rptr. 124 (1960) (retail store); *Hayes v. Richfield Oil Corp.*, 38 Cal.2d 375, 380, 240 P.2d 580 (1952) (service station and parking lot); *Boothby v. Town of Yreka City*, 117 Cal.App. 643, 649, 4 P.2d 589 (1931) (polling place); *Burroughs v. Ben's Auto Park, Inc.*, 27 Cal.2d 449, 453, 164 P.2d 897 (1945) (parking lot); *Rau v. Redwood City Woman's Club*, 111 Cal.App.2d 546, 549, 245 P.2d 12 (1952) (auditorium); *King v. New Masonic Temple Assn.*, 51 Cal.App.2d 512, 515, 125 P.2d 559 (1942) (auditorium).

[21]   Restatement (Second) of Torts § 359, Comment a. (1965).

[22]   *See, generally, Prosser and Keeton on Torts* (5th Ed., 1984), § 63.

Again, a concealed hazardous waste condition which is dangerous would probably trigger a disclosure duty in the context of a leasing transaction.

3.2.2 Disclosure Duty of Brokers

Real estate brokers also have disclosure duties which are triggered by transactions in which they are involved. Such duties may be applicable under the laws of many states.

The Seller's Broker. Under **California** law, for example, a seller's real estate broker has long had the same common law duty of disclosure as the seller (see § 3.2).[23] Nondisclosure under that duty constitutes fraud. However, the broker's duty has been expanded in the context of residential transactions to apply in negligence cases as well.

In *Easton v. Strassburger*,[24] the court found that the seller's broker was affirmatively obligated to perform a competent inspection of residential property and to disclose to the buyer all material facts affecting the value or desirability of the property revealed or which should have been revealed by the inspection. The breach of that duty in the *Easton* case resulted in a negligence judgment against the broker who failed to disclose to the purchaser the existence of landfill and soil problems. "Red flag" signs of those problems should have been apparent to the broker upon a competent inspection of the property. Serious collapse of the soil occurred soon after the sale. The seller was also liable for failing to disclose the defective soil condition to the broker and the purchaser. Even though the broker was found only five percent responsible for the ultimate damage, the broker was jointly and severally liable for the full amount (and the broker was, of course, the "deep pocket").

The duty established by the *Easton* case was later codified and clarified by the **California** legislature in a law which requires the listing and cooperating brokers to conduct a "reasonably competent and diligent visual inspection of the property" and to disclose to a "prospective purchaser" of residential property comprising one to four dwelling units "all facts materially affecting the value or desirability of

---

[23]   *Lingsch v. Savage*, 213 Cal.App.2d 729, 29 Cal.Rptr. 201 (1963); *Cooper v. Jevne*, 56 Cal.App.3d 860, 128 Cal.Rptr. 724 (1976).

[24]   152 Cal.App.3d 90, 199 Cal.Rptr. 383 (1984).

the property that such an investigation would reveal . . ."[25] This duty applies to sale, lease with option to purchase, ground lease and real property sales contract transactions for such residential property. While the *Easton* case expressly left open the question whether the duty also applies to commercial transactions, the statute has been interpreted as limiting the negligence duty of listing and cooperating brokers to transactions involving residential properties of one to four dwelling units.[26] The common law fraud standard still applies, of course, to both commercial and residential transactions.

With respect to cases governed by the **California** Civil Code provision, a reasonably competent *visual* inspection might or might not reveal the presence of hazardous substance conditions on or under a property, depending upon the existence and nature of visible indications regarding subsurface conditions or the possible presence of hazardous materials in the construction of a building.

The Buyer's Broker. The duties of the *buyer's* broker or a *dual* agent may be broader. Such realtors owe a fiduciary duty to the buyer and may be found negligent as fiduciaries for failing to inspect a property and disclose material facts. A **California** appellate court has ruled that an

> agent must exercise reasonable skill and care for the benefit of the principal in the performance of agency duties, and will be liable for any damages suffered by the principal as a result of the agent's negligence. . . . Those duties may include inspecting the property and disclosing any material defects to the principal.[27]

Under that standard, the court stated that the jury could have found the buyer's broker negligent for failing to pursue further investigation after

---

[25]   Cal. Civil Code § 2079 *et seq.*

[26]   *Smith v. Rickard*, 205 Cal.App.3d 1354, 254 Cal.Rptr. 633 (1988).

[27]   *Id.*, at 1364. However, another California appellate court has disagreed with that statement and has ruled that a buyer's broker has no duty to inspect. *Murray v. Hayden*, 211 Cal.App.3d 311, 259 Cal.Rptr. 257 (1989). Thus, the issue appears to be unresolved. However, publication of the *Murray v. Hayden* opinion was quickly vacated, eliminating that case as authority.

an initial visual inspection and to disclose to the buyer the potential existence of root rot in a commercial avocado orchard.

In another case, the owner of a mobil home sued the manufacturer because formaldehyde vapors from the construction materials resulted in eye irritation and respiratory problems. The jury ruled in favor of the plaintiff, and the verdict was upheld on appeal on the ground that the formaldehyde vapors constituted a breach of the manufacturer's express warranty against substantial defects.[28] Based on that case, it has been said that

> the existence of formaldehyde in a residential dwelling may be a "substantial defect" that would affect the "value or desirability" of the dwelling and therefore its existence must be disclosed to a buyer. Also, since formaldehyde insulation is not uncommon, the broker may be required to make a reasonable investigation to discover its existence.[29]

If this is true with respect to formaldehyde, it may also be true regarding other hazardous materials commonly utilized in construction, now or in the past (e.g., asbestos). The visual inspection standard of the **California** Civil Code provision might limit the responsibility of listing and cooperating brokers in this connection, but the fiduciary duty of the buyer's broker or a dual agent may be broader as discussed above.

Thus, it appears at this time under **California** law that the buyer's broker or a dual agent are the most at risk for any failure to inspect for and disclose hazardous substance conditions, and that listing brokers are also at risk at least in residential transactions where a reasonably competent visual inspection would have revealed such a condition. In addition, known material facts must be disclosed in both commercial and residential transactions. While the disclosure laws relevant to brokers focus primarily on residential real property transactions, further development can be anticipated also in the context of nonresidential properties as purchasers seek defendants to share in the cost of cleanup

---

[28] *Troensegaard v. Silvercrest Industries. Inc.*, 175 Cal.App.3d 218, 220 Cal.Rptr. 712 (1985).

[29] Miller & Starr, *Current Law of California Real Estate* (1st Ed.), Vol. 1 Part 2 (1987 Supplement), § 4:24, pp. 68-69.

required by environmental laws or to compensate for personal injuries caused by toxic materials which were allegedly present at the time of sale.

See § 3.3.2 below for a discussion of **California's** new consumer information booklet ("Environmental Hazards: Guide for Homeowners and Buyers").

3.2.3 When Does a Seller, Landlord or Broker Have "Knowledge" Requiring Disclosure?

The common law disclosure duties discussed above become applicable when the seller, landlord or broker has "knowledge" of a material, dangerous or defective condition which must be disclosed in connection with the sale or lease of real estate. Disclosure duties under various statutes are also generally applicable when a person has "knowledge." Those statutes usually do not define what is meant by that term. The question often arises whether a party must undertake any investigation or perform any due diligence in order to obtain knowledge or to confirm its existence.

As noted in § 3.2.2, landlords (under some circumstances) and brokers (always) have a duty to perform inspections to obtain knowledge. If they do not have actual knowledge, they will be charged with the information which should have been learned during such an inspection, and liability may follow from any negligent failure to discover and disclose. Even without an affirmative duty to inspect and discover new information, however, what may be "known" warrants further consideration.

Actual or Constructive Knowledge. Generally, knowledge may be either "actual" or "constructive." The constructive knowledge principle is set forth, for example, in the **California** Civil Code as follows:

> Every person who has actual notice of circumstances sufficient to put a prudent man upon inquiry as to a particular fact, has constructive notice of the fact itself in all cases in which, by prosecuting such inquiry, he might have learned such fact.[30]

---

[30]   Cal. Civil Code § 19.

This principle typically comes into play to determine when a statute of limitations commences to run under the discovery rule, *i.e.*, when the claimant knew or should have known, with the exercise of reasonable diligence, of the facts giving rise to the claim. The principle has also been applied in cases under the California Public Liability Act, which imposes liability on cities for dangerous or defective conditions on public property where appropriate city personnel had "knowledge or notice" of the condition and failed to remedy it within a reasonable time. Even though the Public Liability Act did not define "knowledge," the courts have found under the quoted Civil Code provision that constructive notice is sufficient. The courts have ruled that the constructive notice principle requires "reasonable diligence in making inspections for the discovery of unsafe or defective conditions."[31] When knowledge is imputed under this principle, "it has the same legal effect as though there was actual knowledge."[32]

It could be argued, by analogy to the Public Liability Act cases, that a seller, landlord or broker is on inquiry notice whenever he has actual notice of circumstances sufficient to put a prudent person on inquiry of the presence of hazardous substance contamination on or beneath a property, or of hazardous materials (such as asbestos) in the construction of a building. The seller, landlord or broker would be charged with knowledge of the facts which a reasonably diligent inquiry or inspection would reveal, resulting in "knowledge" which may have to be disclosed.

However, for inquiry notice to exist, there must be an obligation to undertake an inquiry. The courts have stated that there must be a

> specific duty to perform which required [the person] to inform himself of pertinent facts or a right [must be] involved, the protection of which has required that he proceed with diligence and as a person of reasonable prudence would proceed to ascertain facts affecting his right. It may be said generally that the doctrine applies only to situations in which failure to make inquiry would

---

[31] *Fackrell v. City of San Diego,* 26 Cal.2d 196, 206, 157 P.2d 625 (1945); *Bady v. Detwilder,* 127 Cal.App.2d 321, 334, 273 P.2d 941 (1954).

[32] *Dolch v. Ramsey,* 57 Cal.App.2d 99, 105, 134 P.2d 19 (1943).

amount to dereliction of duty or a failure to take ordinary care of one's own concerns.[33]

As we have seen, landlords and brokers do have inspection duties under the common law in connection with real estate transactions, and thus, will be charged with constructive knowledge of hazardous conditions whenever actual notice exists of circumstances sufficient to put a prudent person upon inquiry. In addition, landowners are generally obligated under tort law principles to exercise due diligence to inspect and maintain their properties to avoid any unreasonable risk of harm to occupants or invitees. Thus, based on what landowners should know about their property generally, they may be charged with constructive knowledge of hazardous conditions when they sell the property. When that information is material, the sellers will be exposed to liability under the common law for any failure to disclose.

As another category of constructive knowledge, all persons are charged with knowledge of the existence and content of documents and instruments recorded in the official real estate records of each jurisdiction. Copies of relevant records can be obtained from the recorder's office or from a title insurance company.

Imputed Knowledge. Wholly aside from any duty to inspect or discover *new* information about the condition of a property, knowledge may already exist or may be chargeable, especially in a corporate context. The actual or constructive knowledge of a corporation's agents and employees is imputed to the corporation, at least as to information obtained in, and relating to, the course and scope of such agency or employment and after a reasonable time for communication of the information to the principal or employer.[34] Thus, in order to determine what a corporation "knows" and must disclose in connection with a real estate transaction, appropriate inquiry should be made of corporate personnel. This would include personnel whose duties involve safety or maintenance or who would otherwise be expected to learn of any hazardous substance contamination or other dangerous or defective

---

[33]   *Sterling v. Title Insurance & Trust Co.*, 53 Cal.App.2d 736, 749, 128 P.2d 31 (1942); *Hobart v. Hobart Estate Co.*, 26 Cal.2d 412, 437-439, 159 P.2d 958 (1945).

[34]   *See, generally,* 3 Cal.Jur.3d, *Agency*, §§ 135 *et seq.*

condition of the property involved. In addition, a corporation will be charged with knowledge of the content of its corporate records in its possession.[35] Thus, relevant corporate records should also be reviewed.

Likely Attitude of the Courts. One cannot expect the courts to be very sympathetic toward sellers or landlords who claim ignorance of hazardous waste contamination at their properties. In most cases, the seller or landlord will probably have known enough to give rise to inquiry notice of the condition, or the knowledge of agents or employees may be imputed to the owner. The likely attitude of the courts has been exhibited in past cases concerning more mundane matters than hazardous waste. In one case, a court was disinclined to "quibble" over whether the knowledge requirement should be described as "knowledge" or "actual knowledge" or "constructive knowledge" or "knowledge or its equivalent," and the court found that knowledge of a defective condition in three or four bathroom sinks was knowledge that the defect was general throughout an entire apartment building.[36] In another case, a landlord claimed lack of knowledge of a defective railing on his property when accused of violating a local repair ordinance. The court responded:

> We can hardly believe that the City intended that the landlord could fulfill his duty under the ordinance as to the instant defective railing by staying away from his own property and insulating himself in his own ignorance.[37]

Given the courts' reactions in these cases, it appears likely that landowners will not be able to prevail easily on claims of ignorance of dangerous conditions such as hazardous waste contamination. Accordingly, sellers and landlords should be prepared to undertake appropriate due diligence and to make disclosures regarding such matters to prospective purchasers and tenants.

---

[35] *Edgar Rice Burroughs, Inc. v. Commodore Products & Artists, Inc.*, 167 Cal.App.2d 463, 475-478, 334 P.2d 922 (1959).

[36] *Anderson v. Shuman*, 257 Cal.App.2d 272, 274, 64 Cal.Rptr. 662 (1967).

[37] *McNally v. Ward*, 192 Cal.App.2d 871, 880-881, 14 Cal.Rptr. 260 (1961).

3.3   State Cleanup, Disclosure and Reporting Laws

A number of states evidently have not been satisfied with the status of disclosure obligations under the common law. Those states have enacted statutes seeking to ensure that hazardous substance conditions will be taken care of or at least disclosed at the time of property transfers.

One purpose for such laws is to make sure that transferees will be on actual or constructive notice of hazardous substance conditions. In this way, the disclosure obligations placed on landowners complement the increased due diligence standard placed on purchasers by the innocent landowner defense discussed in Chapter 1. That defense is thus being squeezed from both directions. It will be a remarkable case indeed which sustains the application of that defense, particularly with regard to any transaction occurring since the enactment of the environmental laws involved.

The laws which will be discussed in this section can be categorized into three types: (i) laws requiring cleanup or governmental approval prior to the transfer of real estate, (ii) laws requiring disclosure to the prospective buyer or lessee or reporting to a governmental agency at the time of a transfer, and (iii) laws requiring recordation of hazardous substance-related information in the official real estate records in order to impart actual or constructive notice to prospective transferees.

States other than those mentioned below may also have similar laws. In addition, local jurisdictions may have adopted ordinances along these lines. For instance, the city of **Los Angeles, California**, has adopted a municipal ordinance which applies to any property upon which there has been an unauthorized release or disposal of a hazardous substance. The ordinance prohibits the sale, transfer or other conveyance of such property without the prior approval of the County Health Department and recordation with the County Recorder of a hazardous substance clearance report including a site characterization study, any required site mitigation plan, and a site clearance certificate to the effect that mitigation measures have been completed to the satisfaction of the applicable state or federal authorities.[38] This remarkable ordinance

---

[38]   Los Angeles Municipal Ordinance No. 164154, November 1, 1988.

appears to be patterned after **New Jersey's** Environmental Cleanup Responsibility Act (see below), but is even more stringent in that it applies to any kind of property, not only certain industrial establishments, and it requires approved cleanup prior to sale or transfer, and recordation of a report, in all cases without exception. Apparently, no one has yet challenged the validity of the ordinance.

Other than the preceding reference to a local ordinance, this section will focus on state law. In any real estate transaction, qualified counsel in the state involved should be consulted to determine the full requirements and up-to-date status of such state or local laws.

3.3.1 Transfer-Triggered Cleanup/State Approval Laws

Of the states surveyed, five have laws requiring cleanup of contaminated property or state approval prior to transfer (**New Jersey, Connecticut, Colorado, Iowa** and **Missouri**). These laws represent an unprecedented intrusion of governmental regulation and bureaucracy into private party real estate transactions. **New Jersey's** law is the most stringent and controversial state law of its kind. Several other states have considered adopting such laws, and, while **Connecticut** has come close, none have gone as far. At this point, it looks like **New Jersey's** law may remain as one of a kind (except for any local ordinances like the one discussed above).

The other states in this category (**Colorado, Iowa** and **Missouri**) require prior state approval of transfers of hazardous waste disposal sites, but without extensive statutory provisions. Presumably the power of approval includes the right to disapprove, or to approve upon satisfaction of conditions which might include cleanup measures.

New Jersey

The Environmental Cleanup Responsibility Act (ECRA)[39] was enacted in 1983. It represents a significant effort by New Jersey to attack its hazardous waste problem, which is the most serious in the nation in terms of the number of sites listed on the federal Superfund NPL.

ECRA applies to any "industrial establishment" which includes any property operated for the "generation, manufacture, refining,

---

[39]   N.J. Rev. Stat. § 13:1K-6 *et seq.*

transportation, treatment, storage, handling, or disposal of hazardous substances or wastes on-site."[40]   Such establishments must also be covered by designated federal Standard Industrial Classification numbers.

When a transfer agreement regarding an industrial establishment is entered into, notice must be given within five days to the Department of Environmental Protection (DEP).   Then, within 60 days prior to cessation of operations, sale (including change in ownership by the sale or transfer of stock[41]), or transfer of the industrial establishment, the owner or operator must submit to the DEP for approval either:

(1) A "negative declaration" which states that "there has been no discharge of hazardous substances or wastes on the site, or that any discharge has been cleaned up . . . and there remains no hazardous substances or wastes at the site";[42] or

(2) A cleanup plan accompanied by a bond or other financial security to guarantee performance.   The obligation to implement the cleanup plan can be assumed by the transferee.[43]

Implicit in the foregoing is an obligation on the part of the owner or operator to investigate the site for possible contamination so that a truthful negative declaration can be made or cleanup plan developed.

Transfer of an industrial establishment is contingent upon compliance with these provisions. A violation may constitute grounds for voiding the sale or transfer of the property by the transferee *or* by the DEP, and renders the owner or operator strictly liable for clean up and removal costs. The transferor may also be liable for any damages suffered by the transferee and for damages resulting from failure to

---

40   *Id.*, §§ 13:1K-8(f) and 13:1K-9.

41   *See, e.g., Cooper Development Co., Inc. v. First National Bank of Boston,* 762 F.Supp. 1145 (D.C.N.J. 1991) (the requirements of ECRA were triggered by the dissolution of a parent corporation and the liquidating distribution to its shareholders of its 85% interest in the stock of a subsidiary corporation which owned a contaminated facility).

42   N.J. Rev. Stat. § 13:1K-8(g).

43   *Id.*, § 13:1K-9.

implement a cleanup plan. Civil penalties of up to $25,000 per day are recoverable for violations.[44]

The required cleanup and approval process under ECRA has resulted in substantial delays in the closing of real estate transactions. It is this factor which has made the law so controversial and which has given other states pause when considering similar legislation.[45]

The New Jersey Supreme Court has ruled that there is an implied private right of action for a buyer to sue a seller who has conveyed property in violation of ECRA. Such an action may be for damages, without voiding the sale, as an alternative to rescission.[46]

Connecticut

The Transfer of Industrial Establishments Act was enacted by Connecticut in the wake of ECRA, but is less stringent. Unlike ECRA, the Standard Industrial Classification numbers are not used in defining the term "industrial establishment." Rather, the term includes any property which generates more than 100 kilograms of hazardous waste per month or upon which hazardous waste is recycled, handled or disposed of for a third party. Before such an industrial establishment may be transferred, its owner or operator must submit a negative declaration to the transferee and to the commissioner, or the transferee must certify to the commissioner that any discharge will be contained in accordance with required plans and procedures. While the transferor's notice must be given to the prospective transferee prior to the transfer, the information is given to the commissioner within 15 days *after* the transfer, and no prior approval of the state is required.[47]

A transferor who fails to comply with these provisions may be held strictly liable for cleanup and removal costs, as well as direct and

---

[44] *Id.*, § 13:1K-13.

[45] However, for an argument that **New Jersey's** approach has been largely successful, that the criticisms of it are not warranted by experience, and that ECRA is worthy of adoption by other states, see Wagner, *Liability for Hazardous Waste Cleanup: An Examination of New Jersey's Approach*, 13 Harvard Environ.L.Rev. 245 (1989).

[46] *Dixon Venture v. Joseph Dixon Crucible Co.*, 584 A.2d 797 (N.J. 1991).

[47] Conn. Gen. Stat. § 22a-134a.

indirect damages. A person who knowingly provides false information faces a penalty of up to $100,000.[48] Unlike ECRA, this statute does not render a transfer voidable in the event the requirements are violated.

Colorado

A substantial change in ownership or in the operation or design of a hazardous waste disposal site must be submitted for prior approval to the board of county commissioners or the governing body of the municipality where the site is located.[49]

Iowa

Before changing the use of, or selling, conveying, or transferring title to, a registered abandoned or uncontrolled disposal site, a person must obtain the written approval of the director of the Department of Environmental Quality.[50]

In addition, the grantors or transferors of property must submit to the county recorder, together with each deed or other instrument, a written statement on a prescribed form (the Real Estate Transfer -- Groundwater Hazard Statement) regarding the presence and location, or the absence of, any wells, solid waste disposal sites, underground storage tank, or hazardous waste on the property, and related details. The statement must be submitted before the deed or other instrument will be recorded. The county recorder transmits such statements to the Department of Natural Resources.[51]

Missouri

The written approval of the director of the Department of Natural Resources is required in order to sell, convey, or transfer title to a registered abandoned or uncontrolled hazardous waste disposal site, or in order to change its use.[52]

---

48   *Id.*, § 22a-134d.

49   Colo. Rev. Stat. § 25-15-206.

50   Iowa Code § 455B.430.

51   *Id.*, § 558.69.

52   Mo. Rev. Stat. § 260.465.

3.3.2 Transfer-Triggered Disclosure or Reporting Laws

Nine of the states surveyed have disclosure or reporting laws which are triggered by real estate transfers (**California, Illinois, Indiana, Massachusets, Minnesota, North Carolina, Pennsylvania, Washington** and **West Virginia**).

California

Disclosure Obligations of Sellers, Lessors and Lessees of California Real Property. Effective January 1, 1988, the California legislature amended its Superfund law to include a new section requiring disclosure of hazardous substance conditions in connection with real property transactions.[53] As originally enacted, the section applied to sellers of nonresidential real estate and to lessees of residential or nonresidential real estate. Each seller had a duty to make a disclosure to his buyers prior to sale, and each lessee had an ongoing duty to make disclosures to the owner upon learning that any hazardous substance release had come to be located on or beneath the property. Enforcement measures included civil penalties, actual damages and, in the case of violation by a lessee, the lessor had the right to void the lease.

That section was adopted concurrently with the amendments to the California Superfund law which incorporated the CERCLA definitions of PRPs and defenses, including the innocent landowner defense. That defense was not previously available under the California Superfund law. The legislative history clearly shows that the two amendments were related. As long as the innocent landowner defense was to be adopted, the California legislature wanted to make sure that information regarding hazardous substance conditions would be disclosed to purchasers so that the new defense would not in fact become available to them. In that way, the legislature could look like it was trying to be fair to innocent parties and yet ensure that there would be no innocence so that the dwindling California Superfund resources would be preserved.

The legislative history also indicates an intention to protect the interests of purchasers by having the required information given to them before the sale occurs. The legislature apparently thought that the prospective purchaser could avoid environmental risks at that point by

---

[53]   Cal. Health & Safety Code § 25359.7.

walking away from the transaction (and if not, then the purchaser would not be "innocent"). However, the legislature did not include any provision for a "cooling off" period after the seller provides the disclosure. Thus, the purchaser might be contractually bound to buy the property notwithstanding the disclosure, unless the purchaser has included appropriate contingency language in the purchase agreement

With respect to leased property, the legislature believed that the lessee would most likely be the party to know of hazardous substance releases. Thus, lessees were required to make ongoing disclosures to their landlords, who would then have the information to disclose upon selling the property, precluding the availability of the innocent landowner defense for the purchaser. This objective was viewed seriously enough to include the provision allowing a landlord the right to void a lease for nondisclosure by a lessee. The civil penalty sanction of $5,000 per violation was not thought to be sufficient incentive for lessees to comply.

There was an immediate outcry against the new disclosure section, chiefly from lessees and leasehold mortgage lenders who feared that landlords might use the lease voidance provision for ulterior purposes (e.g., in order to terminate an old, below market lease). In addition, the statute was not well drafted and contained numerous ambiguities. As a result, the section was amended twice in 1988.[54] While the amendments resolved some of the issues and shortcomings, others remain (e.g., there is still no cooling off period for purchasers). The most important change was the deletion of the lease voidance provision. The legislature instead provided that nondisclosure by a nonresidential lessee could be treated as an event of default under the lease, curable by the lessee taking remedial action. The legislature exacted its pound of flesh for this softening of the statute, however. The disclosure obligation of each

---

[54] By Assembly Bill No. 924 and Senate Bill No. 1496, effective February 18, 1988, and September 22, 1988, respectively, as urgency legislation.

owner of nonresidential real property was expanded to apply not only in sales but also in leasing transactions.[55]

The disclosure section, as amended to date, contains the following specific disclosure obligations and sanctions for noncompliance:

(a) *Sellers or Lessors of Nonresidential Real Property* must, prior to the sale or lease, give written notice to the buyer or lessee of the presence of any hazardous substance release which the seller or lessor knows or has reasonable cause to believe has come to be located on or beneath the property. Sanctions for nondisclosure include actual damages and, in the case of actual knowledge of a material amount of hazardous substance release and a knowing and willful failure to disclose, civil penalties of up to $5,000 for each separate violation.[56]

(b) *Lessees of Residential or Nonresidential Real Property* who know or have reasonable cause to believe that any release of any hazardous substance has come or will come to be located on or beneath that real property, must give written notice to the owner or lessor within a reasonable period of time, either prior to the release or following the discovery by the lessee or renter of the presence or believed presence of the hazardous substance release. Sanctions for nondisclosure include actual damages and, in the case of knowledge of a material amount of hazardous substance release (or of a release required to be reported to a state or local agency) and knowing and willful failure to disclose, civil penalties of up to $5,000 for each separate violation.[57]

With respect to *nonresidential* leases only, the knowing and willful nondisclosure by a lessee who has knowledge of a material amount of hazardous substance release (or of a release required to be reported to a state or local agency), may be treated by the owner or lessor, upon

---

[55] For a detailed discussion of Cal. Health & Safety Code § 25359.7, its background, purposes, and the many questions raised, *see* Oppenheimer/Nanney, *Recent Developments Regarding Hazardous Substance Disclosure Obligations of Lessees, Lessors and Sellers of Real Property,* California Continuing Education of the Bar, Supplemental Program Materials: *Fundamentals of Real Property Practice* (Jan/Feb 1989).

[56] Cal. Health & Safety Code § 25359.7(a).

[57] *Id.,* § 25359.7(b).

written notice to the lessee or renter, as an event of default under the lease or rental agreement. The lessor's remedies in such a case are determined by the provisions of the lease or rental agreement. However, the lessee or renter has a statutory right to cure the default by promptly commencing and completing the removal of the hazardous substance release, or by taking other appropriate remedial action, as reasonably approved by the owner or lessor.[58]

It is important to note that the disclosure obligation under this statute applies with respect to *any* hazardous substance release. While there is a "materiality" standard on most of the sanctions for noncompliance, there is *no* materiality or "reportable quantity" standard limiting the disclosure obligation in the first instance or limiting the liability for actual damages for nondisclosure (although one might ask what damages would arise from the release of an immaterial quantity of a hazardous substance). It appears that the legislature wanted *all* relevant information to be disclosed, without screening, so that the recipients would be able to assess for themselves the importance of the information. Thus, in California real estate transactions involving sophisticated parties who wish to be in full compliance with the law, notices are being given which include every conceivable hazardous substance release that might be present on or under the property. As a result, this disclosure law may be the most stringent of its kind anywhere in the United States.

The statute requires disclosures only between the parties to a sale or lease. Although the state may recover civil penalties for noncompliance, there is no provision for making reports to the state or for recordation of any notice given pursuant to the law.

Transferors of Residential Real Property. With specified exemptions, a Real Estate Transfer Disclosure Statement must be delivered to the

---

[58] *Id.,* § 25359.7(b)(2)(A) and 25359.7(b)(3). The method of cure could be costly and may be of little comfort for a lessee who was not responsible for the release but must undertake remedial action if preservation of the lease is desired. Thus, it is advisable for California lessees to implement compliance programs in order to avoid a deemed default which might arise from nondisclosure.

prospective transferee by the transferor of residential real property.[59] The information required to be included is set forth in the prescribed form of Disclosure Statement, including a broad sweep of information regarding the nature, attributes and condition of the residential property. Unlike the hazardous substance release disclosure law, there is a cooling off period provided to the transferee after receipt of the Disclosure Statement.

It was presumably the existence of this disclosure law which led the legislature to omit residential sales transactions from the hazardous substance release disclosure law. However, the required Disclosure Statement form did not originally call for disclosures concerning the presence of hazardous substance contamination. Certain items on the former version of the Disclosure Statement (i.e., items regarding any landfill, any notices of abatement or citations, or any lawsuits against the seller affecting or threatening to affect the real property) might have reached the issue of hazardous waste if it was present in landfill on the property or was the subject of an abatement notice or citation or a lawsuit affecting the property. Otherwise, the common law duty to disclose material facts (see § 3.2) apparently governed disclosure of hazardous waste conditions in connection with the sale of residential real property in California.

Effective January 1, 1990, the Disclosure Statement form was amended so that it specifically calls for the disclosure of hazardous substance conditions in residential transactions. The seller is required to disclose "whether he or she is aware of any substances, materials, or products which may be an environmental hazard such as, but not limited to, asbestos, formaldehyde, radon gas, lead-based paint, fuel or chemical storage tanks, and contaminated soil or water on the subject property."[60] In addition, effective July 1, 1990, counties or cities may adopt local ordinances requiring additional disclosures on forms prescribed by the state statute, or may require other disclosures pursuant to an ordinance adopted before that date.

---

[59]   Cal. Civil Code § 1102 et seq.

[60]   Legislative Counsel's Digest, AB 584 (Assembly Member Hauser); 1989 Stats., c. 171.

This disclosure law applies only between the parties to the transaction. No report to the state or recordation of the Disclosure Statement is called for by the law.

Effective January 1, 1990, sellers of residential real property subject to the Disclosure Statement requirement must also disclose as soon as possible prior to transfer of title any actual knowledge of any former federal or state ordinance locations within a neighborhood radius of one-mile of the property. Former ordinance locations are those once used for military training and may contain potentially explosive munitions.[61] A similar disclosure duty to prospective tenants was imposed on landlords of residential dwelling units, also effective January 1, 1990, or as soon thereafter as practicable for then-existing tenancies.[62]

In May 1991, the California Department of Real Estate and the Department of Health Services published a consumer information booklet entitled "Environmental Hazards: Guide for Homeowners and Buyers." The booklet discusses basic information about asbestos, formaldehyde, lead, radon, hazardous wastes and household hazardous waste, and includes a listing of federal and state agencies. Giving this booklet to a transferee of residential real property will satisfy the seller's and broker's disclosure duties regarding common environmental hazards. But this does not relieve the seller or broker from any obligation to disclose the existence of known environmental hazards on or affecting the real property involved.[63]

Transferors of Hazardous Waste or Border Zone Property. Whenever property has been designated by the Department of Health Services as a "hazardous waste property" or a "border zone property," the owner must, upon entering into any purchase, lease or rental agreement, execute and deliver a written notice containing the following statement:

---

[61]   Cal. Civil Code § 1102.15.

[62]   *Id.*, § 1940.7.

[63]   Cal. Bus. & Prof. Code § 10084.1; Cal. Civ. Code § 2079.7; Cal. Health & Safety Code § 25417.

The land described herein contains hazardous waste or is within 2000 feet of land that contains hazardous waste. This condition renders the land and the owner, lessee, or other possessor of the land subject to the requirements, restrictions, provisions, and liabilities contained in Chapter 6.5 (commencing with Section 25100) of Division 20 of the Health and Safety Code. This statement is not a declaration that a hazard exists.[64]

Owners of Buildings with Asbestos-Containing Construction Materials. California's asbestos notification law is discussed in § 4.3.2 of Chapter 4. In this context, that law requires the mailing of notice to any new owner designated to receive notice under the law "within 15 days of the effective date of the agreement under which a person becomes a new owner."[65] This appears to call for notice triggered by a transaction, but to be given afterwards. It is doubtful that the provision would apply to a purchase and sale transaction, because the seller would no longer be an owner subject to the law. However, the persons who must be notified include lessees and management agents (who are also treated as "owners" for purposes of this law). Thus, an owner of a building covered by the law must provide the notice to new lessees or agents promptly following the effective date of the new lease or management agreement. Of course, the presence of asbestos in the building might have been disclosed beforehand for other reasons, but compliance with the notice procedure under this law may also be required.

Illinois

Illinois law provides that persons wishing to transfer any interest in property which has been used as a hazardous waste disposal site must (i) provide prior written notice of the transfer to the Illinois Environmental Protection Agency, and (ii) inform the buyer or transferee of any conditions imposed by the Agency upon the use of the property.[66]

---

[64]   Cal. Health & Safety Code § 25230(a)(2).

[65]   *Id.,* § 25915.2(c).

[66]   Ill. Rev. Stat. ch. 111-1/2 para. 1021(n).

In addition, Illinois has enacted the Responsible Property Transfer Act of 1988 which is a comprehensive disclosure law.[67] The effective date of the Transfer Act was delayed until November 1, 1989, and it applies to transactions occurring after January 1, 1990.

The Transfer Act applies to the transfer of any parcel of land (1) upon which a facility is located which is required to submit hazardous chemical inventory forms under the federal Emergency Planning and Community Right-to-Know Act of 1986,[68] or (2) which has an underground storage tank requiring registration with the State Fire Marshal.

With specified exemptions, the Transfer Act applies to transfers by deed or other instrument, or by lease for a term exceeding 40 years including all renewal options. The law also covers transfers of the trust powers or more than 25 percent of the beneficial interests in an Illinois land trust, or a transfer for security purposes of any beneficial interest in such a trust.

In connection with all covered transfers, the transferor must complete and deliver to the buyer and any lender a prescribed form of Environmental Disclosure Document for Transfer of Real Property, which calls for detailed information about the nature of the property, the nature of the transfer, the environmental status and condition of the property and operations conducted there, and the prior ownership and uses of the property. The Disclosure Document also contains notice for the parties regarding potential liabilities under the Illinois Environmental Protection Act, including copies of some of its liability provisions.

The Transfer Act provides for a ten-day cooling off period in favor of the buyer *or* lender if the Disclosure Document reveals "environmental defects in the real property which were previously unknown," or if the transferor fails to deliver the Disclosure Document after demand.[69]

---

67   *Id.*, ch. 30 para. 901 *et seq.*

68   42 U.S.C. § 11022.

69   Ill. Rev. Stat. ch. 30 para. 904(c).

Significantly, within 30 days after the transfer takes place, the Disclosure Document must be "recorded in the office of the recorder of the county in which such property is located and filed with the Environmental Protection Agency."[70] Recordation with the county recorder is the joint responsibility of the transferor and transferee.

Stringent sanctions apply for noncompliance, including civil penalties of up to $1,000 for the violation, plus $1,000 per day while the violation continues. Any false statement or certification on a Disclosure Document made with actual knowledge of falsity will result in civil penalties of up to $10,000 for the violation, plus $10,000 per day while the violation continues. The parties who fail to record the Disclosure Document will be jointly and severally liable for a civil penalty of up to $10,000. Actions to recover such penalties and compel compliance with the Transfer Act may be commenced by the Illinois Attorney General or the State's Attorney in the county where the violation occurred. Such actions are initiated upon such attorney's own motion or upon the request of the Environmental Protection Agency or *any citizen* of the county. Actions are authorized by any person who suffers damages as a result of any violation of the Transfer Act, and attorneys' fees are recoverable by the prevailing party.[71]

Indiana

Indiana has adopted the Responsible Property Transfer Law,[72] which "takes effect on January 1, 1990, and applies to transfers of property that take effect, or that are scheduled to become final, after December 31, 1989."[73] The Transfer Law appears to be quite similar to Illinois' Transfer Act.

The Transfer Law applies to the transfer of any parcel of real property that has not been subject to bonding or other financial assurances released by the appropriate governmental agency after compliance with applicable state laws and that (1) contains a facility which is required to submit hazardous chemical inventory forms under

---

70   *Id.*, para. 906.

71   *Id.*, para. 907.

72   I.C. 13-7-22.5.

73   Sec. 2, Senate Enrolled Act No. 541 (P.L. 166-1989, May 22, 1989).

the federal Emergency Planning and Community Right-to-Know Act of 1986, (2) contains an underground storage tank (UST) for which notification is required under Subtitle I of RCRA and analogous Indiana law, or (3) is listed on the Comprehensive Environmental Response, Compensation and Liability Information System (CERCLIS) in accordance with Section 116 of CERCLA.[74]

With specified exemptions, the Transfer Law applies to transfers by deed, contract for sale or other instrument of conveyance, or by lease for a term exceeding 40 years, including all renewal options. The law also covers assignment of more than 25 percent of the beneficial interest in a land trust, or a mortgage or collateral assignment of a beneficial interest in a land trust. Exempted transfers include tax deeds, reconveyances of property that is security for debt, foreclosure sale deeds, easement, and other enumerated transfers.[75]

Transferees include buyers, mortgagees, grantees or lessees of real property or assignees of more than a 25 percent interest in a land trust.[76]

In connection with covered transfers, the transferor must complete and deliver a prescribed form of Environmental Disclosure Document for Transfer of Real Property to each other party to the transfer at least 30 days beforehand (unless all the other parties waive that requirement, in which event the Disclosure Document must be delivered before the transfer becomes final).[77] The Disclosure Document must include, among other things, detailed information about the nature of the property, the nature of the transfer, the environmental status and condition of the property, and the prior ownership and uses of the property.

The Transfer Law provides for a ten-day cooling off period in favor of the prospective transferee if the Disclosure Document reveals "environmental defects in the property that were previously unknown" to the transferee, or if the transferor fails to deliver the Disclosure

---

74   I.C. 13-7-22.5-6.

75   *Id.*, 13-7-22.5-7.

76   *Id.*, 13-7-22.5-8.

77   *Id.*, 13-7-22.5-10.

Document after demand.[78] However, once a transfer has taken place, it may not be voided under the Transfer Law.[79]

Within 30 days after the transfer takes place, the Disclosure Document must be recorded in the office of the recorder of the county in which the property is located and filed with the Department of Environmental Management. Recordation of the Disclosure Document is the joint responsibility of the transferor and transferee.[80]

Noncompliance with the Transfer Law by a transferor is a Class B infraction.[81] Knowingly false statements on a Disclosure Document by a transferor is a Class A infraction, and each day the false statement remains uncorrected is a separate infraction.[82] Failure to record the Disclosure Document is a Class A infraction.[83] A prosecutor of any such infraction may obtain an order requiring the defendant to comply with the Transfer Law.[84] Civil actions are authorized for the recovery of consequential damages based upon a violation of the Transfer Law, and a party may recover reasonable costs and attorney's fees.[85]

Massachusetts

The conveyance or leasing of any interest in property on or in which hazardous waste has been disposed of is prohibited until notice of such disposal is recorded in the registry of deeds. In addition, the use of such land for anything other than a disposal facility is prohibited until such notice is recorded.[86]

---

[78]   *Id.*, 13-7-22.5-11; I.C. 13-7-22.5-12, I.C. 13-7-22.5-13.

[79]   *Id.*, 13-7-22.5-14.

[80]   *Id.*, 13-7-22.5-16.

[81]   *Id.*, 13-7-22.5-17.

[82]   *Id.*, 13-7-22.5-18.

[83]   *Id.*, 13-7-22.5-19.

[84]   *Id.*, 13-7-22.5-20.

[85]   *Id.*, 13-7-22.5-21.

[86]   Mass. Gen. L. ch. 21c § 7.

Minnesota

Before any transfer of ownership, an owner who knows or should have known that the property was used as the site of a hazardous waste disposal facility, or was subject to extensive contamination by release of a hazardous substance, must record an affidavit with the county recorder of the county in which the property is located. The affidavit must disclose "the identity, quantity, location, condition and circumstances of the disposal or contamination to the full extent known or reasonably ascertainable," as well as any use restrictions affecting the property.[87]

Within 60 days after the change of any information required to be disclosed, a new affidavit must be recorded, and the owner or subsequent owner who removes the hazardous substances involved may record an affidavit indicating that such removal has been accomplished.[88]

Failure to record such an affidavit will not affect or prevent the transfer of ownership. However, "any person who knowingly fails to record an affidavit as required . . . shall be liable . . . for any release or threatened release of any hazardous substance from a facility located on that property."[89]

North Carolina

When the possession of an inactive hazardous substance or waste disposal site is transferred, the deed, lease or other instrument of transfer must contain a statement that the property has been used as a hazardous substance or waste disposal site.[90]

Pennsylvania

Conveyances of property upon which hazardous waste has been disposed of must include in the deed an acknowledgement of that fact and a description of the location and types of wastes present at the property. This applies when the hazardous waste has been disposed of by the grantor or when the grantor has actual knowledge of the disposal.

---

[87]   Minn. Stat. § 115B.16(2).

[88]   *Id.*

[89]   *Id.*, § 115B.16(4).

[90]   N.C. Gen. Stat. § 130A-310.8.

Violation of this requirement may result in civil liability for cleanup costs and in civil and criminal penalties.[91]

Washington

Before selling any interest in real estate, the seller must give a written disclosure to the buyer regarding any significant release of any hazardous substances known to the seller to have occurred at the property within the last 20 years. Any buyer injured by the failure of the seller to make such a disclosure may recover damages unless that right has been expressly waived by the buyer. Implementing regulations are to specify what quantities of releases are deemed significant for purposes of the disclosure requirement.[92]

West Virginia

West Virginia has a disclosure law which applies to the sale or lease of any land which has been used for the storage, treatment or disposal of hazardous waste. Upon selling or leasing such property, owners who had any interest in the property when it was used for that purpose, or who have actual knowledge that property was used for such purpose, must disclose in the deed, lease, or other instrument, that the property was used for the storage, treatment, or disposal of hazardous waste.[93]

In a unique provision, West Virginia also imposes a disclosure obligation on any grantee or lessee who intends to use the property for storing, treating, or disposing of hazardous waste. Such transferees must disclose that intention in writing to the owner within 30 days prior to the transfer with a full description of the proposed method of storing, treating or disposing of such waste, the kind of waste to be involved, the proposed location of the activity, and any other information required by the Director of the Department of Natural Resources to be included in such disclosures.[94]

---

[91]   35 Pa. Cons. Stat. §§ 6018.405 and 6018.601-607.

[92]   Wash. Rev. Code §§ 70-105B.160(4) and (5).

[93]   W.Va. Code § 20-5E-20(a).

[94]   *Id.*, § 20-5E-20(b).

3.3.3 Laws Requiring Recorded Notice

Several of the states discussed in the previous section have laws requiring that hazardous substance disclosures be recorded in connection with real estate transactions. A number of additional laws in those and other states require recordation of similar notices, and in some cases reports to state agencies, without regard to the pendency of any transaction. However, one of the apparent purposes for such laws is to make sure that future transferees will be placed on actual or constructive notice of the hazardous substance condition and any applicable use restrictions. In this way, such laws are transaction-oriented. These statutes relate to properties which are or have been used and regulated as hazardous waste treatment, storage or disposal facilities (TSDFs).

These laws appear to be patterned generally after the RCRA requirement that the owner or operator of a hazardous waste disposal unit which has been closed must record, on a deed or other instrument which would normally be examined in a title search (to notify future purchasers), a notice that the land has been used to manage hazardous wastes, that its use is restricted under federal regulations, and that a survey showing the type, location and quantity of hazardous wastes disposed of has been filed with the Regional Administrator of the EPA and the appropriate local governmental agency with jurisdiction over land use.[95] However, some of the state laws apply at stages other than closure of a hazardous waste facility, such as when the facility is originally permitted or registered for that use.

Some of the laws contemplate that record notices may be updated as circumstances change (e.g., to reflect that the hazardous waste has been removed). Those laws which do not provide for updated information would appear to place a permanent stigma on the property without regard to its current condition.

In addition, there are numerous laws governing regulated industries or activities requiring reports, certifications or applications of various kinds to governmental agencies at the time of a transaction whereby there is a commencement, closure or change in ownership or operation of the business or activity. For instance, operating permits may have to

---

[95]   40 C.F.R. § 264.119(b).

be transferred, or new permits obtained, at the time of a transaction. Examples of regulated industries with such requirements include hazardous waste facilities, injection wells, underground storage tanks, oil and gas wells (onshore and offshore), unit operations and geothermal wells. Thus, a transaction may trigger reporting obligations under such laws and regulations, and they should not be overlooked by the parties. However, a listing of such laws is beyond the scope of this book. This § 3.3.3 focuses instead on laws requiring the recording of hazardous waste related information in the official real estate records.

California

California's Hazardous Waste Control Law includes a provision authorizing the state Department of Toxic Substances Control (DTSC) to require, as a condition of the issuance of a permit for a hazardous waste facility, the

> execution and recording of a written instrument which imposes an easement, covenant, restriction, or servitude upon the present and future uses of all or part of the land on which the hazardous waste facility subject to the permit or grant of interim status is located and on all or part of any adjacent land held by, or for the beneficial use of, the owners of the land on which the hazardous waste facility subject to the permit or grant of interim status is located . . . The easement, covenant, restriction, or servitude shall state that the land described in the instrument has been, or will be, the site of a hazardous waste facility or is adjacent to the site of such a facility, and may impose those use restrictions as the department deems necessary to protect the present or future public health.[96]

An owner of such land may request the modification or removal of the easement, covenant, restriction or servitude. After a public hearing, the DHS may agree to grant such a request, in which case an instrument

---

[96] Cal. Health & Safety Code § 25202.5. The DHS's Toxic Substances Control Program was transferred to the newly formed California Environmental Protection Agency in 1991 and is now known as the Department of Toxic Substances Control (DTSC).

reflecting that agreement must be recorded in the county where the land is located.[97]

Upon closure of a hazardous waste facility, the owner or operator must record a notation on the deed to the facility or on another instrument normally examined during a title search that: (1) the land has been used to manage hazardous waste, (2) its use is stricted; and (3) the survey plat and record regarding the waste disposed of at the facility have been filed with the local authority with jurisdiction over zoning or local land use.[98] The owner or operator must also submit to the state DTSC a certification that the required notation on the deed has been recorded together with a copy of the document on which the notation has been placed.[99]

In addition, whether or not a property has been formally permitted as a hazardous waste facility, the DHS may initiate a proceeding to have any property upon which a significant disposal of hazardous waste has occurred (creating an existing or potential significant hazard to present or future public health or safety) designated as a "hazardous waste property" or a "border zone property."[100] Upon such determination, the Director of the DHS must order the owners of the land to execute and record an instrument which imposes an easement, covenant, restriction or servitude upon the present or future uses of the land as required by the statute, and if the owners fail to do so, the restriction will be issued by order of court which will be recorded.[101] The designation may be removed later if "the waste no longer creates a significant existing or potential hazard to the present or future public health or safety."[102]

Indiana

A restrictive covenant is required for property intended as a landfill for the disposal of hazardous waste. The covenant must be recorded in

---

[97]   *Id.*, § 25202.6.

[98]   22 Cal. Code of Regulations §§ 66264.119(b)(1) and 66265.119(b)(1).

[99]   *Id.*, § 66264.119(b)(2) and 66265.119(b)(2).

[100]   Cal. Health & Safety Code § 25222.

[101]   *Id.*, § 25230(a) and (b).

[102]   *Id.*, § 25234(a).

the appropriate county by the Department of Environmental Management.[103]

Louisiana

Landowners who know that hazardous waste disposal has occurred on their property, or the state has identified the property as a solid or hazardous waste site, must record notice in the mortgage conveyance records.[104]

Maine

Once a closure plan for a hazardous waste facility has been approved, the board must file a notice with the register of deeds in the county where the facility is located. The notice must include the types of hazardous wastes and their treatment and disposal on the land involved, as well as any restrictive covenants required by the board regarding use of the property. Such restrictions can be removed later upon petition of the landowner.[105]

Missouri

Missouri law provides for the registration of hazardous waste disposal sites. When the director places a site used for hazardous waste disposal on the registry, he must file a notice to that effect with the recorder of deeds in the county where the site is located. When the site is properly closed, the director must file this finding also.[106]

North Carolina

When a site is granted a permit for use as a landfill or hazardous waste disposal facility, the owner must file a certified copy of the permit in the office of the register of deeds in the county where the land is located.[107]

---

[103]   Ind. Code § 13-7-8.5-5.

[104]   Act of July 9, 1989. West's La. Sess. Law Serv. (No. 6) 1514.

[105]   Me. Rev. Stat. Ann. Tit. 38 § 1319-S.

[106]   Mo. Rev. Stat. § 260.470.

[107]   N.C. Gen. Stat. § 130A-301.

Ohio

After closure of a hazardous waste disposal unit, the owner or operator must submit within 60 days to the local zoning authority and the Director of Environmental Protection a record of the type, location, and quantity of hazardous wastes disposed of there. This information, including the fact that hazardous wastes have been disposed of at the property and that its use is restricted, must be recorded on a deed to the property or another instrument which would normally be examined during a title search. Any subsequent removal of the hazardous waste may also be recorded in the real estate records.[108]

Tennessee

When a property is placed on the list of inactive hazardous substance sites, the Commissioner of the Department of Public Health must notify the register of deeds in the county where the property is located. The notice of this listing must then be recorded by the register of deeds. Any subsequent containment or cleanup must also be recorded.[109]

Texas

Before any person may dispose of industrial solid waste or municipal hazardous waste, a statement must be recorded in the county real estate records which describes the location and other details of the planned disposal.[110]

Washington

Any owner of land which is the site of a significant release of any hazardous substance, as found by the Department of Ecology, must record a notice with the auditor of the county in which that site is located. The notice must include information specified in the statute. Any owner who fails to record a required notice is subject to a damage action which may be brought by any other person with an interest in the property and who is injured by such noncompliance. The Department

---

[108] Ohio Admin. Code § 3745-55-19.

[109] Tenn. Code Ann. 68-46-212(d).

[110] Tex. Admin. Code § 335.5.

may itself record the notice when it has discovered the release. A certificate of completion of remedial action may also be recorded.[111]

3.4 Toward a Broad Disclosure Policy

The simple days of *caveat emptor* are gone. A system of disclosure rules has developed which is complex, rapidly changing and fraught with peril. Each disclosure duty, from common law to various statutory requirements, must be observed. One of those duties might apply even if others do not. Some properties are being permanently stigmatized with recorded notices.

Despite these developments, property owners remain generally reluctant to give bad news to prospective buyers or lessees. It is a natural human impulse to "puff" what one is selling rather than to impart negative information. Even when an owner realizes that disclosures must be made, the impulse still is to communicate as little as possible regarding those matters which might detract from the desired transaction. Thus, owners often ask counsel to advise as to the minimum which must be disclosed. The determination of the minimum disclosure requirement can be a dangerous exercise, and the answer in various states may be different.

In view of the broad disclosure requirements and the potential fraud liability for partial disclosures, it is often the best policy for transferors to disclose virtually everything they know about a property. That policy has the advantage of simplicity, although it is the reverse of *caveat emptor*. It protects against liability for failure to disclose some piece of information which, in hindsight, a court might determine should have been disclosed. A broad disclosure policy is particularly compelling when the information concerns the presence of hazardous wastes at a property. Except in obvious cases, such a condition may be viewed as a "latent" or "concealed" and "material" condition which must be disclosed under common law principles. Even if not under the common law, many of the new statutes discussed above may require disclosure. In sum, there is great exposure to liability for failure to disclose hazardous waste conditions, and transferors must keep that in mind when considering what information to share with prospective transferees.

---

[111] Wash. Rev. Code §§ 70-105B.160(1), (2) and (3).

Finally, it should be noted that there are other transfer-triggered disclosure laws relating to environmental conditions, but which are not summarized in this chapter because they do not relate to hazardous waste. For example, **California** realtors (or sellers acting without an agent) must disclose to the buyer whether the property is located within a designated geologic or earthquake hazard zone, but only if an official special studies map of the applicable area, prepared by the State Geologist, is reasonably available and notices are posted at the offices of the county recorder, assessor and planning commission identifying the location of the map.[112] Guidelines for the preparation of maps of seismic hazard zones are to be developed by January 1, 1992, and when the official maps are completed, the State Geologist is to provide copies to the applicable jurisdictions and notices are to be posted regarding the availability of the maps to sellers and their realtors.[113] Booklets entitled "Homeowner's Guide to Earthquake Safety"[114] and "Commercial Property Owner's Guide to Earthquake Safety"[115] may be given to a prospective transferee as sufficient information regarding general geologic and seismic hazards, without altering any duty of a seller or broker to disclose the existence of known hazards on or affecting the property.

Similarly, under federal law, mortgage lenders must investigate and disclose to the prospective purchaser or lessee (or ensure that the seller or lessor has disclosed) that the property is located in a designated flood hazard zone.[116] Under a new law effective July 1, 1991, sellers must make a disclosure if the property is located in a designated fire hazard

---

[112] Alquist-Priolo Special Studies Zone Act, Cal. Public Resources Code § 2621.9.

[113] *Id.*, §§ 2695, 2696.

[114] Cal. Civil Code § 2079.8; Cal. Bus. & Prof. Code § 10149; Cal. Public Resources Code §§ 2621 et seq.

[115] Cal. Civil Code § 2079.9; Cal. Bus. & Prof. Code § 10149; Cal. Public Resources Code §§ 2621 et seq. and §§ 2690 et seq.

[116] Flood Disaster Protection Act of 1973, 42 U.S.C. § 4104a; 12 C.F.R. § 339.5; *Small v. South Norwalk Savings Bank*, 205 Conn. 751, 535 A.2d 1292 (Conn. 1988) (Bank was held liable for negligent failure to comply with flood hazard zone disclosure requirement).

area.[117] Another example is the requirement that termite reports be provided to residential buyers.

Such disclosure laws should not be overlooked by the parties to a real estate transaction.

---

[117] Cal. Public Resources Code §§ 4124, 4136.

CHAPTER FOUR

OTHER DISCLOSURE AND REPORTING LAWS

4.1   Introduction

4.2   Federal Disclosure and Reporting Laws

    4.2.1 CERCLA and SARA

    4.2.2 RCRA

    4.2.3 TSCA

    4.2.4 CWA

    4.2.5 OSHA

    4.2.6 Disclosures Required Under Securities Laws

4.3   State Disclosure and Reporting Laws

    4.3.1 California's Proposition 65

    4.3.2 California's Asbestos Notification Law

    4.3.3 California's Business Plan Requirements

    4.3.4 Other California Reporting Laws

    4.3.5 Disclosure and Reporting Laws of Other States

    4.3.6 Local Regulations

4.4   Conclusion

4.1   Introduction

In addition to disclosure and reporting laws which are triggered by transactions (see Chapter 3), there are other hazardous substance disclosure and reporting laws which are the ongoing obligation of operating businesses or landowners regardless of any transaction. Those laws are relevant to the parties to a real estate transaction because previous disclosures or warnings to private parties or reports to governmental agencies provide an important source of information which might be reviewed during environmental due diligence. The absence of such disclosures and reports should not be relied on as indicating that there are no environmental problems, however. Companies often are not in compliance with disclosure and reporting laws, and hazardous conditions might exist which are not subject to any such requirement.

Information developed during environmental due diligence (e.g., from soil testing) might itself incidentally trigger a reporting requirement. This might not be desired by one or more of the parties to a transaction. The reporting laws represent a chief reason why many parties are reluctant to permit or undertake environmental due diligence, for fear of what might be found and the spectre of governmental involvement following an obligatory report. That attitude, of course, only results in deferral of discovery. The contamination, when ultimately uncovered, is likely to have become more widespread and more costly to remedy; and it might not be someone else's problem at that time, particularly in view of the extensive liability provisions of the environmental laws. Any risk can be assessed, confronted and appropriately allocated at the time of a transaction as long as the parties are not overly fearful of reporting requirements.

The disclosure and reporting laws are also important when the transaction involves the acquisition of a going business rather than real estate alone. The compliance of the business with various laws, including environmental laws and reporting requirements, should be investigated as a part of acquisition due diligence.

The following summaries are not intended to be comprehensive. Counsel should be consulted in each case for the full scope of the laws and regulations which might apply to any particular circumstances.

4.2   Federal Disclosure and Reporting Laws

A number of federal laws require notices or reports to governmental agencies with respect to hazardous substance releases.

4.2.1   CERCLA and SARA

CERCLA provides that any person who is in charge of a "facility"[1] must notify the National Response Center immediately upon gaining knowledge of any release of a "reportable quantity" of a hazardous substance.[2] The Administrator of the EPA by regulation designates the reportable quantities for the various hazardous substances identified

---

[1]   "Facility" is defined broadly to include any building or other place "where a hazardous substance has been deposited, stored, disposed of, or placed, or otherwise come to be located." 42 U.S.C. § 9601(9).

[2]   *Id.*, § 9603(a).

under CERCLA. In the absence of such a regulation as to a particular substance, the statute provides for a reportable quantity of one pound.[3] Further, the threshold quantity must be released within a 24 hour period to be reportable.[4] As a practical matter, it is often difficult or impossible to know if a threshold quantity of a hazardous substance has been released within that time frame and is hence reportable, particularly when an old release is discovered.

This CERCLA reporting requirement does not apply to federally permitted releases or to the application of pesticide products registered under FIFRA.[5] A report is also not required under CERCLA if the release is reported (or specifically exempted from reporting) under RCRA.[6] Where the release is of a continuous nature and it has been reported, further reporting is done annually or in the event of any significant increase in the quantity of releases over previously reported rates.[7] Releases of petroleum products are not covered to the extent the petroleum involved is excluded from the definition of "hazardous substance" (as discussed in §§ 1.2.2 1 and 1.2.7 of Chapter 1).

Sanctions for noncompliance or reporting of false or misleading information include criminal fines and up to three years in prison (or five years for repeat offenses). The federal Court of Appeals for the Sixth Circuit recently upheld the conviction of a person under the Clean Air Act and CERCLA for failing to report the release of more than one pound of asbestos during a demolition project.[8] The federal Court of Appeals for the Second Circuit has upheld the conviction of a maintenance foreman, a relatively low-level employee, for failing to report a hazardous substance release (involving the disposal of waste cans of paint) which he had supervised. That employee was sufficiently "in charge" of the facility for the reporting requirement to apply to

---

[3] *Id.*, § 9602.

[4] 40 C.F.R. Part 302.

[5] 42 U.S.C. §§ 9603(a) and (e).

[6] *Id.*, § 9603(f)(1).

[7] *Id.*, § 9603(f)(2).

[8] *U.S. v. Buckley*, 934 F.2d 84 (6th Cir. 1991).

him.[9] Thus, compliance by employees at many levels of a company can be called into question under CERCLA.

Title III of SARA added the Emergency Planning and Community Right-To-Know Act of 1986, which established local emergency planning agencies, and which requires certain businesses to prepare inventory reports listing hazardous chemicals in their possession, to assist in development of local emergency response plans, to prepare annual reports of releases of hazardous substances, and to report immediately certain ultrahazardous releases.[10]

In particular, the Act mandated the establishment of state commissions, planning districts and local committees for the administration of an extensive planning and reporting program.[11] Those agencies must develop comprehensive emergency response plans.[12] The Act applies (i) to those "extremely hazardous substances" listed by the Administrator of the EPA, who must also establish threshold planning quantities for each such substance (two pounds in the absence of regulations), and (ii) to those facilities which have on hand any listed substances in excess of the respective threshold amounts.[13]

The owner or operator of those facilities which handle listed substances in excess of threshold quantities, and which must prepare Material Safety Data Sheets (MSDS) under the Occupational Safety and Health Act of 1970, must submit (i) an MSDS for each regulated chemical (or a list of such chemicals), and (ii) hazardous chemical inventory forms to the applicable local emergency planning committee, the state emergency response commission and the local fire department. Such owners and operators are required to submit new MSDS as necessary to keep the reported information up-to-date, and the inventory forms must be updated annually.[14] The apparent purpose for these reporting requirements is to ensure that the appropriate authorities who

---

9   *U.S. v. Carr*, 880 F.2d 1550 (2d Cir. 1989).

10   42 U.S.C. §§ 11001 *et seq.*

11   *Id.*, § 11001.

12   *Id.*, § 11003.

13   *Id.*, § 11002.

14   *Id.*, §§ 11021 and 11022.

must respond to emergencies will have information on hand regarding which extremely hazardous substances are likely to be encountered in a release from a particular facility. That information can be critical to the quick selection of an appropriate response action for the protection of the public health and safety.

In addition, even if CERCLA already requires a report to the National Response Center, the owner or operator of a facility must immediately notify the community emergency coordinator for the local emergency planning committees in the event of a release of a "reportable quantity" of an extremely hazardous substance. That quantity is established by regulations (or is one pound in the absence of regulations). Releases which result in exposure to persons solely within the facility need not be reported under the Act.[15]

Enforcement orders may be issued under the Act, and civil penalties of up to $25,000 per day may be imposed for noncompliance with an order. In addition, civil penalties of up to $25,000 per day (or $75,000 for repeat offenses) may be assessed for violation of the reporting requirements. A knowing and willful violation may result in a criminal fine of up to $25,000 and two years in prison (or up to $50,000 and five years for repeat offenses).[16] Suits may also be commenced by state or local governments or by *any citizen* for the enforcement of the Act or collection of civil penalties for violations.[17]

In sum, the CERCLA and SARA reporting requirements were designed to provide necessary information to facilitate emergency response to fresh releases and to compile data regarding the nature and quantities of ongoing hazardous substance releases. It does not appear that these reporting requirements apply to past releases (e.g., those which occurred when a property was under prior ownership and which might be discovered during environmental due diligence). Under CERCLA, it would usually not be known whether the release occurred within a 24-hour period; and under SARA, an old release probably would not involve a current emergency of the kind contemplated by the

---

[15]   *Id.*, § 11004.

[16]   *Id.*, § 11045.

[17]   *Id.*, § 11046.

emergency notification provisions. However, a prospective purchaser, lessee or lender should be interested in the hazardous substance activity and reports of a company subject to the CERCLA or SARA reporting requirements.

4.2.2   RCRA

A comprehensive program for regulation of underground storage tanks was enacted as Subtitle I of RCRA, and petroleum is a specifically regulated substance under that law.[18] Each UST owner must "notify the State or local agency or department designated . . . of the existence of such tank, specifying the age, size, type, location and uses of such tank."[19] Pursuant to regulations, each UST owner or operator must report "releases and corrective action taken in response to a release from" such UST.[20] Thus, the discovery of UST leakage, including that which began long before discovery, may have to be reported under RCRA.

The UST program may be enforced by order. Civil penalties of up to $25,000 per day may be imposed for noncompliance. In addition, civil penalties of up to $10,000 per day per UST may be assessed for failure to comply with the release reporting requirements or for knowing failure to report the existence of any UST or for providing false information.[21]

4.2.3   TSCA

The Toxic Substances Control Act (TSCA) requires manufacturers and processors of chemical substances to maintain records and submit reports to the Administrator of the EPA.[22] Civil penalties of up to $25,000 per day may be imposed for violation of the reporting requirement, and, in addition, a knowing or willful violation may result

---

18   *Id.,* § 6991 *et seq.*

19   *Id.,* § 6991a(1).

20   *Id.,* § 6991b(c)(3).

21   *Id.,* § 6991e.

22   15 U.S.C. § 2607.

in a criminal fine of up to $25,000 per day and imprisonment for up to one year.[23]

4.2.4   CWA

The Clean Water Act (CWA) prohibits "the discharge of oil or hazardous substances" into or upon the "navigable waters" and "adjoining shorelines" of the United States in any harmful quantity as determined by regulations.[24] Any person in charge of a facility, upon learning of such a discharge, must "immediately notify the appropriate agency of the United States Government of such discharge," and failure to give such notice may result in a criminal fine of up to $10,000 and imprisonment for up to one year.[25] Reports under this statute may be relevant to a transaction involving land located on a waterway, on a coastline, or on wetlands.

4.2.5   OSHA

The federal Occupational Safety and Health Act (OSHA) requires employers to maintain and make available to the Secretary of Labor records regarding compliance with the Act. In addition, employers must "promptly notify any employee who has been or is being exposed to toxic materials or harmful physical agents in concentrations or at levels which exceed those prescribed by an applicable occupational safety and health standard . . ., and shall inform any employee who is being thus exposed of the corrective action being taken."[26]   OSHA has, for example, implemented extensive regulations regarding occupational exposures to asbestos[27] and demolition or renovation activity which might disturb asbestos,[28] including various reporting requirements. Additional reporting requirements exist under the EPA's National Emissions Standards for Hazardous Air Pollutants (NESHAP) program regarding renovation or demolition work involving asbestos.   The records of past reports or the cost of future compliance should be of

---

23   *Id.*, § 2615.

24   33 U.S.C. § 1321(b)(3).

25   *Id.*, § 1321(b)(5)

26   29 U.S.C. § 657

27   29 C.F.R. § 1910.1001

28   *Id.*, § 1926.58.

interest to prospective transferees of properties with asbestos-containing construction materials.

4.2.6   Disclosures Required Under Securities Laws[29]

Federal securities laws may require environmental disclosure at various times. For those corporations which are public reporting companies, environmental disclosures are required in the periodic reports (such as the annual report on Form 10-K and the quarterly report on Form 10-Q) filed with the Securities and Exchange Commission (the "SEC"). In addition, the requirements of many of the registration statement forms (such as the S-1 form) require environmental disclosure in connection with the registration of securities under the Securities Act of 1933. The basic requirements are contained in Items 101, 103 and 303 of Regulation S-K. There are also SEC releases and interpretative letters which discuss these requirements.

Item 101 of Regulation S-K states that:

> Appropriate disclosure also shall be made as to the material effects that compliance with Federal, State and local provisions which have been enacted or adopted regulating the discharge of materials into the environment, or otherwise relating to the protection of the environment, may have upon the capital expenditures, earnings and competitive position of the [company] and its subsidiaries. The [company] shall disclose any material estimated capital expenditures for environmental control facilities for the remainder of its current fiscal year and its succeeding fiscal year and for such further periods as the [company] may deem material.

Under Item 101, a company which has reason to believe that its costs beyond the two-year period discussed in Item 101 will be materially higher than its costs during such two year period may have an obligation to develop (and disclose) estimates of future costs.[30] Furthermore, costs

---

[29]   This § 4.2.6 was written by Janet Hoffman, Baker & Hostetler, McCutchen Black, Los Angeles, California.

[30]   Securities Act Release No. 6130 (September 27, 1979).

necessary to compensate for and remedy previous noncompliance with environmental regulations should also be disclosed.[31]

Item 103 requires the disclosure of information with respect to material pending or contemplated legal proceedings, other than ordinary routine litigation incidental to the business, and in particular requires a description of:

> [A]n administrative or judicial proceeding . . . arising under any Federal, State or local provisions that have been enacted or adopted regulating the discharge of materials into the environment or primary [sic] for the purpose of protecting the environment . . . if:
>
> A.   Such proceeding is material to the business or financial condition of the [company];
>
> B.   Such proceeding involves primarily a claim for damages, or involves potential monetary sanctions, capital expenditures, deferred charges or charges to income and the amount involved, exclusive of interest and costs, exceeds 10 percent of the current assets of the [company] and its subsidiaries on a consolidated basis; or
>
> C.   A governmental authority is a party to such proceeding and such proceeding involves potential monetary sanctions, unless the [company] reasonably believes that such proceeding will result in no monetary sanctions, or in monetary sanctions, exclusive of interest and costs, of less than $100,000; provided, however, that such proceedings which are similar in nature may be grouped and described generically.

The SEC interprets the term "proceeding" broadly. Proceedings which must be disclosed include administrative proceedings initiated by the company, if a governmental authority is a party, and administrative

---

[31]   *In re Occidental Petroleum Corp.*, Exchange Act Release No. 16950 (July 2, 1980).

consent orders.[32] However, designation as a PRP is not required to be disclosed under Item 103 unless the PRP also has knowledge that a governmental agency is contemplating a proceeding.[33]

Item 303 of Regulation S-K (Management's Discussion and Analysis of Financial Condition and Results of Operations), requires disclosure of certain forward-looking information about the company. Disclosure is required of known trends, demands, commitments, events or uncertainties if they are (1) reasonably likely to occur, and (2) reasonably likely to have a material effect on the company's financial condition or results of operations. The SEC has provided an example of a situation in which Management Discussion and Analysis (MD&A) disclosure would be required. The example given was that of a PRP with no available statutory defenses which is unsure that its insurance covers its potential liability and which is unsure whether it can obtain contribution from other PRPs. The release states that:

> Based upon the facts of this hypothetical case, MD&A disclosure of the effects of the PRP status, quantified to the extent reasonably practicable, would be required. For MD&A purposes, aggregate potential cleanup costs must be considered in light of the joint and several liability to which a PRP is subject. Facts regarding whether insurance coverage may be contested, and whether and to what extent potential sources of contribution or indemnification constitute reliable sources of recovery may be factored into the determination of whether a material future effect is not reasonably likely to occur.[34]

The May 18, 1989, release also makes clear that companies are required in the MD&A section to disclose any material potential capital expenditures necessary to comply with recently adopted legislation, including environmental legislation, even though final regulations implementing such legislation have not yet been adopted.

---

[32]   *In re U.S. Steel Corp.*, Exchange Act Release No. 16223 (September 27, 1979); Securities Act Release No. 6130 (September 27, 1979).

[33]   Securities Act Release No. 6835 (May 18, 1989).

[34]   Securities Act Release No. 6835 (May 18, 1989).

Given the disclosure requirements discussed above, a public company's periodic reports may be a valuable potential source of information regarding the company's environmental record. A prudent purchaser of either the stock of a public reporting company which holds real estate, or of real estate from a public reporting company, would do well to review the company's most recent reports of Forms 10-Q and 10-K, although the purchaser should be cognizant of the fact that the seller may not have complied with the reporting requirements.

In addition to providing a potential source of information for purchasers of the real property of public reporting companies, the federal securities laws, and in particular Rule 10b-5 promulgated under the Securities Exchange Act of 1934, may require a shareholder selling its stock in a corporation which owns contaminated real property to disclose that fact to the purchaser if it is material. A purchaser of all of the stock of a corporation subject to material undisclosed environmental liabilities may have a cause of action against the seller of the stock under Rule 10b-5. It is beyond the scope of this book to discuss the elements of a Rule 10b-5 cause of action in detail. However, purchasers and sellers of stock should be aware that the securities laws apply to such transactions and can provide remedies unavailable otherwise.

Many state securities laws and regulations contain provisions similar to Rule 10b-5, and should also be consulted if a stock transaction is contemplated in connection with a company which owns or leases real estate which might have environmental problems.

The SEC and the EPA are increasingly sharing information. The EPA provides the SEC with information about companies identified as PRPs or which are the subject of civil or criminal enforcement proceedings under the environmental laws. The SEC reviews this information to determine whether such companies are complying with their reporting and disclosure requirements under the securities laws. Likewise, the EPA obtains information from the SEC about the net worth of companies which are the subject of EPA enforcement actions, for the purpose of calculating appropriate penalties.

4.3   State Disclosure and Reporting Laws

Many states have laws requiring reports of hazardous substance releases along the lines of the federal rules discussed above. One state,

California, has been especially active with respect to disclosure laws and has unique provisions which will be highlighted below.

4.3.1   California's Proposition 65

California's Safe Drinking Water and Toxic Enforcement Act of 1986[35] was adopted by initiative measure (Proposition 65) and has two chief components. It prohibits any person in the course of doing business from "knowingly" discharging or releasing any chemical "known to the state to cause cancer or reproductive toxicity into water or onto or into land where such chemical passes or probably will pass into any source of drinking water,"[36] and it prohibits such persons from "knowingly and intentionally" exposing any individual to such a chemical "without first giving clear and reasonable warning to such individual."[37] This section focuses on the warning requirement.

Proposition 65 List.   Most environmental laws define "hazardous substances" by reference to other laws or hazard criteria. While many substances have been identified under those laws and placed on various lists, additional substances may qualify as hazardous. Thus, it can be unclear whether a particular substance is regulated. Proposition 65 takes a different approach. It covers only those substances which have been (i) specifically identified as causing cancer or reproductive toxicity and (ii) published by the Governor on a list which is updated at least annually.[38]   The first list was published on February 27, 1987, and contained 27 cancer-causing chemicals and two additional chemicals known to cause reproductive toxicity. The list has grown considerably since then. As of July 1, 1989, the list contained 261 cancer-causing chemicals and 30 additional reproductively toxic chemicals.[39]   As of

---

[35]   Cal. Health & Safety Code § 25249.5 *et seq.*

[36]   *Id.,* § 25249.5.

[37]   *Id.,* § 25249.6.

[38]   Id., § 25249.8.

[39]   *California Regulatory Notice Register,* Office of Administrative Law, Register 89, No. 26-Z, pp. 2066-2072 (6-30-89) (including chemicals listed through July 1, 1989) ["Register 89 No. 26-Z"].

April 1, 1991, the list contained 373 cancer-causing chemicals and 106 additional reproductively toxic chemicals.[40] As of January 1, 1992, the list contained 377 cancer-causing chemicals and 121 additional reproductively toxic chemicals.[41]

Warnings and Safe Harbor Regulations. Warnings must be given when exposure is anticipated by a "person in the course of doing business," which is defined to exclude persons with fewer than ten employees.[42] The warning requirement applies as to a particular chemical 12 months after it is listed.[43] Thus, Proposition 65 warnings were first required to be given as of February 27, 1988, for the initial 29 chemicals listed. The warning requirement applies or will apply in the future to additional chemicals based on their various dates of listing. For example, tobacco smoke was added to the list on April 1, 1988, and warnings regarding tobacco smoke became required as of April 1, 1989. Similarly, Vitamin A (in daily dosages in excess of 10,000 International Units) was added to the list of reproductively toxic chemicals as of July 1, 1989, so that warnings became required commencing July 1, 1990.[44] Aspirin was added to the list of reproductively toxic chemicals (especially during the last three months of pregnancy) as of July 1, 1990, so that warnings became required as of July 1, 1991.[45]

Warning is not required "if the person responsible can show that the exposure poses no significant risk assuming lifetime exposure at the level in question" for cancer-causing substances, or that "the exposure will have no observable effect assuming exposure at one thousand (1,000) times the level in question for substances known to the state to cause reproductive toxicity," and, in any action brought to enforce the warning requirement, the burden is on the defendant to prove that the exemption

---

40 *Id.*, Register 90, No. 13-Z, pp. 455-463 (4-1-91) ["Register 90, No. 13-Z"].

41 *Id.*, Register 91, No. 52-Z, pp. 1805-1814 (1-1-92).

42 Cal. Health & Safety Code § 25249.11(a).

43 *Id.*, § 25249.10(b).

44 Register 89 No. 26-Z, at p. 2071.

45 Register 90 No. 13-Z, at pp. 461 and 463.

applies.[46]   Some assistance in this regard may be derived from
implementing regulations which define the "significant risk" levels for a
number of the chemicals listed under Proposition 65, resulting in a "safe
harbor" if the exposure in question is less than the defined risk level.

Warnings "need not be provided separately to each exposed
individual and may be provided by general methods such as labels on
consumer products, inclusion of notices in mailings to water customers,
posting of notices, placing notices in public news media, and the like,
provided that the warning accomplished is clear and reasonable."[47]
Thus, since February 27, 1988, the California populace has been deluged
with warning notices in newspapers, in mailings together with utility
bills, and in posted signs at many places, including gas stations,
restaurants and other buildings.   Since April 1, 1989, many office
buildings have posted warning signs at all entrances which usually read
as follows:

WARNING

**This facility permits smoking, and tobacco smoke is
known to the State of California to cause cancer.
(Health & Safety Code § 25249.6)**

Regulations implemented under Proposition 65 would allow a
general warning which says only that "This area contains a chemical
known to the State of California to cause cancer."[48] This regulation has
been attacked as not requiring the specific information ("clear and
reasonable" warning) contemplated by Proposition 65.   Responding to
this concern, an extensive and controversial revision of those regulations
is under review by the Cal-EPA's Office of Environmental Health and
Hazard Assessment.

Other regulations implementing Proposition 65 have been adopted
on an emergency basis by Cal-OSHA as a part of the hazard

---

46   Cal. Health & Safety Code § 25249.10(c).

47   *Id.*, § 25249.11(f).

48   22 Cal. Code of Regulations § 12601.

communication program for workplace exposures.[49] These regulations make it clear that where Cal-OSHA's hazard communication program and Proposition 65 overlap, the employer must comply with the hazard communication program, which is deemed to be compliance with Proposition 65. However, some chemicals are regulated by Proposition 65 but not by Cal-OSHA's hazard communication standard (e.g. tobacco smoke). In such cases, the employer must comply with either the regulations under Proposition 65 or the hazard communication regulations for the workplace exposures involved. Of course, Proposition 65 and its implementing regulations continue to apply with respect to any exposed persons who are not employees and are not covered by the hazard communication standard.

What Benefit? One wonders what benefit the public actually derives from the plethora of notices. People really do not have much choice about many of the exposures. Most people need to use their automobiles and must pump gas into them notwithstanding the warning signs at gas stations. Most people who work in enclosed offices or other buildings are not in a position to quit their jobs even though tobacco smoke is circulated through ventilation systems and warnings are posted. Southern California Gas Company includes a Proposition 65 notice with its billings approximately every two months, because natural gas contains small amounts of benzene, a listed substance, which might result in an exposure in the case of a gas leak. There are obviously much greater dangers from a gas leak than the potential exposure to benzene, and the notice does not really accomplish anything. Gas company customers who repeatedly receive the notices simply throw them into the trash.

Some commentators have suggested that a real benefit of Proposition 65 has been the quiet assessment conducted by many companies and their modification of operating procedures and chemical usage to avoid the emission of listed chemicals so that warnings need not

---

[49] 8 Cal. Code of Regulations § 5194(a)(6) (Hazard Communication). Cal-OSHA was required to incorporate Proposition 65 into its hazard communication program as a result of litigation. *Cal. Labor Fed., AFL-CIO v. Cal. Occupational Safety and Health Standards Board*, 221 Cal.App.3d 1547, 271 Cal.Rptr. 310 (1990).

be given.[50] Be that as it may, the consuming public must ultimately pay the cost of the paperwork and trash removal caused by Proposition 65, regardless whether that cost is warranted by any benefit. The exercise must be followed nonetheless to avoid the potential liability which attaches to noncompliance (unless a company can prove that the exposure involved poses no "significant risk").

Enforcement. Proposition 65 may be enforced by court order, and violations are subject to the assessment of civil penalties of up to $2,500 per day for each violation. Each individual who is not warned when required may represent a separate violation. Thus, potential civil penalties can mount rapidly. Enforcement and civil penalty actions may be brought by the government *or by any person in the public interest,* after 60 days notice to the state Attorney General and the local district attorneys and city attorney, if the government has not acted to commence and diligently prosecute the violation.[51] Such a person may receive a "bounty" in the amount of 25 percent of the civil penalties collected.[52]

A number of lawsuits have been filed in the wake of Proposition 65. Several lawsuits have sought to compel more vigorous implementation and enforcement by the state, and indeed the Governor has been required to update and add to the Proposition 65 list of regulated chemicals faster than he wished.[53] The California Attorney General commenced legal action in 1988 attacking a warning system using an "800" toll free telephone number (rather than posted signs or warning labels on products) which was established by a number of supermarket

---

50 Los Angeles Times, p. D1, "Quiet Legacy of Once-Hated Proposition 65" (Jan. 28, 1992).

51 *Id.,* § 25249.7.

52 *Id.,* § 25192(a)(2).

53 *See, e.g., AFL-CIO v. Deukmejian,* Sacramento County Superior Court, Case No. 348195; *AFL-CIO v. Deukmejian,* Sacramento County Superior Court, Case No. 502541; *AFL-CIO v. Deukmejian,* Sacramento County Superior Court, Case No. 359223; *Nicolle-Wagner v. Deukmejian,* Los Angeles County Superior Court, Case No. C733003.

and retail chains and manufactures of non-cigarette tobacco products.[54]
The Attorney General's position was upheld by court rulings that the toll
free telephone number system is an inadequate method of compliance
with Proposition 65.[55] The tobacco company defendants promptly
settled, agreeing to pay $150,000 and to label their products with
Proposition 65 warnings. Two years later, the supermarket and retail
chain defendants settled, agreeing to pay $750,000 in fines and penalties
for their alleged post noncompliance (the labeling by the product
manufactures cured the problem prospectively).[56] In contrast, in 1988,
the Solano County District Attorney filed suit against several developers
and the California Building Industry Association under the unfair trade
practices law claiming that they are *over-warning* prospective buyers of
homes when the conditions warned about do not pose a sufficiently
significant health risk, resulting in desensitization to such warnings.[57]
Thus, businesses are exposed to costly Proposition 65 penalties for failing
to warn, or costly unfair trade practice penalties for over-warning. This
is a real dilemma when it may be unclear whether the "significant risk"
threshold triggering the warning requirement is present in a given set of
circumstances.

Cases have been initiated by environmental groups under the bounty
provisions of the law, but these cases generally have been taken over by
the government during the 60-day notice period. For example, after
such a notice from a coalition of environmental groups, the Attorney
General commenced action against Gillette, the manufacturer of Liquid
Paper correction fluid, and 22 distributors of that product, alleging that
bottles of correction fluid do not have proper warning labels about the
risk of exposure to trichloroethylene (TCE), a Proposition 65-listed

---

54   *People v. Safeway Stores*, San Francisco County Superior Court, Case No.
     897576.

55   For the most recent ruling to this effect, by an appellate court, *see
     Ingredient Communication Council, Inc. v. Lungren*, No. C007628, 1992
     WL 13836 (Cal. Ct.App.3d Dist., 1-28-92).

56   *Id.*, settlement filed Nov. 26, 1990. Reported at p. 1037, Toxics Law
     Reporter (1-16-91).

57   *People v. Webb and Associates*, Solano County Superior Court, Case No.
     103136. This case was reportedly near settlement in the Fall of 1990
     (nature of settlement unknown).

carcinogen contained in the fluid. That chemical enhances the speed at which the fluid will dry when applied on paper. An alternative Liquid Paper product (sold "just for copies") contains water instead of the chemical but takes longer to dry. The environmental groups believed that users of Liquid Paper should be given the informed choice between the products. Potential civil penalties in the case were estimated to exceed $100 million.[58] Gillette quickly settled the lawsuit by agreeing to market a safe version of the product within four months, to allow customers to exchange bottles of the fluid, to advertise the hazard and safer alternatives and to pay $300,000 in penalties.[59]

Other examples of enforcement actions under Proposition 65 include: a series of actions against companies emitting ethylene oxide (a sterilizer used on food and chemical products), resulting in several settlements for significant amounts[60]; an action regarding the sale of paints, solvents and resins, resulting in a settlement requiring warnings and the payment of $50,000[61]; a suit arising from exposure to asbestos from an abatement project without appropriate warnings[62]; a series of cases against manufactures of water repellants, paint strippers and spot removers (containing perchloroethylene), resulting so far in a settlement involving the reformulation of spot remover products as well as $150,000 for attorneys' fees incurred by the Sierra Club and the Environmental Defense Fund plus another $50,000 toward a trust fund to help finance

---

[58]   *Los Angeles Times*, Part II, p. 8 (Sept. 8, 1989).

[59]   *Id.*, Part I, p. 3 (Sept. 29, 1989).

[60]   *See, e.g., People v. Baxter Bentley Laboratories*, and *People v. Baxter Healthcare Corp.*, Los Angeles and Orange Counties, reportedly settled for $600,000; *People v. Griffith Micro Science*, Los Angeles County Superior Court No. BC006063, reportedly settled for $1.1 million, including $250,000 in cash and $840,000 in relinquished pollution credits arising from installation of smog control equipment; *People v. Botanicals International*, Los Angeles County Superior Court No. BCOO6060, reportedly settled for $500,000; *People v. Santa Maria Chili, Inc.*, Santa Barbara County Superior Court No. SM 64010, reportedly settled for $225,000.

[61]   *People v. PPG Industries*, Solano County Superior Court No. 103914.

[62]   *Thomas v. Berkeley Horticultural Nursery*, Alameda County Superior Court No. 638680-5.

future enforcement actions[63]; an action against a closed tannery which reportedly emitted the largest amount of perchloroethylene into the air annually in the San Francisco Bay region[64]; action against three companies manufacturing household products containing paradichlorobenzene, such as mothballs, room fresheners and diaper pail deodorizers, resulting in settlements for product labeling with Proposition 65 warnings, refund offer to consumers who received no such warning when purchasing the products, with newspaper advertisements regarding that offer, plus $27,000 from one of the companies[65]; as action against a biotechnology firm arising from chloroform emissions[66]; actions against dishware manufacturers for lead in glaze coatings[67]; an action against manufacturers and retailers of leaded crystal products[68]; and a class action and an Attorney General

---

[63] Reported at p. 100, *BNA's California Environment Reporter* (2-4-91); The Los Angeles Times, p. A3 (1-17-91); *Id.*, p. A18 (7-6-90).

[64] *Citizens for a Better Environment and International Ladies' Garment Workers' Union v. Sawyer of Napa Inc.*, Napa County Superior Court No. 61687, filed 2-11-91. It was recently reported that this was the first Proposition 65 case to be tried in court, and that the trial court ruled in favor of the defense after a four-week trial, on the grounds that knowing or intentional exposures to a listed chemical beyond the no significant risk level did not occur. *See BNA's California-Environment Reporter*, pp. 161-163 (3-2-92); *California Environmental Insider*, pp. 1-2 (2-29-92).

[65] *People v. Willert Home Products*, San Francisco County Superior Court No. 924886; *People v. Excell Products Corp.*, San Francisco County Superior Court No. 924887; and *People v. Sanitoy Inc.*, San Francisco County Superior Court No. 924888; See The Los Angeles Times, p. A3 (10-17-90).

[66] *People v. Bio-Rad Laboratories, Inc.*, Contra Costa County Superior Court No. 90-05401, filed 12-12-90, reportedly settled for $550,000 in penalties under Proposition 65 plus another $150,000 to the Bay Area Air Quality Management District, with an agreement to cease the use of chloroform.

[67] Filed in San Francisco Superior Court according to the California Environmental Insider, p. 10 (11-15-91).

[68] The Los Angeles Times, p. E1 (6-13-91).

suit against many wineries and merchants due to the lead-containing foil caps on corked wine bottles.[69]

Relevance to Transactions. All this controversy is chiefly of relevance to ongoing businesses which must comply with Proposition 65. The parties to a real estate transaction may, however, wish to review present and past Proposition 65 notices regarding the property involved. If the business is also being acquired, the status of compliance and possible successor liability for penalties should also be considered. In addition, if a property has not been properly posted with warning signs where exposures are anticipated, Proposition 65 liability would arise when prospective transferees visit the property and are not warned, just like anyone else.

4.3.2   California's Asbestos Notification Law

Consistent with the expansion of its disclosure laws, California enacted an asbestos notification law, effective January 1, 1989.[70] That law provides that each "owner" of any "building" constructed prior to 1979 who knows that the building contains "asbestos-containing construction materials" must give written notice to that owner's "employees" working within the building, and a copy of that notice must be provided to all other owners with whom the owner has privity of contract.[71]

"Owner" is broadly defined to include each owner, lessee, sublessee, or owner's agent of all or part of a building. "Building" means all or any part of a "public and commercial building," defined as any building

---

[69]   *Lockhon v. Ernest and Julio Gallo Winery,* San Diego County Superior Court No. 641038 (order allowing class action to proceed filed 12-5-91); *See also People v. Gallo Vineyards, Inc.,* San Diego County Superior Court No. 640951 ($900,000 settlement approved 12-5-91). Another suit also arises from lead foil on wine bottles, this one against liquor stores, *Armendarize v. Safeway Stores,* San Diego County Superior Court No. 638657.

[70]   Cal. Health & Safety Code §§ 25915 *et seq.* Extensive revisions to this notification law were enacted as urgency legislation effective September 27, 1989. See 1989 Stats., c. 948 (A.B. 1564). Additional substantive amendments have been made, effective January 1, 1992. See 1991 Stats., c. 731 (A.B. 1940).

[71]   *Id.,* §§ 25915 and 25915.5.

except school buildings, apartment complexes of fewer than ten units and residential dwellings. "Asbestos-containing construction material" refers to any manufactured construction material, including structural, mechanical and building material, which contains more than one-tenth of one percent asbestos by weight. "Employee" is broadly defined to include all employees and contractors engaged in any employment or the performance of any services on other than a casual or incidental basis in any building subject to the new law.[72]

The written notice must be given to each individual employee and to each other owner with whom the owner has privity of contract, within 15 days of the receipt by the owner of information identifying the presence or location of asbestos-containing construction materials in the building, and annually thereafter; to new employees, within 15 days of commencement of work in the building; and to new owners (with whom the owner has privity of contract), within 15 days of the effective date of the agreement under which a person becomes a new owner.[73] If the asbestos is located in limited areas of a building under designated conditions, the owner may provide a more limited form of notice or may provide notice only to the employees working within or entering those areas, such as building maintenance employees or contractors.[74] Special provisions limiting the notice requirement under designated conditions apply to owners of units within a residential common interest development.[75]

The notice must include (i) the results of any asbestos survey of the building; (ii) specific locations where asbestos is present; (iii) handling restrictions and safety instructions; (iv) the results of bulk sample analysis or monitoring; and (v) the potential health risks, although items (iii) and (v) can be limited if the owner claims no special knowledge of

---

[72]   *Id.*, §§ 25919 through 25919.5.

[73]   *Id.*, § 25915.2(a), (b) and (c).   In addition to the initial and annual notices, supplemental notices must be provided within 15 days of the close of the 90-day period after the required notice is given or any subsequent 90-day period during which new information is obtained. *Id.*, § 25915.2(a).

[74]   *Id.*, § 25915.2(f), (g) and (h).

[75]   *Id.*, § 25915.2(d).

such matters.[76] If the asbestos is completely encapsulated and asbestos fibers are not being released and have no reasonable possibility to be released from the material in its present condition, then a more limited form of notice may be given.[77] The owner must make available to employees and other owners for review and photocopying all asbestos survey and monitoring data and any asbestos management plan prepared for the building.[78] Conspicuous warnings must be posted in each area where any construction, maintenance or remodeling work is conducted with a potential for employees to come into contact with, or to release or disturb, asbestos or asbestos-containing construction materials. The content of the warning notice is specified in the statute.[79]

Criminal misdemeanor penalties of up to $1,000 or one year in the county jail, or both, will apply to any owner who knowingly or intentionally fails to comply with the statute or presents any false or misleading information to employees or other owners. Those penalties became operative on July 1, 1989.[80]

Interestingly, the law does not require that asbestos surveys or air monitoring be undertaken or that asbestos management plans be prepared. Only the disclosure of known information is required. The law will apply, of course, when asbestos surveys are done for other reasons and relevant information becomes known.

---

[76]   *Id.*, § 25915(a) and (b). Alternative, more limited, contents are allowed for notices involving any building with respect to which an owner has elected to implement an asbestos management plan. *Id.*, § 25915.1. The content of such a plan must meet specified criteria for purposes of this disclosure law. *Id.*, § 25915.1(b).

[77]   *Id.*, § 25915.2(e).

[78]   *Id.*, § 25917. Where there are multiple owners of a building or part of a building, the owners may designate which owner is to provide the location in the building for the survey, monitoring or management plan materials to be made available. *Id.* In addition, one of the owners may be designated to prepare any required notices and the other owners may rely on that form of notice and use it under specified conditions. Id., § 25916.5.

[79]   *Id.*, § 25916.

[80]   *Id.*, § 25919.7.

Application to Mixed-Use Buildings. Given the unusual and confusing definition of the word "building" for purposes of the asbestos notification law, it is uncertain whether apartment buildings of ten or more units are included, and, if so, what is included if the residential dwellings contained in such buildings are excluded. The answer may be discerned from the fact that any *part* of a building may be a "building." Larger apartment complexes typically have management offices and work shops where leasing and maintenance personnel are employed. Those parts of an apartment building are not residential in nature. Thus, employees working in those areas may be entitled to notice under the law even if the residential tenants are not.

However, in cases where employees are notified in an apartment building or a mixed use building (e.g., a building with both commercial and residential tenants, which is not uncommon in urban areas), consideration should be given to notifying the residential tenants as well as the employees and commercial tenants. A residential tenant might well claim that the information should have been disclosed based on general tort principles, particularly where knowledge of a potentially hazardous condition existed. For example, the United States Navy was held liable under Maine law for the negligent failure to warn the families of shipyard workers at Portsmouth Naval Shipyard of the danger of exposure to asbestos fibers in work cloths. The daughter of a worker had died of mesothelioma caused by such exposure.[81] Moreover, asbestos is a listed substance under Proposition 65, and that law might provide another basis for such warnings where asbestos exposure is anticipated.[82] (The asbestos notification law itself applies if asbestos is *present*, without regard to whether releases have occurred or are threatened.)

Application to Absentee Owners. The asbestos notification law on its face applies only to owners who have their own "employees" working in a building. Other "owners" must only be given a *copy* of the notice

---

[81]   *Dube v. Pittsburgh Corning*, 870 F.2d 790 (1st Cir. 1989).

[82]   As noted in the preceding section, at least one lawsuit has been commenced under Proposition 65 for failure to provide warnings during an asbestos abatement project.

given to employees.[83] In the absence of employees, there would be no notice to copy and mail to any other owners. Nowhere does the statute require that notice be provided to other owners independently of notice to one's own employees. The legislature was obviously concerned with the safety and health of employees. Therefore, the law applies to owners with employees, and the only apparent reason for supplying copies of employee notifications to other owners is so that they will in turn be required to notify their employees.

The notification procedure should ordinarily ensure that all employees working in a building will receive the required notice, but not necessarily. An absentee landlord (having no employees in the building) would have no apparent duty under the statute to notify its tenants (who are defined as other "owners" for purposes of this law). This result appears to be inconsistent with the policy objective of disseminating asbestos information to all employees working in the building, including tenants' employees. The statute, even after extensive amendments, simply does not contemplate the absentee owner situation. A court would essentially have to rewrite the applicable provisions in order to bridge that omission by interpretation, but a court might be inclined to do so in order to give effect to the legislative purpose.[84]

It should be noted, however, that the term "employee" is so broadly defined that if an absentee owner hired a contractor to perform any significant services at the building, the law would be triggered, requiring notice to the contractor with copies to other owners. Thus, a true "absentee" owner might be hard to find.

---

[83]   Upon receipt of such a copy, the other "owners" would be on notice of the presence of asbestos and would in turn be required to notify their employees working in the building.

[84]   In this regard, it could be argued that the 1989 amendment adding § 25915.1 (asbestos management plans) reflects the assumption of the legislature that notices to other owners are on an equal footing with notices to an owner's own employees. That section states that an owner who has adopted an asbestos management plan may comply "by providing notices to other owners and all employees of that owner working within the building," suggesting that other owners must be notified in any event, although the statute could have been written more clearly if that was the intention.

The asbestos notification law is of importance due to the common presence of asbestos in buildings constructed before 1979. The parties to a real estate transaction may wish to determine whether the law applies to the property involved and, if so, to determine the status of compliance and to review the information compiled for employees and other owners.

4.3.3 California's Business Plan Requirements

In a law reminiscent of the federal Emergency Planning and Community Right-To-Know Act of 1986, California requires certain businesses to establish and implement a business plan for emergency response to a release or threatened release, to adopt training programs for their employees, and to submit to the administering agency detailed inventories and other information concerning the location, type, quantity and the health risks of hazardous materials routinely stored, handled or otherwise used by such businesses.[85] The businesses subject to the law include those handling a quantity of hazardous material at any one time during the reporting year equal to or exceeding a total weight of 500 pounds, or a total volume of 55 gallons, or 200 cubic feet at standard temperature and pressure for compressed gas. Businesses which are most commonly affected include dry cleaners, woodworking shops, auto body and paint shops, jewelry stores, chemical manufacturers and metal plating shops, among others. Failure to comply with this law can create exposure to significant statutory penalties.

Qualified local ordinances may entitle a city or county to an exemption from the state law, in which event businesses located in such cities or counties must comply with the local ordinance.[86]

The law also requires any business which handles any hazardous material to report immediately upon discovery any release or threatened release of a hazardous material. The report must be made to the local administering agency and to the state Office of Emergency Services.[87]

California has enacted another new law providing that the business plan requirements must be met before any city or county may issue a

---

[85] Cal. Health & Safety Code § 25500 et seq. (Hazardous Materials Release Response Plans and Inventory.)

[86] *Id.*, § 25505.2.

[87] *Id.*, § 25507.

final certificate of occupancy after January 1, 1989. This should at least ensure compliance by businesses moving into newly constructed locations. In addition, after July 1, 1989, cities and counties may not permit the construction of a facility within 1,000 feet of a school without requiring a risk management and prevention plan.[88]

These requirements, and related business records, plans and reports, should be of interest to a prospective transferee of either the business or the real estate where the business has been conducted.

4.3.4   Other California Reporting Laws

The *Hazardous Waste Control Law* (HWCL) contains several notice or reporting provisions. The Department of Toxic Substances Control (DTSC) (formerly the Toxic Substances Control Program of the state Department of Health Services, but now a part of the new Cal-EPA) is authorized to issue an order requiring the owner or operator of any facility or site at which hazardous waste is or has been stored, treated or disposed of to conduct monitoring, testing, analysis and reporting. Such an order may be issued whenever the department believes that the presence of the hazardous waste or any release "may present a substantial hazard to human health or the environment," and the purpose would be to "ascertain the nature and extent of the hazard."[89] Any intentional or negligent violation or false report may result in civil penalties of up to $25,000 for each separate violation, or $25,000 per day for continuing violations.[90]

Any owner, lessor or lessee who knows, or has probable cause to believe, that any "significant" disposal of hazardous waste has occurred on land owned or leased by such person, *or* that the land is within 2,000 feet of such a significant disposal, must apply to the DHS for a determination whether the land should be designated a "hazardous waste property" or a "border zone property."[91] Such properties are subject to

---

[88]   *See* 1988 Stats., c. 1589 (AB 3205), amending or adding numerous sections of the Government Code, Health and Safety Code and Public Resources Code.

[89]   Cal. Health & Safety Code § 25187.1(a).

[90]   *Id.*, § 25189.

[91]   *Id.*, § 25221(a).

severe use restrictions.[92] However, the application requirement applies only if the person intends within one year "to construct or allow the construction on that land of a building or structure to be used for a [prohibited] purpose."[93]

Generators or managers of hazardous waste must comply with the notice and reporting provisions of RCRA and with DTSC regulations regarding non-RCRA hazardous waste.[94] Generators of hazardous waste and owners of treatment, storage or disposal facilities must submit notification statements (containing specified and extensive information about the activity) by January 1, 1988, and subsequently whenever there has been a substantial change in the information; significant civil penalties apply to noncompliance.[95]

The HWCL (pursuant to the *Toxic Injection Well Control Act of 1985*) requires injection well users to file with the DHS a hazardous waste injection statement containing detailed information as prescribed, and noncompliance is subject to severe civil penalties.[96]

Consistent with CERCLA and RCRA, the DTSC may require reports relating to hazardous substances, wastes or materials from owners, operators, generators, storers, treaters, disposers and transporters of such substances or related facilities.[97]

Persons who discharge liquid hazardous wastes or hazardous wastes containing free liquids into any surface impoundment must make reports as required by the local Regional Water Quality Control Board.[98]

Owners or operators of land treatment units must at least annually submit information to the DTSC, including sufficient soil samples to

---

[92]   *Id.*, § 25232 (*see* Chapter 5).

[93]   *Id.*, § 25221(a).

[94]   *Id.*, § 25153.6.

[95]   *Id.*, § 25158.

[96]   *Id.*, § 25159.13.

[97]   *Id.*, § 25185.6.

[98]   *Id.*, § 25208.7.

detect whether hazardous substances are migrating from the treatment zone.[99]

Used oil recyclers must submit annual reports to the DTSC containing extensive information about their activities, including the disposition of any used oil received but not recycled.[100]

Under the *Hazardous Waste Source Reduction and Management Review Act of 1989*, generators who, by site, routinely generate more than 12,000 kilograms of hazardous waste, or more than 12 kilograms of extremely hazardous waste, within a calendar year, must prepare source reduction plans and waste management performance reports by September 1, 1991, and periodically thereafter.[101]

The *Underground Storage Tank Act* requires that any unauthorized leakage or release which escapes from containment must be reported by the operator of the UST to the designated local agency. The report must be made within 24 hours after the release either was detected or should have been detected, to be followed by a full written report within five working days. If the leakage or release does not escape from secondary containment and is cleaned up within eight hours after it is detected or should have been detected, then the operator need record the event only in its monitoring reports.[102]

The *Aboveground Petroleum Storage Act* requires the owner or operator of an aboveground storage tank which contains crude oil or its fractions to report, immediately upon discovery, to the city and county, any spill or release of one barrel (42 gal.) or more which must be reported to the Office of Emergency Services pursuant to Water Code § 13272.[103] Also, a Spill Prevention Control and Countermeasure Plan may be required under this law.[104]

---

[99]   *Id.*, § 25209.4.

[100]   *Id.*, § 25250.17.

[101]   *Id.*, §§ 25244.14 *et seq.*; *see* stats. 1989, c. 1218 (SB 14).

[102]   *Id.*, §§ 25294 and 25295.

[103]   *Id.*, § 25270.8.

[104]   *Id.*, § 25270.7.

The *Porter-Cologne Water Quality Act of 1970* provides that any person who actually discharges or proposes to discharge any waste into any waters or land which *could affect* the quality of the waters of the state must file a report with the applicable Regional Water Quality Control Board.[105] In addition, any person who (without regard to fault) causes or permits any hazardous substance or sewage to be discharged in or on any waters of the state must immediately notify the Office of Emergency Services pursuant to the spill reporting provisions of the state toxic disaster contingency plan and must also notify the appropriate Regional Water Quality Control Board. Regulations establish "reportable quantities." Failure to provide such notice is a misdemeanor punishable by up to $20,000 and imprisonment for up to one year.[106] A similar reporting requirement applies with respect to the spill of any oil or petroleum product, in which case the punishment is not less than $500 nor more than $5,000 per day for each day of failure to notify and up to one year in prison.[107] Regional boards may also require monitoring, recordkeeping and reporting by persons who discharge pollutants or dredged or fill material into navigable waters.[108]

The *California Superfund* law requires annual reporting and tax returns (on March 1 of each year to and including March 1, 1991, for the preceding calendar year) to the State Board of Equalization by every person who disposed (onsite or offsite) of more than 500 pounds of hazardous waste during the preceding calendar year. The report must be submitted on forms prescribed by the board which call for information regarding the amounts of hazardous waste disposed of in several specified categories.[109] The data compiled from these reports is submitted to the Governor each year.[110] The information is also used for the calculation of a hazardous waste disposal tax, the proceeds of

---

105 Cal. Water Code § 13260.

106 *Id.*, § 13271.

107 *Id.*, § 13272.

108 *Id.*, § 13383.

109 Cal. Health & Safety Code, former §§ 25342 and 25345(e).

110 *Id.*, former § 25344.

which help finance the California Superfund program.[111] Failure to file the annual report and tax return may result in a civil penalty of up to $500 per day, and a knowing failure to file is a crime punishable by a fine of up to $25,000 per day and up to one year in prison.[112] As a result of extensive amendments in the hazardous waste disposal tax and fee provisions, effective January 1, 1991, this tax applies only through calendar year 1990. For 1991 and subsequent years, the Cal-Superfund tax was eliminated and the base rate for another disposal fee was doubled, in effect merging the Superfund tax into the other fee program.[113]

The *California Pipeline Safety Act of 1981* requires pipeline operators to report immediately to the local fire department and the Office of Emergency Services whenever there is a rupture, explosion or fire involving a pipeline; violations may result in civil penalties of up to $10,000 per day (up to a maximum of $500,000 for any related series of violations), or in the case of a knowing and willful violation, criminal fines of up to $25,000 for each offense and up to five years imprisonment.[114]

It should come as no surprise that the *Radiation Control Law* requires persons who acquire, possess or use a source of ionizing radiation to maintain records as required by the DTSC, including records showing the radiation exposure of all individuals for whom personnel monitoring is required by the DTSC, and that such records must be submitted to the DTSC upon request.[115]

The *Labor Code* provides that employers who use any carcinogen, including asbestos and vinyl chloride, must submit to the Occupational Safety and Health Standards Board a written report of any incident resulting in the release of a potentially hazardous amount of a carcinogen into any area where employees may be exposed.[116] The

---

[111] *Id.*, § 25330(d).

[112] *Id.*, former § 25343.

[113] *Id.*, § 25174.1; *see also* Cal. Rev. and Tax Code § 43051.

[114] Cal. Govt. Code §§ 51018, 51018.6 and 51018.7.

[115] Cal. Health & Safety Code §§ 25825 and 25826.

[116] Cal. Labor Code § 9030.

Labor Code also requires reporting by employers prior to the commencement of asbestos-related work such as renovation or demolition which might disturb asbestos.[117] Similar reporting requirements exist under the rules of the various air quality management districts which require advance notice of asbestos-related work.

The *California Hazardous Substances Act* regulates the manufacture, importation and sale of hazardous substances, and, among other things, requires warning labels on products (such as art or craft materials) containing toxic substances.[118]

The *Air Toxic "Hot Spots" Information and Assessment Act of 1987* also contains reporting provisions. Operators of facilities which manufacture, formulate, use or release hazardous substances must submit a comprehensive emissions inventory plan to the applicable air pollution control district, and those operators classified in the high priority category must submit health risk assessment plans to the district.[119] This law specifically acknowledges that toxic air pollutants are a source of contamination and a health risk, especially regarding areas in the vicinity of a source of toxic emissions. Indeed, upon approval of a health risk assessment plan, the district may require the facility operator to notify *all exposed persons* of the results of the assessment.[120] The district also may require any air emission permit applicant or holder to submit information regarding the nature of the emissions.[121]

Pursuant to the *California Corporate Criminal Liability Act of 1989,*[122] corporations or managers who have actual knowledge of a "serious concealed danger" which is subject to the regulatory authority of an "appropriate government agency" involving a product or business practice must, within 15 days of acquiring knowledge (or immediately where there is imminent risk of great bodily harm or death): (1) give

---

[117]   *Id.,* § 6501.5; 8 C.C.R. § 1529(r)(1)(A).

[118]   Cal. Health & Safety Code § 28796.

[119]   *Id.,* §§ 44340 and 44360.

[120]   *Id.,* § 44362.

[121]   *Id.,* § 42303.

[122]   Cal. Penal Code § 387 (Stats. 1990, c. 1616, effective January 1, 1991).

written notice to the Division of Occupational Safety and Health in the Department of Industrial Relations (unless the manager knows that the Division has been informed already), which in turn forwards the notice to any other appropriate government agency, and (2) give written notice to affected employees (unless the manager knows that the employees have been warned already). The disclosure requirement does not apply if the hazard is abated within the 15-day notice period (unless other applicable regulations require disclosure nonetheless).

Noncompliance is punishable by imprisonment in county jail for up to one year, or by fine of up to $10,000, or both; or by imprisonment in state prison for up to 16 months, or by fine of up to $25,000, or both; but if the defendant is a corporation, the fine may be up to $1,000,000.

This may be the strongest corporate accountability law in the nation. It has been called the "Be a Manager, Go to Jail" law. The intent of the legislature was to "up the ante" on product or workplace hazards, to overcome the kind of cost-benefit analysis which has led some companies to permit product defects or workplace hazards to continue uncorrected and without appropriate warnings. The threat of significant criminal fines and imprisonment may increase the pressure. Hazardous substance conditions may trigger the notice requirements of this law.

This law has been criticized because of the severe criminal sanction which can apply in cases of mere negligent noncompliance. Efforts are being made to amend the law to require at least "gross negligence" or "reckless disregard" of the safety of others before prosecution is permitted. It remains to be seen whether such efforts will be successful.

Pursuant to *Senate Bill 198*,[123] all employers in California must have a comprehensive written injury and illness prevention program. One of the elements of such a program is a system for communications both to and from employees regarding workplace safety hazards, with assurance of no reprisals against employees for reporting unsafe work practices or conditions. Documentation is required to establish compliance with this law. Cal-OSHA's General Industry Safety Orders

---

[123]   Stats. 1989 c. 1369 (SB 198), amending various sections of the Cal. Labor Code, including § 6401.7, and the Cal. Insurance Code, effective July 1, 1991.

implement the requirements of SB 198.[124] In addition, a guide for developing a workplace injury and illness prevention program has been published by Cal-OSHA.

Relevance to Transactions. The parties to a real estate transaction should be interested in any disclosures, warnings, reports or plans under any of these laws, or any other similar laws or regulations, with respect to the property involved. Further, some of these reporting requirements may apply in the event of the discovery of a past release during environmental due diligence or otherwise by a subsequent innocent owner or operator.

4.3.5   Disclosure and Reporting Laws of Other States

Reporting rules similar to the federal and some of the California requirements are mirrored in the laws of many other states. Several examples follow (see also those mentioned in Chapter 3).

Arizona

Any owner or operator of a facility who obtains knowledge of any release (except a permitted release) of a hazardous substance must immediately notify the Director of Environmental Quality if the release is of a "reportable quantity" of the substance as determined under CERCLA or by the Director. A violation of this reporting requirement may result in civil penalties of up to $10,000.[125]

In addition, any operator of a UST must notify the department and the owner of the tank of each release from the tank no later than 24 hours after the release is detected, to be followed by a written report to the department within 14 days. The written report must include the identity and quantity of the released substance, the time period during which it occurred, and the corrective measures taken or anticipated. "Reportable quantities" are determined by reference to the federal UST program under RCRA.[126]

---

[124]   *See* 8 Cal. Code of Regulations § 3203.

[125]   Ariz. Rev. Stat. Ann. § 49-284.

[126]   *Id.*, § 49-1004.

Massachusetts

As soon as any owner or operator of a site has knowledge of a release or a threatened release of oil or hazardous substance, the Department of Environmental Quality Engineering must be notified immediately unless the release conforms to the terms of a currently valid permit or license issued by the department or unless the release is in connection with the application of a pesticide product registered under FIFRA.[127]

New York

Pursuant to implementing regulations, New York's Environmental Conservation Law provides that any person who owns or controls any hazardous substance (and any employees, agents or contractors of such a person) must promptly notify the Department of Environmental Conservation upon obtaining knowledge of the release of a "reportable quantity" of a hazardous substance into the environment.[128]

Oregon

Oregon's CERCLA analogue provides that any defendant who would otherwise have a defense to Superfund liability will lose the benefit of that defense if he "[o]btained actual knowledge of the release and then failed to promptly notify the department and exercise due care with respect to the hazardous substance concerned . . ."[129]

In addition, "[a]ny person owning or having control over any oil or hazardous material who has knowledge of a spill or release shall immediately notify the Emergency Management Division as soon as that person knows the spill or release is of a reportable quantity."[130]

4.3.6   Local Regulations

The ordinances and regulations of local jurisdictions represent another important source of reporting requirements in the event of hazardous substance releases. For example, fire codes often have such provisions, and some municipalities also must be notified in the event of

---

[127]   Mass. Gen. L. ch. 21E § 7.

[128]   N.Y. ECL § 40-0111.

[129]   Or. Rev. Stat. § 466.567(4)(a).

[130]   *Id.*, § 466.635.

leakage from USTs. Such local regulations are too numerous and various to summarize here. Nevertheless, the parties to a real estate transaction should consider those regulations as well as federal and state requirements of the kind discussed above.

4.4 Conclusion

In recent years, an extensive and complex disclosure and reporting system has developed with regard to hazardous substances. The maze of federal, state and local laws and regulations can be confusing and can result in technical violations even by companies endeavoring to comply with the law.

Recently adopted legislation in California recognizes that "the current hazardous materials reporting system creates a hodgepodge of data" and that businesses have a variety of reporting requirements creating compliance problems. Therefore, the legislature mandated the development of a manual of reporting duties and forms by July 1, 1991, as well as a feasibility study due on the same date regarding the proposed creation of a "single comprehensive" hazardous materials reporting form for businesses to submit to the appropriate state and local agencies, in order to improve both compliance and the usefulness of the reported information.[131] It remains to be seen whether this effort will be successful.

Regardless of whether the reporting system is improved, it will continue to engender reluctance on the part of some property owners to allow extensive environmental due diligence. While the wisdom of that reluctance can be debated, it is real. Sophisticated buyers, lessees and lenders usually will not consider a property unless it is fully available for environmental assessment. The same is true with respect to acquisitions of stock of companies which own or lease potentially contaminated property. Thus, owners who fear disclosure and reporting requirements too much may not be able to find willing buyers, lessees or lenders and may have to face eventual cleanup anyway.

---

[131] Cal. AB 854 (Assembly Member Killea, D-San Diego), § 2 which was adopted as Stats. 1989, c. 938; *see* Cal. Health & Safety Code § 25503.2.

CHAPTER FIVE

LAND USE RESTRICTIONS AND
BUILDING PERMIT REQUIREMENTS

5.1   Introduction

5.2   Land Use Restrictions

5.3   Building Permit Requirements

5.1   Introduction

Prospective purchasers who intend to develop real estate need to know whether the land may be used lawfully for their desired purposes. Lenders who finance such projects are equally interested. A network of land use restrictions may apply to any real property. While a full discussion of that subject is beyond the scope of this book, this chapter notes the existence of land use restrictions related to hazardous waste, and Chapter 6 discusses wetlands regulation.

Similarly, even if the land may be used for the intended purposes, any developer must be able to obtain building permits for construction. This chapter will also discuss whether hazardous waste may pose an obstacle to the issuance of building permits.

5.2   Land Use Restrictions

As indicated in § 3.3.3 of Chapter 3, a number of states restrict the use of hazardous waste sites, to the point of requiring notice of that fact to be filed or recorded in the real estate records of the applicable jurisdiction. Typically, permissible use is restricted as the appropriate state agency may see fit for the protection of public health and safety.

California has a more detailed statute, the Hazardous Waste Disposal Land Use Law, which reaches not only hazardous waste sites, but also neighboring lands. The state Department of Health Services (DHS) is authorized by law to designate real property as either a "hazardous waste property" (if a significant disposal of hazardous waste creating a significant existing or potential hazard to public health or safety is present at the site) or a "border zone property" (if the property is within 2,000 feet of a hazardous waste property).[1]

A proceeding for the designation of a property as a "hazardous waste property" or a "border zone property" may be initiated by the DHS whenever it obtains information showing that a significant disposal of hazardous wastes has occurred at a property.[2] The DHS must commence an examination and make a determination on that issue upon the request of *any interested person.*[3] Finally, any owner, lessor or lessee of property who knows or has reasonable cause to believe that a significant disposal of hazardous waste has occurred there (or within 2,000 feet), and who intends within one year to construct or allow the construction of a building or structure for a use which would be prohibited for a border zone property, must apply to the DHS for a determination whether the land should be designated as a hazardous waste property or a border zone property.[4]

A designated hazardous waste property may not be developed for any "new use" and may be used, modified or expanded only in connection with any industrial or manufacturing facilities which existed on such land as of January 1, 1981.[5] A designated border zone property may not be developed for use as (and existing structures may not be modified for new use as): (i) a residence, (ii) a hospital for humans, (iii) a school for persons under 21 years of age, (iv) a day care center for children, or (v) any permanently occupied human habitation (other than those for industrial purposes).[6] Variances may be obtained allowing such properties to be used for otherwise prohibited purposes.[7] However, local authorities are free to adopt even more restrictive land use regulations which would then be controlling.[8]

---

1   Cal. Health & Safety Code §§ 25220 et seq.

2   *Id.,* § 25222.

3   *Id.,* § 25149.3.

4   *Id.,* § 25221.

5   *Id.,* § 25232(a).

6   *Id.,* § 25232(b).

7   *Id.,* § 25233.

8   *Id.,* § 25236(b).

A knowing violation of the use restrictions may result in a civil penalty of up to (i) 25 percent of the fair market value of the land and improvements, (ii) 25 percent of the sale price of the land and improvements, or (iii) $50,000.00, whichever is established and greatest.[9]

In January 1991, the DHS issued an Interim Final manual entitled "Border Zone Property Determination: Guidance for Preparation of a Preliminary Endangerment Assessment." This manual sets forth the department's policies and procedures for implementing the Hazardous Waste Disposal Land Use Law.

Whether a property has been designated as a hazardous waste property or a border zone property, or might be subject to that designation, is of great importance to the parties to a real estate transaction and should be considered in the course of environmental due diligence. The applicable use restrictions, under the state law or more restrictive local regulations, may prohibit development or limit it in ways not desired by the parties.

5.3   Building Permit Requirements

As indicated above, **California** law sets forth a procedure for the determination whether a property is a "hazardous waste property" or a "border zone property." Not surprisingly, once such a proceeding has been initiated, the state law prohibits the issuance of a building permit for development for a restricted purpose pending the determination by the DHS.[10]

Local ordinances or policies may provide additional restrictions. For example, the **City of San Francisco** mandates a soil analysis report for the possible existence of hazardous waste before building permits may be issued for developments involving the disturbance of at least 50 cubic yards of soil in designated areas of the city. In addition, the Director of the Department of Public Works may require such analysis in connection with any building permit application whenever there is reason to believe that hazardous wastes may be present. The soil sampling and analysis must satisfy criteria set forth in the ordinance.[11]

---

[9]   *Id.*, § 25196.

[10]   *Id.*, § 25149.3(d).

[11]   San Francisco Public Works Code §§ 1001 and 1002.

When the soil analysis report reveals the presence of hazardous waste, the building permit applicant must do the following before the Director of Public Works may act on the permit application: (1) submit a site mitigation report prepared by a qualified person, assessing whether the hazardous waste poses any significant environmental or health safety risk and, if so, recommending mitigation measures, (2) complete the site mitigation measures identified in the report, and (3) certify to the city that the site mitigation report indicated that the hazardous wastes posed no significant environmental or health and safety risk *or* that all recommended mitigation measures have been performed *or* that the site was on the NPL or was a California Superfund site and the applicable federal or state agency has certified that site mitigation is complete.[12]

The seller or the seller's agent in any sale or exchange of real property in the designated areas of the city must provide a written summary of the applicable code provisions and obtain a signed acknowledgement of receipt from the buyer. However, the buyer will be subject to the ordinance even if such notice is not provided.[13]

The San Francisco ordinance is in its own way just as stringent as New Jersey's ECRA (see Chapter 3), although the ordinance operates at the building permit stage rather than upon change of ownership.

Another example is the **City of Santa Fe Springs**, which has adopted a similar approach as a matter of policy, although not reflected in any published ordinance. According to its Director of Environmental Management, that city requires that, prior to issuance of any conditional use permit or development plan approval, developers must:

> (1) have a qualified and licensed environmental consultant perform an environmental audit, including any necessary soil and other tests, to determine whether the property contains any hazardous wastes or toxic substances which could affect the quality of the ground or surface waters of the property;

---

[12]   *Id.*, §§ 1004 and 1005.

[13]   *Id.*, § 1010.

(2) provide written representations to the city that, based on reasonable inspection, the developer has no knowledge or reason to believe that any hazardous materials were ever used, generated, stored or disposed of at the property (except as otherwise stated in the audit report), and the developer is not in violation of any notification, remediation or other requirements of federal, state or local law concerning the environmental condition of the property;

(3) obtain all permits and approvals which the city or any other governmental agency may require as to the environmental condition of the property; and

(4) acknowledge that any city approvals do not imply that any applicable permit or other requirements of any other federal, state or local jurisdiction have been satisfied and that it is the developer's sole obligation to comply with all such requirements.

If the audit report shows that hazardous wastes or toxic substances are present, the owner must clean up the property before any building permit may be issued. If the owner fails to do so, the city will refer the matter to the DHS or the applicable Regional Water Quality Control Board.

A sampling of other California cities indicates that such policies are becoming more widely adopted, at least on an informal basis. Developers should endeavor to ascertain at an early planning stage the applicable policies of the local jurisdiction. However, a number of city attorneys believe that the same result can and would be reached under other existing policies and ordinances, such as regulations for the abatement of nuisances. Moreover, any project requiring an Environmental Impact Report under the California Environmental Quality Act (CEQA) could involve an assessment of existing hazardous waste conditions and the potential impact of the proposed development on the environment and public health and safety as a result of the presence or disturbance of any such hazardous wastes. It would appear that development approvals could be denied based on such considerations. Perhaps for this reason, many cities are content simply to implement CEQA or their nuisance ordinances and feel no need to adopt more explicit hazardous waste policies at the building permit stage.

Other local jurisdictions throughout the nation may have similar ordinances, policies or informal requirements regarding the issuance of building permits for property which might be contaminated.

To the extent that local jurisdictions have or adopt policies such as those noted above, environmental issues will not be avoidable by anyone wishing to obtain a building permit or plan approval for the development of property. Thus, environmental assessments are a practical necessity in such jurisdictions for any owner or prospective purchaser who intends to improve the property. Construction lenders are equally affected. In such cases, the reluctance discussed in Chapter 4 on the part of some owners to allow environmental assessments (for fear of triggering reporting requirements) must certainly be overcome if a real estate transaction or development project is to proceed.

CHAPTER SIX

WETLANDS REGULATION

6.1   What are Wetlands?

In general, *wetlands* encompass lands which are transitional between water and land environments. These lands are environmentally sensitive, provide essential habitat for many species, and are critical to preserving water quality and maintaining groundwater and food supplies. Most population centers border on wetlands because historically settlements arose near water sources. As populations and cities have grown, they have tended to occupy and destroy the very wetlands which have provided sustenance for human life and wildlife. In recent decades, wetlands have been disappearing at an alarming rate. Accordingly, legislation to protect such areas from development has been adopted by the federal and many state governments. A number of local jurisdictions also have ordinances with a similar purpose.

The term "wetlands" has been defined in different ways by the federal and state governments. See **Table 6-1** at the end of this chapter for sample definitions. Those definitions, and others, are very broad and include land subject only to episodic water saturation. Wetlands need not be on a coastline or riverbank, but can be well inland, wherever a natural pond may appear, as long as aquatic life or vegetation requiring saturated soil is supported at least seasonally.

161

Thus, land that appears completely dry may in fact fall within a state or federal definition of a wetland. Such a determination could be crucial in light of the various federal and state laws restricting the development of wetlands. It is therefore important for real estate professionals to be familiar with the applicable statutes governing the land in question and to know whether the land is subject to wetlands restrictions.

Statutes regulating the development of wetlands have come into existence in response to the increasing recognition of the need to preserve them. These statutes, both federal and state, generally require developers to obtain a permit prior to commencing specified activities. As a result, the wetlands statutes have created a clash between the competing interests of environmentalists and developers.

There has been much controversy over the definition of wetlands and the proper scope of governmental regulation. After President Bush's 1988 campaign pledge of "no net loss" of wetlands, it appeared that regulation of the subject would expand, and the Federal Manual for Identifying and Delineating Jurisdictional Wetlands, issued in March 1989, contained broad wetlands criteria. Since then, however, the political battle has intensified, with developers and agricultural interests lobbying against broad wetlands regulation. An interagency agreement in 1990 between the EPA and the U.S. Army Corps of Engineers (Corps) appeared to back away from the President's commitment; on September 26, 1990, the Corps adopted an exception to the wetlands law appearing to favor the agricultural community; and in August 1991 a revised draft Manual, which would narrow the scope of wetlands, protection, was released for review. Environmentalists have fought back, opposing the revisions and any relaxation of wetlands protection.[1] The

---

[1]   This high-stakes political controversy has been regularly reported in the press. *See, e.g.,* a series of articles in The Los Angeles Times: "Environmentalists Criticize Bush Over Wetlands Agreement," p. A19 (2-8-90); "Effort to Change Wetlands Definition Sparks Protests," p. A4 (3-29-91); "Wetlands Law Swamped by Rising Tide of Criticism," p. A1 (7-5-91); "Bush Offers New Wetlands Policy; Critics Assail It," p. A1 (8-10-91); Coalition Warns of Wetlands Loss," (11-12-91); "Wetlands Studies Withheld, Officials Say," p. A5 (11-17-91); "Experts Assail Proposed Rules for Wetlands," p. A1 (11-22-91); "Restore Nation's

EPA has recently announced that the revised Manual will probably not be ready until the Fall of 1992. It remains to be seen how this battle will be resolved.

6.2   Federal Regulation of Wetlands

At least eight federal statutes pertain to wetlands,[2] the most important being the *Clean Water Act of 1977* (CWA).[3]   The stated mission of the CWA is to "restore and maintain the chemical, physical, and biological integrity of the Nation's waters."[4]   Although wetlands are not expressly mentioned, the act provides the main avenue for restricting the development of wetlands by forbidding the discharge of dredged or fill materials into the "navigable waters of the United States" unless authorized by a permit issued by the Corps pursuant to section 404 of the CWA.[5]   The term "navigable waters," as defined by the Code of Federal Regulations (C.F.R.), has caused great controversy. The federal courts have given a broad interpretation to the term by requiring the Corps to exercise its jurisdiction "to the maximum extent permissible under the Commerce Clause of the Constitution . . . not limited to the traditional tests of navigability."[6]   Pursuant to this statutory interpretation, the C.F.R. includes "wetlands" within its definition of "waters of the United States."[7]

The Corps' broad jurisdiction over wetlands was upheld by the United States Supreme Court in *United States v. Riverside Bayview Homes, Inc.*[8] where a unanimous court held that 80 acres of low-lying, marshy land near the shores of Lake St. Clair in Macomb County,

---

Wetlands, Report Urges," p. A7 (12-12-91); and "Pollution, Floods Foreseen in Wake of Wetlands Plan," p. A4 (1-17-92). Federal and state legislators have also been active in the wetlands controversy, introducing a number of bills on the subject.

2   *See* **Table 6-2**.

3   33 U.S.C. §§ 1251-1376.

4   *Id.*, § 1251.

5   *Id.*, § 1344.

6   *See, e.g., Natural Resources Defense Council, Inc. v. Callaway*, 392 F.Supp. 685, 686 (D.D.C. 1975).

7   33 C.F.R. § 328.3(a)(3).

8   474 U.S. 121, 131 (1985).

Michigan, was a wetland adjacent to a navigable waterway, that such wetlands are part of the "waters of the United States," and that the land was subject to the CWA's section 404 permit process. The courts have also determined that the Corps has jurisdiction over artificially created wetlands holding that "federal jurisdiction is determined by whether the site is presently wetlands and not by how it came to be wetlands."[9] However, in a case involving the application of the section 404 permit process to an isolated wetland, the court ruled that the imposition constituted a material expansion of the coverage of the CWA, which the Corps had no power to effect pursuant to an internal policy directive rather than by following the public notice and comment process under the Administrative Procedure Act.[10]

The Corps has issued regulations for a nationwide permit program for 27 categories of projects viewed as having little impact on wetlands or other jurisdictional waters, reducing the paperwork and processing required to obtain a permit and exempting some activities altogether.[11] In April 1991, the Corps proposed amendments which would add 13 new nationwide permit categories, relax the criteria on a number of the existing categories, and expand the acceptable forms of mitigation under some circumstances. These amendments are controversial, much like the proposed amendments to the Federal Manual for Identifying and Delineating Jurisdictional Wetlands (discussed above).

In addition to the Corps, the EPA has concurrent jurisdiction over all wetlands pursuant to its veto power under section 404(c) of the CWA. As such, the EPA has the power in certain circumstances to veto the

---

[9]   *Bailey v. United States Army Corps of Engineers*, 647 F.Supp. 44, 48 (D. Idaho 1986). *See also Leslie Salt Co. v. U.S.*, 896 F.2d 354 (9th Cir. 1990) (the Corps has jurisdiction even where the wetlands were artifically created in part due to the actions of a government agency, Caltrans, distinguishing *U.S. v. City of Fort Pierre*, 747 F.2d 464 (8th Cir. 1984) where the court ruled that the Corps' jurisdiction did not apply to wetlands of its own creation).

[10]   *Tabb Lakes, Ltd. v. U.S.*, 715 F.Supp. 726 (E.D. Va. 1988), affirmed 885 F.2d 866 (4th Cir. 1989).

[11]   Those regulations are codified at 33 C.F.R. Part 330. The Corps' authority to establish nationwide permits was upheld in *Shelton v. Marsh*, 902 F.2d 1201 (6th Cir. 1990).

Corps' approval of a permit.[12] That power may be limited where the project is a necessity without practical alternatives.[13]

Developers should be aware that approval of a permit to develop a wetland is sometimes conditioned on the successful completion of a mitigation project. For example, in *Newport Galleria Group v. Deland*, the approval of a permit to develop a wetland was conditioned on the developer creating an off-site artificial swamp to replace the wetlands.[14]

There are several federal economic incentive programs to protect wetlands. One example is the Department of Agriculture's Water Bank Program which gives the Secretary of Agriculture the power to enter into ten-year contracts with landowners to pay land and crop values in exchange for the landowner's promise to continue wetland preservation.[15] The 1986 Tax Reform Act also encourages the preservation of wetlands by providing that any gain on the disposition of converted wetlands shall be treated as ordinary income (if capital gains treatment were otherwise available), and that any loss on such disposition is a long-term capital loss.[16] A third program designed to discourage development of wetlands is the Erodible Land and Wetland

---

[12]   *See, e.g., Newport Galleria Group v. Deland*, 618 F.Supp. 1179 (D.D.C. 1985). The applicability of section 404(c) and the EPA's veto power over after-the-fact permits has been the subject of litigation. *Russo Development Corp. v. Thomas*, No. 87-3916 (D.N.J. Nov. 6, 1989). *See also Bersani v. Robichaud*, 850 F.2d 36 (2d Cir. 1989) (upholding the EPA's veto of a section 404 permit in a case where an alternative site had been available when the developer entered the market to search for a site for a shopping mall, but was purchased by another developer and was no longer available at the time of the permit application).

[13]   *James City Attorney v. EPA*, No. 89-156-NN (D.E.Va. Nov. 6, 1990) (EPA's veto to the filing of a creek to create a water reservoir was invalid where the veto was based on an EPA presumption that alternatives existed; the county desperately needed the reservoir for water supply and no practical and available alternatives existed).

[14]   *Newport Galleria Group v. Deland*, 618 F.Supp. 1179, 1181 (D.D.C. 1985).

[15]   Water Bank Program For Wetlands Preservation, 16 U.S.C. §§ 1301-1311.

[16]   26 U.S.C. § 1257.

Conversion and Reserve Program[17] which allows the Secretary of Agriculture to withdraw crop insurance, price supports, farm storage facility loans, or disaster payments to "any person who in any crop year produces an agricultural commodity" on converted wetland.[18] In a further effort to protect wetlands from development, the federal government has enacted a wetlands acquisition program entitled the Emergency Wetlands Resources Act of 1986.[19]

Most of the controversy involving governmental regulation of wetlands, however, has involved the government's refusal to compensate an owner of a wetland whose permit to develop the wetland has been denied or conditioned on an onerous mitigation requirement. In recent years, much litigation has arisen as to whether and under what circumstances the denial of permission to develop a privately owned wetland constitutes a regulatory taking in violation of the 5th and 14th Amendments of the U.S. Constitution.

In the typical case, the owner of the wetland claims that the regulation renders the property worthless and thus effectuates a "regulatory" taking. Recent case law suggests that federal and state governments that "take" wetlands pursuant to regulations under the CWA or state legislation may be required to compensate the owners of the property, if the owner can make a sufficient showing on the facts.[20]

---

[17] 16 U.S.C. §§ 3801-3845.

[18] *Id.*, § 3821. A federal appeals court has held that environmental groups have standing to challenge the Secretary of Agriculture's exemption of land from this wetland conservation law. *Nat'l Wildlife Fed. v. Agri. Stab. and Conserv. Service*, 901 F.2d 673 (8th Cir. 1990).

[19] *Id.*, §§ 3901-3932.

[20] *Florida Rock Industries, Inc. v. United States*, 791 F.2d 893, 905 (1986), *cert. den.* 479 U.S. 1053 (1987) ("We think, however, the record reveals a substantial possibility that a taking should be held to have occurred under correct legal standards, so a remand is necessary."). On remand, the developer won a takings judgment for $1 million. *Florida Rock Industries, Inc. v. U.S.*, No. 266-82L (U.S. Cl.Ct. July 23, 1990). That case is again on appeal. *See also Loveladies Harbor, Inc. v. U.S.*, 15 Cl.Ct. 381 (1990), $2.6 million just compensation awarded, 21 Cl.Ct. 153 (1990) (this case is also on appeal); *Ciampitti v. U.S.*, 22 Cl.Ct. 310 (1991) (no taking); *Lucas v. South Carolina Coastal Council*, No. 23342 (S.C. Supreme Court Feb. 11, 1991) (no taking). Although not involving

The owners of wetlands face a heavy burden of proof that denial of a permit to fill wetlands or an onerous mitigation requirement constitutes a taking. In order to do so, the owners must show that the regulation either prohibits any economically viable use of the land, restricts the use of the land in a manner that does not substantially advance the purposes behind the regulation, or interferes with investment backed expectations to the extent that a taking occurs.[21]

Consistent with the general increase in the use of enforcement mechanisms under environmental laws, a developer was recently convicted and sentenced to pay a $200,000 fine and to serve three years in prison for knowingly filling in wetlands without a section 404 permit, the first such conviction under the CWA.[22] A number of other prosecutions are pending for the same violation by other developers.

---

wetlands, *see also First English Evangelical Lutheran Church of Glendale v. County of Los Angeles*, 482 U.S. 304, 107 S.Ct. 2378, 96 L.Ed.2d 250 (1987) (holding that land use regulations may result in a "taking" requiring compensation, so that the property owner was entitled to compensation when regulations precluded the reconstruction of buildings destroyed in a flood in a mountain canyon resulting from a forest fire which denuded watershed areas).

[21] Klock and Cook, *The Condemning of America: Regulatory "Takings" and the Purchase by the United States of America's Wetlands*, 18 Seton Hall L. Rev. 330, 355 (1988).

[22] *United States v. Pozsgai*, Cr. 88-00450 (E.D.Pa. July 13, 1989); upheld on appeal, *U.S. v. Pozsgai*, 897 F.2d 524 (3d Cir. 1990); *cert. den., Pozsgai v. U.S.*, 111 S.Ct. 48 (1990). *See also U.S. v. Key West Towers, Inc.*, No. 87-10034-Civ.-King (S.D. Fla. Aug. 10, 1989) (developer ordered to restore illegally filed wetlands to natural state and either to pay a civil penalty of $250,000 or deed the affected parcel to a charitable organization for maintenance as a wetland); *U.S. v. Sumitomo Construction Co.* (D. Guam May 22, 1990), 55 FR 22111 (5-31-90) ($1.3 million civil penalty and order to restore or mitigate loss of wetlands); *U.S. v. Jones*, No. S-90-0216 (D.C. Md. May 25, 1990) (settlement by property owner for $1 million fine plus $1 million contribution to National Fish and Wildlife Foundation, for filling of 300 acres of wetlands); *U.S. v. Ellen*, No. S-90-0215 (D.C. Md. May 25, 1990) (indictment against the contractor in the Jones case, for violations of the Clean Water Act and the Rivers and Harbors Act).

6.3   State Regulation of Wetlands

Several states have enacted comprehensive wetland statutes to supplement federal protection programs while other states rely on a variety of environmental statutes to deter the development of wetlands. In the absence of a wetland statute, a state's power to protect wetlands from development derives chiefly from its power to object to the issuance of federal section 404 permits. A state has the authority to object to a section 404 permit when the proposed discharges onto, or fill of, wetlands would violate state water quality standards[23] or would be inconsistent with a state's approved Coastal Zone Management Program.[24] A permit may not be issued in the face of such an objection until the state agrees or the Secretary of Commerce determines that the proposed activity is consistent with the federal Coastal Zone Management Act or is "necessary in the interest of national security."[25] In addition, under the 1977 amendments to the CWA, the EPA may authorize state operated permit programs; however, the scope of such state authority does not include traditionally navigable waters, which remain under federal jurisdiction.[26]

State wetland statutes generally contain a declaration of policy, a statement of findings, definitions, and provisions for agency authority and jurisdiction, mapping (identification of wetlands), permit procedures, and penalties. Some states have separate statutes for inland and coastal wetlands, while others have one to cover both or only have a statute that covers one or the other. States generally, through their statutes, implement a program whereby filling, dredging, draining and other developing activities require a permit while certain activities such as agriculture, mining, public utility projects, and construction and maintenance of public road systems are exempted. Some of the more recent statutes address the takings issue. A number of courts have upheld the constitutionality of state wetlands statutes or local wetlands ordinances on the basis that protection of such environmentally sensitive

---

[23]   33 C.F.R. §§ 320.3(b), 325.2(b)(2).

[24]   *Id.*, § 320.3(b).

[25]   *Id.*, § 325.2(b)(2)(ii).

[26]   33 U.S.C. § 1344(g)(1).

areas falls within the government's police power.[27]   Thus, in the wetlands context, the presumption in favor of police power regulation is strong, and, as a result, cases such as *Nollan v. California Coastal Commission*[28] might not provide a basis for an argument that the application of wetlands regulation to a particular property is not justified.

California

California does not have a comprehensive wetland protection act but depends on approximately 59 statutes to protect its wetlands.[29]   The *California Environmental Quality Act* (CEQA)[30] which is patterned after the *National Environmental Policy Act* (NEPA),[31] is California's basic charter for protection of the environment in connection with projects requiring governmental permits or approvals, and as most developments on wetlands require a permit, CEQA is involved.   In practice, California depends mainly on four statutes which provide direct permit authority over wetlands.   The California Coastal Act of 1976[32] protects coastal area wetlands up to 1000 yards landward from mean high tide.[33]   The San Francisco Bay Conservation And Development Commission protects the San Francisco Bay within 100 feet of the bay.[34] The Tahoe Regional Planning Agency partially protects the Lake Tahoe

---

[27]   *See, e.g., Just v. Marinette County*, 56 Wis.2d 7, 201 N.W.2d 761 (1972) (a county's shoreland zoning ordinance properly required a conditional use permit before wetland property could be filled).

[28]   483 U.S. 825, 107 S.Ct. 3141, 97 L.Ed.2d 677 (1987) (holding that conditions for issuance of building permits must be related to the purposes of the permit requirement, so that the California Coastal Commission could not condition a permit on the grant of a beach access easement).

[29]   Dennis, *Status and Trends of California Wetlands*, Cal. Legis. Comm. Reports, KA223, 1984s, v.1.

[30]   Cal. Pub. Res. Code §§ 21000 *et seq.*

[31]   42 U.S.C. §§ 4321 et seq.

[32]   Cal. Pub. Res. Code §§ 30000 *et seq.*

[33]   *Id.*, § 30103.

[34]   Cal. Gov't. Code § 66610.

region,[35] and the Suisun Marsh Preservation Act protects the Suisun Marsh in the San Francisco Bay's Delta Area.[36]

New York

The state of New York has two comprehensive wetlands acts, the *Freshwater Wetlands Act*[37] to protect inland wetlands and *the Tidal Wetlands Act*[38] to protect coastal wetlands. The acts are very similar and should be read in conjunction with one another. One major difference between the acts is that the freshwater act may be enforced by localities, with the state intervening only if local authorities fail to enact an ordinance protecting their wetlands. Indeed a locality may regulate wetlands whether or not it has filed a map identifying them. The crux of both acts is that, with limited exceptions, most development on a wetland requires a permit. Also, areas adjacent to wetlands that impinge on or otherwise greatly affect the wetland are regulated if within 100 feet of the wetland. Some notice is provided by the state or locality by publication of a map showing the land subject to regulation. An interim permit procedure is available for any area where mapping has not been completed. Permit applicants have the burden of demonstrating that the proposed activity is in accordance with the act and any decisions may be appealed to an administrative board. The major exceptions to the permit process are agricultural and recreational activities.

Illinois

Illinois is one of only two coastal states[39] which do not have coastal wetlands protection programs approved by the EPA pursuant to the Coastal Zone Management Act (CZMA).[40] Illinois does have some direct statutory protection through the *Illinois Natural Enhancement*

---

[35]   *Id.,* §§ 67000 *et seq.*

[36]   Cal. Pub. Res. Code § 29010.

[37]   N.Y. ECL §§ 24-0101 *et seq.*

[38]   *Id.,* §§ 25-0101 *et seq.*

[39]   The other state is **Texas.**

[40]   16 U.S.C. § 1451. Illinois is considered a coastal state because it borders the Great Lakes. 16 U.S.C. § 1453(4).

Program[41] enacted pursuant to the *Illinois Conservation Enhancement Act.*[42]

Michigan

Since October 1, 1980, activities on Michigan's wetlands have been governed by the *Goemaere-Anderson wetland protection act.*[43] The act, following the general trend, requires a permit for filling, dredging, developing or draining a wetland. Permits are issued for periods of up to five years. Permissible activities include recreational activities as well as farming, horticulture and silviculture. In addition, the act contains a notice provision whereby, as wetland inventories are completed under the act, "owners of record as identified by the current property tax roll shall be notified of the possible change in the status of their property."[44] Finally, the act contains a provision acknowledging the possibility of a taking without just compensation and provides a procedure for handling such claims.

New Jersey

New Jersey recently enacted a Freshwater Wetlands Protection Act (effective July 1, 1988)[45] to complement The Wetlands Act of 1970, its coastal wetlands act.[46] New Jersey's freshwater act differs from the general trend in that it contains a provision expressly creating a "rebuttable presumption that there is a practicable alternative to any nonwater-dependant regulated activity that does not involve a freshwater wetland."[47] In order to rebut the presumption, the applicant for a freshwater wetlands permit must demonstrate, among other things, that the proposed project cannot be done in another way or another place which would lessen or avoid adverse impact on an aquatic ecosystem.[48]

---

[41]   Ill. Rev. Stat. ch. 5, paras. 2403-1 *et seq.*

[42]   *Id.*, paras. 2401-1 *et seq.*

[43]   Mich. Comp. Laws §§ 281.701 et seq.

[44]   *Id.*, § 281.720.

[45]   N.J. Stat. Ann. §§ 13:9B-1 *et seq.*

[46]   *Id.*, §§ 13:9A-1 *et seq.*

[47]   *Id.*, § 13:9B-10.a.

[48]   *Id.*, § 13:9B-10.b.

Included in the statute's definition of regulated activities are dredging, filling, excavating, dumping, the placing of obstructions and the driving of pilings onto wetlands. Permit applicants may, prior to applying for a permit, request from the local department a letter of interpretation to determine whether the site is a regulated area. Although a letter stating that the site is not a freshwater wetland may be relied on, subject to EPA revocation, a lack of response from the department does not entitle the applicant to assume that the site is not a freshwater wetland.[49]

A New Jersey court has upheld regulations (implemented under the Freshwater Wetlands Protection Act) requiring that degraded wetlands must be replaced on a two for one basis, but overruled an alternative requirement that each degraded or lost acre of wetlands be compensated by enhancement of seven acres of other wetlands.[50]

Florida

Florida has enacted a comprehensive wetland statute entitled the *Warren S. Henderson Wetlands Protection Act of 1984*.[51] In line with most state wetland statutes, a permit is required for any filling or dredging activity while certain agricultural and mining activities are exempted. In order to receive a permit, the applicant must provide assurances that water quality standards will not be violated and that the project is not otherwise contrary to the public interest. In addition, the Act creates a formal wetlands monitoring system that determines the general location and acreages of wetland areas in the state, identifies the impacts on wetlands created by the issuing of permits and keeps statistics of all decisions made regarding the issuing of permits.

6.4 The Effect of Wetlands Regulation

State and federal wetlands statutes often impose strict land use controls thereby impinging on real estate development and transactions. The value of a piece of property may decline dramatically if it is

---

49   *Id.*, § 13:9B-8.

50   *N.J. Chapter of the Nat'l Assn of Industrial and Office Parks v. N.J. Dept. of Env. Protection*, No. A-3285-88TS (NJ Super.Ct. Appellate Div. May 10, 1990).

51   Fla. Stat. Ann. §§ 403.91 *et seq.*

determined to be a wetland. Thus, prospective buyers and lenders may wish to have a determination made prior to consummating a transaction. Such a determination might be difficult, as the boundaries of wetlands are often not well defined and circumstances change. While many state wetlands statutes have sought clarity through mapping provisions, most have yet to be completed and modifications are constantly occurring. As such, total reliance on maps is not advised, even where available.

The disclosure rules which apply to real estate transactions in general also apply to wetlands.[52] Wetlands pose special problems due to the multitude of wetlands definitions and jurisdictional conflicts between federal, state and local governments. The applicable statutes must be read carefully as even exempted activities often must be "ongoing" and activities conducted on areas near wetlands, known as "transition areas," often require a government waiver if not a formal permit. Therefore, those involved in real estate transactions should review all applicable laws and procedures in order to avoid unwelcome surprises with regard to acquiring or developing wetlands.

---

[52]   *See* Chapter 3.

TABLE 6-1

SAMPLE WETLANDS
DEFINITIONS

Source	Definition
Exec. Order 11,990 (May 24, 1977), *reprinted after* 42 U.S.C. § 4321	[T]hose areas that are inundated by surface or ground water with a frequency sufficient to support and under normal circumstances does or would support a prevalence of vegetative or aquatic life that requires saturated or seasonally saturated soil conditions for growth and reproduction. Wetlands generally include swamps, marshes, bogs, and similar areas such as sloughs, potholes, wet meadows, river overflows, mudflats, and natural ponds.
The United States Fish and Wildlife Service's Wetland Classification System (December 1979)	[L]ands transitional between terrestrial and aquatic systems where the water table is usually at or near the surface or the land is covered by shallow water. For purposes of this classification wetlands must have one or more of the following attributes: (1) at least periodically, the land supports predominantly hydrophytes; (2) the substrate is predominantly undrained hydric soil; and (3) the substrate is non-soil and is saturated with water or covered by shallow water at some time during the growing season of each year.
The *California Coastal Act of 1976*, Cal. Pub. Res. Code § 30121	[L]ands within the coastal zone which may be covered periodically or permanently with shallow water and include salt water marshes, freshwater marshes, open or closed brackish water marshes, swamps, mudflats, and fens.

Table 6-2

33 C.F.R. § 328.3(7)(b)   [T]hose areas that are inundated or saturated by surface or ground water at a frequency and duration sufficient to support, and that under normal circumstances do support, a prevalence of vegetation typically adapted for life in saturated soil conditions. Wetlands generally include swamps, marshes, bogs, and similar areas.

TABLE 6-2
FEDERAL WETLANDS STATUTES

Statute	Description
Clean Water Act of 1977, 33 U.S.C. §§ 1251-1376. Authority: United States Army Corps of Engineers, Environmental Protection Agency.	The CWA seeks to restore and maintain the waters of the United States, including wetlands.
Coastal Barrier Resources Act, 16 U.S.C. §§ 3501-3510. Authority: Secretary of the Interior.	Wetlands associated with coastal barriers are identified as a resource that should be protected and conserved.
Coastal Zone Management Act, 16 U.S.C. §§ 1451-1464. Authority: Secretary of Commerce.	The act sets forth a directive calling for the implementation of programs to provide for the protection of natural resources including coastal wetlands.
Erodible Land and Wetland Conservation And Reserve Program 16 U.S.C. §§ 3801-3845. Authority: Secretary of Agriculture	Part of the 1985 Food Security Act, the act discusses wetlands within the scope of agriculture. The act contains disincentives for agricultural production on wetlands.

Wetlands Regulation

Land and Water Conservation Fund Act, 16 U.S.C. §§ 460l-4 to 4601-11.
Authority: Secretary of the Interior.

The act addresses the need to preserve wetlands in order to protect recreational activities on wetlands.

Rural Environmental Conservation Program, 16 U.S.C. §§ 1501-1510.
Authority: Secretary of Agriculture.

Part of the Agriculture and Consumer Protection Act of 1973 concerning conservation and rural pollution abatement.

Water Bank Program for Wetlands Preservation, 16 U.S.C. §§ 1301-1311.
Authority: Secretary of Agriculture.

Authorizes the secretary to formulate and carry out programs to prevent the serious loss of wetlands.

Emergency Wetlands Resources Act of 1986, 16 U.S.C. §§ 3900-3932.
Authority: Secretary of the Interior.

Comprehensive statute to promote, in conjunction with other federal and state statutes, the conservation of wetlands and to help fulfill international obligations contained in various migratory bird treaties and conventions.

CHAPTER SEVEN

OTHER FEDERAL AND STATE
ENVIRONMENTAL LAWS

7.1   Introduction

7.2   Federal Laws

7.3   California Laws

7.4   Other States

7.1   Introduction

There are numerous federal and state environmental laws in addition to the Superfund laws. Some of them have been mentioned in previous chapters. This chapter will provide brief descriptions of selected federal and California environmental laws which may affect real estate transactions.

7.2   Federal Laws

National Environmental Policy Act (NEPA).[1]   NEPA requires environmental impact review of federal, state and local development projects which are federally funded, and of private development projects which require federally issued permits.

Resource Conservation and Recovery Act of 1976 (RCRA).[2]   RCRA provides standards for controlling hazardous wastes from production through disposal, a so-called "cradle to grave" system. RCRA provides for the permitting of parties who generate, treat, move, store, dispose of or transport hazardous substances. Similar to CERCLA, injunctive orders may be issued against prior or current generators, transporters, owners or operators.

RCRA also contains an underground storage tank program which regulates USTs used for storage of petroleum and CERCLA hazardous

---

[1]   42 U.S.C. §§ 4321 *et seq.*

[2]   *Id.,* §§ 6901 *et seq.*

substances. This UST program forms the basis in federal law for setting design, operation, monitoring, leak response, closure and financial responsibility standards for USTs. A strict liability standard is applied.

RCRA authorizes citizen suits in federal court against any person in violation of the provisions of RCRA or against any present or past generator, transporter, owner or operator of a treatment, storage or disposal facility who has contributed to the storage, treatment, handling, transportation or disposal of any hazardous waste "which may present an imminent and substantial endangerment to health or the environment."[3] Before such an action may be brought, prior notice must be given to the EPA, the applicable state and the prospective defendants, and the action may not be commenced if a federal or state agency has initiated and is diligently pursuing remedial orders or cleanup action.[4] If the "endangerment" standard is satisfied and no governmental agency has acted after notice (so that a private action may be commenced), the relief recoverable includes enforcement orders requiring compliance with RCRA or action to remediate the hazard.[5] Thus, a money judgment is not available (except that the costs of the litigation, including reasonable attorneys' and expert witness fees, are recoverable[6]).

The RCRA citizen suit provision is clearly designed to ensure compliance and cleanup by responsible parties, but it is not designed to provide a method of cleanup cost recovery among private parties. Nevertheless, the citizen suit provision has become an important avenue of redress for petroleum leakage which is excluded from CERCLA. A RCRA claim can be stated, for example, by a landowner against an operator or former owner who contributed to petroleum leakage in order to obtain cleanup at their expense. It may be possible to include other claims, perhaps state law causes of action, with the RCRA case in federal court under the doctrine of pendent jurisdiction. A significant limitation, however, is that, unlike CERCLA, the private action

---

3   *Id.*, § 6972(a)(1).

4   *Id.*, § 6972(b)(2).

5   *Id.*, § 6972(a).

6   *Id.*, § 6972(e).

provisions of RCRA are not retroactive to events occurring before RCRA was enacted.[7]

Clean Water Act (CWA).[8] CWA controls the discharge or threatened discharge of listed pollutants into navigable waters of the United States by imposing cleanup and cost recovery provisions against parties responsible for such discharges. CWA implements a permit system for the controlled discharge of hazardous substances. Cost recovery is available against past or present owners or operators causing unauthorized discharges or threatened discharges. A strict liability standard is imposed, and liability is joint and several. CWA allows the federal government to order the cleanup or abatement of a discharge or threatened discharge, and provides for injunctive relief when a possible pollution hazard is imminent. The important impact of the CWA on the development of wetlands is discussed in Chapter 6.

Clean Air Act (CAA).[9] CAA controls the release of hazardous air pollutants from both stationary and mobile sources, and authorizes the EPA to promulgate national ambient air quality standards and emission standards with respect to air pollutants. CAA implements a permitting system for the controlled emission of air pollutants. CAA requires the preparation and submission of state implementation plans (SIPs) for attaining national air quality standards pursuant to such SIPs.

Toxic Substances Control Act (TSCA).[10] TSCA authorizes federal control of the testing, manufacture, processing and distribution of toxic chemical substances, expressly including PCBs and asbestos. TSCA allows private actions, but only to restrain ongoing violations of the act; civil penalties set forth in TSCA may be assessed only by the EPA.[11]

The Refuse Act of 1899.[12] This law provides for injunctive relief against parties responsible for the discharge or deposit of refuse into waters of the United States.

---

[7]   *Ascon Properties, Inc. v. Mobil Oil Co.*, 866 F.2d 1149 (9th Cir. 1989).

[8]   33 U.S.C. §§ 1251 *et seq.*

[9]   42 U.S.C. §§ 7401 *et seq.*

[10]   15 U.S.C. §§ 2601 *et seq.*

[11]   *Brewer v. Ravan*, 680 F.Supp. 1176 (M.D. Tenn. 1988).

[12]   33 U.S.C. § 407.

Occupational Safety and Health Act (OSHA).[13] OSHA imposes limitations respecting occupational exposure to hazardous substances such as asbestos.

7.3 California Laws

California Environmental Quality Act (CEQA).[14] CEQA is the California counterpart to NEPA (see § 7.2). CEQA requires environmental impact review of development projects "proposed to be carried out or approved by public agencies." Specified exemptions apply, including exemptions for projects which are determined not to result in significant environmental impacts.

Hazardous Waste Control Law (HWCL).[15] HWCL is the California counterpart to RCRA (see § 7.2). Formerly administered by the Department of Health Services (DHS), and now administered by the Department of Toxic Substances Control (DTSC) of the new Cal-EPA, HWCL provides for "cradle to grave" management and regulation of hazardous waste, and permits cleanup orders against the present and prior owners, lessees or operators of contaminated property, or against present or past generators, storers, treaters, transporters or disposers and handlers of hazardous wastes. The DTSC may perform necessary cleanup and recover costs from liable parties. HWCL sets up a permitting system and regulation for those who generate, treat, move, store, dispose of or transport hazardous wastes, and provides closure and post-closure requirements for facilities at which hazardous wastes have been generated, treated, stored or disposed of. Both the state and federal provisions should be reviewed in connection with permitting requirements because HWCL and RCRA are not identical.

The HWCL includes the *Hazardous Waste Disposal Land Use Law,*[16] which authorizes the DHS to designate real property as (i) a "hazardous waste property" if substances creating a hazard or potential hazard to public health or safety are present at the site, or (ii) a "border zone property" if it is within 2,000 feet of a hazardous waste deposit.

---

[13]   29 U.S.C. §§ 651 *et seq.*

[14]   Cal. Public Resources Code §§ 21000 *et seq.*

[15]   Cal. Health & Safety Code §§ 25100 *et seq.*

[16]   *Id.,* §§ 25220 *et seq.*

The use of real property so categorized is restricted, subject to available variances.

Porter-Cologne Water Quality Control Act (Porter-Cologne Act).[17] The California counterpart to CWA (see § 7.2), this act is implemented by the Water Resources Control Board, which oversees a number of Regional Water Quality Control boards (RWQCBs). It regulates hazardous waste disposal by controlling discharges, leaks or threatened discharges, and establishes a permitting system for the controlled discharge of wastes which "could affect the quality of the waters of the state." It authorizes cease and desist orders and cleanup and abatement orders in certain hazardous conditions. RWQCBs may perform cleanup and recover costs from liable parties.

Safe Drinking Water and Toxic Enforcement Act of 1986 (Proposition 65).[18] Proposition 65 prohibits the discharge of detectable quantities of carcinogenic or reproductively toxic chemicals into sources of drinking water. It requires warnings when exposure to such chemicals is anticipated. A list of chemicals covered by Proposition 65 was published by the governor, and is updated at least annually. The warning aspect of Proposition 65 is discussed in Chapter 4.

Hazardous Substances Underground Storage Tank Law.[19] This law establishes standards for the construction, permitting, monitoring, leak response and closure of USTs containing hazardous substances. The law provides that owners or operators may be liable for failure to obtain a permit for a UST; failure to repair or maintain a UST properly; and abandoning or improperly closing a UST. The law requires the reporting of certain unauthorized releases from a UST. The UST program does not exclude petroleum from the list of controlled hazardous substances.

Aboveground Storage of Petroleum Law.[20] This new law regulates aboveground petroleum tank facilities, including inspection and monitoring requirements, and spill reporting provisions. The law also

---

[17]   Cal. Water Code §§ 13000 *et seq.*

[18]   Cal. Health & Safety Code §§ 25249.5 *et seq.*

[19]   *Id.,* §§ 25280 *et seq.*

[20]   *Id.,* §§ 25270 *et seq.*

mandates the preparation of spill prevention control and countermeasure plans.

Air Resources Law.[21] The California counterpart to the federal CAA (see § 7.2), this act controls releases of hazardous air pollutants from both mobile and stationary sources. It is monitored by the California Air Resources Board (CARB) through a number of local or regional air pollution control districts. It implements a system for the controlled emission of air pollutants from specific sources by requiring permits for the construction, modification, replacement or operation of certain potential sources of air contaminants.

Hazardous Materials Release Response Plans and Inventory.[22] California has adopted a series of statutory provisions respecting emergency responses to the release or threatened release of hazardous materials. These provisions require immediate notice of releases or threatened releases of hazardous substances to local and state emergency response agencies; preparation of release response plans by businesses which handle designated threshold amounts of hazardous substances and by local agencies; and development of risk management and prevention programs.

Toxic Pits Cleanup Act of 1984 (TCPA).[23] TCPA requires that surface impoundments of hazardous waste be made safe or closed to eliminate migration of contaminants into water supplies.

Other State and Local Laws. The following are several additional examples of the many ways in which California has enacted provisions regulating hazardous wastes. The Attorney General may bring an action to protect natural resources from pollution, impairment or destruction.[24] Asbestos related work is regulated to ensure that such work is performed only by qualified personnel.[25] Additionally, California voters reactivated the provisions of Cal-OSHA by approving Proposition 97 in

---

[21]   *Id.*, §§ 39000 *et seq.*

[22]   *Id.*, §§ 25500-25541.

[23]   *Id.*, §§ 25208-25208.17.

[24]   Cal. Govt. Code § 12607.

[25]   Cal. Labor Code §§ 6501.5 through 6501.9, 6503.5, 9021.5, and Cal. Bus. and Prof. Code §§ 7058.5, 7065.01, 7118 and 7118.5.

the election of November 8, 1988, and Cal-OSHA resumed operations on May 1, 1989.

Many counties and municipalities have also enacted ordinances designed to control or minimize the presence of hazardous substances. For example, the Los Angeles County Uniform Fire Code contains detailed provisions for the regulation and permitting of hazardous, toxic, flammable and combustible materials handled or stored within its jurisdiction, as well as regulations affecting the manner of construction of buildings and fire safety systems. The Los Angeles City Fire Code contains similar provisions.[26] Los Angeles County also regulates USTs.[27]

7.4 Other States

Other states, and local jurisdictions within those states, may have analogous laws, ordinances, regulations or policies in addition to the Superfund laws. It is important for real estate professionals to be aware of the existence of such rules and the need to comply with their requirements.

---

[26] Los Angeles Municipal Code §§ 57.01.01 *et seq.*

[27] Los Angeles County Code §§ 11.02 *et seq.*

CHAPTER EIGHT

COMMON LAW LIABILITY

8.1   Introduction

In addition to statutory liabilities, traditional sources of common law liability apply in the hazardous waste context. Some of the common law theories provide recourse to a person injured or whose property is damaged by exposure to hazardous substances (so-called "toxic torts"). Others may provide a basis for recovery of cleanup costs under some circumstances. Further, it may be that no statutory claim exists for the desired relief. For example, the petroleum exclusion from the definition of "hazardous substance" precludes a private right of action under CERCLA for cleanup cost recovery in the case of leakage of petroleum (see Chapter 1); and a private action under RCRA for petroleum leakage may only result in a cleanup order, not a money judgment (see Chapter 7). Thus, unless a money claim can be stated under a state statute, the claimant must look to the common law for a remedy. It has been held that a party who is not an identified PRP under CERCLA may still be subject to suit for contribution toward cleanup costs under applicable state law principles.[1] Possible common law liabilities in the environmental context should therefore not be overlooked. This chapter will provide a brief description of such theories of liability.

Litigation regarding hazardous waste typically involves a variety of claims under environmental statutes and the common law, depending upon the circumstances and the relief desired. Each theory of liability has its own elements and available remedies. Careful analysis is required in each case by legal counsel to determine what relief is available under what theories of action in the applicable jurisdiction and how best to proceed.

8.2   Fraudulent Misrepresentation or Nondisclosure; Negligent Misrepresentation

Chapter 3 notes the circumstances under which a seller has a common law duty to disclose material facts concerning the condition, value or desirability of real estate. Failure to disclose under those circumstances will expose the seller to liability for common law fraud. Except where the hazardous waste condition is or should be apparent to a reasonably prudent buyer, this theory of action will likely be applicable in cases of nondisclosure of a hazardous waste condition known to the seller.[2]

It should therefore come as no surprise that an actual misrepresentation that the property in question is "clean" when the seller knows that it is "dirty" may likewise provide the basis for a fraud

---

1   *U.S. v. Hooker Chemicals & Plastics Corp.*, 739 F.Supp. 125 (W.D.N.Y. 1990) (Occidental Chemical Corp., Hooker's successor, was allowed to maintain a cross-claim under state law against Niagara County for contribution or indemnity toward Love Canal cleanup costs even though the County was not a PRP under CERCLA, but, under the facts of the case, Occidental failed to make out a claim for contribution or indemnity under New York law).

2   *See e.g., New Jersey v. Ventron Corp.*, 182 N.J. Super 210 (App.Div. 1981), *aff'd as mod.*, 94 N.J. 473 (1983) (buyers successfully sued seller for fraudulent nondisclosure of pollution).

claim.[3] The elements of such a claim are: "(1) a *false representation* or concealment of a material fact (or, in some cases, an opinion) susceptible of knowledge, (2) made with *knowledge* of its falsity or without sufficient knowledge on the subject to warrant a representation, (3) with the *intent* to induce the person to whom it is made to act upon it; and such person must (4) act in *reliance* upon the representation (5) to his *damage*."[4] These elements encompass two kinds of fraud, including knowingly false statements and those made without reasonable grounds for belief in their truth. Thus, a false statement that the property is "clean" may be actionable fraud either as a knowingly false statement or as a "negligent misrepresentation."

The damages that are recoverable for fraud in connection with a real estate transaction vary from state to state. In California, for example, a plaintiff who was fraudulently induced to purchase property may recover damages calculated on the "out-of-pocket" loss rule, *i.e.*, the difference between the consideration paid and the actual value of the property (as opposed to the "benefit-of-the-bargain" rule which would allow recovery of the difference between the value of the property as represented and its actual value).[5] Plaintiffs may also recover "additional damages" including amounts expended in reliance upon the fraud (e.g., closing costs) and "other consequential damages stemming from the fraud."[6] It has yet to be established in a reported court case under California law whether hazardous waste cleanup costs constitute a recoverable "additional" damage or "consequential" damage of the kind

---

[3] *See, e.g., Gopher Oil Co. v. Union Oil Co.*, 757 F.Supp. 988 (D. Minn. 1990), *affirmed in part and remanded in part*, 1992 U.S. App. LEXIS 1076 (8th Cir. Jan. 28, 1992) (buyer successfully sued seller for affirmative misrepresentation of the condition of the site which was polluted with oil and industrial chemicals).

[4] *South Tahoe Gas Co. v. Hofmann Land Improvement Co.*, 25 Cal.App.3d 750, 765, 102 Cal.Rptr. 286 (1972) (emphasis in original).

[5] Cal. Civil Code § 3343(a).

[6] *O'Neil v. Spillane*, 45 Cal.App.3d 147, 159, 119 Cal.Rptr. 245 (1975); Cal. Civil Code § 3343(a)(1).

contemplated by the statute.[7] It can be argued that such costs ought to be recoverable as a consequential damage because the plaintiff would not have purchased the property had he known the truth, and, hence, the cleanup costs would not have been incurred by the plaintiff absent the fraud. In fraud cases, exemplary or punitive damages are also recoverable.[8]

8.3   Negligence

In view of the strict liability accorded under the Superfund laws, it is often unnecessary to resort to negligence claims. That is particularly true where the plaintiff seeks recovery of cleanup costs from a responsible party. On the other hand, personal injury and property damage claims (other than damages to natural resources) are not redressed by CERCLA,[9] and a negligence cause of action might be important to a toxic tort claimant.

Ordinary negligence applies where the defendant owed a duty of care to the plaintiff, the defendant breached that duty, and the breach was the proximate cause of damage to the plaintiff. Whether a duty of care exists in the first instance depends upon the factual circumstances, the relationship of the parties, and the available case precedents in similar situations. In the context of real property sales, the doctrine of *caveat emptor* generally precludes a negligence claim against a former owner based on the condition of the property, unless the seller has breached a disclosure duty, has committed fraudulent nondisclosure, or is a builder and has breached an implied warranty arising in new residential construction.[10]

---

[7]   Such damages are recoverable under New Jersey law. *See State Department of Environmental Protection v. Ventron Corp.*, 94 N.J. 473, 468 A.2d 150, 156, 166 (1983) (in a fraudulent nondisclosure case, purchasers were entitled to recover as damages from the seller the cost of a hazardous waste containment system and other costs of abating the pollution).

[8]   Cal. Civil Code § 3294; *Channell v. Anthony*, 58 Cal.App.3d 290, 129 Cal.Rptr. 704 (1976).

[9]   42 U.S.C. § 9607(a).

[10]   *See, e.g., Preston v. Goldman*, 42 Cal.3d 108, 227 Cal.Rptr. 817, 720 P.2d 476 (1986). For a discussion of *caveat emptor* and the emergence of common law and statutory disclosure duties, see Chapter 3.

The doctrine of negligence *per se* can assist a plaintiff in establishing that a duty of care existed and was breached. That doctrine applies where a statute or administrative rule regulates the conduct of the defendant and in effect imposes a duty of care for the benefit of a class of persons which includes the plaintiff. Negligence is presumed if the defendant violates such a law or regulation resulting in the injury or death of a protected person.[11]

Negligence *per se* frequently comes into play in toxic tort cases due to the many laws and regulations governing the possession, use, handling, transportation and disposal of hazardous and toxic materials as well as those laws requiring disclosures, warnings and reports (see Chapters 3 and 4). Where a defendant has failed to observe such requirements, an employee or other person may be in a position to claim that he or she was exposed to and injured by hazardous substances, or that property was damaged by such exposure, because the defendant violated safety regulations or gave no warning and, hence, that the defendant was negligent *per se*.[12]

A plaintiff who wins a negligence case is generally entitled to recover any damages which are proven to have been caused by the defendant's wrongful conduct.[13]

8.4 Nuisance

Theories of private and public nuisance apply where hazardous substances are involved. A "nuisance" may consist of "[a]nything which is injurious to health, or is indecent or offensive to the senses, or an obstruction to the free use of property, so as to interfere with the

---

[11] *See, generally*, 46 Cal.Jur.3d, *Negligence* §§ 92 to 111.

[12] In this connection, the failure of a business to implement a business plan or other required hazardous substance control measures may expose the business not only to statutory penalties but also to increased prospects for civil liability under the doctrine of negligence *per se* for personal injury or death or other damages caused by hazardous substance releases, particularly where the harmful effect would have been avoided or minimized had a business plan or other control measure been implemented as required by federal or state law.

[13] *See, e.g.*, Cal. Civil Code § 3333.

comfortable enjoyment of life or property . . . "[14] Thus, by definition, nuisance claims may arise in relation to personal injuries sustained from exposure to toxic materials which are "injurious to health."

In addition, it may be possible to state a claim for recovery of cleanup costs under a nuisance theory. The person who created the nuisance may be liable, even long after that person has sold the contaminated property.[15] The current owner or occupant may also be liable due to control over the land from which the nuisance emanates, even if innocent of involvement in the creation of the harmful condition.[16] The *Restatement Second of Torts* provides the rule:

> § 839. Possessor Who Fails to Abate
> Artificial Condition
> A possessor of land is subject to liability for a nuisance caused while he is in possession by an abatable artificial condition of the land, if the nuisance is otherwise actionable, and

---

[14]   *Id.*, § 3479.

[15]   *U.S. v. Hooker Chemicals & Plastics Corp.*, 722 F.Supp. 960 (W.D.N.Y. 1989) (Occidental Chemical Corp., the corporate successor of Hooker, was held liable under a public nuisance theory for Love Canal cleanup costs incurred by the State of New York even though Hooker had disclosed the existence of the chemical waste dump and had disclaimed liability upon selling the property in 1953; assumption of risk was available as a defense, but not a complete defense, only in diminution of recoverable damages in proportion to contributing causes). *See also U.S. v. Hooker Chemicals & Plastics Corp.*, 748 F.Supp. 67 (W.D.N.Y. 1990) (punitive damages were recoverable on the public nuisance claim).

[16]   *See, e.g., State of New York v. Shore Realty Corp.*, 759 F.2d 1032, 1051, 1053 (2d Cir. 1985) (Purchasers of waste disposal site were liable for cleanup. The responsibility for abating the nuisance was based on the purchasers' exclusive control over the property, not on any wrongful conduct on their part in creating the nuisance); *State v. Charpentier*, 126 N.H. 56, 489 A.2d 594, 598-600 (1985) (Defendant landowner was found liable for nuisance created by a third party because she failed to prevent the dumping of hazardous wastes she knew or had reason to know of and did not take reasonable steps to remove the existing hazard from her property).

> (a)   the possessor knows or should know of the
> condition and the nuisance or unreasonable risk of
> nuisance involved, and
>
> (b)   he knows or should know that it exists
> without the consent of those affected by it, and
>
> (c)   he has failed after a reasonable opportunity
> to take reasonable steps to abate the condition or to
> protect the affected persons against it.[17]

Consequently, a lessee or purchaser may be liable for a harmful condition created by his predecessor or any other person if he fails to abate the condition after a reasonable amount of time.[18] Thus, nuisance law is a form of strict liability.

Of course, to be a nuisance, the condition must be "unreasonable," so that the courts will balance the actual or potential harm against the usefulness of the activity of the defendant.[19] The defendant is likely to lose most such determinations where hazardous waste contamination creates no benefit, only harm.

Until recently, the leading modern case on the subject of nuisance liability for hazardous waste was *Philadelphia Electric Co. v. Hercules, Inc.*[20] That case clarified that private nuisance theory is available only to neighbors, and that a person may pursue a public nuisance theory only if he exercised a right in common with the general public but suffered harm of a different kind. In *Philadelphia Electric*, hazardous waste had leached from a property causing pollution of a nearby river used as a source of drinking water. The purchaser of the contaminated land was *not* entitled to recover abatement costs from the former owner

---

17   Restatement Second of Torts § 839 (1979).

18   *Id.*, § 839, comments (d) and (l). In this regard, California law specifically provides that: "Every successive owner of property who neglects to abate a continuing nuisance upon, or in the use of, such property, created by a former owner, is liable therefor in the same manner as the one who first created it . . . The abatement of a nuisance does not prejudice the right of any person to recover damages for its past existence." Cal. Civil Code §§ 3483 and 3484.

19   *Shields v. Wondries*, 154 Cal.App.2d 249, 316 P.2d 9 (1957).

20   762 F.2d 303 (3rd Cir. 1985), *cert. den.* 474 U.S. 980 (1985).

on a nuisance theory. The purchaser was not a neighbor with standing to sue for private nuisance. As to the public nuisance claim, the purchaser did suffer abatement costs unlike any damage incurred by the general public, but the purchaser was not exercising any right in common with the general public. The public's right had to do with the river's water quality, whereas the purchaser's expenses arose out of its private property rights in its own land, and the contamination on the purchaser's property was the source of the pollution, not the result of it. Accordingly, under *Philadelphia Electric*, nuisance theory appears to be available chiefly to neighbors who incur damages such as personal injuries or abatement costs as a result of any nuisances emanating from adjoining land.[21]

In what appears to be a dramatic expansion of the law of nuisance, the court in *Mangini v. Aerojet - General Corp.*[22] permitted a present property owner to proceed with claims for both public and private nuisance against a former tenant of a former owner of the same property (the former tenant having contaminated the property with hazardous waste during the term of the lease). The court declined to follow *Philadelphia Electric* and ruled that nuisance law in California is not limited to cases involving neighboring properties. The *Mangini* case provides a significant new remedy for present owners against former owners or occupants who caused contamination. This remedy may be particularly important in cases where strict CERCLA liability does not apply (e.g., petroleum contamination not covered by CERCLA). It remains to be seen whether *Philadelphia Electric* or *Mangini* will become the leading authority as this issue is considered by other courts across the country.

8.5   Strict Liability in Tort (Ultrahazardous or Abnormally Dangerous Activity)

The concept of strict liability in tort of a possessor of real estate was originally declared in the old English case of *Rylands v. Fletcher*:

---

[21]   *See*, to the same effect, *Pinole Point Properties, Inc., v. Bethlehem Steel Corp.*, 596 F.Supp. 283, 292 at n.5 (N.D.Cal. 1984).

[22]   230 Cal.App.3d 1125, 281 Cal.Rptr. 827 (1991) (the California Supreme Court subsequently declined to review the case).

We think that the true rule of law is that the person who for his own purposes brings on his land and collects and keeps there anything likely to do mischief if it escapes, must keep it at his peril, and if he does not do so, is *prima facie* answerable for all damage which is the natural consequence of its escape.[23]

Although this theory originally provided recourse against an owner of trespassing cattle, it is now the potential source for claims against owners of contaminated property causing injuries to others. The *Restatement Second of Torts* sets forth the general rule:

§ 519. General Principle

(1) One who carries on an abnormally dangerous activity is subject to liability for harm to the person, land or chattels of another resulting from the activity, although he has exercised the utmost care to prevent the harm.

(2) This strict liability is limited to the kind of harm, the possibility of which makes the activity abnormally dangerous.[24]

In 1983, the Supreme Court of New Jersey found that the disposal of toxic waste is an "abnormally dangerous" activity. The court concluded that the owner of land who used or permitted others to use the land for such activities was strictly liable for resultant damages, including cleanup and abatement costs incurred by the state.[25] More recently, the Supreme Court of New Jersey has ruled that the former owner of property which it sold in 1943 was strictly liable under the doctrine of

---

[23]   *Rylands v. Fletcher*, L.R. 1 Ex. 265, 279-80 (1866), *aff'd*, L.R. 3 H.L. 330 (1868).

[24]   Restatement Second of Torts § 519 (1977).

[25]   *State Department of Environmental Protection v. Ventron Corp.*, 94 N.J. 473, 468 A.2d 150 (1983).

abnormally dangerous activity (radium deposits) to the current owner who purchased the property in 1974.[26]

The federal Court of Appeals for the Fifth Circuit also has found that the storage and disposal of hazardous waste is an ultrahazardous activity and, hence, that a waste disposal company was strictly liable for damages, including a fire at a refinery, caused by hazardous waste which it had disposed of there.[27] California courts likewise have recognized that use of toxic materials may constitute an "abnormally dangerous" activity.[28] However, the federal district court for the Northern District of California has suggested that a cleanup cost recovery claim brought by a purchaser of contaminated land against a former owner based on an ultrahazardous activity theory would likely fail on the merits because "the cost of cleaning up [hazardous waste] and diminished property value, is not the type of harm for which strict liability generally attaches."[29] A Florida court has held that a claim for strict liability for abnormally dangerous activity may not be stated by an owner of commercial land against former owners for contamination, and there was no disclosure duty under the circumstances.[30]

Accordingly, it appears that personal injuries or property damages caused by hazardous waste contamination, and cleanup or abatement costs incurred by the government or a neighbor, are redressable under the doctrine of strict liability in tort due to ultrahazardous or abnormally

---

26   *T&E Industries, Inc. v. Safety Light Corp.*, 587 A.2d 1249 (N.J. Supreme Ct. 1991) (declining to follow *Philadelphia Electric* which limited this liability theory to cases involving neighboring lands, not successive owners of the same property). To the same effect, *see Hanlin Group Inc. v. International Minerals & Chemical Corp.*, No. 89-0089 B (D.C. Maine July 26, 1990) (strict liability claim allowed to proceed against former owner for hazardous waste disposal).

27   *Ashland Oil, Inc. v. Miller Oil Purchasing Co.*, 678 F.2d 1293, 1307-1308 (5th Cir. 1982).

28   *Aherns v. Superior Court*, 197 Cal.App.3d 1134, 243 Cal.Rptr. 420 (1988) (involving PCBs).

29   *Pinole Point Properties, Inc. v. Bethlehem Steel Corp.*, 596 F.Supp. 283, 292 at n.5 (N.D.Cal. 1984).

30   *Futura Realty Inc. v. Lone Star Building Centers, Inc.*, No. 90-821 (Fla. Dist. Ct.App. April 9, 1991).

dangerous activity. But there is a conflict in the case law and it is not clear whether a purchaser may recover cleanup or abatement costs under that theory from a former owner or occupant of the contaminated land.

8.6   Trespass

A physical intrusion onto the real property of another may constitute an actionable trespass. This doctrine applies to both surface and subsurface invasions, as well as those occurring through the air. There is some overlap between the trespass doctrine and the nuisance doctrine, but this is not always so because a nuisance need not involve a physical intrusion (e.g., noise can be a nuisance but not a trespass).[31] Moreover, for a trespass to be actionable, it must involve an intentional or negligent activity on the part of the defendant.[32] Thus, the underground migration of hazardous waste might not constitute a trespass if the activity resulting in the disposal and migration was neither intended nor negligent, but the condition could be a nuisance if left unabated.[33]

8.7   Rescission

Rescission is an available remedy in cases of fraud or mutual mistake of fact, among other circumstances.[34] Thus, a transferee of an interest in contaminated real estate might be in a position to rescind the transaction.[35] In the case of a mutual mistake of fact, the transferor might also be able to do so. This actually occurred in a recent case involving land which was, unknown to either party, contaminated by leaking gasoline tanks. The seller (who was potentially liable under

---

[31]   *Wilson v. Interlake Steel Co.*, 32 Cal.3d 229, 185 Cal.Rptr. 280, 649 P.2d 922 (1982).

[32]   *Id.*

[33]   *See, generally*, the cases cited in *Prosser & Keeton on The Law of Torts*, § 13 (5th Ed., 1984).

[34]   *See, e.g.*, Cal. Civil Code § 1689(b).

[35]   *See Roth v. Leach*, No. 30639 (N.Y. Sup.Ct. Wayne County, Oct. 4, 1990) (buyer allowed to rescind the purchase of a residential lot because the seller had buried hazardous waste and had not disclosed it to the buyer).

environmental laws) preferred to be in control of the cleanup process and successfully rescinded the transaction over the objections of the purchaser (who, for some unexplained reason, wanted to enforce the contract and acquire the property notwithstanding the discovery of the contamination).[36]

Sometimes sellers will reserve a contractual rescission or termination right if, pending close of escrow, the cost of cleanup will exceed reasonable expectations altering the economics of the deal. For example, in one case the cleanup cost was to be determined, and the purchase contract provided as follows: "If the cost of such clean-up work will, in Seller's best judgment, be economically impractical, then Seller, at its option, may terminate this Contract by providing written notice to purchaser no later than six weeks plus five business days following completion of the Soils Study."[37] When the cost estimate came in at approximately $218,000 to $240,000, the Seller terminated the contract under this clause and then offered to complete the sale if the buyer would pay the cleanup cost. The buyer refused and sought to enforce the contract. The trial court upheld the Seller's termination of the contract, but that result was reversed on appeal. The seller's discretion was limited by the implied covenant to act in good faith, and the case was returned to the trial court to determine whether that obligation had been fulfilled when the seller terminated the transaction.

8.8   Contractual or Equitable Indemnity.

Transaction documents might include an allocation of potential environmental liability, including an indemnification clause (see Chapter 18). If so, when hazardous waste is discovered, recourse might be available to a party under express contractual indemnity for expenses incurred in connection with that condition.

Even if there is no such contractual provision, it might be possible to obtain a form of equitable indemnity on a quasi-contract theory based

---

[36]   *Garb-Ko, Inc., v. Lansing-Lewis Services, Inc.*, 167 Mich. App. 779, 423 N.W.2d 355 (Mich. App. 1988). The result in this case might have been different if the purchaser had agreed to indemnify the seller for the cost of cleaning up the leaking USTs.

[37]   *Greer Properties, Inc. v. La Salle Nat'l Bank*, No. 87-C-10983 (N.D. Ill. June 21, 1988), *reversed* 874 F.2d 457 (7th Cir. 1989).

on the notion that a party who has incurred a cost which is justly the obligation of another ought in good conscience to be able to obtain reimbursement in order to avoid the unjust enrichment of the responsible person.[38] The availability of an equitable indemnity cause of action in a hazardous waste situation was upheld in the *Mangini* case.[39]

8.9   Statute of Limitations

CERCLA has expressly preempted any state statute of limitations which would commence sooner than the "federally required commencement date" with respect to any claim under state law for personal injury or property damages "which are caused or contributed to by exposure to any hazardous substance, pollutant or contaminant, released into the environment from a facility"; the statute of limitations in such cases will commence to run on "the date the plaintiff knew (or reasonably should have known) that the personal injury or property damages . . . were caused or contributed to by the hazardous substance or pollutant or contaminant concerned."[40]   Thus, in toxic tort cases, federal law mandates the "discovery rule" rather than the "date of injury rule" which might otherwise apply.   The CERCLA "discovery rule" is even more generous to plaintiffs than the "discovery rule" which exists under some state laws which would look to the date of discovery *of the injury.*   The CERCLA standard goes beyond that.   Not only must the injury be known, but it must also be known that the injury was caused or contributed to by a particular hazardous substance.   Accordingly, a toxic tort claim might have great longevity before it becomes time-barred.

A nuisance or trespass which is abatable is continuing in nature (vs. permanent) and is hence not barred by the statute of limitations if the nuisance or trespass still exists or existed during the limitation period (e.g., within the last three years), even though it may have commenced long before.   A cause of action for equitable indemnity accrues, and the statute of limitations begins to run, when the indemnitee has suffered

---

[38]   *See, e.g., Santa Clara County v. Robbiano,* 180 Cal.App.2d 845, 848, 5 Cal.Rptr. 19 (1960).

[39]   *Mangini v. Aerojet - General Corp.,* 230 Cal.App.3d 1125, 1153-1155 (1991).

[40]   42 U.S.C. § 9658(a)(1) and (b)(4).

loss through payment.[41] Thus, these causes of action may be available to a plaintiff long after other claims are time-barred.[42]

---

[41]   *Mangini v. Aerojet - General Corp.*, 230 Cal.App.3d 1125, 1154 (1991). *See also Arcade Water District v. U.S.*, 940 F.2d 1265 (9th Cir. 1991) (even though the laundry which released chemicals was no longer in operation and the plaintiff's well was also closed, the nuisance was continuing in nature as long as the contamination continued leaching into the plaintiff's well and could be abated, and hence the claim was not time-barred).

[42]   *See, e.g., CAMSI IV v. Hunter Technology Corp.*, 230 Cal.App.3d 1525, 282 Cal.Rptr. 80 (1991) (claims for negligence, negligence per se and strict liability for ultrahazardous activity were time-barred where the plaintiff was on notice of the contamination problem and could have learned the full extent and source of the problem by exercise of reasonable diligence sooner than the allowable limitations period -- the plaintiff did not plead a continuing nuisance cause of action).

PART II

THE IMPACT OF ENVIRONMENTAL LAWS
ON REAL ESTATE TRANSACTIONS

CHAPTER NINE

SELLERS AND BUYERS

9.1   **The Seller's Concerns**

9.2   **The Buyer's Perspective**

9.3   **The Stage Is Set**

9.4   **Profit Opportunities for the Fearless Entrepreneur**

Part I of this book highlights a number of environmental laws, including the Superfund laws, which can have a significant impact on real estate transactions. The potential for liability under those laws has brought environmental concerns into the forefront of matters considered in real estate transactions.

This chapter will outline the impact of such environmental laws on the key players in a real estate transaction, the seller and buyer. The perspectives of other participants (e.g., lenders, brokers and others) are addressed in the upcoming chapters in Part II. How the parties might deal with their respective concerns is discussed further in Part III.

9.1   The Seller's Concerns

Sellers have traditionally expected to sell real estate and then to walk away from it. The only exceptions were when the seller committed a fraud or there was a mutual mistake of fact so that the buyer might be entitled to rescission or damages, or when the transaction was financed in whole or in part by the seller. Otherwise, the seller would have no further involvement with the property. All the benefits and obligations associated with ownership of the property would become the buyer's upon closing of the transaction. The environmental laws have shattered that traditional expectation.

Known Environmental Problems. When hazardous waste contamination is known, the seller has an obligation to disclose it to the prospective buyer (see Chapter 3). The seller may also wish to make a disclosure in order to preserve his own "intervening" landowner status where the contamination preexisted his acquisition of the property. As seen in Chapter 1, such intervening landowners will have federal Superfund liability only if they fail to disclose the condition upon selling the property. The same rule applies under the Superfund laws of a number of states (e.g., **California**,[1] **Oregon**,[2] and **Pennsylvania**[3]). In addition, various statutes may require reports to governmental agencies (see Chapter 4). Such reporting obligations might be triggered by the discovery of hazardous waste while a transaction is pending.[4]

Whenever the problem becomes known, the value and marketability of contaminated property may be adversely affected.[5] The potential liability under the Superfund laws (either by way of governmental or private cost recovery actions), may in some cases exceed the value of a property. In addition, the property may become encumbered by a cleanup cost recovery lien under the provisions of CERCLA or the applicable state Superfund law, and in some states the lien may be a "superlien" (see Chapter 2).

Even where the seller is willing to consider undertaking remedial action, the cost can in some cases run into the millions of dollars. The duration of remedial action can cover many years in serious cases. Substantial delay can be expected also for relatively minor cases, unless a buyer is willing to close the transaction before the cleanup is completed. As shown in Chapter 3, that option is not available for contaminated industrial property in **New Jersey** where cleanup must be completed before the property may be transferred. It may be difficult on any timely basis to obtain the certification of the appropriate governmental agencies that the cleanup has been completed. Buyers are often not willing to buy contaminated property or to wait for the cleanup process

---

[1] California adopts the federal standards for liable parties and defenses. Cal. Health & Safety Code § 25323.5.

[2] Or. Rev. Stat. § 466.567.

[3] 35 Pa. Cons. Stat. Ann. § 6020.701(b)(1).

[4] Thus, sellers may wish to obtain the agreement of the prospective buyer and its consultant to maintain confidentiality regarding the results of an environmental assessment. The seller will want to determine whether reporting is required, at least as long as the seller owns the property.

[5] *See* Chapter 15 regarding valuation and appraisal of contaminated properties.

to be concluded. Thus, desired property transfers can be delayed or frustrated altogether.

If the buyer is willing to close the transaction while the property remains contaminated (in a state where that is permitted), the seller must still be mindful of the prospect for future liability under the environmental laws. The seller's primary concern is that the buyer might not properly manage the risk, leaving the seller exposed to Superfund liability to the government. While the buyer might agree to assume the risk of environmental problems, such agreements are not binding on the government or any other third party. The seller, as a former owner, will remain a PRP in the eyes of the government. Moreover, if the seller has agreed to pay all or some of the cleanup cost after closing of the transaction, the seller may be at risk of excessive cleanup measures. The buyer might want to have a pristine property at the seller's expense. As a result of these considerations, sellers often wish to manage the risk before selling the property, but this is not always possible as a practical matter.

Another source of potential ongoing liability relates to any toxic tort claims of third parties for personal injuries or property damages caused by exposure to hazardous substances. Such injuries might not occur, or the cause of the injury might not be discovered, until sometime in the future.

If the buyer, in addition to assuming the risk of known environmental problems, agrees to indemnify the seller against any environmental liability, that agreement will be only as good as the creditworthiness of the buyer. The seller will remain potentially liable to the government or third parties.

In sum, where contamination is known, the seller may be stuck with an unmarketable property. Even if a buyer is found, the seller may have to sell at a discount and may still face ongoing liabilities under the environmental laws to the government, the buyer and third parties.

Where No Environmental Problems Are Known. One might think that if no environmental problems are known to exist, then the seller has nothing to worry about. To the contrary, the seller should consider the risk that existing hazardous waste contamination might be discovered in the future. If so, claims might be made that at least some of the contamination occurred during the seller's period of ownership or operation of the property. It also might be alleged that the seller is liable as the generator of the waste.

In the event of such a discovery after a sale has been completed, the seller would have concerns similar to those noted above, although the seller would be in a worse position with regard to management of the risk. The amount of the seller's eventual liability will be affected greatly by the propriety of the current owner's management of the problem and the cost-effectiveness of remedial measures taken.

There have been numerous instances in recent years where cleanup cost recovery claims have been made against former owners who sold their properties many years ago, even before the Superfund laws were enacted. Many transactions which the parties thought were long since concluded are being revisited as owners seek contribution from former owners for the cost of cleanup of hazardous waste conditions some or all of which predated the acquisition by the current owner. In such situations, environmental issues were probably not contemplated by the parties and liability will be based on statutory provisions without the benefit of any contractual protections. Parties completing transactions now, with appreciation for the potential environmental liabilities, are in a position to allocate those risks in a negotiated manner.

Thus, in view of the risk of future discovery of contamination, environmental issues have become the subject of intense negotiations in real estate transactions even where the parties in good faith believe that a property is "clean."

Environmental Assessments by Sellers. A former owner has no liability for contamination which may occur after the property is sold. It may not be clear, however, *when* contamination occurred (whether before or after a particular real estate transaction). Sellers therefore should consider undertaking an environmental assessment in order to document the condition of the property at the time of sale (a so-called "base line" assessment). Such information may assist the seller's position that a hazardous substance release must have occurred after the sale (in response to a future claim by the buyer, the government or a third party).

9.2   The Buyer's Perspective

Buying a Liability. A buyer's main concern is that the property being purchased might bring with it an environmental liability. As the owner of contaminated real estate, the buyers could face strict Superfund liability and possibly a cleanup cost recovery lien or superlien even if the contamination occurred completely before the purchase. This prospect is very real when contamination is known to be present, and, as indicated above, potential exposure to liability exists even if no environmental problem is known or disclosed to the buyer at the time of the purchase.

Environmental Assessments.   If   the   buyer   performs   an environmental assessment before acquiring the property and finds no contamination (and none is disclosed), then the innocent landowner defense might be available. However, the buyer will have the burden of proof on that defense, and it may be difficult to overcome the government's likely argument that the assessment was insufficient. It did fail to reveal the problem. To the extent that the assessment reveals the presence of hazardous waste, then the buyer may be able to insist that the seller bear the cost of cleanup, or to cancel the transaction if the purchase agreement contains a condition in this regard and if an acceptable allocation of risk cannot be negotiated.

When assessing the possibility of an undisclosed or unknown environmental problem, the buyer should appreciate that the risk is greater for some kinds of properties than others, but that no property is immune. For example, agricultural properties may be contaminated with the accumulated residue of the application of pesticides. The operation of agricultural properties may also involve machinery and storage tanks which are common sources of contamination. Even though a property may look unused and undeveloped, it may have been used in some way in the past leaving behind soil or groundwater contamination. An empty corner lot in a choice location, on the market at a very attractive price, might have been the site of an old gas station with leaking USTs.

Developed commercial properties have a range of environmental risks including such matters as asbestos (commonly used as an insulation or fireproofing material until the late 1970s); PCBs (formerly used in electrical equipment and transformers); and old, leaking and perhaps abandoned, USTs (used for storage of fuel oil, gasoline or other fuels).

Developed industrial properties (both light and heavy industrial) are perhaps the most likely to have hazardous waste problems arising from the handling and storage of chemicals and other hazardous substances in their operation. The use of cleaning solvents and wastewater disposal may also be a source of pollution. Industrial properties may have leaking USTs and underground pipelines. The possibility of soil and groundwater contamination should be considered in any transaction involving such a property.

Other properties, including residential, can have hazardous substance problems arising from the prior use of the property, the nature of the construction materials used (including asbestos), or the uses of adjoining properties from which hazardous waste may have migrated. One example is Love Canal, the residential neighborhood in New York which was built near a chemical waste dump. There are other such examples, and more awaiting discovery.

Thus, regardless of the apparent nature of the property, the buyer should be careful of hidden environmental problems. See Chapter 16 for a more in depth discussion of environmental assessments.

Available Recourse Against Other PRPs. Buyers are in a better position today than in the old days of *caveat emptor.* If preexisting contamination is discovered after the purchase, the buyer might have recourse against the seller or other prior owners under the new environmental laws or under common law principles. Contractual indemnity rights also might exist if they were negotiated and obtained from the seller. As long as the buyer has not contributed to the contamination after acquiring the property and did not waive possible future environmental claims at the time of purchase, there is a very good prospect under the environmental laws for obtaining relief from the actually responsible parties. On the other hand, such recourse is only as good as the creditworthiness of the defendant(s) when the environmental problem finally comes to light and liability is affixed. There will in any event be a significant drain in time, trouble and expense in dealing with the problem and obtaining any available relief.

Land Use Restrictions. The buyer has an additional range of concerns involving the intended use of the property. Zoning and land use regulations must be reviewed to determine if the property may lawfully be used or developed as desired. For environmental purposes, this includes such matters as land use restrictions or special permitting or variance requirements arising from the presence of hazardous waste or from the location of the property on wetlands (see Chapters 5 and 6).

Operating Permits. The buyer also should be concerned about the transferability or availability of operating permits, both environmental and nonenvironmental. Depending upon the nature of the projected operations, environmental permits might be required from the federal and state agencies which regulate air pollution and water quality concerning projected air emissions or discharges into water sources. In some urban areas such as Los Angeles, there is increasing pressure to solve the air pollution problem, and stricter requirements are being adopted by the air pollution control agencies. This may make it more difficult in the future to obtain or retain operating permits which are necessary for the conduct of a business, and it will probably become more expensive to comply with regulations in order to stay in operation. Numerous other permit requirements might also be applicable, and the buyer should undertake a complete review to determine the feasibility of the desired operations or development.

9.3   The Stage Is Set

In essence, the seller wants to (i) sell the property for the best possible price, (ii) avoid triggering reporting requirements, and (iii) have the buyer assume all environmental risks. The buyer, on the other hand, wants to (a) discount the price to reflect known or potential environmental problems, (b) conduct a sufficient environmental assessment, (c) preserve environmental claims against the seller or others should contamination be discovered in the future, and (d) use or develop the property for the intended purposes. With these conflicting objectives, the stage is set for some very interesting negotiations. Often the gap between the positions is insurmountable, but techniques are available which might make a transaction possible. The elements which should be considered in negotiations are discussed in Chapter 18.

9.4   Profit Opportunities for the Fearless Entrepreneur

The old proverb about one person's loss being another person's gain can apply to contaminated real property. Profit opportunities are available for a new breed of fearless entrepreneur. It may be possible to acquire contaminated property at a discounted price which makes it worthwhile. Private owners may be willing to sell at a substantial discount to someone willing to take over the problem. Other possible sellers include federal or state agencies or financial institutions which may have acquired title to contaminated properties. Another source would be properties owned by bankrupt entities.

The discount from the fair market value of the property if clean must be greater than the cost of remediation. The buyer can clean up the property, perhaps develop it, and resell it for a profit or hold it as a long-term investment. The risk is great, and that kind of project would best be undertaken only by those with a considerable knowledge of environmental assessment methods, cleanup technology, and how to deal with the applicable governmental agencies and obtain any necessary or desirable approvals and certifications. Such expertise may be available from consultants.

The risk of such an endeavor could be lessened if agreements are reached in advance with the government. Indeed, the EPA has received enough inquiries along those lines that it now has a policy. In June 1989, the EPA acknowledged that it has received "numerous requests for covenants not to sue from prospective purchasers of contaminated property."[6] Such purchasers are, of course, endeavoring to clarify the risk and quantify the cost of such an acquisition by seeking the EPA's agreement in advance that proposed remediation will be acceptable and that the EPA will not require further action. In its policy memorandum, the EPA noted that its basic policy is not to become involved in private real estate transactions. Nevertheless, the EPA proceeded to set forth several criteria for entering into such agreements, including:

---

[6]   EPA Policy Memorandum, *Guidance on Landowner Liability under Section 107(a)(1) of CERCLA, De Minimis Settlements under Section 122(g)(1)(B), and Settlements with Prospective Purchasers of Contaminated Property*, June 6, 1989, at p. 25.

a. Enforcement action is anticipated by the Agency at the facility. . .

b. A substantial benefit, not otherwise available, will be received by the Agency for cleanup. . .

c. The Agency believes that the continued operation of the facility or new site development, with the exercise of due care, will not aggravate or contribute to the existing contamination or interfere with the remedy. . .

d. Due consideration has been given to the effect of continued operations or new development on health risks to those persons likely to be present at the site. . .

e. The prospective purchaser is financially viable.[7]

In other words, the EPA has announced that it will consider such agreements if the prospective purchaser has the financial capability to pay for or to undertake the cleanup, no one will get hurt from the projected use of the property while remedial action is underway, and the deal is good for the Superfund because a private party will finance the cost of cleanup which the Superfund would otherwise have to bear.

If those criteria are met, the agreement must contain specified terms, including the following elements:

(1) *Consideration from the purchaser*, including (a) a cash payment toward the EPA's response action, or removal or remedial activities by the purchaser, (b) a waiver of claims against the United States or the Superfund respecting any contamination at the property or costs of response, (c) the filing in the local land records of a notice that hazardous substances were disposed of at the property and the EPA makes no representation as to permissible uses, and (d) the grant of an irrevocable right of entry to the EPA for response actions under EPA oversight and monitoring compliance with the agreement

---

[7]   *Id.*, at 28-31.

(and in return, the EPA will grant a covenant not to sue under CERCLA and RCRA with respect to contamination existing at the time of acquisition by the purchaser);

(2) *Reservation of rights* to assert various claims such as those arising out of the purchaser's own operation of the facility, releases after the date of acquisition, breach of the agreement or lack of due care with respect to the contamination, any criminal liability, and any claims against persons who are not parties to the agreement;

(3) Acknowledgement that the *scope of response actions* which may be undertaken by the EPA is not limited by the agreement, notwithstanding any interference or closure of the purchaser's operations at the property;

(4) Acknowledgement that *the purchaser must comply with all applicable federal and state laws and exercise due care* regarding the hazardous substances at the facility;

(5) *Disclaimer* of any representations or warranties by the EPA about the hazards at the property or its fitness for any particular use; and

(6) *Procedures*, including the approval of the agreement by the Attorney General.[8]

One might expect that the EPA would not assert such rigorous requirements if the seller is a federal agency (such as the Internal Revenue Service, a military department selling off a closed military base, or the EPA itself). In any case, the policy is in place and the opening is there for prospective purchasers to limit the risk of an acquisition by entering into an agreement in advance with the EPA. Whether similar arrangements can be reached with the applicable state agencies may vary from state to state. Such an approach could, together with a sufficient price discount, make it feasible for a purchaser to acquire a contaminated property to occupy and operate, to hold for investment and lease to others, or to turn over at a profit after cleanup is completed.

---

[8]   *Id.*, at 31-35.

For those who think really big, the "doughnut hole" theory is being developed by some environmental consultants. The premise of this theory is that contaminated property depresses the value of surrounding lands, the doughnut. If all of those properties can be acquired at low prices, the cleanup of the contaminated property in the hole of the doughnut should result in appreciated value of the entire project. This can even make it worthwhile to acquire some contaminated properties which would not pencil out by themselves.

An analogous situation would exist in the case of a company which owns several properties, whether or not contiguous, one of which is contaminated. The value of the company is depressed as a result. Subject to successor liability considerations (see Chapter 14), that company may be an attractive target for an acquisition. The cleanup of the one contaminated asset may result in marked appreciation of the value of the entire company.

We can expect to see further development of such entrepreneurial theories and activities in the coming years. It should even be possible to obtain bank financing for such projects where the price is right, the necessary expertise is available, the cleanup prospects are good, and suitable assurances can be arranged with the applicable governmental agencies.

CHAPTER TEN

LENDERS AND LENDER LIABILITY

10.1   The Lender's Perspective

The interests of lenders also are affected by the environmental laws. First, lenders are concerned about the impact of such laws on the borrower and the collateral, essentially the economic viability of a loan. Second, lenders are concerned about their own exposure to liability. Finally, lenders may need to satisfy the standards of secondary markets or loan participants. These matters will be explored in this chapter. How the lender might deal with these concerns is discussed further in Chapters 18 and 19.

10.2 The Lender's Concerns About the Borrower and the Viability of the Loan

Superfund Liability. As an owner or operator of real property, the borrower may be exposed to liability to the federal or state governments, or to private parties, under the Superfund laws and perhaps other environmental laws. That risk can be assessed with respect to contamination which is known or is discovered before the loan commitment becomes final and unconditional. In that case, the lender can make an appropriate credit determination. However, additional risks exist regarding unknown contamination which might be discovered in the future, or further hazardous substance releases which might occur during the term of the loan. Future environmental liabilities might place a crushing financial burden on the borrower. From the lender's perspective, this substantially increases the risk of loan default and could result in the borrower's bankruptcy. This risk cannot be weighed in a vacuum. Lenders therefore typically require that environmental assessments be conducted by their borrowers before loans are made, in hopes that any problems will be discovered.

Environmental assessments have their limits, however. Even if a seller would allow it, which is unlikely, it is simply not practical to dig up every square foot of soil in order to prove a negative. Thus, there will always be the risk of undiscovered contamination, as well as future hazardous waste problems, which might threaten the ability of the borrower to repay the loan.

The Collateral. Lenders obtain mortgages or deeds of trust encumbering real estate as security in the event of loan default. The value of that collateral is critical to the lender. There must be sufficient value to cover the outstanding balance of indebtedness under the loan. Hazardous substance contamination can diminish the value of the collateral or destroy it altogether. This is another reason why lenders often require environmental assessments, in order to determine, insofar as possible, whether the collateral is sufficiently valuable.

Loan to Value Ratios. Lenders usually require that the value of the collateral not only equal the amount of the loan, but exceed it. A typical standard is that the amount of the loan must be no more than 80 percent of the value of the property. The remaining 20 percent represents the borrower's own investment in the property, which provides an incentive to the borrower not to default on the loan. That equity margin also provides a cushion for the lender to cover the increased balance of a debt as interest payments are not made or expenses are incurred by the lender which are chargeable to the borrower and secured by the mortgage or deed of trust (e.g., loan administration costs, attorneys' fees, etc., as provided by the loan documents). Hazardous waste contamination can diminish the value of collateral, resulting in a loan to value ratio problem. The valuation and appraisal of contaminated property is discussed in Chapter 15.

Land Use and Building Permit Restrictions. Lenders are also affected by laws and regulations restricting land use or the availability of building permits (see Chapters 5 and 6). It can be a rude awakening for a borrower who acquires property and subsequently learns that it may not be used or developed for the purposes intended or that substantial delay and costly remedial measures are required before building permits will be issued or construction may resume. Such an outcome will be equally significant to the lender.

This can be a particular problem for construction lenders (with respect to straight construction loans as well as those with both acquisition and construction components). One might think that construction lenders would have less environmental risk than permanent lenders. After all, the construction lender's involvement with a property is supposed to be temporary. Upon completion of construction, the construction loan will be taken out by a permanent loan. The permanent lender faces the long-term risk of discovery of previously unknown contamination or future contamination from the operations of the borrower or from other sources. However, the risk of uncovering contamination not revealed by any assessment is enhanced in a construction situation (e.g., during grading or excavation for foundations or underground parking). Such a discovery can threaten the viability of the project and the prospects for repayment of a partially or fully funded acquisition or construction loan. Construction lenders therefore may reasonably insist on more thorough environmental assessments than might be acceptable to a permanent lender for an already developed property. An element of risk nevertheless will remain, because environmental assessments are rarely as broadly intrusive as the initial stages of construction.

Building Code Requirements. Construction on wetlands or in a flood zone, even if permitted, can involve extra cost due to special building code requirements. For example, the foundations may have to be built to a point above the high water mark. Such extra measures can be costly, and that should be factored into the construction loan, or a financing problem will arise.

Compliance with Environmental Laws. Lenders are also concerned with the borrower's compliance with environmental laws during operations. The borrower must have, or be able to obtain, all required operating permits, both environmental and nonenvironmental. What permits are required of course depends upon the nature of the business, its equipment, its projected handling of hazardous substances, its actual or designed waste discharge or emission requirements, and the applicable laws of the jurisdiction involved. Once operating permits are obtained, the borrower also must comply with any permit conditions or other applicable laws and regulations. Required pollution controls can increase the borrower's cost of doing business, diminishing the portion of operating revenues which will be available for debt service. These matters would be an appropriate subject for review during a lender's environmental and financial assessment of a proposed loan.

In the construction loan context, the lender may wish to have engineers and consultants review the plans for the facility to assess whether the intended storage and handling of any hazardous materials, and the designed methods of waste discharge, emission or disposal, will be in compliance with applicable laws and regulations (e.g., California's Proposition 65, the federal CWA, RCRA, CAA and state analogues, as well as local fire codes and other applicable ordinances). In addition, the borrower's plan for business operations should be reviewed to ensure that proper measures are included for compliance with business plan, reporting, disclosure and warning requirements which may apply to the business (see Chapters 3 and 4). Although the operating phase of the business will be of more direct concern to the permanent lender, the construction lender wants to make sure that the project is properly planned so that a permanent loan can be obtained by the borrower. The construction lender does not wish to be stuck with a loan on a project which, due to poor environmental, or other, planning by the borrower, will not satisfy the lending standards of a permanent lender. This will be easier to deal with when the permanent lender is known and involved from the beginning. However, quite often a construction project is already underway or nearing completion before a permanent lender is identified.

The violation of permitting or operating regulations can result in significant civil penalties, which may accrue on a daily basis while the violation continues. Such penalties can quickly mount into the hundreds of thousands or millions of dollars. Sometimes criminal fines and even prison terms also may be imposed. These sanctions can have a serious impact on the borrower's ability to repay the loan.

Cleanup Cost Recovery Liens. The borrower's interest in the real estate may be, or may become, subject to cleanup cost recovery liens under CERCLA or applicable state lien laws. The lien priority of the lender's mortgage or deed of trust also is at stake. Before making a loan, the lender should review whether there are any existing cost recovery or other liens or encumbrances affecting the property. Lenders also should be mindful of the risk that such liens might be recorded or filed in the future. This is of particular concern in those states with superlien laws (see Chapter 2), as the state's cleanup cost recovery lien may gain priority over the lender's mortgage or deed of trust. Such indebtedness, whether senior or junior in lien priority to the loan, represents an added financial drain on the borrower and an increased risk of loan default.

Toxic Torts. The borrower, as the owner of contaminated collateral, may become liable under common law principles for personal injuries or property damages suffered by others (see Chapter 8). Such liability also may increase the risk of loan default.

Successor Liability. Depending upon the nature of the transaction being financed, the borrower may inherit environmental liabilities as a successor entity (see Chapter 14). This should also be considered by the lender in making a credit determination.

Creditworthiness of the Borrower. Underlying the foregoing comments is the basic concern with the risk of loan default in the face of environmental problems which the borrower may not be able to afford to remedy and also meet debt service obligations. The identity and

217

creditworthiness of the borrower therefore is critical to the lender in any case where environmental issues might arise. A lender may be willing to finance a transaction involving environmental risk for a borrower who has a strong financial standing and is unlikely to default on the loan regardless whether environmental problems come to light. Even a small environmental risk for the borrower might not be acceptable to the lender with respect to a borrower whose financial condition is weak. In addition, the borrower may be a valued customer who expects the lender to take his risky business along with the good or the borrower will take his business elsewhere. Thus, lenders have difficult credit decisions to make in each case when environmental issues come to light.

10.3   Lender Liability under CERCLA

Another major concern of lenders is with their own exposure to liability under environmental laws, especially CERCLA.

10.3.1   The Secured Party Exemption

Lenders are generally not exposed to environmental liability as long as they act only in the capacity of a lender and secured party. CERCLA expressly excludes from the definition of "owner or operator" any person "who, without participating in the management of a . . . facility, holds indicia of ownership primarily to protect his security interest in the . . . facility."[1] This exclusion is obviously intended to protect lenders from CERCLA liability (although the scope of that protection is a matter of intense controversy). The same situation exists under most state Superfund laws as well.

The wording of the exclusion might seem odd to readers in states where a secured party does not obtain an "ownership" interest in real property, only a "security" interest; "ownership" would not be acquired unless the secured party is the successful purchaser at a foreclosure sale ("lien theory" states). However, Congress used the term "indicia of ownership" because of the common law rule in some states viewing a mortgage as an actual conveyance of ownership, with foreclosure being required only to cut off the borrower's equity of redemption ("title theory" states). The statutory language would also appear to cover the contract for sale technique where the seller retains record title until all

---

[1]   42 U.S.C. § 9601(20)(A).

payments have been made, although beneficial ownership passes to the buyer at the time of the transaction; the seller's interest is really that of a secured party. The legislative history indicates that the exemption also includes lease financing arrangements.[2]

Thus, it appears that the purpose of the secured party exemption is to equalize the treatment of lenders notwithstanding differences in state property law, recognizing that lenders in title theory states should not be liable as "owners" any more than lenders in lien theory states who are not owners under state law. This interpretation of the secured party exemption is supported by the available legislative history of CERCLA. The secured party exemption originated with the definition of "owner" in H.R. 85, the Comprehensive Oil Pollution Liability and Compensation Act, which was introduced in 1979. H.R. 85 was passed by the House, but died in the Senate Committee on Environment and Public Works. But an element of H.R. 85 survived and ultimately found its way into the compromise legislation known as CERCLA. That element was the definition of "owner," complete with a secured party exemption:

> (x) "owner" means any person holding title to, or, in the absence of title, any other indicia of ownership of a vessel or facility, but does not include a person who, without participating in the management or operation of a vessel or facility, holds indicia of ownership primarily to protect his security interest in the vessel or facility.[3]

The House Committee on Merchant Marine and Fisheries' report to the House of Representatives explained the definition of "owner" as including those who hold title or possess some equivalent evidence of ownership, but excluding "certain persons possessing indicia of ownership (such as a financial institution) who, without participating in the management or operation of the vessel or facility, hold title either in order to secure a loan or in connection with a lease financing

---

2   *See* House Report 96-172, Part 1, *reprinted in A Legislative History of the Comprehensive Environmental Response, Compensation, and Liability Act of 1980*, Vol. 1 at 546 (1983).

3   H.R. 85(x) as introduced (reprinted in 3 H. Needham, Superfund: A Legislative History 451-476 (1982)

arrangement..."[4] This clearly reflects that the original intent of the definition was to avoid imposing "owner" liability on secured parties even though they may be deemed as title owners under the vagaries of state law.[5]

This was recognized by the court in *U.S. v. Maryland Bank and Trust Co.*[6] The court noted that the secured party exemption originated with H.R. 85[7] and that H.R. 96-172, Part 1, indicates that Congress intended "to protect banks that hold mortgages in jurisdictions governed by the common law of mortgages..."[8] The court explained that "[u]nder the law of Maryland (and twelve other states) the mortgagee-financial institution actually holds title to the property while the mortgage is in force . . . Congress intended by the exception to exclude these common law title mortgagees from the definition of 'owner' since title was in their hands only by operation of the common law."[9]

However, a lender may incur personal liability under CERCLA upon stepping out of the traditional lender's role, either by foreclosing and actually becoming the owner of contaminated property or by becoming overly involved in the management or operation of the contaminated collateral.

10.3.2 Lender as "Owner" After Foreclosure

A lender may become exposed to liability under CERCLA by foreclosing its security interest and actually becoming the owner of a hazardous waste site (subject to the effect of the new EPA "safe harbor" rule discussed in § 10.3.3-4 below). In the leading case on this issue,

---

4   H.R. 172, 96th Congress, 1st Session, Part 1, at 36 (1979) (reprinted in 1980 U.S. Code Cong. & Admin. News 6181).

5   *See* Burkhart, *Lender/Owner and CERCLA: Title and Liability*, 25 Harvard J. on Legis. 317, 338-339 (1988).

6   632 F.Supp. 573 (D.Md. 1986).

7   *Id.*, at 579.

8   *Id.*, at 579-580.

9   *Id.*, at 579. For additional discussion of the origin and intent of the secured party exemption, and the efforts to change that intent, *see* the discussion on **"Clarification of 'Indicia of Ownership'"** in § 10.3.4-4 below.

U.S. v. Maryland Bank & Trust Co.,[10] the lender foreclosed its lien on a property and, as owner, ultimately became exposed to CERCLA cleanup liability of approximately $550,000; the defaulted loan was for $335,000. The court rejected the lender's argument that foreclosure was simply an action taken to protect its security interest in the collateral. The court determined that the lender had purchased the property at the foreclosure sale "not to protect its security interest, but to protect its investment."[11] Moreover, the court viewed the lender's position as contrary to the objectives of the Superfund legislation:

> Under the scenario put forward by the bank, the federal government alone would shoulder the cost of cleaning up the site, while the former mortgagee-turned-owner, would benefit from the clean-up by the increased value of the now unpolluted land. At the foreclosure sale, the mortgagee could acquire the property cheaply. All other prospective purchasers would be faced with potential CERCLA liability, and would shy away from the sale. Yet once the property has been cleaned at the taxpayers' expense and becomes marketable, the mortgagee-turned-owner would be in a position to sell the site at a profit.
>
> In essence, the defendant's position would convert CERCLA into an insurance scheme for financial institutions, protecting them against possible losses due to the security of loans with polluted properties. Mortgagees, however, already have the means to protect themselves, by making prudent loans. [Footnote: The mortgagees also have the options of not foreclosing and not bidding at the foreclosure sale. Both steps would apparently insulate the mortgagee from liability.] Financial institutions are in a position to investigate and discover potential problems in their secured properties. For many lending institutions, such research is routine. CERCLA will not absolve them from responsibility for their mistakes of judgment.[12]

---

[10]   632 F.Supp. 573 (D.Md. 1986).

[11]   *Id.,* at 579.

[12]   *Id.,* at 580.

Maryland Bank would have done better to walk away from the collateral and write off the loan.

The same result would apply under the Superfund laws of many states (for example, **California**, which adopts the federal standards for Superfund liability and defenses). However, the laws of several states are more favorable to lenders. Under the **Connecticut** Superfund law, a mortgagee who acquires title to contaminated property by foreclosure, or deed in lieu of foreclosure, will not be liable "beyond the value of such real estate."[13] The **Maryland** Superfund law exempts "[a] holder of a mortgage or deed of trust who acquires title through foreclosure to a site containing a controlled hazardous substance,"[14] without any apparent limitation on the exemption. In several other states, the potentially responsible parties include only those who actually caused or contributed to, or were otherwise responsible for, the pollution of the site, so that an innocent lender would apparently have no Superfund liability in the first instance. States with such limited standards of liability include **Arizona**,[15] **Maine**,[16] **Michigan**,[17] **New Jersey**,[18] **Rhode Island**,[19] and **Virginia**.[20] In some states, such as **New Hampshire**, the third party defense is not qualified like CERCLA's, so that as long as the lender is itself innocent of any contribution to the contamination, a defense to liability would apparently exist.[21]

---

[13]   Conn. Gen. Stat. Ann. § 22a-452b. The statute does not specify at what point in time the value is determined (e.g., when the property is still polluted at the time of foreclosure, or later after cleanup has been completed). This would make a significant difference on the extent of lender liability. In any case, the lender would not be liable for cleanup costs exceeding the value of the property, whenever determined.

[14]   Md. Health-Envtl. Code Ann. § 7-201(x)(2).

[15]   Ariz. Rev. Stat. Ann. § 49-283.B.

[16]   Me. Rev. Stat. Ann. Tit. 38 § 1367.

[17]   Mich. Gen. Stats. Ann. § 299.608.

[18]   N.J. Stat. Ann. § 58:10-23.11g.c.

[19]   R.I. Gen. Laws § 23-19.1-22.

[20]   Va. Code Ann. §§ 10.1-1406.C, 44-146.37(B) and 44-146.18:1.

[21]   N.H. Rev. Stat. Ann. § 147-B:10a.

10.3.2-1 What if the Lender Promptly Transfers the Property After Foreclosure?

One of the important lender liability issues is whether the secured party exemption can be retained following a foreclosure where the lender promptly retransfers the property. In *Maryland Bank*, the lender still held title to the property at the time of the court judgment, approximately four years after the foreclosure. It is not surprising that the court found that the lender was the "owner" and was no longer entitled to the secured party exemption. In another case, *U.S. v. Mirabile*,[22] a former mortgagee (American Bank and Trust Company) purchased a contaminated site at foreclosure and assigned its interest four months later. That lender was found to be entitled to the secured party exemption because the foreclosure was undertaken in order to protect its security interest. The *Maryland Bank* court characterized that holding as "generous."[23] While there is a factual difference between these cases regarding the duration of the lender's ownership following foreclosure, the reasoning of the two cases is in direct conflict on this issue.

A lender may wish to rely on *Mirabile*, but it is not always possible as a practical matter to sell contaminated property promptly after a foreclosure. Moreover, the strong policy rationale in *Maryland Bank* was adopted, and the reasoning of the *Mirabile* court was rejected, by the court in *Guidice v. BFG Electroplating and Manufacturing Co.*[24] In that case, the lender held record title to a property for eight months and was later sued in a CERCLA response cost recovery action. The court held that a lender who is the successful bidder at a foreclosure sale is liable just like any other bidder would have been, and therefore the lender was a PRP under CERCLA with respect to the period that it owned the property. In view of evidence that disposals and releases of hazardous substances occurred during that period, the lender's summary judgment motion was denied. The *Guidice* case effectively dashed any hopes of reliance on *Mirabile*. Thus, given the weight of authority on this issue, most lenders have become wary of foreclosing on

---

[22]   15 Envt'l L. Rep. 20,994 (E.D. Pa. 1985).

[23]   632 F.Supp. at 580.

[24]   732 F.Supp. 556 (W.D.Pa. 1989).

contaminated real estate. But see the new EPA "safe harbor" rule discussed below.

10.3.2-2   The Lender as Intervening Landowner

As seen in Chapter 1, the only owners who had liability under the original language of CERCLA were the current owner and the owner at the time of the disposal of the hazardous waste. Thus, *intervening* owners (i.e., those who acquired an already contaminated property but no longer own it upon the commencement of a cost recovery action) had no CERCLA liability whatsoever. This was modified somewhat when SARA adopted the disclosure rule imposing liability on intervening owners who actually knew of the contamination and failed to disclose it to the buyer. Thus, it would appear that a lender could foreclose on already contaminated property and sell the property before any cost recovery action is commenced, with appropriate disclosures, and avoid Superfund liability as an intervening landowner.

When viewed in this way, the result reached in *Mirabile* was actually correct.   American Bank and Trust Company foreclosed on the property several months after all business operations had ceased. The property already was contaminated at that time. The bank assigned its rights to the property four months after the foreclosure, well before any cost recovery action was commenced by the United States. There is no indication in the court opinion of any further disposal or releases of hazardous substances occurring during the four months when the bank owned the property. Thus, the bank may have been an *intervening* landowner with no liability under CERCLA.[25] (In contrast, the lender in *Maryland Bank* was still the owner of the property and clearly a PRP when the cost recovery action was commenced.) The *Mirabile* court did not base its ruling on this analysis, however.

Lenders are nevertheless wary of foreclosing on contaminated property. As a practical matter, it may be very difficult to sell the property, especially where a known hazardous waste condition must be disclosed in order to maintain intervening landowner status. If the lender still owns the property when a cost recovery action is

---

[25]   The disclosure rule (imposing liability on intervening landowners who fail to disclose known contamination) was adopted by SARA in 1986, and thus had no application when the *Mirabile* decision was reached in 1985.

commenced, then the lender will be liable as the current owner. Moreover, as pointed out by the *Guidice* court,[26] the terms "disposal" and "release" have broad definitions under CERCLA, including "leaking," "leaching" (i.e., the movement of hazardous waste through the soil), and numerous other descriptive terms.[27] Thus, unless the preexisting contamination is completely static, there is a risk of continuing disposals or releases by further leakage, leaching or movement of the contamination, even during a relatively short period of ownership between a foreclosure and a prompt resale. In that case, the lender may be exposed to liability as the owner at the time of a disposal or release. However, other courts have taken a narrower view of "disposal" and have excluded subsequent migration or movement, limiting CERCLA § 107(a)(2) PRPs to those who owned or operated a contaminated site when the hazardous substances were introduced into the environment.[28] That interpretation enhances the prospects of being an intervening owner without CERCLA liability.

10.3.2-3 The Third Party Defense.

If intervening landowner status does not apply, it might still be possible, under limited circumstances, for a lender to become an "owner" and nevertheless avoid Superfund liability by mounting a *third party defense*. Such a defense might be successful if the contamination was caused *solely* by a stranger to the property (e.g., a midnight dumper) without any contractual relationship between the lender and the responsible parties. The burden of proof will be on the lender. The lender must additionally establish that it exercised reasonable care with respect to the hazardous substances and took reasonable precautions at

---

26   *See also, Tanglewood East Homeowners v. Charles-Thomas, Inc.*, 849 F.2d 1568, 1573 (5th Cir. 1988); *CPC Int'l v. Aerojet-General Corp.*, 759 F. Supp. 1269 (W.D.Mich. 1991).

27   42 U.S.C. § 9601(22) ("release"); 42 U.S.C. §§ 6903(3) and 9601(29) ("disposal").

28   *See, e.g., Ecodyne Corp. v. Shah*, 718 F.Supp. 1454 (N.D. Cal. 1989), citing *Cadillac Fairview/California, Inc. v. Dow Chemical Co.*, 21 ERC 1108 (N.D. Cal. 1985), *reversed on other grounds*, 840 F.2d 691 (9th Cir. 1988).

the site since acquiring ownership.[29] These elements may be difficult to prove, especially if the borrower, while an owner or operator of the property, was responsible for causing or contributing to any of the contamination.

The innocent landowner portion of the third party defense might be available to a lender who can prove that the hazardous substance condition was not known at the time of the foreclosure notwithstanding a sufficient environmental assessment, and that the contamination was caused by third parties who had no direct or indirect contractual relationship with the lender. The difficulties of proof of this defense are discussed in Chapter 1.

10.3.3 Participation in the Management of the Facility

It is also possible for a lender to lose the benefit of the secured party exemption by actively participating in the management or operations of its borrower (even without any foreclosure). In the *Mirabile* case, the court denied Mellon Bank's motion for summary judgment with respect to its liability under CERCLA due to the alleged participation of a bank officer in the management of the borrower at the site. Among other things, it was alleged that the bank officer was frequently on the site and insisted upon various personnel changes, and that the bank had required the borrower to accept the day-to-day supervision of a particular person. Based on these disputed allegations, the court found that there was a triable issue of fact whether Mellon Bank had participated in the management of the borrower sufficiently to lose the secured party exemption and to become liable under CERCLA.[30]

10.3.3-1   *U.S. v. Fleet Factors*

In *U.S. v. Fleet Factors Corp.*,[31] the lender entered into a factoring agreement with the borrower whereby funds were advanced against the assignment of accounts receivable. The security package also included equipment, inventory and fixtures, as well as a security interest in the

---

[29]   *Id.*, § 9607(b); *U.S. v. Maryland Bank & Trust Co.*, 632 F.Supp. 573, 581 (D. Md. 1986).

[30]   *U.S. v. Mirabile*, 15 Environ. L. Rptr. 20994, 20997 (E.D.Pa. 1985).

[31]   29 ERC 1011 (S.D. Ga. Dec. 22, 1988). *See* below for citation to the appellate court opinion in this case.

facility itself. During the term of the factoring agreement, the lender checked the credit of the borrower's customers before goods were shipped to them. This practice continued pursuant to a court approved factoring agreement after the borrower's bankruptcy, until the borrower finally ceased operations. The lender never foreclosed its security interest in the real estate, but did eventually foreclose its lien on inventory and equipment. In the process of the public auction and the removal of the sold equipment, friable asbestos located on connecting pipes was allegedly disturbed. The EPA subsequently inspected the site and incurred approximately $400,000 in connection with the removal and proper disposal of (i) 700 drums of toxic chemicals, nearly 500 of which were rusty and leaking, and (ii) 44 truck loads of asbestos containing materials. Some time after the EPA response action, title to the real estate was conveyed to the local county government at a foreclosure sale for the nonpayment of state and county taxes. Two days after the tax foreclosure, the United States sued the lender, among others, under CERCLA for the recovery of the response costs.

On motions for summary judgment on the issue of CERCLA liability, the United States first contended that the lender was liable as a current owner or operator of the facility. The court determined that a person liable as a current owner or operator must be one as of the time the government's complaint is filed (or must be the owner or operator immediately before the tax foreclosure took place[32]). The court then rejected the government's contention because the lender's contacts with the property had ceased long before the date of the tax foreclosure.

The government's next contention was that the lender was liable as an owner or operator of the facility at the time of the disposal of the hazardous substances because the lender had participated in the management of the facility both while its borrower was in business and later at the time of the auction, thereby losing the secured party exemption. The court ruled, as a matter of law, that the lender had not participated in the management of the facility and therefore had no CERCLA liability in connection with its activities as a lender up to the time of the auction. In a passage which gave some comfort to lenders pending the appeal of the case, the judge stated:

---

[32] 42 U.S.C. § 9601(20)(A)(iii).

> I interpret the phrases "participating in the management of a . . . facility" and "primarily to protect his security interest," to permit secured creditors to provide financial assistance and general, and even isolated instances of specific, management advice to its debtors without risking CERCLA liability if the secured creditor does not participate in the day-to-day management of the business or facility either before or after the business ceases operation.[33]

The court then concluded that the lender's activities, such as checking the credit of the borrower's customers before goods were shipped, did not rise to the level of participation in management sufficient to impose CERCLA liability.

On the other hand, the court did not dismiss the government's claims regarding the involvement of the lender or its agents in the disturbance and release of asbestos containing materials at the time of auction. Disputed facts regarding those allegations could not be resolved without a trial.

At this point, it was thought that a lender would risk loss of the secured party exemption only by foreclosing its security interest and actually becoming the owner of the property (*Maryland Bank, Guidice*) or by actively participating in the day-to-day management of the operations of the facility (*Mirabile, Fleet Factors* [district court opinion]). While this sounds fairly clear and workable, it was only the beginning of one of the most remarkable and controversial developments in the history of lender liability.

First, there was much speculation among legal commentators over exactly what activities a lender could pursue without participating in the day-to-day management and losing the benefit of the secured party exemption. Then, the issue finally become the subject of two federal appellate court opinions, by the Court of Appeals for the Eleventh Circuit in the *Fleet Factors* case and by the Court of Appeals for the Ninth Circuit in *In re Bergsoe Metal*. The decisions in those cases have only intensified the controversy.

---

[33]   *U.S. v. Fleet Factors Corp.*, 29 ERC 1011, 1014 (S.D. Ga. 1988).

In *U.S. v. Fleet Factors*,[34] the Eleventh Circuit took an unanticipated view of the case. As noted above, the district court determined that the secured party exemption was not lost until the lender's agents entered the property to conduct a foreclosure sale of equipment, resulting in disturbance of asbestos. The Eleventh Circuit felt that the standard applied by the district court was too "permissive" a standard for secured lenders.

The court ruled that in order to lose the benefit of the secured party exemption and become liable under CERCLA **as an "owner"** of contaminated property, a lender need only participate in the financial management of a facility to a degree indicating a "capacity to influence" the borrower's hazardous waste practices, even if that influence is not exercised. Participation in financial management which is sufficient to infer such a "capacity to influence" (and, hence, deemed "ownership") may occur under circumstances which would not constitute participation in day-to-day operations sufficient to become liable as an "operator."[35]

Applying this standard, the court reviewed the involvement of the lender in the financial affairs of the borrower and found the facts sufficient to result in loss of the secured party exemption at a much earlier point in time than had been found by the district court:

> Fleet's involvement with SPW [the borrower], according to the government, increased substantially after SPW ceased printing operations at the Georgia plant on February 27, 1981, and began to wind down its affairs. Fleet required SPW to seek its approval before shipping its goods to customers, established the price for excess inventory, dictated when and to whom the finished goods should be shipped, determined when employees should be laid off, supervised the activity of the office administrator at the site, received and processed SPW's employment and tax forms, controlled access to the facility, and contracted with Baldwin to dispose of the fixtures and equipment at SPW. These facts, if proved, are sufficient to remove Fleet from the protection of the secured creditor exemption. Fleet's involvement in the

---

34   901 F.2d 1550 (11th Cir. 1990).

35   *Id.*, at 1557-1558.

financial management of the facility was pervasive, if not complete.[36]

The court also noted that it was not even necessary to rely on an inference that Fleet had the capacity to influence the borrower's hazardous waste practices. Fleet "actively asserted its control over the disposal of hazardous wastes at the site by prohibiting SPW from selling several barrels of chemicals to potential buyers. As a result, the barrels remained at the facility unattended until the EPA acted to remove the contamination."[37] The court further stated that the government's allegations would indicate that Fleet was involved in the operational management of the facility sufficiently to impose CERCLA liability on Fleet, although the court chose to "forego an analysis of Fleet's liability as an operator" and to base its decision on "owner" liability.[38]

The Eleventh Circuit opinion in *Fleet Factors* sent shock waves across the country and has been the subject of intense comment and criticism.[39] The opinion appeared to narrow the secured party

---

[36]   *Id.*, at 1559.

[37]   *Id.*, fn. 13, at 1559.

[38]   *Id.*, at 1556, fn. 6, and at 1559. Because of Fleet's extensive involvement in the operational management of the borrower, and the court's own comments that the case could have been resolved on that basis, it has been suggested by a number of commentators and by the EPA that the standard enunciated by *Fleet Factors* on "owner" liability is mere *dicta*.

[39]   *See, e.g.*, Schmall and Tellier, *Hazardous Lending: Making Loans in the Post-Fleet Factors Era*, 8 California Real Property Journal 1-9 (Summer 1990); Katcher, *Lenders' Liability for Environmental Hazards*, 20 Real Estate Review 72-76 (Fall 1990); Madden, *Will the CERCLA be Unbroken? Repairing the Damage after Fleet Factors*, 59 Fordham Law Review 135-168 (1990); Unterberger, *Lender Liability Under Superfund: What the Congress Meant to Say Was...*, Toxics Law Reporter 541-545 (9-19-90); Hamlin, Prince & Schutz, *The Ability to Control Test: Expanding CERCLA Liability Beyond Lenders?*, Toxics Law Reporter 833-840 (11-28-90); Goodman, *CERCLA's (Insecure) Secured Creditor Exemption*, The Practical Real Estate Lawyer 85-95 (May 1991); Leibow, *A Bright Line Drawn in the Right Place: What Constitutes Acceptable Management Participation Under CERCLA's Security Interest Exemption?*, 19 Cal. Bankr. J. No. 2, 123-159 (1991); Notes, *Cleaning Up the Debris After Fleet Factors: Lender Liability and CERCLA's Security Interest Exemption*, 104 Harvard Law Review 1249-1268 (1991).

exemption and to broaden the environmental responsibility of secured lenders (and perhaps anyone with a "capacity to influence"). The stated policy objectives of the court were to encourage lenders to undertake environmental reviews before making loans and then to monitor and insist on borrowers' compliance with environmental standards, in view of the potential for CERCLA liability.[40]

As a practical matter, the *Fleet Factors* decision faces a lender with the choice of not exercising its rights to exert financial controls in the case of a nonperforming loan or, if it must do so, going further to monitor the debtor's hazardous waste practices as well. In the latter case, the lender's objectives would be to ensure that disposals which might result in liability do not occur during the lender's period of deemed "ownership." Of course, where influence over such practices is actually exercised, CERCLA liability would follow. But the risk of liability would exist even if the lender does not oversee those practices, so that the lender may be better off by taking an active role in the hope of avoiding or limiting the risk. This, in effect, casts secured lenders in the role of environmental police, at least where the lender has crossed the "participation" threshold. Lenders may or may not be equipped to handle this role.

10.3.3-2 *In re Bergsoe Metal*[41]

The Ninth Circuit considered a case which was factually at the other end of the "participation" spectrum. In a bankruptcy case, the Oregon Department of Environmental Quality had found contamination at the site of a lead recycling plant. The builder and operator of the plant, Bergsoe Metal Corporation, had been put into involuntary bankruptcy by a bank creditor. The bank and the bankruptcy trustee for Bergsoe Metal subsequently filed suit against the owners of Bergsoe Metal for the costs of cleaning up the contamination. Those defendants filed a third party complaint against the Port of St. Helens, the municipal entity which held record title to the site, claiming that the Port was liable for cleanup costs under CERCLA.

---

[40]   *U.S. v. Fleet Factors*, 901 F.2d 1550, 1558-1559 (11th Cir. 1990).

[41]   *In re Bergsoe Metal Corporation*, 910 F.2d 668 (9th Cir. 1990).

The Ninth Circuit first determined that the Port was a secured party even though it held record title. The case involved a sale-and-leaseback transaction whereby the site was "sold" to the Port and leased back to Bergsoe Metal. The Port issued revenue bonds which served as the vehicle for financing the construction of the plant. "Rent" under the "lease" was equal to the principal and interest due under the revenue bonds; the Port mortgaged the plant to the bank and assigned all of its rights under the lease to the bank as trustee for the bondholders, and Bergsoe Metal had the right to repurchase the facility for $100 once the bonds had been paid in full. Under these circumstances, the Ninth Circuit had no difficulty in finding that the Part was not really an "owner." The sale-and-leaseback transaction was not a true sale, but was a sophisticated financing transaction. The Port held "indicia of ownership" primarily for security purposes. The true owner was Bergsoe Metal, and the Port was a secured party.

The court then considered whether the Port was nevertheless liable due to loss of the secured party exemption under CERCLA based on alleged "participation" in the management of the facility, including the rights reserved to the Port as lessor in the lease. Under the facts of the case, however, the Port's only participation had been in connection with the initial revenue bond financing and in its subsequent consent to a workout due to its technical position as owner/lessor of the site--the real interested parties to the workout being Bergsoe Metal and the bank as trustee of the bondholders. Regardless of the rights reserved in the documents, the Port had in fact never been involved in the actual management of the facility and therefore did not lose the benefit of the secured party exemption.

In its opinion, the Ninth Circuit noted the ruling of the Eleventh Circuit in *Fleet Factors*, but left

> for another day the establishment of a Ninth Circuit rule on this difficult issue. It is clear from the statute that, whatever the precise parameters of "participation," there must be *some* actual management of the facility before a secured creditor will fall outside the exception. Here there was none, and we therefore need not engage in line drawing... As did the Eleventh Circuit in *Fleet Factors*, we hold that a creditor must, as a threshold matter, exercise

actual management authority before it can be held liable for action or inaction which results in the discharge of hazardous wastes. Merely having the power to get involved in management, but failing to exercise it, is not enough.[42]

This laid to rest the concern raised by some in the wake of *Fleet Factors* that merely having the right in loan documents to become involved in management was enough to lose the exemption. Of course, that was not the holding of *Fleet Factors*. Even under the Eleventh Circuit's standard, there was a period of years where the factoring arrangement was in place, with all the associated documentation and reserved rights, before the borrower had financial difficulties and Fleet actually began to exercise its rights over financial management, resulting in loss of the exemption.

Thus, pervasive participation in financial management may expose a secured party to "owner" liability under CERCLA (*Fleet Factors*), but no such exposure exists when there is **no** participation in management (*Bergsoe*). Where the threshold lies between these extremes remains unclear. Secured parties may take comfort in the fact that the Ninth Circuit did not adopt the "capacity to influence" standard established by the Eleventh Circuit, suggesting that there may be some policy difference between the courts as to where the "participation" threshold lies. However, the Ninth Circuit did not actually reject the Eleventh Circuit standard either, leaving the issue for another day. The existence of such a policy difference therefore must be clarified in future cases.

10.3.3-3 Legislative Response

In response to the growing fear of lender liability following the opinion in *Fleet Factors*, a number of bills have been introduced in Congress which would address the concerns of the financial industry.

H.R. 1450 (Rep. John La Falce). The original version of this bill (H.R. 4494) was introduced in April 1990 by Rep. La Falce. That bill would have amended the CERCLA definition of "owner or operator" to exclude designated lending institutions which acquire ownership or control of a facility to realize on a security interest held in a facility, and

---

[42]   *Id.*, at 672 and fn.3 at 673.

also to exclude corporate or individual fiduciaries administering a trust or estate of which a facility is a part. The bill was reintroduced, with extensive revisions, as H.R. 1450 on March 14, 1991, with the express intention of codifying the January 1991 Draft EPA rule (see § 10.3.3-4 below), although the language of the bill is not identical to the draft or the final EPA rule.

However, as proposed in March 1991, H.R. 1450 would amend CERCLA and define terms for the secured party exemption using some of the language from the draft EPA rule, and would establish that "indicia of ownership" includes any security interest. Note that this would depart from the original intent of the exemption which was needed only in title states as discussed in § 10.3.1 above. H.R. 1450 is still pending in Congress.

S. 651 (Sen. Jake Garn). The original version of this bill (S. 2827) was introduced in June 1990 by Sen. Garn. That bill would have exempted from CERCLA liability those depository institutions, other mortgage lenders and federal banking agencies which acquire a contaminated property through foreclosure *or* which hold, control or manage such property pursuant to the terms of an extension of credit or in a fiduciary capacity, unless the exempt entity is actually at fault in connection with the release or disposal of the hazardous substance or actually benefitted from the response, removal or remedial action. The Garn bill was reintroduced, with extensive revisions, as S. 651 on March 13, 1991. As revised, the Garn bill would:

- amend banking acts;

- limit the strict liability (re hazardous substance releases) of insured depository institutions and mortgage lenders to the "actual benefit" conferred by removal, remedial or other response action by another party (not to exceed the fair market value of the property after the action);

- exclude liability of insured depository institutions and mortgage lenders based solely on unexercised capacity to influence operations;

- limit the exclusion and apply liability if the otherwise exempt entity causes or contributes to the release of hazardous substances, if after foreclosure reasonable steps are not taken to prevent continued releases of hazardous substances known or discovered, or if the otherwise exempt entity actively directs or conducts operations resulting in release of hazardous substances;

- provide additional protections for federal banking or lending agencies, which would extend to the first subsequent purchaser from the agency; and

- require the applicable agencies to develop and promulgate environmental assessment procedures and standards for depository institutions and mortgage lenders, with final regulations within 180 days of enactment of the bill.

S. 651 was not adopted by Congress, but further legislative efforts along these lines are anticipated.

H.R. 1643 (Reps. Owen/Weldon). The original version of this bill (H.R. 2787) was introduced by Rep. Weldon on June 28, 1989. That bill would have amended CERCLA to clarify what specific steps must be undertaken in order to qualify as a Phase I environmental assessment and to provide a purchaser of property with the "innocent landowner" defense. The bill was reintroduced by Reps. Owens/Weldon on March 22, 1991, as H.R. 1643 with a new section on lender liability (the "Superfund Liability Clarification Act"), which would, among other things:

- amend CERCLA to establish that "indicia of ownership" includes any security interest;

- limit the secured party exemption to mortgage lenders, insured depository institutions or Federal lending institutions who comply with environmental procedures and guidelines to be established by EPA.

- define "participation in management" to exclude:

-- selling collateral;

-- complying with environmental guidelines (*e.g.*, Phase I Environmental Audits);

-- engaging in reasonable management of a facility upon discovery of contamination while acting to administer or wind down affairs of the owner or while proceeding diligently to pass title;

-- having the capacity to affect hazardous waste disposal management decisions; and

-- engaging in workout activities or other actions reasonably necessary to protect a security interest;

- impose liability (notwithstanding the exclusion) if the secured party causes or contributes, by act or omission, to a release or threatened release of hazardous substance; and

- require the EPA to promulgate regulations to carry out the amendments.

Like H.R. 1450, this bill would depart from the original intent of the exemption by providing that *any* security interest constitutes "indicia of ownership," in effect treating all states as title states without regard to the differences in property law between title states and lien states. This would amount to a reversal of the original intent of the secured party exemption, from a uniform rule of nonliability for secured parties under the "owner" PRP category, to a uniform rule of liability as "owner," subject only to the exemption.

Another significant consequence of this proposed legislation is the effect it may have on noninstitutional lenders, such as sellers who take back a mortgage or deed of trust to secure payment of the deferred portion of the purchase price, or any other person who is not in the mortgage lending business but who obtains a deed of trust as security. The bill would by definition treat such lenders as "owners" because of their security interest and yet preclude the availability of the secured party exemption to them because they are not defined mortgage lenders, insured depository institutions or Federal lending institutions. This would have a devastating effect on noninstitutional secured parties, and such a person would be ill advised to obtain a security interest in potentially contaminated property if this legislation were to become law in its proposed form. H.R. 1643 is still pending in Congress.

10.3.3-4 EPA "Safe Harbor" Rule

Under pressure from the financial industry, and perhaps fearing overbroad legislative exemption for secured parties, the federal Environmental Protection Agency (EPA) has jumped into the fray. At hearings held in August 1990 regarding the foregoing bills, James Strock (then the EPA's Assistant Administrator for Enforcement, and now the Secretary of the new Cal-EPA) testified that the EPA was reviewing the issue of lender liability under CERCLA and expected to promulgate an administrative rule clarifying the scope of lender liability and defining a "safe harbor" for lenders which would allow them to foreclose on property and accomplish workouts of nonperforming loans without incurring CERCLA liability. In addition, the EPA would clarify the meaning of "participating in the management" to allow lenders to exercise certain rights and remedies in the event of borrower default without losing the secured party exemption. Mr. Strock stated that the subject was complex and required an appropriate balance between the legitimate concerns of the financial industry and the valid public policy objectives of preserving the Superfund and ensuring responsible conduct by secured parties when contamination is suspected or discovered. Mr. Strock suggested that these concerns could be "best addressed promptly through administrative clarification" (rather than legislation).[43] It is apparent that the EPA would prefer to adopt an administrative rule rather than see CERCLA amended by Congress.

Since then, the EPA indeed prepared a so-called "safe harbor" rule, although the rate of progress did not live up to Mr. Strock's optimistic testimony that the rule would be issued promptly. Drafts of an EPA rule were leaked,[44] to varying degrees of consternation. The Proposed

---

[43]   *See* the Statement of James M. Strock, Assistant Administrator for Enforcement, United States Environmental Protection Agency, Before the Subcommittee on Transportation and Hazardous Materials of the House Committee on Energy and Commerce, United States House of Representatives, August 2, 1990, at page 2.

[44]   *See Draft EPA Rule re Lender Liability under CERCLA* (September 14, 1990), reprinted at BNA's Environment Reporter, pp. 1162 et seq. (10-12-90); *Draft EPA Rule re Lender Liability under CERCLA* (January 24, 1991), reprinted at BNA's Environment Reporter, pp. 1908 et seq. (2-22-91).

Rule was formally published for comment in June 1991.[45] After public comment and further revision, the Final Rule was adopted on April 29, 1992, and was codified as new Subpart L under 40 CFR Part 300, §§ 300.1100 and 300.1105 (part of the National Oil and Hazardous Substances Pollution Contingency Plan; Lender Liability Under CERCLA).[46] Representatives of the EPA have informally advised that the EPA was conforming its own enforcement activities to be consistent with the Proposed Rule pending the promulgation of the Final Rule.

A comparison of the drafts of the Proposed Rule shows that the EPA started out with a strong inclination to cast secured lenders in the role of environmental police, including stringent requirements to take environmentally beneficial actions at various stages throughout the life of a loan or risk loss of the secured party exemption. Those requirements were nowhere to be found in the statute and strong objections were raised as a result. Each subsequent draft, and the Final Rule, has been more favorable to lenders. Nevertheless, important concerns and pitfalls remain for lenders.

The Final Rule can be analyzed by focussing on the various stages of a loan.

Pre-Loan Phase. As an example of the shift in favor of lenders, the initial draft of the rule, in September 1990, expressly required that lenders conduct pre-loan environmental assessments of proposed collateral as a condition of the secured party exemption. The January 1991 Draft deleted that requirement, but continued to exert great pressure on lenders by saying that such assessments would be "highly probative" evidence of action consistent with the secured party exemption, a "badge of good commercial practice" and "highly probative for determining whether the totality of the [security] holder's actions undertaken to protect the security interest are consistent with the Section 101(20)(A) exemption."

In contrast, the June 1991 Proposed Rule contained none of that pressure, and the Final Rule states:

---

[45] Proposed Rule and Request for Comment re Lender Liability Under CERCLA (June 5, 1991), published at 56 Federal Register 28798 (6-24-91).

[46] The Final Rule was published at 57 Federal Register 18344 (4-29-92).

Neither the statute nor this regulation requires a holder to conduct or require an inspection to qualify for the exemption, and the liability of a holder cannot be based on or affected by the holder not conducting or not requiring an inspection.[47] ... Nor can liability be premised on a holder's having undertaken or required an inspection, and nothing in this rule should be understood to discourage a holder from undertaking or requiring such an inspection in circumstances deemed appropriate by the holder.[48]

The EPA was apparently forced to recognize that it could not impose a pre-loan inspection requirement, but it encourages such inspections by including them within the safe harbor.

If an inspection reveals contamination, the EPA goes on the indicate that the security holder may, for example, (i) refuse to extend credit, (ii) take other uncontaminated property as security, (iii) proceed to obtain a security interest in the contaminated property (where the contamination is not significant or the risk of default is slight), or (iv) require cleanup as a condition of the extension of credit. Those actions are also within the safe harbor.[49]

During Loan Term. The initial draft of the rule contained language which would have required a lender to undertake environmental "policing" activities during the term of a loan, or risk loss of the secured party exemption. The Final Rule contains a subtle but significant softening of language which apparently deletes the requirement for

---

[47] 40 CFR § 300.1100(c)(2)(i).

[48] EPA Comments, 57 Federal Register at 18376.

[49] EPA comments, 57 Federal Register at 18377. Logically, a prospective lender who has not yet made a loan or obtained a security interest could hardly be deemed an "owner" subject to CERCLA liability. However, there is a risk that a lender could be viewed as an "operator" by actually exerting influence over a prospective borrower's hazardous waste practices, by, for example, requiring cleanup as a condition of the loan. The Final Rule would apply the safe harbor in such instances.

environmental policing activities.[50] However, environmental policing activities are permissible and will not constitute "participating in the management" of the facility. Permissible, safe harbor, activities include:

- requiring the borrower to clean up the vessel or facility during the term of the security interest;[51]

- requiring the borrower to comply or come into compliance with applicable federal, state, and local environmental and other rules and regulations during the term of the security interest;[52]

- securing or exercising authority to monitor or inspect the vessel or facility (including on-site inspections) in which indicia of ownership are maintained, or the borrower's business or financial condition during the term of the security interest; or

- taking other actions to adequately police the loan or security interest (such as requiring a borrower to comply with any warranties, covenants, conditions, representations or promises from the borrower).[53]

---

[50] Compare "...the exemption requires that a secured creditor undertake actions consistent with CERCLA when protecting the security interest..." (in the September 1990 Draft), and "...the exemption requires that the actions undertaken by a security holder in the course of protecting a security interest be consistent with CERCLA..." (in the January 1991 Draft), with "the exemption requires that the actions undertaken by a holder in overseeing or managing the loan or other obligation be consistent with those of a person whose indicia of ownership in a facility is are held primarily to protect security interest ..." (in the Final Rule, 57 Federal Register at 18377).

[51] While it is clear that the EPA encourages lender-required cleanups and would propose to leave the exemption intact, how would a *court* treat such an actual display by the lender of influence and participation in the hazardous waste management of a facility?

[52] The EPA had no choice on this one in view of the *Bergsoe Metals* and *Fleet Factors* cases, as well as the statute itself, which require some actual participation by a lender in management before the exemption would be lost, something more than covenants, default remedies or other provisions contained in loan documents.

[53] 40 CFR § 300.1100(c)(2)(ii)(A).

The Final Rule makes it clear that such requirements "may be contained in contractual (e.g., loan) documents," and "liability cannot be premised on the existence of such terms, or upon the holder's actions that ensure that the facility is managed in an environmentally sound manner."[54]   The "mere capacity, or ability to influence, or the unexercised right to control facility operations" will not be enough to lose the exemption.[55]

What conduct will constitute "participation in the management" during the term of a loan resulting in loss of the secured party exemption? The Final Rule answers this important question as follows:

> A holder is participating in management, while the borrower is still in possession of the vessel or facility encumbered by the security interest, only if the holder either:
>
> (i) Exercises decisionmaking control over the borrower's environmental compliance, such that the holder has undertaken responsibility for the borrower's hazardous substance handling or disposal practices; or
>
> (ii) Exercises control at a level comparable to that of a manager of the borrower's enterprise, such that the holder has assumed or manifested responsibility for the overall management of the enterprise encompassing the day-to-day decisionmaking of the enterprise with respect to:
>
> (A)   Environmental compliance or
>
> (B)   All, or substantially all, of the operational (as opposed to financial or administrative) aspects of the enterprise other than environmental compliance. Operational aspects of the enterprise include functions such as that of facility or plant manager, operations manager, chief operating officer, or chief executive officer.

---

[54]   EPA comments, 57 Federal Register at 18377. As noted above, the part about loan terms is consistent with the rulings in the *Bergsoe Metals* and *Fleet Factors* cases, but the concept stated in the latter part of the last quoted language is not evident from existing case law.

[55]   40 CFR § 300.1100(c)(1).

> Financial or administrative aspects include functions such as that of credit manager, accounts payable/receivable manager, personnel manager, controller, chief financial officer, or similar functions.[56]

The EPA refers to this as the "general test of management participation." To the benefit of lenders, it appears that participation in the financial or administrative management of the borrower's business would be permitted, and that, in order to lose the exemption, there must be a nexus between the control exercised by the lender and the borrower's hazardous waste disposal or hazardous substance handling practices or its environmental compliance in general. The test would not, however, allow lenders to take over operational control of a business, carving out environmental compliance.

There may be a fundamental conflict between this general test and the safe harbor provisions. What if it is necessary for the lender to exercise "decision-making control over the borrower's environmental compliance" (which falls outside of the safe harbor) in order to "ensure that the facility is managed in an environmentally sound manner" (which is within the safe harbor)? Thus, although the Final Rule would provide a significant degree of comfort to secured lenders with respect to their activities during the term of a loan, there may still be difficulty in determining the threshold of impermissible "participation in the management" when the lender's activities have an impact on the borrower's environmental compliance.

Workout Phase. The Final Rule presents little change in concept at the workout phase as compared to earlier drafts. It would be permissible for a lender to work out a troubled loan, but there are pitfalls.

Permitted Workout Activities. Permitted lender activities during the workout phase may include the following:

- restructuring or renegotiating the terms of the security interest;

- requiring payment of additional rent or interest;

- exercising forbearance;

---

[56]   40 CFR § 300.1100(c)(1).

- requiring or exercising rights pursuant to an assignment of accounts or other amounts owing to an obligor;

- requiring or exercising rights pursuant to an escrow agreement pertaining to amounts owing to an obligor;

- providing specific or general financial or other advice, suggestions, counseling, or guidance; and

- exercising any right or remedy the holder is entitled to by law or under any warranties, covenants, conditions, representations or promises from the borrower."[57]

In general, lenders may work out a nonperforming loan to "prevent, cure or mitigate a default" or to "preserve, or prevent the diminution of, the value of the security," and when workout activities are undertaken, the security holder "will remain within the exemption provided that the holder does not by such action participate in the management of the vessel or facility as provided in 40 CFR 300.1100(c)(1)."[58]

Borrower Control. The Final Rule and EPA comments make it clear that the borrower must remain in possession and ultimate decisionmaking control of the operations of the facility during the workout phase. A security holder voids the exemption when it divests the borrower of decisionmaking control over facility operations.

Hidden within the "borrower control" concept is a significant pitfall for lenders. One of the traditional remedies available to lenders upon default is the right to go to court to obtain the appointment of a receiver to take control of the collateral. This is frequently done concurrently with the filing of a judicial foreclosure action, in order to preserve the collateral from waste or misappropriation by the borrower. It could be essential from a remedies standpoint, and even environmentally beneficial, to have a receiver appointed to take control of the security pending the results of litigation or a workout of the troubled loan. The borrower control aspect of the Final Rule may, in effect, face a lender with the risk of losing the secured party exemption if the lender exercises its right to have a receiver appointed by a court with a sufficient degree of authority over the collateral to divest the borrower of

---

[57]   40 CFR § 300.1100(c)(2)(ii)(B).

[58]   *Id.*

decisionmaking control. It would appear to be permissible, however, to have a receiver appointed merely to collect the rents or exercise other financial or administrative functions, as distinguished from operational management encompassing environmental compliance.

This aspect of the Final Rule appears to be illogical in view of other provisions. There is no apparent reason why a lender should be denied the valuable remedy of the appointment of a receiver to take charge of the collateral, particularly where the Final Rule would allow a lender to effect the ultimate divestment of borrower control, foreclosure, and yet retain the exemption (see below). The Final Rule appears to ignore state law principles that a receiver acts with authority of a court and that the lender is generally not liable for the acts of a receiver. It could be argued that it is the court, not the secured party, who has divested the borrower of control when a receiver is appointed, so that the exemption should not be lost. In any case, lenders who seek the appointment of a receiver should consider the scope of the receiver's authority and the effect of the borrower control aspect of the Final Rule.

Foreclosure and Holding for Disposition and Liquidation. With regard to the foreclosure and post-foreclosure phase of a loan, the Final Rule includes astonishing new protections for lenders, but some pitfalls and questions remain.

Foreclosure. The Final Rule contains the remarkable concept that "indicia of ownership" to "protect a security interest" may include full legal title through foreclosure or deed in lieu of foreclosure. Under applicable state property law, a lender who is the successful bidder at a foreclosure sale, or who receives a deed to the property in lieu of foreclosure, becomes the fee title owner of the property. This is actual ownership, not merely an "indicia" of ownership; the foreclosed security interest merges into title and no longer exists.[59] However, it is necessary for the EPA to indulge in the fiction of a continuing security interest in order to support the post-foreclosure safe harbor, without an amendment of the statute. It remains to be seen whether this fiction will be respected by the courts.

---

[59] As noted above, the courts in *Maryland Bank* and *Guidice* would treat a lender who obtains title following foreclosure just like any other owner.

The Final Rule sets forth certain requirements for a secured party to remain within the safe harbor following a foreclosure:

Temporary Acquisition. The acquisition must be temporary, for subsequent disposition, as a necessary incident to protection of the security interest.

Outbidding. The exemption would not be available to a foreclosing lender who has outbid or refused bids from parties offering "fair consideration" for the property. Such actions indicate that the property is no longer being held "primarily to protect the security interest" and is indicative of investment intent which is not protected by the secured party exemption. *Fair consideration* is defined as:

> an amount equal to or in excess of the sum of the outstanding principal (or comparable amount in the case of a lease that constitutes a security interest) owed to the holder immediately preceding the acquisition of full title (or possession in the case of property subject to a lease financing transaction) pursuant to foreclosure and its equivalents, plus any unpaid interest, rent or penalties (whether arising before or after foreclosure and its equivalents), plus all reasonable and necessary costs, fees, or other charges incurred by the holder incident to work out, foreclosure and its equivalents, retention, maintaining the business activities of the enterprise, preserving, protecting and preparing the vessel or facility prior to sale, or-release of property held pursuant to a lease financing transaction (whether by a new lease financing transaction or substitution of the lessee) or other disposition, plus-response costs incurred under section 107(d)(1) of CERCLA or at the direction of an on-scene coordinator; less any amounts received by the holder in connection with any partial disposition of the property, net revenues received as a result of maintaining the business activities of the enterprise, and any amounts paid by the borrower subsequent to the acquisition of full title (or possession in the case property subject to a lease financing transaction) pursuant to foreclosure and its equivalents. In the case of a holder maintaining indicia of ownership primarily to

protect a junior security interest, fair consideration is the value of all outstanding higher priority security interests plus the value of the security interest held by the junior holder, each calculated as set forth in the preceding sentence.[60]

In limited circumstances, the lender is justified in requiring more than "fair consideration," i.e., where the lender "is required, in order to avoid liability under federal or state law, to make a higher bid, to obtain a higher offer, or to seek or obtain an offer in a different manner."[61]

This bidding limitation may become a trap for the unwary bank officer bidding at a foreclosure sale. It is not unusual for a lender to bid up to the full amount of the secured indebtedness (including principal and accrued interest and other charges).[62] In some cases, a lender might even be inclined to bid a little more if there is substantial equity value over and above the amount of the encumbrance. After all, the lender may wish to obtain the value of that equity instead of allowing a stranger to do so. Lenders would like to profit in some instances, to cover losses on other mortgage loans. But if a third party bids at least "fair consideration," the lender dare not bid even one penny more or the secured party exemption will be lost under the Final Rule.

Thus, if there are any environmental liability concerns, the bidding officer should make the necessary calculation to avoid outbidding or refusing bids which equal or exceed "fair consideration." Alternatively, the bidding officer should be able to establish necessary justification for requiring higher consideration as permitted by the Final Rule in limited circumstances.

Holding for Disposition and Liquidation. In a significant concession to lenders, the Final Rule would allow the secured party to

---

[60]   40 CFR § 300.1100(d)(2)(ii)(A).

[61]   40 CFR § 300.1100(d)(2)(ii).

[62]   This may be a mistake if the lender plans to proceed personally against the debtor for a deficiency judgment on the debt. By bidding the full amount of the debt, it is deemed paid in full and there is no deficiency.

"maintain business activities"[63] in order to "protect or prepare the secured asset prior to sale or other disposition." Other permissible alternatives are to sell, liquidate and promptly wind up operations.[64] The secured party exemption continues unless:

- the security holder fails, within *twelve months* following the acquisition of marketable title (e.g. following the expiration of an applicable redemption period after foreclosure), to list the property and begin advertising the property for sale or disposition on at least a *monthly* basis in a qualified publication or newspaper; or

- the security holder "rejects, or fails to act upon within 90 days of receipt of a written, *bona fide*, firm offer of fair consideration for the property received at any time after *six months* following foreclosure or its equivalents." A "written, bona fide, firm offer" means "a legally enforceable, commercially reasonable, cash offer solely for the foreclosed vessel or facility, including all material terms of the transaction, from a ready, willing and able purchaser who demonstrates to the holder's satisfaction the ability to perform."[65]

This portion of the Final Rule appropriately recognizes that it may take a long time to sell a contaminated property. Flexibility is allowed, as long as marketing efforts are timely initiated and pursued and as long as an offer of "fair consideration" is accepted. There are significant problems, however.

It could be disputed whether the material terms of an offer are "commercially reasonable." The lender would be at risk of losing the exemption if it rejects an offer that could be viewed later by a court as commercially reasonable. With regard to the calculation of "fair consideration," net operating revenues earned after a foreclosure have

---

63   The EPA evidently could not bring itself to use the word "operate," as that would clearly fall within the "operator" category of CERCLA liability. Instead, the EPA uses the phrase "maintain business activities"-- perhaps there is a difference....

64   40 CFR § 300.1100(d)(ii).

65   40 CFR § 300.1100(d)(2)(i) and (ii)(B).

been viewed traditionally as the property of the new owner, and no credit is applicable with regard to the former indebtedness of the defaulting borrower who lost the property to foreclosure. In addition, the secured party-turned-owner would normally like to receive fair market value for the property upon resale. Therefore, when reviewing a purchase offer, a bank officer in this situation may forget to calculate "fair consideration" (or the officer may be unaware of this new requirement). A rejection of an offer which is for less than fair market value, but amounts to "fair consideration," may be a major blunder resulting in loss of the secured party exemption.

Equitable Reimbursement. The EPA comments to the Final Rule indicate that the government may seek equitable reimbursement of response costs, apparently to avoid situations where a secured party by obtain an unfair benefit by virtue of the cleanup of its collateral at the expense of the Superfund. The comment is as follows:

> In addition, should the EPA response action enhance the value of the facility and result in the holder realizing an amount greater than that to which the holder is otherwise entitled, the United States may seek equitable reimbursement under applicable principles of law, of the amount by which the holder has been unjustly enriched or has benefitted as a result of the EPA cleanup.[66]

This notion of equitable reimbursement appears to be an attempt to defeat the very exemption which the EPA is purporting to uphold and indeed expand. If a secured lender is exempt by law from CERCLA liability, then it presumably should have no liability to reimburse the Superfund. Say, for example, that a secured lender never did anything to lose the exemption and a third party acquired the property at a foreclosure sale after an EPA cleanup. If the sale yielded more than it would have if the EPA cleanup had not occurred, is the lender liable to reimburse the government for the amount of the increased yield? This is not in CERCLA, hence the resort to "equity." The EPA's comments do not cite any particular rule of law or equity or case authority which would require a secured party to reimburse anyone for anything taking place on a property before foreclosure under circumstances where the

---

[66]   *See* 57 Federal Register at 18368.

secured party did not step out of the lender's role. It remains to be seen whether the courts will apply the law of unjust enrichment in this context as the EPA seeks.

Government Entities. Federal agencies including the Resolution Trust Corporation and the Federal Deposit Insurance Corporation may face the risk of CERCLA liability by virtue of acquiring ownership or control of contaminated properties in the portfolios of failed financial institutions. As a result, these and other governmental agencies have sought clarification and limitation of their potential CERCLA liability. Pending legislation would address their concern, as discussed above. In addition, the Final Rule provides an expansion of the innocent landowner portion of the third party defense in the case of governmental agencies, by elaborating on the provisions of CERCLA § 101(35)(A)(ii).

That provision allows governmental agencies which acquire contaminated property involuntarily by escheat or "other involuntary transfer or acquisition" or through the exercise of eminent domain, to obtain the benefit of the innocent landowner defense to CERCLA liability apparently without regard to the knowledge of the agency about the condition of the property and without any obligation on the agency's part to have undertaken environmental assessment of the property beforehand. The Final Rule enumerates additional situations which constitute "involuntary" acquisition of property by the government within the meaning of that provision. This would include any situation where the government acquires property as a function of its role as sovereign or is required to act as a conservator or receiver under statutory mandate. Examples include acquiring abandoned property, acquiring security interests or properties from failed private lending and depository institutions, acquiring assets through foreclosure pursuant to a governmental loan or loan guarantee program, or acquiring property pursuant to a forfeiture or seizure law.[67]

Clarification of "indicia of ownership." As discussed in § 10.3.1 above, the secured party exemption was originally intended to equalize the CERCLA liability of lenders in title states (where the holder of a mortgage or deed of trust is deemed under state law to be the owner, subject to the borrower's right of redemption) with lenders in lien states

---

[67]   40 CFR § 300.1105.

(where the holder of a mortgage or deed of trust is merely a secured party, not an owner). As lenders in lien states are not "owners" under state law, the exemption was necessary for lenders in title states so that all lenders would be treated the same under CERCLA, i.e., not liable as "owners," but still possibly subject to liability as "operators" (thus the "participation in the management" exception to the exemption). The Final Rule reverses this original intent and establishes that *any* security interest is an "indicia of ownership," so that secured parties nationwide will have "owner" liability, subject to the exemption.

This gambit by the EPA appears to be based on the *Fleet Factors* opinion which treated the deed of trust in that case as an "indicia of ownership" without any discussion,[68] as if all deeds of trust are of that nature. The *Fleet Factors* opinion reasoned that "participation in the management" must mean something more than "operator" liability because that form of liability is separately stated in the statute, rendering "participation in the management" "meaningless" unless it has a different meaning than "operator" liability.[69]

The court obviously overlooked the difference between lien states and title states and the fact that the case arose out of Georgia, which is a title state. By virtue of the property law of Georgia, Fleet was the owner of the property (subject to the borrower's right of redemption), and the deed of trust clearly constituted an "indicia of ownership." In a title state like Georgia, "operator" liability and "participation in the management" would indeed appear to be redundant if they are the same thing. However, this is not the case in lien states where the beneficiary of a mortgage or deed of trust is not an owner, where a mortgage or deed of trust is not an "indicia of ownership," and where a secured party should have no "owner" liability at all (until becoming the owner upon foreclosure). A secured party in a lien state may be exposed only to "operator" liability during the life of the security interest. Because the statute exempts secured party-owners in order to treat them the same as nonowner secured parties, the "participation in the management"

---

[68] "There is no dispute that Fleet held an 'indicia of ownership' in the facility through its deed of trust..." *U.S. v. Fleet Factors*, 901 F.2d 1550, 1556 (11th Cir. 1990).

[69] *Id.*, at 1557.

exception to the exemption must be congruent with "operator" liability, or else there would not be substantial equality in treatment of secured parties across the country.[70] This compelling explanation of the origin of the secured party exemption and the proper interpretation of the "participation in the management" exception was completely missed by the *Fleet Factors* court.

The EPA apparently would like to perpetuate the misapprehension of the law exhibited by the *Fleet Factors* court in order to treat all security interests as "indicia of ownership" and all secured parties as "owners." This would be quite a convenient "clarification" for the EPA. After all, it is far easier to establish the liability of a secured party by an expanded concept of "ownership" status (regardless of state property law) than it is to prove that a secured party has become an "operator," which may involve much more difficult questions of fact.

The notion that all secured parties should be deemed to be owners has even found its way into the pending legislation, as discussed in § 10.3.3-3 above. Either the Congressional proponents of those bills do not realize what they are doing, or they are deliberately setting out, together with the EPA, to reverse the original intent of CERCLA.

As a policy matter, such a reversal might not be objectionable if the exemption provides a broad and clear enough safe harbor for lenders. It may be worth it for lenders in lien states to become "owners" if that is the price they must pay for the significant advantages of the Final Rule for lenders in all states, such as the theoretical ability to remain within the secured party exemption for an indefinite period of time following a foreclosure. This is an extremely valuable provision which did not exist under prior law. Moreover, the Final Rule is beneficial to the extent that it clarifies and limits the scope of "operator" liability as well as "owner" liability under CERCLA for secured parties. Indeed, the response of the financial industry to the Proposed Rule and Final Rule has been rather muted in comparison to the outcry which greeted the initial draft.

---

[70]   As quoted in § 10.3.1, the original wording of the secured party exemption in H.R. 85 referred to "participating in the management or operation" of a facility, reflecting that Congress itself treated the terms "management" and "operation" synonymously.

Trustees and Fiduciaries.   Some commentators criticized the Proposed Rule because it allowed no relief for trustees or fiduciaries (other than governmental agencies) who are called upon to manage contaminated property in a representative capacity and may be exposed to CERCLA liability as a result.   However, it is difficult to be critical of the EPA in this regard because the secured party exemption has nothing to do with persons acting in a trust or fiduciary capacity rather than as secured parties.   The part of the Final Rule which expands the innocent landowner defense for the benefit of governmental agencies is at least based on statutory language.   There is no similar language in the statute regarding trustees or fiduciaries upon which an interpretation could be based.   The pending legislation would address this issue, however.

What deference will the Proposed Rule receive from the courts? Even if the government conducts its own enforcement actions consistently with the safe harbor set forth in the Final Rule, the question remains whether private litigants will feel likewise constrained and whether the courts will give deference to the Final Rule as an authoritative interpretation of the secured party exemption in private cost recovery actions.   Courts traditionally defer to administrative rules interpreting statutes administered by the agency, at least where the interpretive rule is promulgated relatively contemporaneously with the enactment of the law.   This factor is lacking in this situation.   Indeed, the Final Rule was promulgated long after the statute was enacted and contains significant changes as compared to the interpretation previously given by the EPA.   Under these circumstances, it is doubtful whether the courts will view the Final Rule as authoritative.[71]

However, the Final Rule has been adopted as an amendment to the National Oil and Hazardous Substances Pollution Contingency Plan (NCP), which is a legislative rule under CERCLA.   As such, the rule will have the force of law unless challenged in the Circuit Court of Appeals of the United States for the District of Columbia within 90 days from

---

[71]   *See, e.g.,* O'Brien, *Environmental Lender Liability: Will an Administrative Fix Work?,* BNA's Toxics Law Reporter, pp. 512 et seq. (9-12-90) (suggesting that even if the EPA complies with the rule, it might not be binding on private parties in cost recovery actions, and a legislative solution to the *Fleet Factors* problem may still be required).

promulgation.[72] This is a clear attempt to limit the prospects for challenge and to the enhance the binding effect of the rule on private party cost recovery actions as well as the government's own enforcement efforts.[73] The theory is that any private cost recovery action under CERCLA which seeks to ignore the secured party exemption as clarified by the Proposed Rule would not be "consistent" with the NCP. It is a required element of a cost recovery action that the actions taken by the plaintiff in responding to hazardous substances be consistent with the NCP. However, it remains to be seen whether this approach will work when it comes to the scope of the liable parties (as opposed to the nature of the response action), and legislative action may still be needed notwithstanding the Final Rule.

The Proposed Rule became the subject of litigation even before its final promulgation. Apparently the Bank of Montana-Butte has received a letter from the EPA to the effect that the EPA will not pursue an enforcement action against it consistent with the secured party exemption in the Proposed Rule, and the bank has used the letter to support a summary judgment motion in a private cost recovery action brought against it by the Atlantic Richfield Company. In an opposition brief, ARCO has contended, among other things, that the EPA's letter and its exercise of its own prosecutorial discretion is not entitled to any deference in the lawsuit between private parties, and that the bank's involvement with the property satisfied the "participation in the management" standard of liability set by the *Fleet Factors* case and indeed exceeded that standard. The results of this case may provide a preview of the extent to which courts will defer to the Final Rule.[74]

---

[72] 42 U.S.C. § 9613(a).

[73] In a subsequent article, O'Brien, *EPA's Lender Liability Rule: A Significant Step for the Lending Community*, BNA's Toxics Law Reporter, pp. 246 et seq. (7-24-91), it was suggested that the adoption of the Proposed Rule as a part of the NCP "has provided the best administrative basis for a binding rule." The EPA's comments to the Final Rule include an extensive discussion and justification of the binding effect of the Final Rule.

[74] *See Atlantic Richfield Co. v. Oaas*, No. CV-90-75-BU-PGH (D. Mont. opposition brief filed 1-21-92), reported in Toxics Law Reporter at p. 1166-1167 (2-26-92).

Conclusion. The bottom line of this controversy is that, until further guidance comes from the Congress or the courts, lenders should still be wary of taking action which may be deemed "participation in the management" of a borrower's contaminated facility. While lenders may act to protect their security interests, lenders remain exposed to liability under CERCLA, especially in private cost recovery actions, if they exercise their rights and remedies in a manner which would appear to a court in hindsight as an excessive entanglement in the business affairs of a borrower or the management and operation of its properties, with particular regard to the borrower's hazardous waste disposal practices. Unfortunately, this means that lenders are still at risk if they exercise influence even in an environmentally beneficial manner, despite the attempts by the *Fleet Factors* court and the EPA to encourage such action. Similarly, it remains to be seen whether the courts will allow lenders to retain the benefit of the secured party exemption following foreclosure as provided by the Final Rule.

The specter of CERCLA liability has caused increased loan processing costs and delays, while lenders assess the environmental condition of proposed collateral, and has had a chilling effect on the availability of credit with adverse consequences to the economy. Perhaps the Final Rule will provide a useful and authoritative safe harbor for lenders, encouraging lending activity. Even so, lenders may still be at risk of incurring liability under other federal, state or local environmental laws which may be unaffected by the CERCLA safe harbor rule. Moreover, lenders may incur economic loss even with the benefit of the Final Rule. A lender who has foreclosed on contaminated collateral may, as a practical matter, have to undertake the expense of cleanup to render the property marketable. Lenders still face the difficult choice of writing off a loan and walking away from the collateral or possibly incurring environmental liability or economic loss. Therefore, the safest course of action for a lender who is concerned about contaminated collateral may be to keep hands off the borrower and the collateral, or to refuse to extend financing in the first place.

10.3.4 Generator Liability

A lender considering the acquisition of contaminated property by foreclosure or deed in lieu of foreclosure should be concerned not only with potential liability as an owner or operator of that property, but also as a generator of hazardous waste. The lender is likely to have to undertake some remedial action in order to make the property marketable. The lender may have to arrange for the removal and proper disposal of the hazardous waste. CERCLA identifies as a liable party:

> (3) any person who by contract, agreement, or otherwise arranged for disposal or treatment, or arranged with a transporter for transport for disposal or treatment, of hazardous substances owned or possessed by such person, by any other party or entity, at any facility . . . owned or operated by another party or entity and containing such hazardous substances . . . [75]

Thus, an owner (including a lender-turned-owner) who arranges for the treatment or disposal of hazardous substances will be liable, as a generator of hazardous waste, in the event that cleanup or other response action is required where the hazardous substances are taken and disposed of or treated. Such liability may exist under both CERCLA and RCRA and state analogues.

Accordingly, even if the lender can prove that it has no liability as an owner or operator of contaminated property (e.g., due to intervening landowner status or the third party defense, including the innocent landowner defense), the lender may become exposed to liability in connection with necessary cleanup efforts.

10.4 Other Theories of Lender Liability

Lender liability is the subject of a huge body of law in addition to the law and case precedents under CERCLA. There are many ways that a lender can incur liability in connection with the extension of credit (or the refusal to do so) or the manner of administration of a loan, essentially the business dealings between lenders and borrowers. This general body of lender liability law is beyond the scope of this book. However, there a two recent developments of note in the environmental liability area.

In *O'Neil v. QLCRI, Inc.,*[76] a septic tank had failed causing the release of raw sewage into a river in violation of the federal Clean Water

---

[75]   42 U.S.C. § 9607(a)(3).

[76]   750 F.Supp. 551 (D.R.I 1990).

Act (CWA) and the common law of nuisance. Later, a credit union extended financing secured by mortgages on the property with the sewage problem. The plaintiff, the Attorney General of the State of Rhode Island, alleged that the credit union had a close relationship with the borrower and "had 'influence or control' over the principal polluters because [the credit union] knew of the sewage problem and could have conditioned the loans on the fixing of the sewage problem."[77] Because the credit union failed to impose any such condition, the state charged that the credit union could be held liable at trial under the common law theory of "aiding and abetting" the borrower's CWA and nuisance law violations. The court permitted the state to pursue that theory in the action, noting that, under the Restatement (Second) of Torts § 876(b), a party may be liable for aiding and abetting harm to third parties from the tortious conduct of another if that party "knows that the other's conduct constitutes a breach of duty and gives substantial assistance or encouragement to the other so to conduct himself..."[78] That common law doctrine is available for use in conjunction with statutory violations, such as the one under the CWA in the case, as well as violations of state common law.

The disturbing implication of the *O'Neil* case is that, particularly in circumstances where a lender has a close relationship with a borrower, the lender may have to exert its influence and control to ensure the borrower's compliance with any number of environmental laws in order to avoid liability for aiding and abetting the borrower's violation of those laws, but if the lender does so, the risk of liability under CERCLA due to "participation in the management" is increased under existing law as discussed in § 10.3.3 above. The other choice is to decline to extend financing. This increases the chilling effect of environmental liability on the availability of credit, which is not good for the economy.

As noted in § 10.3.3, pending legislation and the EPA's Final Rule on Lender Liability Under CERCLA may provide a safe harbor for lenders to undertake environmentally beneficial action such as that contemplated by the *O'Neil* case without incurring CERCLA liability. Until the law is authoritatively clarified in that way, lenders are at risk of

---

[77]   *Id.*, at 554.

[78]   *Id.*

incurring environmental liability under a combination of statutory and common law theories, whether or not they become actively involved in environmental oversight of borrowers.

In another development, regulations have been promulgated under federal money-laundering statutes which apparently would impose liability on lenders for the manner in which borrowers or depositors use their ill-gotten money when the lender fails to comply with the required reporting of cash transactions. An emerging theory under these regulations is that if the cash is used to support an enterprise which is conducting activities resulting in the unlawful disposal or release of hazardous substances, the lender may become liable for the consequent environmental contamination. Lenders should be able to avoid this potential source of liability by scrupulously complying with cash transaction reporting requirements.

10.5 Loan Participations and Secondary Markets

Loan Participations. Lenders are often not alone in financing transactions. Some loans are large enough to require participations with other lenders because the amount exceeds the maximum loan which banking regulations permit the lender to make. Even if loan limits are not reached, sometimes a lender will desire to participate a sizable loan simply in order to spread the risk. In either case, the lender must be concerned not only with its own internal credit and risk-assessment standards, but also with those of the other financial institutions which the lender will seek as participants. Loan participants will have their own environmental standards which must be satisfied or they will decline to go forward with a transaction. The lead lender must be aware of those standards when reviewing the borrower's loan proposal or project design.

Secondary Markets. Similarly, lenders often do not intend to hold a loan for very long, but to sell it on the secondary market by assigning the note and its security, perhaps retaining only the loan servicing function. This is a typical practice in connection with large portfolios of residential mortgage loans. The assignee of such loans assumes the risk of loan default and the prospect of foreclosure and acquisition of ownership of the collateral. Thus, financial institutions and others in the secondary market are equally concerned about environmental issues and have their own standards which originating lenders must satisfy.

The major secondary markets involve the Federal National Mortgage Association (Fannie Mae) and the Federal Home Loan Mortgage Corporation (Freddie Mac). These institutions buy loan portfolios consisting of loans secured by single family or multi-family residential properties. As a result of environmental concerns, they have adopted assessment and property appraisal policies which must be followed by originating lenders in order to ensure that their loans will be qualified for sale in this secondary market.[79]

There is a more limited secondary market with respect to commercial loans, sometimes involving a single loan rather than a loan portfolio. How environmental concerns are handled in this market and how the risks are allocated between the originating lender and those who purchase the loan(s) is usually negotiated on a case-by-case basis.[80]

10.6 Weighing the Risks

Lenders essentially face the following environmental risks: (i) the increased risk of the borrower's loan default, (ii) reduced value of the collateral, (iii) having to forego "dirty" collateral in order to avoid incurring cleanup liability without a provable defense, (iv) incurring cleanup liability as an owner or operator even without foreclosure (as a result of overly active participation in the management of the borrower's affairs), (v) incurring cleanup liability as a generator of hazardous waste upon disposing of it, and (vi) new laws or court interpretations in the future which might impose even greater risks on secured parties. These risks, and the potential magnitude of liability in a given situation, must oe weighed when making a credit determination. Even a small risk of a huge liability or loan loss might be unacceptable to a lender.

---

[79] *See* Appendix A (FNMA Environmental Hazards Management Procedures) and Appendix B (FHLB Thrift Bulletin; Environmental Risk and Liability) at the back of this book.

[80] For additional discussion of environmental assessment standards established by secondary markets, *see* Chapter 16. *See also* Teutsch, *Environmental Hazards: A Real Estate Lender's View*, Mortgage Bankers Association of America, at pp. 40-46 (July 29, 1988).

As a result of these risks, many sophisticated lenders have adopted detailed policies and procedures for assessing such risks before making loans (see Chapter 16). Prospective borrowers are sometimes required to fill out extensive questionnaires eliciting broad disclosure of information regarding the condition of the property and the status of compliance with environmental laws. Lenders also often require environmental provisions in their loan documentation (see Chapters 18 and 19). Finally, lenders should exercise care in the manner of loan administration, to avoid "participating in the management" of the borrower or the property.

CHAPTER ELEVEN

LESSORS AND LESSEES

11.1   Lessors

Lessors, as owners of real estate, have all the CERCLA liabilities flowing from that status as set forth in previous chapters. Lessors have no exemption from such liability merely because the property is leased and the lessee is in possession and control of the property. The third party defense is not available because of the contractual relationship existing between the lessor and lessee. Thus, lessors are exposed to strict liability under CERCLA as a result of activities of their lessees.[1]   A lessor might, however, have a CERCLA claim for contribution against a lessee who actually caused the contamination requiring response or remedial action.

The same strict liability exists under the Superfund laws of many states. A lessor might not have liability under those state Superfund laws which require fault as a basis for liability where the hazardous substance release was caused solely by a lessee (see Chapter 1).

Unlike a seller who severs any relationship with a property upon conveying it to a buyer, a lessor has a continuing interest in how the property is used due to the potential for environmental liability. As a result, lessors are concerned about the business operations of their lessees, and in particular the handling and disposal of hazardous substances.

From an environmental liability viewpoint, the ideal lessee would be one who does not store, use, handle, treat or dispose of hazardous

---

[1]   *See, e.g., U.S v. Monsanto Co.*, 858 F.2d 160 (4th Cir. 1988), *cert. den.*, 109 S.Ct. 3156 (1989).

substances, and a lessor might wish to prohibit such activities. However, hazardous materials are common and they are frequently essential to the conduct of business. Even in an office environment, a general prohibition against the possession or use of hazardous substances would preclude the use of photocopying machines, correction fluid, refrigerators, fluorescent lighting, other kinds of electronic equipment, as well as cleaning compounds and many other ordinary products. Thus, there is no such thing as a "clean" lessee, and it would be unrealistic for a lessor to prohibit the possession or use of hazardous substances by lessees. This is even more the case for heavier commercial or industrial properties where hazardous chemicals and materials constitute essential ingredients of product manufacturing processes.

This is not to say, however, that a lessor is totally at the mercy of a polluting lessee. Appropriate limitations and controls can and should be negotiated and included in leases, depending upon the nature of the property and the projected business operations of the lessee. In that regard, the lessor will be concerned with the lessee's compliance with all environmental laws and regulations concerning the storage, use, handling, treatment and disposal of hazardous substances. In addition, the lessee should have all required environmental (and nonenvironmental) permits. The lessee should also have appropriate business plans and reporting procedures where it will handle the threshold amounts of hazardous substances triggering such requirements under federal or state law (see Chapter 4). The lessor should be provided with copies of all such plans and reports.[2] Violation or breach of any of these requirements should be an event of default under the lease so that the lessor will be able to take steps to require compliance or to terminate the lease and avoid any further environmental risk. Moreover, the lessor may wish to be indemnified against any environmental liability arising out of the lessee's activities. Such contractual indemnity provisions would supplement and clarify the

---

[2]   Under **California** law, for example, a lessee which must have a business plan is required by law to provide written notice to the owner of the property that the business plan requirement applies and has been complied with, and the lessee must upon request provide a copy of the business plan to the owner or the owner's agent. Cal. Health & Safety Code § 25503.6.

CERCLA right of contribution which would exist already in favor of the lessor with respect to contamination caused by a lessee. These and other contractual protections are discussed further in Chapter 18.

11.2 Lessees

Operator or Generator Liability. Lessees may have strict liability under CERCLA as the current operator of contaminated property or as the operator at the time of the disposal of hazardous waste, or as a generator of hazardous waste.[3]

What About Intervening Operators? There is no provision in CERCLA for liability on the part of an intervening operator. The disclosure rule adopted by SARA expressly applies to "owners" who transfer "ownership," which apparently excludes an intervening operator from the defined categories of PRPs.[4] Thus, a lessee of previously contaminated property whose lease expires or is terminated before any cost recovery action is commenced would apparently not be a PRP subject to suit, regardless of any disclosures.[5] This makes sense because a lessee would have no relationship with, and no occasion for making a disclosure to, a subsequent lessee.

What About Sublessors or Assignors? The foregoing rationale is not so clear, however, when a lessee has subleased the property or assigned the lease. In such a case, the lessee would have a relationship with the sublessee or assignee and disclosure would be an appropriate rule. While a disclosure obligation may exist at that time under other principles of law, CERCLA does not appear to provide for it or even to contemplate that situation.

On the other hand, a disclosure rule would be unnecessary if a sublease or assignment does not alter the lessee's status as a PRP. If a lessee has vacated the property and turned over possession to a sublessee or assignee, it would appear that the lessee is no longer operating the property and would have no CERCLA liability. One cannot be overly

---

[3]   42 U.S.C. §§ 9607(a)(1), (2) and (3).

[4]   *Id.*, § 9601(35)(C).

[5]   Such an intervening lessee might, however, be the generator of hazardous waste disposed of elsewhere. Liability would follow that status in the event of any release of hazardous waste from the disposal facility.

confident of that position, however. At least one court has found a sublessor liable as an "owner" because it "maintained control over and responsibility for the use of the property and, essentially, stood in the shoes of the property owners."[6] That decision was reached before SARA adopted the "operator" category of PRPs, and it was necessary for the court to characterize a sublessor's interest as that of an owner for liability to apply at all. The courts might be inclined to use the same rationale to find a sublessor liable as an owner even if it is not an operator any longer. That theory would appear to be weaker in the case of a lease assignment where the element of control and responsibility on the part of the assignor may be lacking. An assignor might therefore be able to claim intervening operator status, especially where the lessor has released the assignor and has agreed to look only to the assignee of the lease for performance of the lessee's obligations.

Thus, it is problematic whether a lessee who has subleased or assigned a lease could claim to be an intervening operator with no CERCLA liability, as long as the lease remains in effect. Even though the statutory language is unclear on the point, the courts may well wish to impose liability under those circumstances consistent with the policy of CERCLA to shift cleanup costs from the Superfund to those with a present or past connection with the property even if innocent of actual involvement in the hazardous substance release. Accordingly, sublessors should be concerned about the hazardous substance activities of sublessees, just as lessors are concerned about their lessees.

Strict Liability and Defenses Under CERCLA. A lessee who is liable under CERCLA as an operator (or perhaps as an owner in the case of a sublease), will have strict liability for hazardous substance cleanup costs unless one of the limited defenses applies. The third party defense will not be available if the owner contaminated the property before leasing it, because the owner is not an unrelated party. The contractual relationship between the lessor and lessee will preclude the lessee from claiming the third party defense, just as that relationship prevents the lessor from avoiding liability when the lessee causes the contamination. However, the third party defense will be available when a stranger to the

---

6   *U.S. v. South Carolina Recycling and Disposal, Inc.,* 14 Envt'l. L. Rep. 20895, 20897 (D.S.C. 1984).

property causes the contamination, if the lessee has exercised due care with respect to the contamination and has taken appropriate precautions.[7]

As a result of strict CERCLA liability and limited defenses, lessees should (just like prospective purchasers) conduct environmental assessments of property before leasing it. In addition, appropriate contractual protections should be negotiated from the lessee's perspective. This may include representations and warranties from the lessor concerning the condition of the property at the commencement of the lease term, as well as indemnification from the lessor regarding any hazardous substance condition which predates the lease or is caused by anyone other than the lessee.

11.3   Common Law Liability of Lessors and Lessees

As indicated in Chapter 8, the basic common law duty of occupiers of land is to repair or warn of concealed dangerous conditions. As stated in the leading **California** case of *Rowland v. Christian*[8]:

> Where the occupier of land is aware of a concealed condition involving in the absence of precautions an unreasonable risk of harm to those coming in contact with it and is aware that a person on the premises is about to come in contact with it, the trier of fact can reasonably conclude that a failure to warn or to repair the condition constitutes negligence.

This general duty will apply to a lessor upon leasing the property to a lessee, and to a lessee while in possession of the property during the term of the lease. The duty will doubtless apply in situations where the concealed dangerous condition consists of hazardous waste.

Thus, lessees should be concerned about whether the lessor has satisfied the common law duties of repair or disclosure, and the lessor should be concerned with the lessee's satisfaction of the same duty during the term of the lease.

---

[7]   42 U.S.C. § 9607(b)(3).

[8]   69 Cal.2d 108, 119, 70 Cal.Rptr. 97, 443 P.2d 561 (1968).

11.4   Environmental Risk Allocation

As suggested in the foregoing comments, lessors typically wish the lessees to have full responsibility for their own activities and to indemnify their lessors with respect to those activities. In turn, lessees do not wish to assume environmental liabilities arising out of the activities of the owner or other tenants. The subject of environmental risk allocation is discussed further in Chapter 18.

CHAPTER TWELVE

BROKERS

Real estate brokers[1] are not identified as PRPs under CERCLA except where a broker is itself an owner or lessee of real estate or the generator or disposer of hazardous waste. Brokers should have no CERCLA or state Superfund liability while acting solely in the capacity of a broker in a real estate transaction.

However, brokers have professional duties of inspection and disclosure as set forth in Chapter 3. Those duties will encompass hazardous substance conditions as well as any other material or defective condition of the real estate involved. Thus, while brokers normally have no direct liability under environmental laws, they may become exposed to professional negligence liability as a result of environmental matters which are not properly handled during a real estate transaction.

It is therefore becoming common for real estate brokers to obtain extensive disclosures from the seller regarding the seller's knowledge of the condition of the property as to both environmental and other matters. This information will then be made available to the buyer. In this way, the broker assists the seller in performing disclosure obligations; it is the professional duty of the seller's broker to assist the seller in that way. Of course, brokers may not rely completely on what the seller discloses, but must also inspect the property and disclose material facts which a reasonably competent inspection would reveal.

It is not, however, the duty of a real estate broker to undertake at its expense a full-blown environmental assessment of a property or to be an environmental expert. Rather, the broker's professional duty is to inform the parties to a transaction (or whichever party the broker represents) of the existence of environmental laws and concerns, and to recommend that steps be taken to assess the risk through qualified environmental consultants and counsel as appropriate to the circumstances. Further, the parties should be informed of any potential

---

[1] For convenience, this chapter refers only to brokers, but that term should be understood to include real estate agents as well.

environmental problem (such as the existence of an old UST, or the known or suspected use of asbestos in the construction of the building) which may be noted by the broker during an inspection. The broker should also have a basic understanding of, and should inform the parties of, the potential liabilities which they may face under the environmental laws after the transaction is concluded, between one another and with respect to third parties. The broker should refer the client to legal counsel for further assistance in this regard. The broker may assist in negotiating the essential terms of the transaction, including how potential environmental liabilities might be allocated between the parties, although legal counsel often becomes more involved at that stage.

The broker should have no liability once it has performed a competent inspection and has informed the parties, especially the purchaser, of (i) any material facts or defects which come to light from the inspection or from the seller's disclosure, and (ii) the basic environmental concerns mentioned above. Any further assessment of environmental matters then becomes the informed choice and the responsibility of the principals in the transaction as assisted by qualified environmental professionals.

Unfortunately, it is not entirely clear under available court precedents exactly how far a broker must go in its inspection of a property in order to be safe from a claim that the investigation was not sufficiently competent and up to professional standards. Thus, there is great potential for litigation in this area. A broker who fails to inspect property or to provide information as indicated is open to a claim of professional negligence. The significant environmental liabilities which might be incurred by parties to a real estate transaction will provide a great incentive for them to look for someone to sue, and a real estate broker who has been lax in this area will become a prime target.

As a result of that potential for suit, it is a wise practice, and one which is becoming more common, for brokers to protect themselves by documenting the discharge of their professional duty in the environmental area. This is done by providing any necessary environmental disclosures in writing. Brokers should also consider providing written advice to their clients about environmental concerns in general and the essential nature of potential liabilities which may arise under environmental laws in connection with the ownership and operation of real estate. The statement should include an appropriate disclaimer of environmental expertise on the part of the broker, together with a recommendation that the client consult with expert environmental consultants and counsel as needed for further explanation of rights and potential liabilities, for assistance in detecting and assessing such risks in the particular transaction, and for expert advice as to how such matters should be handled in the transaction. The written advice should include a form of acknowledgement for the client to sign to the effect that the broker has made specified disclosures regarding the condition of the property; that the broker is not, and is not expected to be, an environmental expert; that the client has not relied on such expertise from the broker; and that the broker has suggested that the client obtain advice from qualified environmental consultants and legal counsel. Brokers sometimes also ask their clients to sign a release and covenant not to sue if environmental problems are later discovered. The enforceability of such a release would appear to be questionable, however, if the broker was in fact negligent in inspecting and making disclosures regarding the property or has not properly and fully advised the parties of the environmental risks.

As long as the broker has obtained such documentation, it should be maintained in the broker's records of the transaction for a lengthy period. How long such records should be kept is difficult to say. One of the insidious characteristics of hazardous waste is that it may lurk unknown for many years before discovery. Because of the fiduciary relationship existing between brokers and their clients, the statute of limitations applicable to professional negligence of real estate brokers in many states is based on the rule of discovery. Under that rule, the statute of limitations on the plaintiff's claim will not commence to run until the plaintiff discovered or reasonably should have discovered the facts giving rise to the cause of action. As this is an indefinite period, brokers should maintain their transaction records for an indefinite period. In those states where the statute of limitations is based on the "date of the injury," instead of its subsequent discovery, or where a statute of repose has been enacted in favor of brokers,[2] the broker will have a better idea how long the records of each transaction should be maintained.

---

[2] For example, **California** has adopted a statute of repose for brokers in residential transactions. An action against a broker for breach of statutory inspection and disclosure duties may not be commenced more than "two years from the date of possession, which means the date of recordation, the date of close of escrow, or the date of occupancy, whichever occurs first." Cal. Civil Code § 2079.4.

CHAPTER THIRTEEN

EXCHANGE ACCOMMODATORS

Tax deferred exchanges under Section 1031 of the Internal Revenue Code often involve the services of exchange accommodators. Companies providing such services typically take record title to real property during the course of the exchange. Because of the potential environmental liabilities arising from ownership of contaminated real estate, exchange accommodators are concerned about their exposure to such liability.

Superfund Liability. The chief concern arises under CERCLA and state Superfund analogues which impose strict cleanup liability on owners and operators of contaminated real property. Presumably, an exchange accommodator would not become involved with the operation of a property. Nor would the accommodator have any involvement with the generation, treatment, transportation or disposal of hazardous substances. Thus, the risk of liability would relate only to the accommodator's status as a temporary owner of the property for purposes of accommodating the tax deferred exchange between other parties.

Accommodators are exposed to a risk of Superfund liability by virtue of having an ownership interest in contaminated real estate. As with other owners, accommodators may become potential targets in a cleanup cost recovery action. It is, however, worth analyzing the scope of that general risk.

Potentially Responsible Owners. As detailed in Chapter 1, there are up to three potentially liable owners in each case, including:

> (1) The owner of the property at the time the contamination occurred[1];
>
> (2) The current owner of the property (that is, the owner at the time of commencement of a cost recovery action, or if title has passed to a unit of

---

[1]   42 U.S.C. § 9607(a)(2).

the state or local government due to bankruptcy, foreclosure, tax delinquency, abandonment or similar means, the owner immediately beforehand)[2]; and

(3) Any intervening owner who obtained actual knowledge of the contamination and failed to disclose it to the buyer.[3]

These are the potentially liable owners under CERCLA and state analogues such as **California's** Superfund law.[4]

The Limited Risk of an Accommodator as Owner. Assume, for example, that all parts of an exchange transaction take place concurrently, with the accommodator holding title to real estate for at most a few minutes between recordation of deeds. Superfund liability would potentially exist if:

(1) Any hazardous substance was disposed of at the property during those few minutes;

(2) A cost recovery action was filed during those few minutes; or

(3) The accommodator actually knew of preexisting contamination and failed to disclose it to the buyer.

The risk of any of these grounds applying as a matter of fact would appear to be quite limited or none in many cases. The likelihood of Risk No. (1) occurring in any given few minutes would depend largely upon the nature of the business conducted at the property, which might or might not involve ongoing disposals or releases of hazardous substances. An accommodator ought to be able to gain some level of comfort on this point by making appropriate inquiry before taking title even for a few minutes.

Any chance of Risk No. (2) occurring is remote indeed, unless a federal or state agency has already incurred cleanup costs and is poised

---

2   *Id.*, §§ 9601(20)(A) and 9607(a)(1); *U.S v. Fleet Factors Corp.*, 29 ERC 1011 (S.D. Ga.Dec. 22, 1988).

3   42 U.S.C. § 9601(35)(C).

4   Cal. Health & Safety Code § 25323.5.

and ready to file a cost recovery action the instant that the deed to the accommodator is recorded.

Risk No. (3) seems to be completely within the control of the accommodator, as it depends upon his actual knowledge. An appropriate disclosure would avoid this risk.

The potential exposure should be the same in a delayed exchange transaction. At the first closing, the first property is transferred to its ultimate buyer. During the delay period while the parties look for the second property, the accommodator holds only the proceeds of the sale of the first property. When the second property is identified, it is acquired and transferred at the second closing. Each time, the accommodator would hold record title to any given property for only a short while during the closing.

Thus, whether an exchange is simultaneous or delayed, an accommodator might be willing to undertake environmental risks as a business matter. Naturally, the accommodator would want the transaction documents to include an indemnity provision in favor of the accommodator should any environmental claim be made.

Even though the potential for environmental liability might be small, a number of companies which formerly provided exchange accommodation services no longer do so. They simply do not wish to become a target at all. On the other hand, there are companies who are eager for the business notwithstanding the risk.

Avoidance of Record Title. It is possible to structure an exchange transaction so that record title to a contaminated property passes directly by deed from one exchange party to the other *without* passing title through the accommodator. This would avoid the status of record ownership and the resulting potential for environmental liability. The federal courts and the Internal Revenue Service have validated exchange transactions involving direct deeds.[5] One reason mentioned in those cases for utilizing a direct deed is to avoid the payment of state documentary transfer taxes twice (once with the deed to the

---

[5]   *See W.D. Haden Co. v. Commissioner,* 165 F.2d 588, 590 (5th Cir. 1948); *Biggs v. Commissioner,* 69 T.C. 905 (1978), *affirmed* 632 F.2d 1171 (5th Cir. 1980); Private Letter Ruling 8008113; and Private Letter Ruling 8912023.

accommodator and again with the deed which reconveys title to the appropriate exchange party or buyer). If the direct deed approach can be used in order to avoid double documentary transfer taxes, the avoidance of record title by an accommodator for environmental reasons becomes a welcome side effect.

It should be noted that the accommodator still must function as an owner, not as a mere escrow, with the contractual right to direct the disposition of the property. The Superfund laws look to owners, not merely the holders of record title.[6] Thus, direct deeds do not avoid the risk entirely. But the position of an accommodator can only be enhanced if his name does appear in the record chain of title.

This approach is actually being used. In a recent transaction known to the author, the property involved with the first leg of an exchange was contaminated. The parties therefore were not in a position to insist that the accommodator join the group of potential Superfund defendants identifiable by a simple chain of title search. The transaction was completed using a direct deed. The accommodator never took record title to the contaminated property, and documentary transfer tax was paid only once to the county recorder.

Environmental Assessments. If the parties insist that the accommodator take record title, or if the accommodator is otherwise particularly concerned about potential environmental liability, protection might be achieved by undertaking a sufficient environmental assessment (at the expense of the exchange parties) to gain the benefit of the innocent landowner defense.[7] This assumes that no contamination is revealed by the assessment and that its sufficiency can be proven. Of course, in order to preserve that defense, the accommodator must be careful to make an appropriate disclosure to the buyer should the existence of contamination come to light in the short time before the closing is completed and the property is retransferred.

In sum, exchange accommodators risk having to defend against Superfund cost recovery actions. But the level of risk should be low or

---

[6] *See*, e.g., *U.S. v. Carolawn Co.*, 21 ERC 2124, 2128 (D. S.C. 1984) (ruling that a party might have continued as an owner even after the transfer of record title).

[7] 42 U.S.C. § 9601(35)(A) and (B).

nonexistent in many cases, and it should be possible for an accommodator to determine the scope of the environmental risk and to minimize or avoid it by structuring the exchange transaction appropriately.

CHAPTER FOURTEEN

CORPORATE OFFICERS, DIRECTORS, SHAREHOLDERS AND SUCCESSORS

14.1 Limited Liability of the Corporate Form--The General Rule

The corporate form has been used traditionally as a means of limiting the liability of shareholders. They risk loss of their investment, but have no personal liability if the assets of the corporation are insufficient to satisfy its obligations.[1] Similarly, officers, directors, agents and employees have no personal liability for the debts of the

---

[1]   18 CJS *Corporations* § 580.

corporation.[2] This principle has encouraged capital formation and the conduct of business ventures of all kinds.

Naturally, there are exceptions to the general rule, and a number of them are quite technical. This chapter will focus on two common law exceptions: (i) liability for one's own wrongful acts, and (ii) liability when proper corporate form has not been maintained or has been misused so that the corporate entity will be disregarded. Apart from these exceptions, corporate shareholders, officers, directors, agents and employees traditionally have not expected to incur any personal liability in the absence of a voluntary personal guaranty of corporate debts. The environmental laws have altered that expectation dramatically and have increased the risk of personal liability for the cost of cleaning up hazardous waste.

14.2 Exception: Direct Personal Liability for One's Own Wrongful Acts

Under the common law, all persons have direct, personal liability for their own participation in conduct which is tortious, wrongful, criminal or otherwise in violation of law, and this includes corporate shareholders, officers, directors, agents and employees. The corporate form has never provided any protection against direct liability for one's own breach of civil or criminal law.[3]

Such liability does not, however, apply to lawful conduct. Much of the hazardous waste which must now be cleaned up was disposed of years ago, before that activity became heavily regulated. Where there was nothing illegal or wrongful about the disposal at the time, common law liability grounded on fault does not provide a remedy. Other legal principles are required in order to impose liability on persons innocent of wrongdoing. As a result, the environmental laws have adopted strict liability standards.[4]

---

[2]   19 CJS *Corporations* § 839.

[3]   As to shareholders, *see, generally,* 18 CJS *Corporations* §§ 5e and 714. With respect to corporate officers, directors, agents and employees, *see* 19 CJS *Corporations* §§ 845 and 931-932.

[4]   *See* Chapter 1.

14.3   Exception: Derivative Shareholder Liability Upon Disregard of the Corporate Entity--The Traditional Theory

A method is available under the common law for imposing personal liability on shareholders for corporate obligations without regard to any wrongful conduct on the part of the shareholder. In order to do so, the circumstances must justify a court's disregard of the corporate entity. Legal annals are replete with cases where corporate creditors have attempted, sometimes successfully, to "pierce the corporate veil" and to obtain personal recourse against shareholders. Such cases are very fact-specific, and a detailed discussion of those precedents is beyond the scope of this book. A statement of the general rule will suffice for our purposes:

> Before [the corporate veil will be pierced] it must be made to appear that the corporation is not only influenced and governed by [a] person, but that there is such a unity of interest and ownership that the individuality, or separateness, of such person and corporation has ceased, and that the facts are such that an adherence to the fiction of the separate existence of the corporation would, under the particular circumstances, sanction a fraud or promote injustice.[5]

Numerous factors have been utilized by the courts in deciding such cases, including:

> . . . commingling of funds and other assets . . . the treatment by an individual of the assets of the corporation as his own . . . the failure to maintain minutes or adequate corporate records . . . the identical equitable ownership in the two entities; the identification of the equitable owners thereof with the domination and control of the two entities . . . the failure to adequately capitalize a corporation; the absence of corporate assets, and undercapitalization; the use of a corporation as a mere shell, instrumentality or conduit for a single venture or the

---

[5]   *Arnold v. Browne*, 27 Cal.App.3d 386, 394, 103 Cal.Rptr. 775 (1972), disapproved on other grounds in *Reynolds Metals Co. v. Alperson*, 25 Cal.3d 124, 158 Cal.Rptr. 1, 599 P.2d 83 (1979).

business of an individual or another corporation . . . the disregard of legal formalities and the failure to maintain arm's length relationships among related entities . . . the diversion of assets from a corporation by or to a stockholder or other person or entity, to the detriment of creditors, or the manipulation of assets and liabilities between entities so as to concentrate the assets in one and the liabilities in another . . . and the formation and use of a corporation to transfer to it the existing liability of another person or entity."[6]

When such factors apply, it may be said that the corporation is the mere *alter ego* of the dominating person and is to be disregarded as a separate entity. That person will thereupon have personal liability for corporate debts and obligations. This is a particular risk for closely held corporations where the owner might not be sophisticated enough to maintain the corporate form properly.

Nevertheless, there must be a corporate debt or obligation of some kind in order to impose liability for it on the shareholders. In connection with hazardous waste, the environmental laws discussed in Part I of this book have established strict liability even where no liability would have existed under the common law. Those liabilities may be imposed on the shareholders personally based on common law principles when the circumstances warrant piercing the corporate veil. This cannot be done under the common law, however, where the corporate form has been properly maintained. In order to impose personal liability on the shareholders of a valid corporation, there must be a way to circumvent the corporate shield. The environmental laws and court decisions to date have approached this problem in two ways. First, they have imposed strict liability directly on persons who have operated contaminated real estate or generated hazardous waste, in effect accomplishing an end run around the corporate veil. Second, a federal rule of law is developing concerning when the corporate veil may be pierced in environmental cleanup cases. As will be seen below, some federal courts have applied a standard which makes it much easier for the veil to be pierced than it would be under traditional standards.

---

[6] *Id.*, at 394-395.

14.4   The New Exception: Direct Personal Liability Under CERCLA as an "Operator" of Contaminated Real Estate or as a "Generator" of Hazardous Waste

As discussed in Chapter 1, owners of contaminated property are just one of several categories of PRPs under CERCLA and many of the state Superfund laws.   Strict liability for cleanup of hazardous substance releases is also imposed on *operators* of contaminated real estate and on those who operated the property at the time of the disposal of hazardous waste.[7]   In Chapter 11, we have seen that operators may include lessees. That term may also include corporate officers, employees and shareholders who manage or operate the property.   In addition, strict liability is imposed on *generators* of hazardous waste, including those who arranged for its treatment, transportation or disposal.[8]   Generators similarly may include any corporate personnel involved in such activity. The cases collected in this section focus mainly on the operator category of liability.

In order to gain an understanding of this controversial area, it is necessary to highlight several of the leading operator liability cases, which can be grouped roughly into three categories: (1) those cases which require some degree of active involvement in the management of a facility before a person will be found liable as an operator, (2) those cases which find that "capacity to control" is sufficient to impose liability, and (3) those which reject both of the preceding lines of authority and require a traditional basis for piercing the corporate veil before personal liability may be imposed.

Cases Requiring Active Participation in Management

In *State of New York v. Shore Realty Corp.,*[9] a corporation was formed for the purpose of acquiring contaminated real estate for development.   The state subsequently commenced a CERCLA action against both the corporation which owned the property and the sole shareholder who was also a corporate officer.   The corporation was, of course, strictly liable as the current owner of the property.   In addition,

---

[7]   42 U.S.C. §§ 9607(a)(1) and (2).

[8]   *Id.,* § 9607(a)(3).

[9]   759 F.2d 1032 (2d Cir. 1985).

the shareholder was found personally liable as the operator of the property. The court stated that "an owning stockholder who manages the corporation, such as [the defendant], is liable under CERCLA as an owner or operator . . . [The defendant] is in charge of the operation of the facility in question, and as such is an 'operator' within the meaning of CERCLA."[10] The court acknowledged that the alleged facts were insufficient to warrant piercing the corporate veil under the common law, which courts do only "reluctantly." Nevertheless, the officer and shareholder was held personally liable without piercing the corporate veil based on a broad interpretation of "operator" liability under CERCLA.

Similarly, in *U.S. v. Conservation Chemical Company*,[11] the founder, chief executive officer and majority shareholder of a company in the business of storing, treating and transporting hazardous waste was held personally liable under CERCLA as an operator (without piercing the corporate veil) because he personally conceived of the waste treatment processes, supervised the construction, hired and supervised employees, and generally "administered the affairs of the corporation."[12]

In *U.S. v. Carolawn Co.*,[13] a plant manager was liable because "to the extent that an individual has control or authority over the activities of a facility from which hazardous substances are released or participates in the management of such a facility, he may be held liable for response costs incurred . . . notwithstanding the corporate character of the business."[14]

In *Quadion Corporation v. Mache*,[15] the defendants were the former shareholders of a closely held corporation which owned a die casting facility. The stock had been sold to the plaintiff's predecessor-in-

---

[10]   *Id.*, at 1052.

[11]   628 F.Supp. 391 (W.D.Mo. 1985).

[12]   *Id.*, at 420. To the same effect, *see U.S. v. Mottolo*, 629 F.Supp 56 (D.N.H. 1984).

[13]   14 Environ. L. Rptr. 20699 (D.S.C. June 15, 1984).

[14]   *Id.*, at 20700.

[15]   738 F.Supp. 270 (N.D.Ill. 1990).

interest. The plaintiff later discovered that the real property was severely contaminated with deposits of PCBs. The contamination allegedly occurred while the defendants had owned the stock of the corporation and were in possession of the facility. The plaintiff sought contribution under CERCLA toward cleanup costs, alleging that the defendants were liable as the "owner or operator" of the facility at the time of disposal of hazardous substances. The defendants contended that, as mere shareholders when the contamination occurred, they had no personal liability and moved to dismiss the action.

The court noted that shareholders of a closely held corporation may be held responsible under CERCLA even in the absence of facts which would warrant the piercing of the corporate veil.[16] In order to determine whether an individual is liable under CERCLA, a very fact specific inquiry must be conducted requiring an evaluation of the totality of the circumstances. Courts examine evidence of an individual's authority to control such matters as the waste handling practices of the corporation, whether the individual holds the position of officer or director, and the distribution of power within the corporation. In addition, courts will look for evidence of responsibility undertaken for waste disposal practices, including evidence of responsibility undertaken and neglected, as well as affirmative attempts to prevent unlawful hazardous waste disposal or abate hazardous waste damage. Because such a fact intensive inquiry was required, the court determined that liability could not be determined at a summary proceeding and required trial on the merits. Accordingly, the defendants' motion was denied.

In *Mobay Corporation v. Allied - Signal, Inc.,*[17] the current owner of a contaminated site incurred significant cleanup costs and initiated a cost recovery action under CERCLA against a number of defendants, including a corporate parent of a corporation which had owned and operated the site at the time contamination occurred. The court ruled that a parent corporation may be liable for the actions of its subsidiary, without piercing the corporate veil, if the parent exercised control over

---

16   The court cited another case for this proposition: *Kelly v. Thomas Solvent Co.,* 727 F.Supp. 1532, 1542-1545 (W.D.Mich. 1989).

17   761 F.Supp. 345 (D.N.J. 1991).

or actively participated in the subsidiary's activities."[18] Summary judgement was denied because material issues of fact remained regarding the extent of the parent's active participation in the management and control of the subsidiary.

The court in *U.S. v. Cordova Chemical Co.*,[19] ruled that the personal liability of a corporate officer under CERCLA had to be determined at trial on the merits because the issue is heavily fact-specific. Factors to be weighed include:

> a corporate individual's position in the company; degree of authority; percentage of ownership; role in board decision-making and daily management; knowledge of and responsibility for waste disposal policy; and personal involvement with, neglect of and ability to control hazardous waste matters.

> The absence or existence of one or more of these factors does not necessarily determine liability. Rather, a combined assessment of all of these factors determines whether a corporate individual should be held personally liable under CERCLA due to involvement in hazardous waste practices or due to neglect thereof when placed in the context of the individual's pervasive control and active involvement over other aspects of the company.[20]

Corporate officer defendants won in *Massachusetts v. Blackstone Valley Electric Co.*[21] The court noted that it is not necessary to pierce the corporate veil to impose CERCLA operator liability on corporate officers or directors. "To hold an officer liable, however, he must have personally participated in the conduct that violated CERCLA."[22] The court dismissed the case against the officers due to insufficient evidence that they had personally participated in any disposal of hazardous waste.

---

18   *Id.*, at 354.

19   21 ELR 20805, 1991 U.S. Dist. LEXIS 4183 (W.D. Mich. Mar. 26, 1991).

20   *Id.*

21   777 F.Supp. 1036 (D.Mass. 1991).

22   *Id.*, at 1039.

The disposal had occurred before those officers became involved with the site.

In an analogous context, the court in *Liquid Chemical Corporation v. Department of Health Services,*[23] considered operator liability under California's Hazardous Waste Control Law (HWCL) (the state equivalent of RCRA). The court upheld the finding of an administrative law judge that a corporate officer was personally liable for a $250,000 fine. That officer was the president and the only corporate officer and was clearly responsible for the overall operation of the facility. He was therefore liable as an operator and was individually responsible for ensuring compliance with the HWCL.

In *Gopher Oil Co. v. Union Oil Co.,*[24] the current property owner pursued a cost recovery action under CERCLA against Union Oil, the corporate parent of the prior owner during the time contamination occurred. Oil and industrial chemicals which were leaked, spilled and intentionally dumped at the site included motor oil and lubricating oil; petroleum hydrocarbons such as benzene, toluene, xylene; solvents such as trichlorethylene, diclorethane and methyisobutyl ketone; and pesticide compounds such as DDD, DDE and DDT. After an advisory jury trial, the court found Union Oil liable as an operator because it had exercised extensive control over the subsidiary's operations for many years. Among other things, Union Oil controlled the sales of the subsidiary's finished products; hired, fired, reassigned and promoted personnel, sometimes against the wishes of the subsidiary's management; set pay grades and job classifications consistent with Union Oil policy; handled the payroll; monitored and assisted the subsidiary's workplace safety and environmental compliance; and approved all significant business decisions.

In *CPC International, Inc. v. Aerojet-General Corp.*[25] the court stated that CERCLA operator liability can be imposed on a parent corporation without piercing the corporate veil.

---

[23]   227 Cal.App.3d 1682, 729 Cal.Rptr. 103 (1991).

[24]   757 F.Supp. 988 (D.Minn. 1990), *affirmed in part and remanded in part,* 1992 U.S.App. LEXIS 1076 (8th Cir. Jan. 28, 1992).

[25]   777 F.Supp. 549 (W.D. Mich. 1991).

> [A] parent corporation is directly liable under section 107(a)(2) as an operator only when it has exerted power or influence over its subsidiary by actively participating in and exercising control over the subsidiary's business during a period of disposal of hazardous waste. A parent's actual participation in and control over a subsidiary's functions and decision-making creates "operator" liability under CERCLA; a parent's mere oversight of a subsidiary's business in a manner appropriate and consistent with the investment relationship between a parent and its wholly owned subsidiary does not.
>
> Factors to consider in assessing whether a parent corporation operated its subsidiary include the parent's participation in the subsidiary's board of directors, management, day-to-day operations, and specific policy matters, including areas such as manufacturing, finances, personnel and waste disposal. In addition, determining the origin and business function of the subsidiary in the context of the parent corporation's business may be helpful in determining whether the parent has operated be wholly owned subsidiary. Other evidence may be less probative if it is simply indicative of the actions of a prudent investor, rather than an active operator, including monitoring of a subsidiary's financial performance consolidation of corporate business matters the such as accounting and legal work, and cooperation between the subsidiary and the parent in research. In the final analysis, each case must be decided on its own unique facts and circumstances.[26]

Applying those factors, the court found CPC International directly liable under CERCLA as an operator with regard to the activities of a subsidiary corporation because CPC actively participated in and exercised significant control over the business and decision-making of the subsidiary. Some of the factors which the court considered

---

[26]   *Id.*, at 573.

"particularly probative" were: CPC's 100% ownership of the subsidiary; CPC's active participation in, and at times majority control over, the board of directors which was chaired at all relevant times by a CPC official; CPC's involvement in major decision-making and day-to- day operations through CPC officials who served within the subsidiary's management (including the president and chief executive officer); CPC's active participation and control in the subsidiary's environmental matters (including formulating environmental compliance policies, participating in meetings with regulators and directing responses to inquiries from regulators); CPC's active participation in the labor problems of the subsidiary; and financial control through approval of budgets and major capital expenditures. Applying similar factors, the court found that Aerojet had operator liability, although the facts also established sufficient grounds for piercing the corporate veil and finding Aerojet liable as an owner (see the discussion on this case in § 14.5 below).

In *U.S. v. Kayser-Roth Corp.*,[27] the government sought to recover cleanup costs incurred in response to a spill of trichloroethylene (TCE) at a textile plant. The defendant was the corporate parent of a dissolved subsidiary which formerly owned the plant. The government contended that Kayser-Roth was liable as an "operator" of the plant when the spill occurred. The Court of Appeal for the First Circuit held that a parent corporation may be held directly liable under CERCLA as an "operator" of property owned by a subsidiary corporation. The court surmised that Congress, by including "operators" as a category of PRPs in addition to owners connected by the conjunction "or," implied that a person who is an operator of a facility is not protected by the legal structure of ownership. Thus, corporate status, while relevant in determining ownership, cannot shield a person from operator liability.

The court went on to say that to be an operator requires more than merely ownership and the ability or authority to control. Instead, active involvement in the activities of the subsidiary is required. The court found that Kayser-Roth did in fact exercise pervasive control over the operations of the subsidiary, including (1) total monetary control including collection of accounts, (2) restricting the budget of the

---

[27]   910 F.2d 24 (1st Cir. 1990), *cert. den.* 111 S.Ct. 957 (1991).

subsidiary, (3) funnelling of all governmental contact, including environmental matters, through Kayser-Roth, (4) requiring that all of the real estate transactions, sales or leases, of the subsidiary be approved by Kayser-Roth, (5) requiring that all capital transfer or expenses greater than $5,000 be approved by Kayser-Roth, and (6) placing Kayser-Roth personnel in most of the director and officer positions of the subsidiary so that Kayser-Roth's corporate policies would be implemented precisely. In particular, Kayser-Roth had approved the installation of the cleaning system that used the TCE which was spilled. Kayser-Roth had the power to control the use of the TCE and to prevent and abate damage. Thus, the court found that Kayser-Roth was liable as an operator.

In *Riverside Market Development Corp. v. International Building Products, Inc.,*[28] the site of an asbestos product manufacturing plant had been allegedly contaminated with hazardous wastes consisting of asbestos and by-products of asbestos manufacturing. The current owners of the site pursued a CERCLA claim against the former owner and its two shareholders (one of whom held 85% of the stock and the other the remaining 15%). The trial court found that issues of fact existed as to whether the minority shareholder was liable under CERCLA as an operator of the asbestos plant; it was alleged that he had been actively involved in the daily operations of the plant, including spending approximately 40% of his work week at the plant supervising operations and even operating plant machinery, and he negotiated supply contracts for raw materials.[29] However, the court found that the majority shareholder was not liable as an operator, and dismissed the action against him, because he resided out-of-state, spent very little time at the plant and was not personally involved in plant operations. The rulings of the trial court were affirmed on appeal.

---

[28]   1990 WL 72249, 1990 U.S. Dist. LEXIS 6375 (D.E.La. 1990), *affirmed* 931 F.2d 327 (5th Cir. 1991) *cert. den.*, 112 S.Ct. 636 (1991).

[29]   For another case where a minority shareholder faced a CERCLA action, *see U.S. v. McGraw-Edison Co.,* 718 F.Supp. 154 (W.D.N.Y. 1989) (a minority shareholder who allegedly actually participated in the day-to-day operations of the company was exposed to CERCLA operator liability; further discovery was needed regarding the minority shareholder's involvement in company operations).

In *Jacksonville Electric Authority v. Eppinger and Russell Co.,*[30] the current owner filed a CERCLA cost recovery action against the former owner of the site, a wood treatment company, and against Tufts University which had received ownership of a majority of the stock of that company through a testamentary bequest of an alumnus. The court stated that a parent corporation can be liable as an operator "when the parent exercises actual and pervasive control of the subsidiary to the extent of actually involving itself in the daily operations of the subsidiary. Actual involvement in decisions regarding the disposal of hazardous substances is a sufficient, but not a necessary, condition to the imposition of operator liability."[31] The court found that the university had no "material involvement" in the daily operations of the wood treatment company so that it was not liable as an operator under CERCLA.

"Capacity to Control" Cases

Some cases have gone further in suggesting that the "capacity to control" (even if not exercised) is sufficient for the imposition of CERCLA liability.

In *U.S. v. Northeastern Pharmaceutical & Chemical Co.,*[32] the president and majority shareholder of a manufacturing company which generated hazardous waste actually lived in another state and delegated operational control to a company vice-president. Both the president and vice-president were sued under CERCLA and RCRA and both were found personally liable as operators (the vice-president was also found liable as a generator). The court pointed out that the absentee president "had the capacity and the general responsibility as president to control the disposal of hazardous wastes at the NEPACCO plant . . . and the capacity to prevent and abate the damage caused by the disposal of hazardous wastes . . . "[33] On appeal, the liability of the absentee president was upheld under RCRA because of his "ultimate authority to

---

[30]   776 F.Supp. 1542 (M.D.Fla. 1991).

[31]   *Id.,* at 1547-1548.

[32]   579 F.Supp. 823 (W.D.Mo. 1984), *affirmed in part, reversed in part,* 810 F.2d 726 (8th Cir. 1986), *cert. den.* 484 U.S. 848, 108 S.Ct. 146 (1987).

[33]   *Id.,* 579 F.Supp. at 849.

control the disposal of NEPACCO's hazardous substances" (but not under CERCLA because the disposal site was located elsewhere, on land neither owned by NEPACCO nor operated by its officers).[34]

Similarly, in *Kelley v. ARCO Industries, Inc.*,[35] the court suggested that the CERCLA liability of a corporate officer or director could be based upon the individual's power to control corporate policy and responsibility for health and safety practices including hazardous waste disposal, so that the person has the ability to prevent the contamination (the "prevention test").

Following the *NEPACCO* case, a court imposed personal liability on a company president as an operator. In *U.S. v. Mexico Feed and Seed Co.*,[36] the government cleaned up PCB contamination and sought cost recovery from the former corporate lessee and its president. The president was found to have been "in charge of and directly responsible for all of the [company] operations, and, hence, possessed ultimate authority to control the disposal of the hazardous substances. Therefore, as owner and operator at the time of the disposal of the hazardous waste at the Mexico site, [the president] is liable under CERCLA."[37] Likewise, the court in *Columbia River Service Corp. v. Gilman*[38] ruled that corporate officers, directors, shareholders and employees can be held liable as operators under CERCLA based on a fact intensive inquiry regarding such factors as the individual's "capacity to timely discover discharges; capacity to prevent and abate damage; power to direct activities of persons controlling the mechanism causing pollution."[39]

---

34   *Id.*, 810 F.2d at 745.

35   723 F.Supp. 1214 (W.D.Mich. 1989).

36   764 F.Supp. 565 (E.D.Mo. 1991).

37   *Id.*, at 571.

38   751 F.Supp. 1448 (W.D.Wash. 1990).

39   *Id.*, at 1454.

A number of other cases have also indicated that capacity to control is a prime factor and may be sufficient for the imposition of CERCLA liability.[40]

If the "capacity to control" theory prevails as the law of the land, the corporate form will provide very little protection against liability in hazardous waste cases. Virtually every majority shareholder has the capacity to control the affairs of the corporation, and sometimes even minority shareholders own enough stock to "control" the corporation. Moreover, corporate officers and managers typically have the "capacity to control" the activities within their areas of responsibility.

Traditional Corporate Veil Cases

Some courts have had more respect for the corporate form, and have not wished to go as far in imposing personal liability without a more traditional basis for doing so.

In *In re Acushnet River and New Bedford Harbor Proceedings re Alleged PCB Pollution*,[41] the government argued that a parent corporation should be held liable under CERCLA for the hazardous waste of its subsidiary based on minimal involvement in the affairs of the subsidiary (such as electing the subsidiary's board of directors). That position, which would render the corporate form meaningless, was rejected by the court. Instead, the court applied more traditional factors for piercing the corporate veil. The court looked for "suggestions of pervasive control" by the parent over the subsidiary, or an indication that the subsidiary was a "mere instrumentality" with respect to the

---

[40]   *See, e.g., U.S. v. Bliss*, 667 F.Supp. 1298, 1306 (E.D.Mo. 1987) (plant supervisor and chief executive officer had "ultimate authority for decisions regarding disposal" and actually arranged for the disposal of hazardous waste, and were found personally liable as generators under section 107(a)(3) of CERCLA, without piercing the corporate veil); *Idaho v. Bunker Hill Company*, 635 F.Supp. 665, 672 (D.Idaho 1986) (while the "normal" activities of a parent corporation "do not automatically warrant finding the parent an owner or operator," the corporate parent was an "operator" where it was aware of its subsidiary's waste disposal practices and the releases, and it had the "capacity to control" those matters and to prevent and abate the damage caused by the disposal and release of hazardous wastes).

[41]   675 F.Supp. 22 (D.Mass. 1987).

disposal of the parent's hazardous waste in order to pierce the corporate veil and impose CERCLA liability on the parent corporation for the hazardous waste activities of the subsidiary. The court found no such control or shell corporation and declined to pierce the corporate veil in that case.

Another recent case has also exhibited respect for the corporate form and resisted an attempted end run around it. In *Joslyn Corp. v. T.L. James & Co.*,[42] the present owner of a contaminated property commenced a private action under CERCLA against the corporate parent of the former owner, on the ground that the parent had CERCLA liability as an "owner or operator" of the site. The court refused to give an expansive reading to the "owner or operator" categories of PRPs, and the court declined to follow the line of cases discussed above which imposed direct liability on corporate officers or shareholders without first piercing the corporate veil. The court stated as follows:

> [T]his court holds that the corporate form, including limited liability for shareholders, is a doctrine firmly entrenched in American jurisprudence that may not be disregarded absent a specific congressional directive. Neither the clear language of CERCLA nor its legislative history provides authority for imposing individual liability on corporate officers or direct liability on parent corporations. Though it is recognized that CERCLA was enacted in the "waning hours of the 96th Congress," and was "the product of apparent legislative compromise [that] is not a model of clarity," . . . this court will not read into the statute a provision disregarding decades of corporate law. The court's conclusion is buttressed by the fact that Congress has, in the past, specified that shareholders or controlling parties are to be held responsible for the acts or debts of a valid corporation . . . Absent a similar provision in CERCLA, this court finds no direct liability against James Company.[43]

The court in *Joslyn Corp.* went on to apply traditional factors and ruled that the parent corporation had not dominated the finances,

---

[42]   696 F.Supp. 222 (W.D.La. 1988).

[43]   *Id.*, at 226.

policies and practices of its subsidiary and that the corporate veil therefore would not be pierced.[44] This ruling by the district court was upheld on appeal. The Court of Appeals for the Fifth Circuit held that Congress, in enacting CERCLA, did not intend to abrogate the general corporate law rule of limited liability. Without express Congressional directive to the contrary, the common law principles of limited liability of corporate shareholders continues to apply even in CERCLA cases. In order for James Co. to be liable, Joslyn would have to use the traditional technique of piercing the corporate veil. Upon review of the facts, the court found no justification for disregarding the corporate entity and holding James Co. liable.[45]

Nevertheless, the weight of authority to date supports end runs around the corporate veil. As a practical matter, these rulings have eliminated the traditional common law restrictions on liability. Thus, any corporate shareholder, officer, director or employee who is personally involved in the management of a company may be exposed to strict CERCLA liability for cleanup costs as an "operator" of the contaminated facility even if innocent of any wrongdoing. Similarly, any corporate personnel arranging or supervising arrangements for the disposal, treatment or transportation of hazardous substances may be exposed to strict CERCLA liability as a generator. At least the latter category of PRP is more palatable because it applies to those who had some actual involvement in the handling of hazardous waste.

14.5 The Emerging Federal Law for Piercing the Corporate Veil in Environmental Cleanup Cases

As indicated above, the traditional means for imposing liability on shareholders (including innocent shareholders) is to pierce the corporate veil. Recent federal court cases have noted the need for a uniform federal rule of decision with respect to piercing the corporate veil in

---

44   *Id.*, at 232.

45   *Joslyn Mfg. Co. v. T.L. James & Co., Inc.*, 893 F.2d 80 (5th Cir. 1990), *cert. den.*, 111 S.Ct. 1017 (1991). See also *In re Southern Timber Products, Inc.*, Appeal No. 89-2 (EPA Judicial Hearing, Nov. 13, 1990) (the EPA Judicial Hearing Officer, in a RCRA case, rejected a claim of personal liability of a corporate officer in the absence of circumstances justifying piercing the corporate veil under a traditional standard).

CERCLA cases. In that regard, the *Acushnet River* court stated as follows:

> In attempting to eliminate the dangers of hazardous wastes, CERCLA presents a national solution to a nationwide problem. One can hardly imagine a federal program more demanding of a national uniformity than environmental protection. Congress did not intend that the ability of the executive to fund the cleanup of hazardous waste sites should depend on the attitudes of the several states toward parent-subsidiary liability in general, or CERCLA in particular. The need for a uniform federal rule is especially great for questions of piercing the corporate veil, since liability under the statute must not depend on the particular state in which the defendant happens to reside.[46]

That court then adopted and applied a fairly traditional standard for piercing the corporate veil. The court had a specific policy reason for doing so, namely the objective of encouraging, rather than discouraging, private investment in contaminated properties:

> Under traditional principles, a corporation which wants to put a waste site or past generation site to productive use can do so by creating a well capitalized, non-fraudulent, separate corporate subsidiary. The ability to work through the subsidiary justifies the initial investment, which will delimit the extent of the risk. Under the [government's] proposed rule, a corporation which wanted to reclaim and make productive a waste site could not do so without risking all its corporate assets if it appeared more than passively interested in the performance of its subsidiary. Patently, the [government's] rule would discourage investors, and reduce the number of solvent parties from which the [government] will be able to seek clean up costs and damages.[47]

---

[46] *In re Acushnet River and New Bedford Harbor Proceedings re Alleged PCB Pollution*, 675 F.Supp. 22, 31 (D.Mass. 1987).

[47] *Id.*, at 32.

Another case, *U.S. v. Nicholet, Inc.,*[48] acknowledged the same need for a uniform federal rule, and then adopted the following rule concerning when the corporate veil may be pierced in CERCLA cases:

> Where a subsidiary is or was at the relevant time a member of one of the classes of persons potentially liable under CERCLA; and the parent had a substantial financial or ownership interest in the subsidiary; and the parent corporation controls or at the relevant time controlled the management and operations of the subsidiary, the parent's separate corporate existence may be disregarded.[49]

The *Nicholet* court then applied those standards to the allegations of the government's complaint and found that a cause of action was stated against a parent corporation. The government had alleged that, during the time a subsidiary corporation owned contaminated property, the parent corporation "held a majority and then all of [the subsidiary's] stock," the parent "actively participated in the management of [the subsidiary's] operations at the site while asbestos, a hazardous substance, was being disposed of there," that the parent "was familiar with [the subsidiary's] waste disposal practices and had the capacity to control the disposal and resultant releases and to abate damages from such releases," and that the parent "benefited from [the subsidiary's] waste disposal practices."[50] The court opinion contains no description of the alleged "active participation" in the operations of the site, as if the details were not important in view of the other factors alleged.

The *Nicholet* court implicitly rejected the more traditional formulations in the *Acushnet River* and *Joslyn Corp.* cases. Instead, the court adopted the operator liability standard of such cases as *State of New York v. Shore Realty Corp.*, and *U.S. v. Conservation Chemical*

---

[48] 712 F.Supp. 1193 (E.D.Pa. 1989). *See, also, U.S. v. Kayser-Roth Corporation,* 724 F.Supp. 15 (D.R.I. Oct. 11, 1989), *affirmed* 910 F.2d 24 (1st Cir. 1990), *cert. den.* 111 S.Ct. 957 (1991) (successor of parent corporation was held liable as an operator, due to the actual exercise of control over the business of the subsidiary, and also as an owner, under a slightly relaxed veil piercing standard under CERCLA).

[49] *Id.,* at 1202.

[50] *Id.,* at 1203-1204.

Corp., and the capacity to control standard of *U.S. v. Northeastern Pharmaceutical & Chemical Co.*, *U.S. v. Bliss*, and *Idaho v. Bunker Hill Co.*, all of which perform the end run around the corporate veil. Thus, the *Nicholet* court only paid lip service to the corporate veil doctrine in the CERCLA context. Perhaps the court felt that the end run is tantamount to piercing the corporate veil.

In a more recent case, Tufts University inherited the stock of a wood treatment company and was sued by the current owner of the site formerly occupied by the company. In addition to the operator liability claim against Tuffs (see § 4.4 above), the plaintiff contended that the university had owner liability. But the court declined to pierce the corporate veil and did not impose CERCLA liability because the university's business was separate and distinct from the company's. There was no common business department nor any combination of daily operations. Financial statements were not consolidated. Tufts did not finance the company's operations, nor did the university use any of the property of the company. While some dividends were distributed in excess of net earnings, the company was able to pay its debts and there was no pillaging of the company's assets by the university.[51]

Applying a traditional veil piercing standard under state law, the court in *CPC International, Inc. v. Aerojet-General Corp.*[52] found that Aerojet was liable under CERCLA as an owner. Aerojet "totally dominated" its subsidiary corporation so that there was a "complete identity of interest" and the subsidiary was the "mere instrumentality" of Aerojet. Probative factors included Aerojet's formation of the wholly owned subsidiary for the purpose of acquiring the site; the incorporation was merely a change in form, not in substance, as Aerojet personnel were transferred to identical or similar jobs with the new subsidiary; Aerojet held authority to direct day-to-day operations and policy matters; the subsidiary's board of directors was nonfunctional and held no meetings; Aerojet had total financial control, and the subsidiary had no separate bank account. The facts were egregious enough so that the corporate veil could be pierced under a traditional state-law standard,

---

[51]   *Jacksonville Electric Authority v. Eppinger and Russell Co.*, 776 F.Supp. 1542 (M.D.Fla. 1991).

[52]   777 F.Supp. 549 (W.D.Mich. 1991).

and it was not necessary for the court to consider any relaxed standard.[53]

While results have not been uniform due to the different facts of each case, the message of these cases is that, by giving expansive scope to the term "operator," some courts have included more than those who personally commit wrongful acts and have imposed liability on a higher level of managers or on shareholders under circumstances where no liability would have existed under the common law. Most of those courts have done so purportedly without piercing the corporate veil. The *Nicholet* court called it piercing the corporate veil under a relaxed standard. This line of cases blurs the distinction between direct liability for one's own acts and derivative liability upon piercing the corporate veil and virtually eliminates any protection of the corporate form.

14.6 Policy Differences and Conflict Among the Courts Regarding "Operator" Liability and Piercing the Corporate Veil in Environmental Cleanup Cases

While the courts recognize that a uniform federal standard is needed for piercing the corporate veil in CERCLA cases, widely divergent rulings exist as to what that standard should be. The policy differences are rather pronounced. On the one hand, some courts have interpreted operator liability broadly, or have liberally pierced the corporate veil, or have merged those two concepts. The apparent purpose is to impose cleanup responsibility on private parties and to preserve the Superfund, as intended by CERCLA.

On the other hand, some courts have appreciated, from a long-term perspective, that the preceding view will only discourage private investment and cleanup of contaminated properties, contrary to the objectives of CERCLA. Moreover, as corporate officers and managers are held personally and strictly liable as operators or as generators, individuals will be less willing to fulfill those necessary roles for fear of

---

[53] *Id.*, at 578-579.

the crushing personal liability which may result.[54] If private companies or individuals are unwilling to invest in or manage known or potential hazardous waste sites, the government and the taxpayer will ultimately have to bear more of the burden. Courts taking this viewpoint believe that traditional limitations on liability should be maintained under the corporate form in order to encourage private investment and management of hazardous waste sites, and that the courts should not read more into the word "operator" than Congress explicitly directs.

Logically, the term "operator" merely refers to lessees or tenants who possess and operate real estate, to bring them within the strict liability principle along with owners. The term contains no inference whatsoever that the corporate form should be disregarded when the owner or operator is a corporation. The cases giving an expansive meaning to the term contain little or no reasoning to support their astonishing conclusion that Congress intended, with one word, to overrule a fundamental concept of corporate law.

It is not enough to say that Congress defined "owner or operator" to include any "person" who owns or operates a facility,[55] and that Congress in turn defined "person" to include individuals as well as corporations and other entities.[56] Those definitions do not compel or imply the conclusion that an individual, because he is a person, will be an owner or operator even though the business or activity is conducted in corporate form. The individual is simply not acting in his individual capacity, but as an officer, director, agent or employee of the

---

[54]   Indeed, it would appear that any person accepting a managerial position with any company which owns or operates real property which might even remotely be contaminated, or whose duties would include handling or supervising the handling of hazardous substances, would be well advised to obtain the agreement of the company (and, if possible, its shareholders) to provide indemnification with respect to any personal liability arising under the environmental laws as a result of acts within the course and scope of the agency or employment or as a result of capacity to control the area of responsibility involved. Query how useful indemnification is if liability is very large; directors and officers insurance might be better, if it is available without an environmental liability exclusion.

[55]   42 U.S.C. § 9601(20)(A).

[56]   *Id.*, § 9601(21).

corporation. It is the corporation which is the owner or operator. The same is true when it comes to arranging for the disposal, treatment or transportation of hazardous substances (the so-called "generator" category of PRPs). Corporate personnel do so on behalf of the corporation, not in their individual capacities.

Individual corporate personnel ought to expect, however, to be liable for any crimes or other violations of law which they may commit, as has always been the law. But it is *not* a crime or a violation of law to operate contaminated property or to dispose of hazardous waste, as long as applicable laws and regulations are obeyed.

Congress clearly has chosen to impose strict liability on owners or operators of contaminated property and on generators and transporters of hazardous waste when releases must be cleaned up. When a PRP is a corporation, the shareholders certainly risk the loss of their investment. It is something else entirely to say that shareholders and numerous corporate managers and personnel may also risk personal liability without proof of any violation of law or wrongful conduct on their part. The courts reaching that conclusion have gone too far.

Thus, unless Congress explicitly overrules these aspects of corporate law in the CERCLA context, the traditional rules regarding the corporate form should still apply. In that case, the term "operator" says nothing about either piercing the corporate veil or end runs around it.

The issue of CERCLA operator liability, whether viewed in theory as an end run around the corporate veil or as directly piercing that veil or as neither, has been considered so far mostly by the federal district courts (i.e., at the trial court level) and as has been shown, the courts are not in agreement. The policy differences have so far not been resolved by the few federal appellate court opinions on the subject. Indeed, the opinions of the Court of Appeals for the First Circuit[57] and the Fifth

---

[57]   *U.S. v. Kayser-Roth Corp.*, 910 F.2d 24 (1st Cir. 1990), *cert. den.* 111 S.Ct. 957 (1991) (applying a broad view of operator liability under CERCLA).

Circuit[58] appear to be at odds, yet the U.S. Supreme Court declined to hear the appeals of those cases.

Only time will tell how the policy differences will be resolved as litigation in this area continues. At the present time, however, corporate shareholders, officers, directors, agents and employees who fulfill management or supervisory functions or who are involved personally with the generation, treatment, transportation or disposal of hazardous waste, should appreciate that they are at risk of personal liability under CERCLA and other environmental laws and that the time-honored concept of limitation of liability through use of the corporate form may provide little or no protection. Apparently, the only persons involved with a company who have nothing to fear are purely passive investors who have no capacity to control under circumstances where the corporate form will be respected by the courts.

14.7 Corporate Successor Liability

Stock Transactions. When the stock of a corporation is transferred to a new owner, there is no change of the corporation's assets and liabilities. Those liabilities may include environmental cleanup costs and monetary penalties. The new owner risks loss of the investment if the liabilities of the corporation exceed its assets (at the time of the acquisition or in the future). Additionally, for reasons discussed above, the new owner may also incur direct personal liability for cleanup costs if the owner becomes an operator of the property, or if the corporate veil can be pierced, with respect to times after the stock acquisition. The seller of the stock obtains an agreed price for his investment, and avoids any ongoing status as an operator of contaminated property; however, the seller remains potentially liable as an operator of the property at the time of any hazardous substance disposal, or if the corporate veil can be pierced with respect to times when the seller owned the corporation.

Thus, the acquisition of the stock of a corporation which owns or operates contaminated real estate merely passes along potential environmental liabilities to the new owner. While the risk to the seller is

---

[58]   *Joslyn Mfg. Co. v. T.L. James & Co., Inc.*, 893 F.2d 80 (5th Cir. 1990) *cert. den.* 111 S.Ct. 1017 (1991) (upholding traditional corporate law principles even in CERCLA cases).

certainly diminished with respect to future events (and the seller has the proceeds of sale), the seller remains at risk of being named as a defendant in a cleanup cost recovery action as to past events and contamination.

Mergers and Consolidations. The same analysis applies to corporate mergers and consolidations where the surviving corporation succeeds by operation of law to the assets and liabilities (including environmental liabilities) of the disappearing corporation. For instance, in *Anspec v. Johnson Controls, Inc.,*[59] the current owner of a contaminated property was permitted to pursue a cleanup cost recovery action under CERCLA against the corporate successor by merger of the corporation which formerly owned the site when the pollution allegedly occurred.[60]

Similarly, in *GRM Industries v. Wickes Manufacturing Company,*[61] Wickes acquired all of the stock of Gulf & Western Manufacturing Co. (G&W) twelve years after G&W had last used a large hazardous waste underground storage tank and two years after G&W had sold the site to GRM's predecessor. GRM sought reimbursement of the cost of removal of the tank and hazardous wastes. Wickes contended that it had never owned or operated the site. However, the court pointed out that G&W, as a corporate entity, continued to retain all its liabilities despite the change in ownership of its stock. The court determined that it was too soon in the litigation to tell whether Wickes should be held liable as the corporate successor of G&W, a potentially liable party, and Wickes' motion to dismiss was denied. (The court did not set forth the potential factual basis for successor liability on Wickes' part, such as a subsequent merger of G&W into Wickes.)

This is of academic interest where the merged corporations are ultimately owned by the same people, but some corporate reorganizations do involve an actual transfer of ownership.

Asset Transactions. In order to avoid the risk of inheriting unknown liabilities which might be acquired along with corporate stock,

---

[59]   922 F.2d 1240 (6th Cir. 1991).

[60]   *See also Smith Land & Improvements Corp. v. Celotex Corp.*, 851 F.2d 86 (3d Cir. 1988), *cert. den.*, 488 U.S. 1029, 109 S.Ct. 837 (1989).

[61]   749 F.Supp. 810 (W.D.Mich. 1990).

transactions are often structured instead as asset acquisitions. In such cases, the purchaser of assets generally does not succeed to the liabilities of the seller. Thus, the buyer would not be liable for a number of possible environmental claims, such as toxic tort or other common law claims and some statutory claims (e.g., for monetary penalties) which might be maintained against the seller with respect to events occurring before the sale. While this may avoid the transfer of some liabilities, the purchaser nevertheless will become liable as the current owner or operator of contaminated real estate, and that automatic PRP status cannot be avoided. In addition, the new owner will be liable for conditions existing (e.g., nuisances) and events occurring (e.g., toxic torts) after the acquisition. On balance, however, asset transactions have definite advantages with regard to avoidance of successor liability.

Recharacterization of Asset Transactions. The preceding paragraph notes that purchasers of assets "generally" do not inherit the liabilities of the seller. As with most rules, there are exceptions. *Philadelphia Electric Company v. Hercules, Inc.,*[62] summarizes those exceptions as follows:

> [W]here (1) the purchaser of assets expressly or impliedly agrees to assume obligations of the transferor; (2) the transaction amounts to a consolidation or *de facto* merger; (3) the purchasing corporation is merely a continuation of the transferor corporation; or (4) the transaction is fraudulently entered into to escape liability, a successor corporation may be held responsible for the debts and liabilities of its predecessor ... A fifth circumstance, sometimes included as an exception to the general rule, is where the transfer was without adequate consideration and provisions were not made for creditors of the transferor ... [Another exception is] the more controversial "product-line" exception in products liability cases.[63]

With respect to the *de facto* merger exception, the court commented as follows:

---

62   762 F.2d 303 (3rd. Cir. 1985), *cert. den.* 474 U.S. 980 (1985).

63   *Id.,* at 308-309.

In determining whether a particular transaction amounts to a de facto merger as distinguished from an ordinary purchase and sale of assets most courts look at the following factors:

(1) There is a continuation of the enterprise of the seller corporation, so that there is continuity of management, personnel, physical location, assets, and general business operations.

(2) There is a continuity of shareholders which results from the purchasing corporation paying for the acquired assets with shares of its own stock, this stock ultimately coming to be held by the shareholders of the seller corporation so that they become a constituent part of the purchasing corporation.

(3) The seller corporation ceases its ordinary business operations, liquidates, and dissolves as soon as legally and practically possible.

(4) The purchasing corporation assumes those obligations of the seller ordinarily necessary for the uninterrupted continuation of normal business operations of the seller corporation.[64]

Based on those factors, the *Philadelphia Electric* court determined that an asset acquisition was a *de facto* merger and that the purchaser therefore had successor liability for pollution of groundwater and a river.

It is hard to distinguish the factors used by the *Philadelphia Electric* court for the *de facto* merger doctrine from the other exception (to the general rule of nonliability) where the purchaser of assets is a "mere continuation" of the selling corporation. There is obviously some overlap between the exceptions.

The general rule and its exceptions have been applied in a number of recent cases. In a case where an asset purchaser expressly assumed the liabilities of the seller, except for liabilities arising from the seller's use and disposal of PCBs, the court applied the traditional *de facto* merger doctrine to impose CERCLA liability on the asset purchaser for

---

[64]   *Id.*, at 310.

the PCB contamination.[65] In contrast, the general rule of nonliability of an asset purchaser was upheld in a hazardous waste case where none of the traditional exceptions applied under the facts of the case, and summary judgment in favor of the asset purchaser was affirmed.[66]

In another case, key employees of a corporation formed a new corporation and acquired substantially all the assets of the first corporation, which then dissolved and distributed its assets to its shareholders. The new corporation then changed its name to be substantially identical to the name of the dissolved corporation. Although ownership had changed, the business continued in essentially the same manner as before. The United States brought suit under CERCLA against the new corporation due to hazardous waste disposal by the predecessor corporation. The court applied a broadened version of the "mere continuation" doctrine. Factors weighed by the court under that approach included "whether the successor: (1) retains the same employees; (2) retains the same supervisory personnel; (3) retains the same production facilities in the same location; (4) continues producing the same products; (5) retains the same name; (6) maintains continuity of assets and general business operations; and (7) whether the successor holds itself out to the public as the continuation of the previous corporation."[67] Applying these factors, the court determined that the new corporation was liable under CERCLA as the successor of the dissolved corporation.

Applying the same factors enunciated in the preceding case, another court also found an asset purchaser liable under CERCLA under the "mere continuation" doctrine. Important factors were that "[t]he company retained the same employees and management operated out of the same physical facilities and continued the same waste hauling business, held itself out to the public as the same company and retained virtually all of the operating assets. The fact that [the asset purchasing

---

[65] *In re Acushnet River & New Bedford Harbor Proceedings re Alleged PCB Pollution*, 712 F.Supp. 1010 (D.Mass. 1989).

[66] *Louisiana-Pacific Corp. v. Asarco, Inc.*, 909 F.2d 1260 (9th Cir. 1990).

[67] *U.S. v. Distler*, 741 F.Supp. 637, 642-643, 31 ERC 1092, 1096 (W.D.Ky. 1990).

corporation] did not retain the same officers or board members is not fatal, as noted by Distler, as long as the other factors are present."[68]

The "mere continuation" doctrine caught another asset purchaser in a CERCLA case where the same location was kept, the purchaser used the seller's logo, and there was continuity in employees, including a key employee of the seller,[69] so that summary judgment was not available on the successor liability issue.

However, at least two other courts have declined to apply either the *de facto* merger doctrine or the expanded version of the "mere continuation" doctrine (known as the "continuing business enterprise" exception), and have refused to impose CERCLA liability on asset purchasers where there was no continuity of shareholders (i.e., there was a true change in ownership of the business)[70] or where there was no commonality of directors and shareholders.[71]

The point of this line of cases for purposes of our discussion is that there are circumstances under which the courts will not respect the form of an asset transaction and will recharacterize it as necessary in order to impose successor liability on the purchaser under one or more exceptions to the general rule of nonliability.

This should not be a problem in cases where the sale of assets is a bone fide arm's length transaction with an actual change of ownership for fair value, especially in the case of a pure real estate acquisition of a location for the purchaser's own business which is different from the seller's. However, asset transactions frequently involve more than the real estate alone and include some or all of the seller's business. In such cases, the purchaser should be mindful of the risk of successor liability and may wish to structure the transaction and the nature of his new business in a way which will minimize the risk of attack. Some

---

[68] *U.S. v. Mexico Feed and Seed Co.*, 764 F.Supp. 565 (E.D.Mo. 1991).

[69] *U.S. v. Western Processing*, 751 F.Supp. 902 (W.D.Wash. 1990).

[70] *Sylvester Brothers Development Co. v. Burlington Northern Railroad*, 772 F.Supp. 443 (D.Minn. 1990).

[71] *U.S. v. Chrysler Corp.*, 31 ERC 1997 (D.Del. August 28, 1990) (although the asset purchaser in this case was found liable under an express assumption of liability clause in the transaction agreement).

commentators have suggested that the risk can be minimized by structuring the transaction as a cash-for-assets acquisition and by making changes to the enterprise and its product lines or otherwise altering the business in ways sufficient to interrupt its continuity.[72] But it might be difficult to change the enterprise where, as a practical matter, the purpose of the acquisition is to acquire and continue a going business.

14.8 Restructuring to Avoid Environmental Liability-- A Dangerous Proposition

One of the exceptions to the general rule that purchasers of assets are not liable for the seller's debts relates to fraudulent transfers for the purpose of avoiding liability. That exception was applied in a recent case involving environmental contamination in the vicinity of Battle Creek, Michigan.[73] In that case, the Michigan Department of Natural Resources notified the Thomas Solvent Company that its Battle Creek facilities were suspected sources of groundwater contamination in a well field which was the primary water supply for more than 35,000 people in the Battle Creek area. The company was asked to investigate and clean up the contamination. Thomas Solvent Company then proceeded to transfer its non-Battle Creek assets into four newly created corporations. The state and federal governments sued on the theory that the transfers were fraudulent and also sought to impose successor liability on the transferee corporations. The court found that Thomas Solvent Company had greatly reduced its assets by spinning off the four new corporations and that the restructuring was accomplished with the actual intent to hinder, delay or defraud creditors, including the state and federal governments with respect to potential CERCLA liability. In addition, the restructured companies were a mere continuation of the Thomas Solvent Company. The court granted summary judgment to the plaintiffs on the fraudulent transfer and successor liability claims.[74]

---

[72]   *See, e.g.,* J. Russell/J. Richardson, *Avoiding Corporate Successor Environmental Liability,* 14 Chemical Waste Litigation Reporter 870 (Oct. 1987).

[73]   *Kelley v. Thomas Solvent Co.,* 725 F.Supp. 1446, 29 ERC 1119 (W.D.Mich 1988).

[74]   *Id.,* at 1128, 1132. For similar results in other cases, *see Abbot Laboratories v. Thermo Chem Inc.,* 1991 U.S. Dist. LEXIS 11789 (W.D. Mich. Aug. 20, 1991); *U.S. v. Mottolo,* 695 F.Supp. 615 (D.N.H. 1988).

Thus, any corporate restructuring after notice of potential environmental liability will be suspect and should be undertaken only with great care, if at all, by the parties and their counsel.

CHAPTER FIFTEEN

APPRAISAL AND VALUATION OF ENVIRONMENTALLY IMPAIRED REAL ESTATE

Paul A. Quintiliani

Cohen, Kerhart, Quintiliani
Real Estate Appraisers & Consultants

15.1 Introduction

Environmental contamination is an issue of increasing concern among buyers and sellers of real estate. Most real estate investors recognize that the value and marketability of a contaminated site is affected, but the degree to which the property's value is impacted is often in dispute. As such, members of the appraisal profession are being asked more frequently to quantify the value implications resulting from hazardous contamination.

Though contaminated properties have existed for many years, it is only recently that a body of knowledge establishing practical and theoretical appraisal procedures has emerged. The purpose of this chapter is to provide an overview of the appraisal process as it relates to contaminated real estate. As environmental issues are only now being afforded widespread consideration, there are professional disagreements on which procedures to apply. It is not the intent of this chapter to provide a definitive guide to appraising contaminated properties. Rather, the objective is to raise issues which should be considered and to identify how various forms of contamination affect the value of real estate.

15.2 Classifying Contaminated Properties

The first step in any appraisal assignment is to identify the problem. This is particularly essential when contamination is the issue. Different forms of contamination have measurably different impacts on the value of a property. Consider the following examples:

> An industrial building containing 5,000 square feet possesses asbestos contamination which must be removed. The firm contracted for removal services has indicated that abatement will require 90 days and result in a total expenditure of $75,000.

> An industrial building containing 5,000 square feet possesses subsoil DDT contamination which must be removed before it permeates the local aquifer. Several remediation companies were contacted to determine the extent of the contamination. No precise estimates can be determined at present, and the timing and cost of cleanup are unknown.

These examples illustrate the complexities encountered when appraising hazardous or contaminated properties. Both industrial buildings possess hazardous substances, but the risks and uncertainties associated with the DDT-affected property are clearly greater, even to unsophisticated investors. Therefore, the implications as to property value must be similarly differentiated.

The first analytical requirement for the appraiser is an understanding of the extent to which a property is contaminated, and the degree to which the cleanup technology has been successfully utilized in other instances. This does not imply that appraisal professionals should determine the presence or absence of hazardous contamination. This is beyond the customary training of most appraisers. However, the appraiser should be knowledgeable of the severity of the contamination and should clearly understand the cleanup procedures required. That information would be obtained from environmental consultants hired by one or more of the parties to a real estate transaction.

When appraising contaminated sites it is often useful to categorize the property by (1) the degree of contamination; (2) the proven success and regulatory conformance of the proposed cleanup technology; and (3) the probable future risks and uncertainties remaining after cleanup, including residual stigma. Placing the subject site within this typology helps the appraiser to conceptualize the problem and will assist when comparing market sales to the property being appraised.

Categorizing a property requires knowledge of various forms of contamination and the hazards associated with each. However, these categories should be viewed as conceptual boundaries rather than absolutes. The process of making these conceptual distinctions involves discussions with remediation companies, conversations with governmental and regulatory oversight agencies, as well as interviews with probable buyers. The following typology is adequate for most appraisal applications.

CLASSIFICATION OF CONTAMINATED PROPERTIES

Contamination Level	*	Cleanup Process	*	Remaining Stigma
------------------------	*	-------------------------	*	-----------------------
Low to Moderate	*	Proven and Accepted	*	Low to Moderate
	*		*	
Moderate to High	*	Tested but Questioned	*	Moderate to High
	*		*	
High to Severe	*	Untested and Disputed	*	High to Severe

The appraised property can possess any given combination of the elements identified above. However, it would be unusual for a property with low to moderate contamination levels to have a remaining stigma that is classified as high to severe. This conclusion would typically be inconsistent, although unique forms of contamination may make such a categorization appropriate.

15.3 The Effects of Contamination on Value

Contaminated real estate can suffer a loss in value for various reasons. The most obvious reduction in value would be the cost to remove or remediate the existing contaminants. However, other losses can occur, with the most notable being a reduction in parcel utility and residual stigma after cleanup efforts have been concluded.

15.3.1 Quantifying Remediation Costs

The cost to remove existing contaminants is one of the reasons contaminated properties are worth less than similar nonimpacted sites. A prudent and knowledgeable buyer would make an allowance for cleanup costs when purchasing a contaminated site. The amount of the cleanup allowance is directly affected by the level of contamination and remediation technology to be employed. The allowance should include (1) the investigative studies required to determine the extent of contamination; (2) the known remediation costs presented by a qualified contractor; and (3) contingencies for future costs that may arise.

Determining an appropriate cleanup allowance requires careful coordination between the appraiser and qualified remediation experts. Quantifying the cost of the investigative studies and the known remediation expenditures is typically a basic accounting function. However, contingencies for future costs are inherently more subjective, though this is often the largest cost category.

Contingencies are an essential element in the cleanup allowance. There is a contaminated site in Southern California, for example, that had an initial projected cleanup cost of $2,000,000 in 1987. Had the property been appraised in 1987 without some contingency for future expenditures, the value of the site would have been grossly overstated. Currently, cleanup expenditures are approaching $10,500,000, with further expenditures likely if the contamination seeps into the aquifer.

When making provisions for future contingencies, it is necessary to understand the proven success of the cleanup technology, regulatory conformance of the remediation strategy, and possible movement of the contamination. One must also be aware that current remediation requirements can change. All these factors are elements to consider when establishing a contingency allowance. Experienced professionals in the remediation field are often the best source of information, as are comparisons of projected versus actual costs of other contaminated sites.

It is also important when establishing contingency allowances to avoid incorporating stigma elements. Residual stigma, or the property's reduced marketability after cleanup, is a conceptually separate factor which should be isolated from the cost to cure contamination. Stigma results from buyer perceptions of future risks and uncertainties, which is partially a function of unknowns in the regulatory environment.

The contamination typology developed previously in this chapter is useful in estimating contingencies. There are many instances in which remediation technologies are proven and accepted. Throughout Southern California, for example, a substantial number of gas stations have been redeveloped to more productive uses even though underground tanks are leaking and must be removed. The method of remediating these properties is widely accepted and frequently employed. Therefore, a contingency allowance may not be warranted. Asbestos removal is similarly proven and accepted. However, more severe forms of contamination produce greater cost uncertainties. It is not uncommon in these instances for actual costs to exceed projections by a wide margin.

15.3.2 Losses in Parcel Utility

A loss in parcel utility is the usual consequence of a property that must be remediated, even when only low levels of hazardous materials are present. Consider the prior example of the 5,000 square foot industrial building that contains asbestos. If the user of this facility is a manufacturer who operates three eight-hour shifts, then production must be curtailed during the 90-day cleanup period. In other words, the right of use and occupancy is temporarily diminished. Therefore, the loss in property value is likely to exceed the cost to cure the existing contamination.

Other forms of contamination can produce more substantive losses in utility. For example, there is a property in Southern California that has such extensive amounts of subsurface contamination that permanent monitoring wells will need to be maintained for a period of at least 30 years. These monitoring wells will not only require expenditures for ongoing maintenance and observation, they will also limit potential developments because the integrity of the monitoring wells must be preserved. These monitoring wells are analogous to permanent easements placed intermittently over the property. Furthermore, the cleanup of this property will require six to eight months of ongoing efforts, which will seriously curtail operations and preclude any additional development on the site during that time.

Another example would be any property which has been designated as a "hazardous waste" or "border zone" property under California's Hazardous Waste Disposal Land Use Law (see Chapter Five); or any property subject to similar use restrictions under the laws of any state or local jurisdiction. The existence of contamination may also affect the availability of building permits or development approvals (see Chapter Five).

The examples above illustrate that contamination can result in lost utility that is both temporary and permanent. The form and magnitude to which a parcel is affected is dependent upon the level of contamination present, the remediation technology employed, and any use or development restrictions imposed by applicable laws or regulations.

Environmental contamination can affect the utility of the land, the utility of the improvements, or both elements simultaneously. The distinction depends upon how a property is contaminated. For example, if an industrial building contains interior chemical holding tanks which were not cleaned or removed by the prior tenant, only the utility of the building is affected. Upon removal of these tanks, assuming no other contamination is present, the property will possess normal utility. Therefore, the existing contamination does not directly affect the land component of the improved parcel.

It is essential to make distinctions about which component of the economic unit is impacted (land or improvements). If only the improvements are negatively affected, then removing these improvements can potentially eliminate the residual stigma because future risks and uncertainties are eliminated similarly. Therefore, there is no theoretical basis for a stigma reduction.

15.3.3 Contamination and Residual Stigma

Even after a contaminated parcel has been cleaned to currently required levels, the site still may not sell for the price it would have received had contamination never been present. A contaminated property can be negatively affected by residual stigma, or loss in value resulting from potential buyers' perception of future risks and uncertainties.

Residual stigma may be minimal to nonexistent, or residual stigma may be greater than the value of the property without hazardous contamination. However, residual stigma is a very real element when appraising contaminated sites.

One example of residual stigma can be found in Southern California. There is a property located in a thriving industrial market that has subsurface DDT contamination. Though the property was cleaned to Environmental Protection Agency and Regional Water Quality Board standards, the current owner has been unable to give the property away at any price. This is somewhat unusual given that surrounding improved properties sell over $100 per square foot. The residual stigma in this instance appears to be greater than the value of the property assuming no contaminants. The implication is that the owners may have to pay someone to take the property off their hands. Negative value can be a reality in cases of severe contamination.

However, it is inappropriate to assume categorically that contamination leads to residual stigma. All the forces that generally affect real estate (social, economic, political and environmental) must also be considered. In Utah, for example, certain properties located in an area known to possess high levels of uranium tailings have actually commanded premiums because the contaminated region was designated as a hazardous waste disposal zone. Major waste treatment and disposal companies subsequently made purchases at prices in excess of surrounding land values.

Additionally, residual stigma may be so minimal that its measurement is not possible. This is particularly true in cases where cleanup technologies are proven and prior contamination levels are low to moderate. For example, sites with underground service station tanks that minimally contaminated the soil are likely to have little residual stigma. Asbestos contaminated office buildings are somewhat similar, although recent studies have shown that asbestos affected properties experience higher vacancy levels even after removal of the contaminants.

The conclusion being advanced is that residual stigma is affected by the contaminants located on the property and the technology available to remove the hazardous substances. All factors being equal, it is logical to assume that the more frequently a remediation technology is employed, proven successful and accepted by regulatory authorities, the less the corresponding residual stigma. However, certain external factors can offset stigma, such as actions taken by governmental agencies. Therefore, all elements normally considered in the appraisal of non-contaminated properties must be analyzed for contaminated sites as well.

15.4 Applications to the Appraisal Process

As previously indicated, this chapter is not intended to provide the reader with a step-by-step approach to appraising real estate that possesses environmental contamination. However, it is appropriate to demonstrate the relationship between the theoretical concepts developed herein and the appraisal process. Within the framework established, it is possible to analyze and quantify the impacts of contamination on value.

Many types of value can be concluded in an appraisal. Most typical is "market value," which can be defined as follows:

> The most probable price, as of a specified date, in cash, or in terms equivalent to cash, or in other precisely revealed terms, for which the specified property rights should sell after reasonable exposure in a competitive market under all conditions requisite to fair sale, with the buyer and seller each acting prudently, knowledgeably, and for self-interest, and assuming that neither is under undue duress.[1]

A critical element of the above definition is that the subject property will transfer. If the property is contaminated on the date of value, then it is assumed that all impacts of the contamination will be reflected in the final value estimate, as a knowledgeable buyer will invariably make an assessment of all site characteristics.

One method of appraising real estate is to compare properties with similar characteristics to the property being appraised and then make adjustments for various elements of comparability (i.e., time, financing terms, location, size and physical characteristics). Therefore, it would be

---

[1]   *The Dictionary of Real Estate Appraisal, 2nd Edition,* American Institute of Real Estate Appraisers, pp. 192-193 (1989).

most preferable when appraising contaminated sites to use recent sales of similarly contaminated sites in the defined market area. However, while this approach is conceptually valid, it has only limited practical application. Properties with severe forms of contamination do not lend themselves to direct comparisons for the following reasons:

1. There are only a limited number of actual transactions which can be gathered for properties with severe levels of contamination. Most potential buyers will avoid properties with high contamination levels. Why buy trouble?

2. Obtaining accurate information on sites with contamination is difficult at best. The appraiser is typically unable to verify the extent of the contamination, or the projected costs to remove the hazardous materials (including contingency allowances).

3. Different forms of contamination can have different impacts on the residual stigma. Oil contamination that does not permeate groundwater systems is not comparable to DDT contamination which has seeped into nearby wells. Making adjustments for these differences is highly subjective.

4. Different forms of contamination can require different cleanup methods. This produces dissimilar impacts on the utility of the comparable properties.

Unless the appraiser is able to verify factually all of these elements, the comparisons will be meaningless. And, even if this information is known, the differences between similarly contaminated properties will likely make comparisons inappropriate. The point is that each contaminated property is so unique in terms of the cost-to-cure, the loss in utility and residual stigma that it is not possible to combine all these elements into a single adjustment or series of adjustments.

In these circumstances, it is more useful to avoid making aggregate comparisons by accounting for as much of the value loss through analysis of the subject property. The objective is to isolate residual stigma by first deducting the remediation costs and utility losses. A demonstration of this technique is provided in the following example.

Assume there is a 10-acre vacant commercial parcel that has underground diesel fuel contamination caused by the corrosion

317

and rupture of a fuel line that services an adjacent property. The line rupture was not detected for several years and approximately 100,000 gallons of fuel has seeped into the soil and now threatens to contaminate the groundwater. Were the property not contaminated, its market value is estimated to be $50 per square foot, or $21,780,000.

To date, approximately $150,000 has been expended in consultation studies to determine the magnitude of the problem. The consultants have indicated that an additional $50,000 will be expended before cleanup can commence. Estimates for removing the contamination are dependent upon whether future studies confirm groundwater contact.

The known remediation costs are $1,000,000 if no groundwater contamination is present, and $6,000,000 if groundwater contamination is involved. Conversations with the consultants revealed that these cost projections are their most probable estimates and include a 15 percent contingency allowance. The consultants confirmed that actual costs may increase substantially because the remediation technology has not been widely used and the regulatory agencies overseeing the cleanup may not permit the proposed levels of contamination remaining after the abatement process. The property owner had acquired several other bids from qualified environmental companies. The highest bids were for $4,000,000 assuming no groundwater contamination and $10,000,000 assuming groundwater contamination.

The cleanup process will take six months to complete. After completion, monitoring wells will be located along the western boundary of the property, and the wells must be maintained for at least 30 years. These wells will prohibit development of one-fifth of the property, although they will not diminish the utility of the remaining developable area.

In the analysis process, the appraiser determines that the known costs assuming no groundwater contamination, plus an additional 100 percent contingency are appropriate. A further allowance has been made for possible groundwater contamination of $2,500,000. This results in the following adjustments.

Estimated Market Value Before Contamination	$21,780,000
Less Cleanup Costs:	
Remaining Consultation Studies	$ 50,000
Known Costs	1,000,000
Contingency Allowance	1,000,000
Possible Water Contamination Allowance	2,500,000

Total Cleanup Costs	$ 4,550,000
Market Value Adjusted for Cleanup Costs	$17,230,000

The remediation effort is projected to continue for six months. Research was conducted into properties that had no development permits in place versus sites available for immediate development to determine whether discounts are appropriate. The research indicated that a 10 percent adjustment is warranted for properties that cannot be immediately developed.

After cleanup, approximately one-fifth of the site (or two acres) will not be developable, even for such low intensity uses as parking. This land area is determined to have no contributory value. Therefore, a deduction of $4,356,000 has been applied (two acres X $50 per square foot). The adjustments applied for utility losses are summarized below.

Market Value Adjusted For Cleanup Costs	$17,230,000
Less Utility Losses:	
Development Delays	2,178,000
Diminished Site Area	4,356,000

Total Loss Of Utility	$ 6,534,000
Market Value Adjusted for Utility Losses	$10,696,000

To determine the residual stigma associated with the subject, sales of other contaminated sites that had been cleaned prior to sale were gathered and compared to sales of uncontaminated sites in each property's market area. Potential buyers were also surveyed for their criteria when purchasing previously contaminated sites. Based upon these investigations, a residual stigma discount factor of 25 percent was concluded.

Market Value Adjusted for Utility Losses	$10,696,000
Less Stigma Factor (25 percent)	5,445,000

Indicated Market Value	$ 5,251,000

The example above illustrates one method of appraising properties impacted with substantial contamination where direct market comparisons cannot be applied. This approach is particularly useful when contamination levels are high or remediation technologies are unproven because it allows the analyst to isolate each factor that reduces the property's market value separately. However, the adjustments applied and the manner in which each was derived is included only for illustration. Each contaminated property is unique. Therefore, it is not adequate to make broad generalizations or apply simple formulas in the appraisal process. This class of properties demands more quantitative analysis and research.

15.5 Summary

Hazardous contamination is increasingly important in the appraisal of real estate. Methodologies for quantifying the value implications, however, have only recently emerged. This chapter has identified some of the conceptual issues that should be addressed when appraising contaminated property and has offered some practical frameworks for analyzing the problems created.

Contamination clearly affects property values more than the related cleanup costs. As noted in this chapter, impacted properties also suffer from losses in parcel utility (either temporary or permanent), as well as residual stigma. The significance of each form of value reduction is dependent upon the contaminants present and their severity.

As all members of the real estate community become more educated in the problems associated with contamination, the appraisal of these properties will become increasingly necessary. This chapter has provided one method of analyzing impacted properties that accounts for specific elements that affect a property's value, including cleanup costs, losses in utility and residual stigma. Certainly other appraisal techniques can be employed. It is unrealistic to assume that a formula approach is adequate for this class of real estate. However, it is essential that all elements affecting a property's value be isolated and integrated into the final value estimate.

PART III

PROTECTIONS AGAINST ENVIRONMENTAL LIABILITY

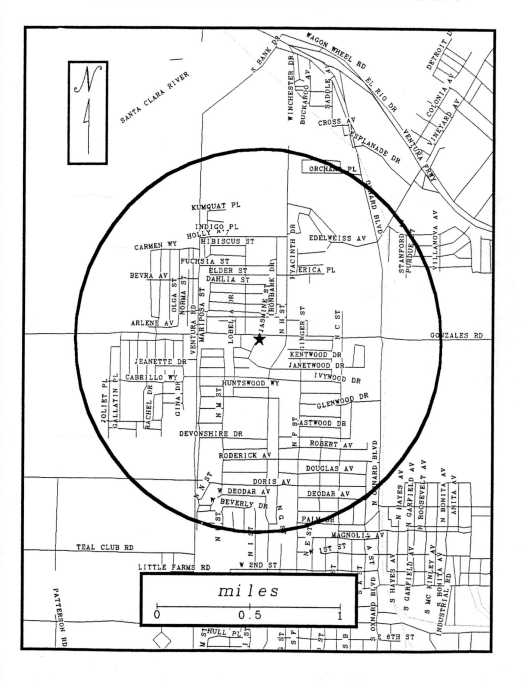

CHAPTER SIXTEEN

ENVIRONMENTAL ASSESSMENTS

Ronald D. Miller, Esq., Vice-President
VISTA Environmental Information, Inc.

16.1   Introduction

Now that we have seen the kinds of environmental laws which create risks in real estate transactions (Part I) and how those risks affect the interests of the various parties to a real estate transaction (Part II), our focus shifts in Part III to the available methods of gaining protection against environmental liability.

The reader should understand that environmental risk *cannot be eliminated* from real estate transactions given today's statutory scheme. All real property transactions can involve environmental risks. Even the vacation cottage whose previous owner's hobby involved toxic chemicals such as photography, painting, or wood refinishing might have a pit used for disposal of the hobbyist's waste. Moreover, under a technical reading of CERCLA and SARA, no landowner is exempt from liability except under limited circumstances where due diligence has been properly conducted. Therefore, the only way to eliminate risk is not to own or operate any real estate or business.

On the other hand, proper environmental due diligence can effectively *reduce* risk. Real estate transactions and business investments, by their very nature, include all kinds of risks. The investor commonly employs techniques to identify, minimize and allocate these risks. This chapter is intended to set forth the techniques that can be used to identify, and therefore minimize, exposure to environmental risks and liability for the real estate lender and investor through a series of logical investigatory steps collectively known as environmental assessments. The goal here is to illustrate how to close real estate and business deals efficiently in the face of environmental risks and how to minimize the risk of incurring unanticipated cleanup liability. Effective environmental due diligence can also help the investor and lender avoid acquiring interests in property with impaired value.

Divergent views have developed over the terms "assessment" versus "audit." In the past, environmental consultants generally preferred to use "preliminary assessment" to label the work performed to investigate the environmental condition of real estate. On the other hand, attorneys generally preferred the term "audit," as it implies a more thorough and comprehensive investigation. Some attorneys, particularly those assisting in the investigation, preferred the term "assessment" so that the client would not expect a more thorough inquiry than was intended. Writers have occasionally drawn a distinction based on whether real estate alone is being acquired (in which case its condition is assessed), or whether a going business is also being acquired (in which case additional records and information would be audited for possible successor environmental liability along with the assessment of the condition of the premises upon which the business is conducted).

Over the past few years, consensus has developed on terms to describe the investigatory process. Most environmental professionals now agree that the term "assessment" refers to the process used to determine the environmental condition of real estate. An assessment is like a photographic snapshot--its description of conditions is limited to a specific time and place. On the other hand, an "audit" is the process used to determine the ongoing compliance of an environmentally active facility. An environmental audit takes into account all existing permits and activities in an effort to determine whether the facility is in compliance with all applicable federal, state and local environmental laws and regulations.

What is most critical, however, is the sufficiency of the investigation to meet the client's legal and technical needs. Perhaps divergent terminology serves to highlight the importance of establishing a defined written protocol for the investigation. Written protocols will be discussed below in greater detail.

This chapter will outline the basic issues which should be addressed in order to identify environmental risk through the assessment process. Auditing is beyond the scope of this book. Further, this book is not intended as a step by step guide for self-help. Therefore, this chapter should be used as a preparatory and/or review tool to establish or assess a program for identifying environmental risk. It is suggested that lenders and purchasers consult with both an environmental attorney and an environmental consulting firm to assure adequate technical and legal assessment of and protection from environmental risk and liability.

16.2 The Threshold Question: On Which Transactions Should a Party Conduct an Environmental Assessment?

The question of establishing which property and transaction types should require an environmental assessment, and determining the extent of that assessment, is probably the quintessential issue of environmental due diligence. Under the federal laws that create liability, no exceptions are made for certain classifications of purchasers and properties. The only legislative guidance on the issue of which transactions require an assessment and the scope of the assessment required can be found in the *Joint Explanatory Statement of Conference,*[1] regarding the innocent landowner defense set forth in SARA. The *Joint Explanatory Statement* articulates that "[t]hose engaged in commercial transactions should,

---

[1] H.R. Rep No. 962, 99th Cong., 2d Sess., H 9083 *et seq.* (October 3, 1986) (hereinafter the "*Joint Explanatory Statement*").

however, be held to a higher standard than those who are engaged in private residential transactions."[2] Therefore, by implication, this passage seems to indicate that the statutory duty to conduct some level of environmental due diligence applies to all transactions.

Therefore, given that any type property, no matter how big or small, can be contaminated, attorneys often have taken the position that no transaction should be commenced without an environmental assessment. On the other hand, their clients often have differing views on the reality of this requirement. For example, lenders often cite competitive pressure as the reason for not requiring assessments on all transactions. Lenders fear that if loan applicants are faced with an additional closing cost, the applicants may go to the competing lender down the street and seek financing without environmental assessment requirements. Likewise many real estate purchasers and developers often feel that the risk does not justify the cost of the assessment and therefore, have preferred to close deals without any environmental investigation whatsoever.

This contrast has resulted in a compromise in real estate purchasing and lending practices. Generally, under current practices, two factors determine which transactions will be subject to an environmental assessment: economics and property type.

16.3   Economics of Environmental Due Diligence

Environmental due diligence can be defined as an investigation of the environmental condition of real estate that is appropriate under the circumstances. One key variable affecting the scope of the assessment is the dollar value of the transaction. The higher the dollar value, the greater level of due diligence will likely be required and the scope of the assessment should be modified accordingly. Legislative support of the economics theory can be found in the *Joint Explanatory Statement* through the distinction between private residential transactions which presumably are of a smaller dollar value than commercial transactions whose participants are to be held to a higher standard because of the greater value of the transaction. To this extent, many lenders have established environmental due diligence policies that require assessments

---

2   *Joint Explanatory Statement*, at H 9085.

for transactions over a certain dollar threshold. The author is aware of policies using $250,000, $500,000 and $1,000,000, as economic thresholds for requiring environmental assessments in lending transactions.

While the economic threshold approach seems sensible and defendable under the federal statutory scheme, several factors create good reason to question that approach. First, the value of a loan or parcel of real estate has nothing to do with the likelihood of environmental contamination. A metal plating firm seeking a $50,000 loan to finance inventory probably has more risk than a $1,000,000 mortgage loan on a single family residence. Moreover, that $50,000 loan, if foreclosed upon or if the lender becomes an operator during a workout can create a multimillion dollar liability. Second, the *Joint Explanatory Statement* specifically sets forth the definition that "good commercial or customary practice with respect to an inquiry in an effort to minimize liability shall mean that a reasonable inquiry must have been made in all circumstances, in light of the best business and land transfer principles."[3] This sentence, particularly the portion stating that an inquiry must have been made "in all circumstances" seems to imply that some level of inquiry should always be conducted. Further, this statement can be read to define the standard for the scope of the assessment. "Good commercial practices" may mean the "best" available at the time of the acquisition. Therefore, while it seems that the value of a transaction may reasonably be used as a threshold for determining which transactions require an assessment, legislative analysis indicates that such strategies may be legally deficient if no investigation is made of properties under the threshold. Instead, it seems more sensible always to require some type of investigation while varying its scope according to the transaction economics and property type.

16.4 Classification of Properties and Types of Properties

While it might be the preference of lenders and purchasers to form due diligence and assessment practices based neatly on transaction values, a more effective approach requires adjusting assessment practices dependant upon the *type* of property while considering both its present and previous uses. A chain of title report is often very useful in the identification of previous uses and will be discussed in greater detail

---

[3]   *Id.*

below. Because the risk of contamination is largely dependant upon what type of activity occurred on the property, it seems logical and consistent with the statutory scheme set forth above to require more thorough and expensive investigatory techniques for those properties having the greatest likelihood of contamination. While all types of property can be contaminated, the following sets forth a general hierarchy of environmental risk related to the property classification:

1. Industrial Property

2. Commercial Property

3. Agricultural Property

4. Undeveloped Property

5. Multi-Family Residential Property

6. Single Family Residential Property

While the classification of the subject property itself should be the primary focus, sound assessment practice should also include review of the uses of neighboring properties, because of the migratory nature of environmental contaminants.

Industrial Properties are obviously the most likely to be environmentally impaired as a result of previous operations on the property. First, many industrial properties have been contaminated as a result of disposal, storage or spillage of hazardous waste. Because no laws prohibited onsite waste disposal until the late 1960s, many companies conveniently disposed of waste onsite. Further, industrial facilities often contain underground storage tanks and underground pipelines that may have leaked in the past or continue to leak at present. Finally, the presence of high risk neighbors in industrially zoned areas warrants additional research into neighborhood environmental problems. Therefore, the scope of the assessment should be modified accordingly. For example, environmental consultants are trained to study internal records and conduct interviews to determine previous and present waste streams including the points of ultimate disposal for each industrial process. They also study the blueprints and sketches of a facility to determine locations of underground storage tanks and pipelines. The environmental consultants also use surveys and government records to determine whether any neighbors have impaired the subject property.

Therefore, any environmental due diligence policy should require fairly extensive testing and assessment procedures for industrial properties.

Commercial Properties encompass a wide variety of uses. For this purpose, Standard Industrial Classifications (SIC) codes can help classify the various types of commercial property in order to determine the scope of the assessment. Clearly, commercial properties that host or have hosted gas stations, automotive repair shops and dry cleaners have significantly greater risk and will require more extensive assessments. On the other hand, office buildings and retail centers have somewhat less risk and may require a less extensive assessment. Remember, however, that many seemingly innocuous properties such as commercial office buildings can involve significant risks as a result of the presence of asbestos or construction on top of old leaking underground tanks.

Agricultural Properties are often significantly impaired as a result of the accumulated residue of pesticides and/or fertilizers. Even proper application and use of these common agricultural aides have resulted in extensive soil and groundwater problems. Further, improper disposal or storage of pesticides and/or fertilizers can result in the creation of toxic hot spots. Agricultural properties commonly have above or below ground storage tanks for machinery fuel uses, and many also have oil wells that may result in hydrocarbon contamination. Finally, many agricultural properties have been used as disposal sites for septic wastes or may have been leased to individuals, corporations and governments for household and industrial waste disposal. The contamination of agricultural property is compounded by the fact that most of these properties are served by private water wells on the property which may render the property useless if contaminated.

Agricultural property assessments should therefore take these unique risks into account. In addition to the standard investigatory techniques, assessments for these properties should encompass soil and groundwater testing. Special effort should focus on soil in the area of barns and storage buildings. Further, the assessment should attempt to determine the existence and location of underground storage tanks and oil wells through physical inspection or interviews with current residents. Interviews should include questions about unique uses such as disposal of septic, household and industrial waste. Review of title records may show oil and gas easements or leases and government environmental records might indicate whether the property has been used for waste disposal or hydrocarbon production.

Undeveloped Properties can be broken down into two types: never developed/rural property and urban/previously developed property. Even undeveloped/rural property can be environmentally impaired by neighboring sources of environmental contamination or by the midnight dumper. Urban and/or previously developed properties present additional risks that previous uses may have left behind soil or groundwater contamination.

Determination of whether an undeveloped property was previously used for some environmentally risky purpose will of course be a threshold issue to be addressed by the assessment. For this purpose, aerial photographs and title histories are particularly useful. The physical inspection should also search for the effects of the midnight dumper. Government environmental records should be used to determine whether impairment from neighboring sources of environmental risk deserves further exploration.

Multi-Family Residential Properties are generally less risky in terms of the likelihood of contamination, yet the magnitude of the risk may be increased tremendously. For example, if a problem is discovered, liability to tenants can multiply the total loss, especially in today's increasingly litigious society where claims are made for fear of cancer and related complaints. Loss of rental income compounds the problem of contaminated multi-family residential properties. Thus, asbestos and radon can become significant risks for multi-family residential properties. For the same reasons, neighboring environmental risks should be carefully researched. In addition, maintenance rooms or buildings serving multi-family residential properties have been commonly contaminated by improper storage of chemicals, paints and fertilizers used for building or grounds maintenance. Finally, many apartment complexes and mobile home parks have been constructed on top of old solid waste landfills that may contain hazardous and other noxious waste.

A special risk attends multi-family residential properties. The Federal National Mortgage Association (FNMA or Fannie Mae) has imposed a very specific set of assessment procedures that disqualifies these properties from financing if they cannot pass specific threshold qualities (see FNMA Environmental Hazards Management Procedures in Appendix A). Therefore, even if the purchaser does not intend to finance the property by a FNMA lender, a future purchaser may be precluded from FNMA financing, thereby requiring alternative financing which may result in a reduction of the purchase price of the property.

Accordingly, any assessment of multi-family properties should meet minimum standards set forth by Fannie Mae. Further, specific emphasis should focus on identification of asbestos and excessive radon levels to avoid risks associated from litigious tenants. Government environmental records and title histories should be checked to determine if the land was previously used for disposal purposes. Finally, the maintenance plant/facility should be carefully audited for evidence of previous improper storage or disposal of maintenance materials.

Single Family Residential Properties also pose environmental risks. While most lenders and purchasers have not yet addressed the issue for single family properties, environmental risks associated with individual homes warrant some form of inquiry. It may be true that the EPA and the U.S. Justice Department have never attempted to recover cleanup costs from a single family homeowner; but a lender who forecloses on a single family home identified as the source of the contamination might not get similar treatment. Moreover, there is no statutory exclusion for the single family homeowner from cleanup liability. On the contrary, the *Joint Explanatory Statement*, as discussed above, even provides support for the argument that Congress intended that some level of due diligence be conducted in private residential transactions.

Single family residential properties have risks beyond radon and asbestos. For example, many homes built prior to the 1960s have old underground storage tanks used for heating oil before the days of natural gas. In many cases, single family homeowners purchased new gas furnaces after gas service became available and simply left the old storage tank in the ground with the oil in it. This often results in leakage contaminating nearby water wells and surrounding soil. Offsite liability can be created from this source if neighboring property is also affected. Improper septic service has also caused significant contamination of single family properties and their wells. Another problem is the potential for drastic devaluation of single family residential property upon publicity of neighboring sources of environmental contamination.

Therefore, the risk attendant to single family residential properties warrants an environmental investigation even though the scope of the assessment may be somewhat less comprehensive than assessments of other types of real estate. Single family properties constructed before 1979 should be inspected for asbestos insulation or fireproofing. Single family properties located in parts of the country where radon gas may be a problem should also be tested for that potential hazard. Inspection for old underground tanks and poorly designed septic fields should be undertaken with respect to older homes. Finally, government environmental records should be checked to determine if any neighbors present significant risk of contaminating or devaluing the property.

In sum, this section has illustrated that some level of environmental due diligence should be performed on all types of real property regardless of the value of the transaction. Therefore, the real issue to be addressed is not whether to perform and assessment but instead, to define the extent of the assessment depending upon the nature of the subject property. However, two common elements always apply:

1.   The property should be characterized by both past and present use which can be ascertained from title records and other historical data.

2.   Government environmental records should be reviewed to isolate neighboring risks of contamination and potential for value impairment.

16.5   The Due Diligence Team

Effective environmental due diligence programs incorporate the skills of various disciplines. Because environmental risks affect many aspects of a real estate transaction, involvement of a team in designing the assessment program helps to ensure efficient and effective coordination. A coordinated approach to environmental auditing best ensures that the results of the assessment will be useful to the parties.

Environmental consultants play a critical role in both designing the protocol and implementing the program. A skilled environmental consultant will help establish the protocol by identification of techniques that are workable in the field. The experience of the environmental consultant can be drawn upon to identify particular risks that are common to certain localities or types of property. Because the environmental consultant will most often be called upon to conduct the assessment, it is important to include the consultant in the planning process. Finally, the environmental consultant will be able to guide the protocol by including such factors as availability of records, limitation of certain auditing techniques and local practices that may affect environmental risks.

Attorneys also play a critical role in the environmental due diligence process. Generally, the parties seek the assistance of attorneys to identify and allocate many possible risks associated with a real estate transaction. If the attorney fails to counsel the client as to the environmental risks, the attorney does not serve the client well. The attorney's role should include assistance with establishing an assessment practice that complies with lender, secondary mortgage market and innocent landowner defense requirements. The attorney may also be called upon to advise whether a specific assessment, as conducted, complies with specific requirements of the established protocol. The attorney's skills can also be used to ensure that the documentation of the assessment is effective for the goals of the assessment. Finally, the attorney may be used in an effort to preserve confidentiality of the information revealed by the assessment under the attorney-client privilege.

Appraisers are the most commonly overlooked party that should be a member of the due diligence team. While consultants and attorneys generally address issues to avoid or allocate cleanup liability, the appraiser's skills are necessary to incorporate consideration of environmental risks on the value of the property. Until only recently, lenders and purchasers have assessed the value of real estate without regard to environmental risk. However, it is now clear that cleanup costs, liability to neighbors, tenants and employees, and even stigma from discovery of neighboring environmental risks, may dramatically affect the value of the subject property (see Chapter 15). While appraisers generally cannot be expected to conduct the assessment, they should be required to consider environmental risk and impairment on the value of the subject property. Therefore, the appraiser should be included in the due diligence team to ensure the development of a report that will help the appraiser realistically value the property.

The client should also be included in the due diligence team. First, the client might not fully understand the risk of cleanup liability and the risk of value impairment. Explanation of these risks helps justify the cost and effort required to design and implement an effective assessment strategy. Moreover, in the end, it is the client who is ultimately responsible for any cleanup costs and suffers any loss of value if contamination is discovered subsequent to the purchase of the property. From this perspective, the limitations of the due diligence process can be acknowledged step by step to avoid hard feelings or lawsuits later. In short, the team concept, although initially more time consuming and costly, should pay off in terms of effectiveness.

16.6   Selecting the Experts

It is critical to the success of the assessment program that the proper experts be selected to design and implement the strategy. While this section focuses on the selection of the environmental consultant, similar considerations apply for each expert of the due diligence team. First, it is important to consider the nature of the expert's practice to determine relevance to the skills necessary to the assessment process. Most environmental consulting firms have less than 10 years experience in business. While this fact alone does not preclude consideration of a young company, intense growth in demand for real estate assessments has exceeded supply of qualified firms and individuals. Moreover, even fewer environmental firms have long term experience in environmental auditing. Many firms whose primary experience includes work in remotely related fields such as systems engineering, drilling operators, laboratory services are new in the business of assessing properties. While this type of experience is helpful, the firm should be asked to demonstrate experience and proficiency specifically in performing real estate assessments.

The firm's reputation and references should also be verified. The process of checking references in evaluating a potential consulting firm has become a fairly standard practice. Good sources to check include environmental attorneys, trade groups, colleagues in your industry and state and federal agencies. Specific inquiry should be made as to:

1.   The firm's ability to meet deadlines;

2.   The fees charged for services;

3.   The thoroughness of the work;

4.   The professionalism displayed by staff and presented in reports; and

5.   The relative ease of coordinating and working with the firm.

The size of the firm may also be a consideration in hiring an environmental consultant. Generally, it is better to focus on hiring an individual consultant who is well qualified rather than on the size of the consulting firm. Therefore, a small firm may be able to provide as good or better service on small local projects if the individual within the firm is well qualified. However, if the assessment program will require coordination throughout many states, then it may be advisable to work with larger firms to help ensure consistent practices and results.

Local knowledge is also critical to successful assessment. For example, government records and title history data vary widely and an effective assessment can usually be provided by a firm with thorough knowledge of the local records available in a particular jurisdiction or state. Local consultants are more likely to be aware of practices specific to a given locality that may give rise to peculiar environmental risks. Finally, a local reputation is helpful to enhance cooperation of local government agencies if necessary.

Insurance is also another interesting issue. While professional liability coverage is largely unavailable for environmental consultants, several firms have claimed that coverage has been secured. To this extent, it is wise to have the attorney review the coverage to ensure that the policy covers the type of risk that would result from an error or omission in the assessment. Most reputable firms will not guarantee the result of the assessment, therefore minimizing the importance of the liability insurance policy. However, a new insurance product has recently become available so that the results of an assessment by a qualified consultant can be insured. The policy excludes coverage for contamination revealed by the assessment and provides coverage for contamination which is missed and later discovered during the policy period. *See* § 21.5 of Chapter 21 for additional discussion about this kind of insurance.

Credentials should also be considered in hiring an environmental consultant. While there are no licenses per se, use of a registered geologist or registered engineer is probably the most relevant national certification available. Some states are now developing certification programs. For example, the State of California certifies environmental auditors with the designation Certified Environmental Assessor (CEA) if the applicant meets the educational and experience qualifications.

Cost and response time parameters should also be considered. Typically, Phase I assessments cost between $2,000 and $5,000 depending upon the firm and the scope of work to be performed. Moreover, because the timing of real estate transactions is critical, estimates, if not guarantees, of response time should be required.

Finally, samples of the firm's work product should be obtained and reviewed. Sample reports give a good indication of the thoroughness of a firm's work and its ability to communicate the results. Specific review should be given by each due diligence team member to ensure that the report meets at least the minimal requirements of that member's role in the assessment process.

16.7   Determining Industry Standards

Probably the most surefire way to defeat the entire purpose of the assessment process is to design a strategy or protocol of lesser standards than those readily available and well documented standards currently used in lending and real estate practice. A major portion of the determination as to whether the purchaser qualifies for the innocent landowner defense will turn on whether the assessment was at least as thorough as that required and commonly used in practice at the time of acquisition. If a court must decide whether the purchaser made "all appropriate inquiry," definition of what is appropriate would be determined by prevalent standards set by the American Society for Testing and Materials (ASTM), Fannie Mae and the former Federal Home Loan Bank Board (now the Office of Thrift Supervision). Surveys of local lending and real estate practices may also become relevant. Finally, publications of the Mortgage Bankers Association, proposed legislation and case law might be used to establish the meaning of "all appropriate inquiry." While the reader should consult actual documents for specific guidance, a summary of key components of these sources is summarized here.

Fannie Mae took the lead in establishing a specific policy and protocol for environmental assessments for its multi-family lending program back in 1986. Under its *Environmental Hazards Management Procedures*, revised in 1988 (attached as Appendix A), Fannie Mae requires (1) a review of government records, (2) interviews with people who are familiar with the site, and (3) an inspection of the site called a "Phase I Assessment." If an investigation results in an inconclusive Phase I report, a Phase II report requiring a more detailed review and physical sampling of the site is required. Fannie Mae also requires ongoing confirmation that the property is being maintained in an "environmentally sound manner."

Fannie Mae has established a formal protocol for Phase I environmental assessment. The protocol requires:

1.   Documentation of information sources used to perform the assessment.

2.   Inquiry into the presence of

    a.   asbestos

    b.   polycholrinated byphenyls (PCBs)

    c.   radon

    d.   underground storage tanks

    e.   waste disposal facilities

    f.   lead paint

    g.   urea formaldehyde

    h.   foam insulation (UFFI)

    i.   lead levels in drinking water.

If there are obvious problems or if the environmental status of the property is uncertain, then Fannie Mae will not finance the property unless a Phase II report indicates that the property is environmentally sound. The purpose of the Phase I assessment is to determine quickly whether enough information exists to evaluate the status of the property

339

clearly, while the purpose of a Phase II assessment is to determine the presence or absence of an uncertain liability or to quantify the extent of an observed or suspected liability. Fannie Mae specifically requires that a Phase II assessment be performed by a qualified environmental consultant but does not require that a Phase I assessment be conducted by an environmental consultant. Further, Fannie Mae does not set out a specific protocol for the Phase II assessment. However, the procedures cite examples of Phase II work to be performed including:

1. Bulk asbestos sampling and analysis, and if required, development of abatement and maintenance programs.

2. Underground storage tank leak testing.

3. Soil sampling and analysis.

4. Groundwater sampling and analysis.

5. Testing of suspected PCB contaminated soil and/or facilities.

6. Investigation of the status of Superfund or RCRA enforcement actions related to neighboring properties.

While acknowledging that properties failing to meet a particular standard may in some cases be corrected through remedial actions and retested, Fannie Mae sets forth a specific list of conditions rendering the property ineligible for financing. Please refer to Appendix A for specific situations and additional details.

The Federal Home Loan Bank (FHLB) issued a thrift bulletin on February 6, 1989, to savings and loan institutions intended to raise awareness of environmental risks and to serve as a guideline for development of policies of reasonable due diligence to protect institutions from financial risk created by environmental contamination. While it does not specifically require a savings and loan institution to follow any specific course of action, the guidance serves as documentation of an industry standard by which the meaning of "all appropriate inquiry" might be reasonably measured.

One key provision set forth in the thrift bulletin articulates that some level of due diligence should be performed in all real estate transactions. The bulletin states that for single family properties where cursory inspections or records research disclose high potential for environmental risk, then Phase I reports are likely necessary. The bulletin also lists specific property types that require Phase I assessments. Please refer to Appendix B for a copy of the thrift bulletin that defines the protocol and identifies various types of properties requiring assessments. The FHLB has defined and established a protocol for Phase I and Phase II assessments as follows:

1. A Phase I Environmental Risk Report is a qualitative assessment of the property. A typical Phase I Report includes, but is not limited to:

    a. A historical review of the use and improvements made to the subject site.

    b. A review of building, zoning, planning, sewer, water, fire, environmental and other department records that would have information on or have an interest in the property and neighboring sites.

    c. A review of the Department of Health Services, Solid Waste Management Board, Regional Water Quality Control Board, Air Quality Management District, and other Boards or Agencies records and files whose actions may affect the subject property and neighboring properties.

    d. An investigation of the subject property and neighboring properties with regard to the Environmental Protection Agency's National Priority List or Comprehensive Environmental Response Compensation and Liability Information System (CERCLIS) list and similar state lists.

    e. An inspection of the site and all improvements with particular attention to the use of hazardous materials in the structures or operating equipment.

f. A verification as to whether present or past owners or tenants have stored, created or discharged hazardous materials or waste, and review of whether appropriate procedures, safeguards, permits and notices are in place.

g. An analysis of old aerial photographs to determine the construction or destruction of buildings and the existence of ponds and disposal areas on the property over time.

h. Interviews with neighbors to determine prior uses of the subject property (if appropriate and only if deemed acceptable by the parties involved in the transaction). Confidentiality must be recognized.

i. A review of building records and a visual inspection of the building(s) to determine if asbestos containing materials may be present.

j. A review of scientific literature to determine the potential existence of radon in the soil.

k. A written report summarizing the findings.

2. Phase II Environmental Risk Report

A Phase II Report is performed if "red flags" are apparent to the lender or if they are disclosed during the Phase I investigation. This report consists of all Phase I activities plus combinations of the following field tests and activities.

a. Testing of underground storage tanks for content and integrity.

b. Soil gas analysis to identify the potential for petroleum hydrocarbons and volatile organic compounds such as industrial solvents and dry cleaning chemicals.

c. Bulk soil sampling.

d. Groundwater sampling if groundwater may be impacted by land activities.

e. Limited surface water sampling if there is a pond, lagoon or stream on the property.

f. A comprehensive review of the regional and local geology to determine the pathways leaked chemicals would follow in the event of a spill or leak.

g. A list of individual groundwater wells or subsurface water bodies that may be affected by a spill or leak.

h. A comprehensive inspection of the building for asbestos-containing building materials. This should include collecting and analyzing samples of the building material for friable asbestos. It is strongly recommended that inspections be performed by EPA-certified inspectors and analyses be completed according to EPA guidelines.

i. If no listed hazardous materials or waste are found, an appropriate verification should be provided.

j. A written report summarizing the finding[s].

Because this bulletin was based upon industry standards as developed by the California League of Savings Institutions, it serves as strong indication of the meaning of "customary or commercial practice" with respect to "all appropriate inquiry."

The ASTM has served as a forum for the development of a national standard for real estate site assessments. In 1990, a working group composed of the Mortgage Bankers Association, Fannie Mae, Freddie Mac, National Association of Homebuilders and other industry groups requisitioned the ASTM. Since that time, over 500 experts from the environmental consulting, legal and banking industries have issued several successive drafts of a standard. The current version, which has passed an initial vote, includes a two part process. First, the ASTM "Transaction Screen," which consists of a brief owner/operator questionnaire, site checklist and government records check, is performed to allow identification of "red flags" that indicate potential presence of environmental hazards. The second part consists of a standard for the full Phase I assessment.

Because ASTM standards are well recognized by legislatures, courts and regulatory bodies, it is likely that the ASTM standard, when finally adopted, will serve as the prevailing national standard for the scope of work for real estate site assessments. Copies of the draft standard may be obtained by contacting the ASTM.[5]

The American Bankers Association recently published a guide setting forth several examples of environmental due diligence strategies which were developed by experts in the field.[6] Each author submitted a sample protocol for a Phase I assessment and, while no consensus on a single approach was developed, the protocols set forth in that document may also serve as evidence of "good commercial or customary practice" of "all appropriate inquiry" within the mortgage lending and mortgage banking industries.

Legislation was introduced in 1989 by Congressman Curt Weldon (H.R. 2787) and reintroduced in 1991 by Congressman Wayne Owens (H.R. 1643) to assist the real estate and lending industries by defining "all appropriate inquiry" (please refer to Appendix C for a copy of the bill as reintroduced). Essentially, this bill provides for the establishment of a rebuttable presumption of innocence if the purchaser, at the time of the acquisition, conducts a Phase I Environmental Audit which consists of a review of the following:

1. A 50 year chain of title search;

2. Aerial photographs;

3. Recorded environmental cleanup liens;

---

[5] American Society for Testing and Materials, 1916 Race Street, Philadelphia, Pennsylvania 19103-1187 [(215) 299-5400].

[6] *Managing Environmental Risk: A Practical Guide for Bankers*, American Bankers Association (1989).

4. Federal, state and local government environmental records; and

5. A visual site inspection.

The legislation specifically requires that the purchaser maintain a compilation of the information reviewed in order to preserve its innocence defense. Recognizing that the lack of definition of environmental due diligence and "all appropriate inquiry" has resulted in the failure of many lenders and purchasers to implement effective policies, this legislation is intended to create a definition of environmental due diligence. The goal is to assist lenders and purchasers to incorporate the legal concept of environmental due diligence into workable lending and real estate practices.

Case Law unfortunately has not yet developed to a point where effective guidance from the courts can be used to develop an environmental due diligence strategy. However, two cases provide some guidance on the subject. In *U.S. v. Serafini,*[7] the defendants in 1969 acquired a vacant parcel of real estate where over 1000 barrels of toxic waste were buried. The defendants claimed that they never saw the property prior to purchasing it. In response to the U.S. Justice Department's lawsuit for cleanup liability, the defendants argued that in 1969 there was no or very little concern about environmental contamination and that it was common practice to purchase property without any inspection whatsoever. The court ruled in part that the scope of "all appropriate inquiry" should be determined at the time that the property was purchased and not by current standards. The court then denied the government's motion for summary judgment, requiring the matter to go to trial on the issue whether no inquiry at all constituted "all appropriate inquiry" in 1969.

Another case also provides some guidance for establishing an effective environmental due diligence policy. In *BCW Associates v. Occidental Chemical Corp.,*[8] the defendant performed a Phase I assessment that indicated that no environmental risks were evident on the property. However, the facts developed during the trial gave clear

---

[7] 706 F. Supp. 346 (M.D.Pa. 1988).

[8] 3 Toxics L. R. 943 (E.D. Pa. Sept. 30, 1988).

indication that the defendant was aware of additional environmental contamination or a very strong likelihood of such problems. Because the defendant failed to investigate the matter further after gaining knowledge of the likelihood of contaminants, the court precluded the defendant's use of the innocent landowner defense. Arguably, this case stands for the proposition that purchasers must act upon red flags revealed by the Phase I assessment and any actual knowledge of potential risks despite clearance of risk in the assessment report.

While neither of these cases provides significant guidance to those conducting environmental due diligence, future litigation will result in a body of case law further defining "all appropriate inquiry."[9]

16.8   Phase I Assessments -- Exploring the Components

The purpose of a Phase I assessment is to provide a qualitative analysis of an initial screening of properties. The real goal here is to develop sufficient information to determine quickly and inexpensively that the environmental integrity of a parcel of real estate is unimpaired by environmental contamination.

For evaluation purposes, Phase I assessments can be separated into two components: (1) acquisition and review of information, and (2) site reconnaissance. Ideally, the information acquisition and review should occur prior to the site reconnaissance to help guide the onsite assessor in the investigation. The information component consists of three distinct subcomponents: (a) government environmental records, (b) historical records, and (c) interviews with site owner/operators and neighbors.

---

[9]   *See also In re Sterling Treating, Inc. v. Becker*, 94 B.R. 924 (Bkrtcy. E.D. Mich. 1989); *U.S. v. Pacific Hide & Fur Depot, Inc.*, 716 F.Supp. 1341 (D. Idaho 1989); Steinway, *The Innocent Landowner Defense: An Emerging Doctrine*, 4 Toxics L.R. 486 (1989).

THE PHASE ONE ASSESSMENT

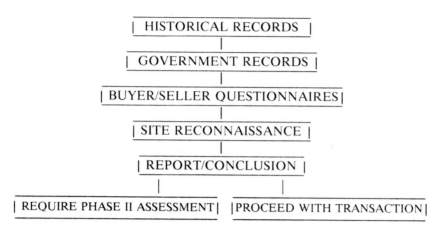

| HISTORICAL RECORDS |
|
| GOVERNMENT RECORDS |
|
| BUYER/SELLER QUESTIONNAIRES |
|
| SITE RECONNAISSANCE |
|
| REPORT/CONCLUSION |

| REQUIRE PHASE II ASSESSMENT | | PROCEED WITH TRANSACTION |

Historical Records. Careful interpretation of the innocent landowner defense focuses on the language requiring that a purchaser make "all appropriate inquiry into the *previous ownership* and *uses* of property consistent with good commercial or customary practice." A fairly obvious and well used technique to determine previous ownership of real estate is the use of title records maintained at the county hall of records and/or private title plants. However, title records do not always indicate the actual owner or user of a property. For example, a property owned by JMM Ltd partnership may actually be leased to ABC Paint Company under an unrecorded lease. On the other hand, many commercial leases are recorded and may indicate the nature of the operation. Once the type of operation is isolated, the SIC code can be used to determine the extent of the audit. Moreover, documents such as pipeline easements, development restrictions and other risks can be identified using title records. Other historical record sources include:

Sanborn/Fire Insurance Maps;

Aerial Photographs;

Building/Tax Department Records;

Cross Index/Street Directories; and

Interviews.

Therefore, beyond prudent lending and real estate practice, the innocent landowner defense specifically requires investigation into previous ownership. Accordingly, historical records dating back a minimum of 40 years should be obtained as a component of the Phase I assessment.

Government Environmental Records. The innocent landowner defense also requires that all appropriate inquiry be undertaken as to the previous *uses* of the property consistent with good commercial or customary practices. An obvious source of information that indicates previous environmentally risky uses of the property can be found in government environmental records. Government records can be used to isolate environmental problems both on the subject property as well as risks in the vicinity of the property. Government environmental records are also critical to establish compliance with requirements set forth by the ASTM, FHLB and Fannie Mae which require documentation of environmental risks, identified in government lists within one mile of the subject property.

There are two categories of government environmental records that should be checked as part of the Phase I assessment. "Primary Sources" of government environmental records consist of listings of known sites of environmental contamination. Purchasing or lending on these properties is extremely risky. The following list contains examples of primary government environmental records:

CERCLIS, the EPA listing of Federal Superfund Sites (including a subset called the NPL);

Sites of Environmental Contamination (maintained by state environmental agencies);

Hydrocarbon (oil & gas) contamination sites (maintained by state environmental agencies);

Leaking Underground Storage Tank (LUST) listings; and

County Level Environmental Records (maintained by county health departments).

The second category of government environmental records consist of listings of properties presenting significant potential for environmental contamination. The following list represents examples of secondary sources of environmental records:

> HWDMS, the EPA's listing of facilities licensed to generate, treat, store or dispose of hazardous waste;
>
> Locations of underground storage tanks (state);
>
> Locations of landfills and other waste disposal facilities (state);
>
> Locations of spills of toxic materials (state, EPA, DOT);
>
> Areas with high potential for radon contamination (state and EPA);
>
> Asbestos records (state);
>
> Locations of above-ground storage tanks (state fire marshall);
>
> Discharge permits - air, surface water, ground water (state and EPA);
>
> PCB (transformer/disposal sites) (state);
>
> Community Right-to-Know disclosures (state and EPA);
>
> Facilities subject to the Toxic Substance Control Act (EPA);
>
> Compliance/Inspection Reports (state and EPA); and
>
> SEC 10-K disclosure (SEC).

These records should be consulted to the extent that they are reasonably available and ascertainable consistent with good commercial and customary practices.

One factor affecting the use of government environmental records is the burden, cost and delay associated with the acquisition of government environmental records. It seems that the usage and extent of the government record search is dependant upon how "reasonably ascertainable" these records are. To ease the burden, cost and time delay associated with the records component of the Phase I assessment, environmental information companies are developing databases to centralize this information. The more sophisticated firms even produce computer generated maps indicating the location of the subject property and the environmental risk sites identified from government record sources within one mile of the subject property.[10]

Buyer/Seller Questionnaires. The third part of the information component of the Phase I audit process includes use and review of a questionnaire to be completed by both the buyer and seller. Arguably, the seller is in a better position to complete the questionnaire due to superior knowledge about the environmental integrity of the property and the neighborhood and about activities that took place while the seller owned the property. Therefore, the questionnaire should be completed by the seller as part of the disclosure requirements of the transaction. It may be difficult to obtain the seller's cooperation in some cases, unless language requiring completion of the questionnaire is inserted into the purchase agreement.

In addition to the seller's disclosure, the buyer/borrower should also be required to complete a questionnaire. Even though the buyer/borrower may not yet be familiar with all of environmental aspects of the property, it is the buyer/borrower who will ultimately be responsible for establishing "all appropriate inquiry." By requiring completion of this questionnaire, the buyer/borrower can begin to familiarize himself with the environmental aspects of a real property transaction while becoming more familiar with the property itself.

Questionnaire formats sometimes call for the seller and buyer to provide a legally binding representation, warranty and certification that the answers are true and correct. While it is certainly preferable to get this kind of representation from the buyer and seller, in many cases it may cause reluctance and conflict detrimental to the transaction and the actual conduct of due diligence. Therefore, in the alternative, it may be wise to prepare a questionnaire that requires the buyer and seller to give answers to the best of their knowledge.

---

[10] For additional discussion of government records in the due diligence process, see *Government Records: An Essential Element of Environmental Due Diligence*, 3 Toxics L. R. 920 (December 21, 1988).

As a general guideline, the following questions should be asked:

1. Do you have any knowledge or indication that hazardous materials have been used on or around the property?

2. Are there any permits affecting environmental conditions or activities issued to the property or its operation?

3. Are any pipes or furnaces wrapped with insulation?

4. When was the building insulated and with what type of material?

5. Are there any underground or above ground storage tanks on the property?

6. Was there ever an oil fueled furnace used on the property?

7. Have the ambient radon levels ever been checked?

8. Does the property rely on a private well for water supply? If so, has the water quality been checked?

9. Are there any storage drums visible on the property?

10. Name all the parties and the type of business occupying the property prior to this transaction.

11. What are the present and intended future uses of the property?

12. Are there any areas on the property used to dispose of waste or other materials, or any areas of uneven settling or unexplainable changes in grade?

13. Does the property now have or did it ever have any oil, gas, water or injection wells?

14. Are there any areas of unnaturally distressed or dying vegetation?

15. Are there any areas of stained soil, asphalt or concrete?

16. How close is the property to any industrial areas?

17. Are there any dumps or landfills near the property?

18. Is the property adjacent to a railroad track or underground pipeline?

19. Is the property within one mile of any known environmental problem such as federal or state Superfund sites, leaking underground tanks, and the like?

20. Are there any indications that any type of hazardous materials have been used, stored or disposed in the neighborhood?

It is advisable to ask questions that can be quantitatively answered by the layman rather than asking questions that call for conclusions or analysis. For example, ask whether the furnace boiler or water heater and associated piping is wrapped with insulation rather than asking if the property contains asbestos. Only a trained professional can determine if the insulation actually contains asbestos and therefore, the lay buyer/seller should not be required to make uninformed conclusions.

Finally, the appraiser can complete a questionnaire as well. For single family residential transactions, it is not unreasonable to ask questions that simply ask for quantitative observation by a staff or fee appraiser. While the appraisal industry has generally sought to avoid the environmental issue altogether, it cannot be maintained that an appraiser has insufficient training or expertise to answer a quantitative questionnaire. For example, if the appraiser cannot answer simple questions such as whether there are any storage drums on the property, whether the piping is wrapped with insulation, the present use of the property, and proximity to industrial areas then arguably that individual is not qualified to conduct an appraisal altogether and alternatives should be sought. If the appraiser is asked to complete a questionnaire, the client should acknowledge the limited skills of the appraiser in environmental assessment and include a statement requiring only that observations as a trained appraiser be incorporated. Cooperation of the appraiser in this function can be extremely valuable and should be included whenever possible.

Site Reconnaissance. After the background information has been acquired and reviewed, completion of the Phase I assessment requires that a skilled field observation be undertaken. It remains unclear as to whether the site reconnaissance function must be performed by an environmental consultant or whether it is sufficient for other competent individuals to perform this task. Industry standards are equally unclear on this point. Fannie Mae only requires that a trained environmental expert perform the Phase II assessment and therefore, by implication, it is reasonable to conclude that the Phase I assessment can be performed by someone other than an environmental consultant. On the other hand, the legislation introduced by Congressman Owens specifically requires that an "environmental professional" perform the Phase I assessment. At a minimum, if the Phase I assessment is to be performed by someone other than an environmental professional, the checklist should be written by or reviewed by an environmental expert. Further, the individuals who are asked to perform the Phase I assessments should be properly trained by environmental experts as well.

The site reconnaissance function consists of a visit to the property to inspect the land and structures built upon the land. As a general guideline, results of the inspection of the following items should be documented:

1. Insulation, flooring and ceiling materials to identify the presence of asbestos or asbestos containing materials (ACM);

2. Transformers, capacitors, fluorescent light ballasts to identify the presence of PCBs;

3. Paint, to determine its current condition and whether it contains lead;

4. Radon level samples;

5. Floor/wall staining;

6. Presence and condition of underground and above ground storage tanks;

7. Presence and destination of floor drains;

8. Presence and condition of storage drums;

9. Current and previous waste disposal practices (e.g. waste stream studies);

10. Evidence of soil/pavement staining or unusual cracking;

11. Unusual gradient changes;

12. Presence of pits, lagoons, ponds or other surface impoundments;

13. Evidence of stressed/unnatural vegetation;

14. Evidence of filling/excavation;

15. Method of wastewater discharges;

16. Method of air emissions;

17. Evidence of contamination on neighboring properties;

18. Interviews with site operators and neighbors about previous activity on the property or in the area; and

19. Type and quality of the water supply.

This list should serve as a general guideline for issues to address while on site. A formal checklist should be developed with the assistance of a qualified attorney and an environmental consultant.

16.9 Phase II Assessments

The goal of the Phase II assessment is to develop additional information as a result of red flags raised during the Phase I assessment or to acquire additional information to assess the environmental integrity of the property confidently. Fannie Mae provides a concise outline of the purpose of a Phase II assessment:

> The Phase II assessment will involve a more detailed physical site inspection and review of historical records. The purpose of Phase II is typically to determine the presence or absence of an uncertain liability (e.g.,

asbestos, or leaking underground storage tanks) or to quantify the extent of an observed or suspected liability (e.g., soils or ground water contamination). Because of the specialized nature of the investigations under Phase II, these assessments must be conducted by a consultant qualified to perform the work.

Examples of the kind of work to be performed in a Phase II assessment would include:

(1) Bulk asbestos sampling and analysis, and, if required, development of abatement and maintenance programs.

(2) Underground storage tank leak testing.

(3) Soil sampling and analysis.

(4) Groundwater sampling and analysis.

(5) Testing of suspected PCB contaminated soil and/or facilities.

(6) Investigation of status of Superfund or RCRA enforcement actions related to neighboring properties.

Lenders should complete and submit the Phase II assessments, see Exhibit 2, with consultant's report attached. No specific protocol is mandatory for the Phase II assessment consultant report. However, it should include a full description of the sampling procedures, the laboratory results and recommendations. The consultant must certify in the report that the assessment was performed diligently and in accordance with all regulatory and good management standards, and that, to the best of its knowledge, the results are complete and accurate. The report must be signed by an officer of the consulting firm that performed the work.

It is essential that all regulatory standards and good management practices be followed at all times and especially where physical sampling and laboratory analysis is involved.

Generally, in addition to filling gaps about the unqualified risks revealed during the Phase I assessment, the Phase II assessment focus is on subsurface environmental quality. Essentially, this process includes sampling and laboratory analysis of groundwater and soil quality. In the early days of environmental due diligence, many strategies called for random soil sampling and groundwater samples on every assessment. However, this approach has been amended to require that these techniques be employed only where some other red flag indicates a likelihood that soil or groundwater may be impaired.

The Phase II assessment also calls for a more in-depth analysis of government records. For example, if a permit is registered to the subject property or a neighboring property, the auditor will likely review agency records to determine current compliance and potential for any additional violations. Moreover, if any known sites of environmental contamination have been identified within a one mile radius of the subject property, the assessor may acquire additional information from the agency as to the severity of the problem and the likelihood of its effect on the subject property through study of groundwater flow maps and the like.

16.10   Documenting Environmental Due Diligence

The environmental due diligence process is intended to serve three basic functions: (1) technical (Is the property impaired?), (2) legal (Does the investigation comply with legal requirements?), and (3) appraisal (Is the value of the property impaired by onsite or nearby contamination?). Therefore, the strategy must be devised and executed in a way that will simultaneously fulfill the needs of all three functions.

The technical and legal requirements have been discussed above. Essentially, the report format should clearly indicate the likelihood of contamination from a technical standpoint. The language and format should be management oriented thereby ensuring proper interpretation and informed decision making. From a legal standpoint, it is clear that due diligence is inadequate under the innocent landowner defense unless all sources of information, investigation techniques and the results are properly documented. In addition, the attorney will want to be certain that the client's reports meet requirements set forth by the originating lender, Fannie Mae and any other parties involved in the transaction.

One important user of the report is often overlooked--the appraiser. The appraiser requires information that he or she can understand and interpret within the valuation function. The appraiser can then translate the results into a dollar figure or range of value impairment that has been caused by the presence of environmental contamination. Specifically, whenever a problem or impairment is noted, the environmental consultant should be required to include a specific section to help the appraiser. If contamination is present, the appraiser needs to know how much it will cost to remedy the problem and when cleanup costs must be paid. Further, the report should include an understandable outline of the owner's remediation plan and associated budgets indicating what actions will be undertaken and when. The report should also include an outline of the environmental consultant's recommended plan and associated budgets, in the event that the owner plans an alternative course of action. Finally, all of the assumptions used to formulate these plans should be articled so that the appraiser accurately assesses impacts on cash flow and market value.11

16.11 Environmental Assessment After Closing the Deal

Monitoring the environmental status of real estate is particularly critical to lenders and landlords. Lenders need to monitor because, even if a "clean" property is used as collateral when the loan was originated, subsequent contamination by the borrower or its tenants will limit the foreclosure option and can potentially render the lending institution liable for the cleanup. Landlords who lease clean property may likewise become liable for a cleanup or lose the value of the property if the tenant contaminates the property. Moreover, Fannie Mae has recognized the importance of ongoing monitoring of environmental compliance and specifically requires the lender to certify from time to time that the borrower is maintaining the property in an environmentally sound manner and in compliance with all applicable laws and regulations.

Setting a specific protocol for the ongoing assessment function is difficult from an overview standpoint. Instead, when the original

---

11   For an excellent discussion of this issue, see *Appraisal Application of an Environmental Auditor's Report*, 1 FOCUS 3, Hazardous Materials Institute (6/30/89). And see Chapter 15 of this book.

environmental assessment is completed it should include a list of issues that should be assessed on an ongoing bases. This list will be specific to the unique characteristics of a property. However, some examples of items requiring ongoing assessment include:

1. Permit status and existence of any violations;

2. Citations issued by government environmental agencies;

3. Compliance with remedial action prescribed in the original audit;

4. Compliance with maintenance actions prescribed in the original audit;

5. Change of tenants and uses of leased buildings; and

6. Status of nearby sources of environmental contamination.

16.12   Managing the Due Diligence Process

A successful environmental assessment strategy requires the cooperation and coordination of the due diligence team. Prior to implementation of due diligence techniques, lending and real estate organizations must formulate a specific policy to address environmental risk.

Preferably, a committee should be appointed consisting of those actively involved in real estate transactions (e.g., loan officers, acquisition managers, legal counsel, risk mangers and upper level management and an environmental consultant who demonstrates specific expertise in environmental due diligence). This committee should then adopt a policy that articulates the specific techniques to be used in every real estate transaction.

Checklists are often helpful in this regard, provided that they are used only by qualified individuals. Consistency is critical. A unified organization-wide policy should be adopted because, in the event less thorough techniques are used in one division, increased risk results to the holding company or parent organization. Setting a due diligence policy and failing to follow it uniformly constitutes strong evidence of investigatory negligence that might be used against the organization in a cleanup action.

After a policy and checklists have been adopted, administrative responsibility should be designated. The individual(s) responsible for implementation of the environmental due diligence strategy should have sufficient training to monitor and implement the policy. There are seminars offered regularly to help train these individuals and keep them abreast of recent developments in due diligence techniques. Finally, the policy should be reviewed and analyzed by the committee at least annually to be sure that the organization maintains the integrity of the policy.

It should be noted, however, that no single policy will *guarantee* successful use of the innocent landowner defense nor will it guarantee that property values will not be impaired by environmental risk. Conversely, failure to conduct an appropriate investigation of the environmental quality of real estate will preclude the use of the innocent landowner defense and will increase the risk of property value losses accordingly.

16.13 Conclusion

This chapter has illustrated the environmental assessment process for real estate transactions. The information presented should serve as general guidance for the issues to be addressed by the environmental due diligence team. It should be clear that some level of the due diligence must be conducted in every real estate transaction. However, the scope of the investigation can be modified depending upon the particular type of property that is the subject of the transaction.

No due diligence policy or procedure can be expected to eliminate environmental risk completely. However due diligence does not require absolute certainty. To this extent, prudent lending and purchasing tactics will reduce economic risk and may eliminate cleanup liability for the true innocent purchaser.

Finally, the scope of environmental assessments will become more intensive in the future. More lenders are requiring environmental assessments today than ever before. Even the legal standard by which the adequacy of the assessment is judged will increase. The *Joint Explanatory Statement* articulates an increasingly higher standard in the future: "Defendants shall be held to a higher standard as public awareness of the hazards associated with hazardous substance releases has grown, as reflected by this Act, the 1980 Act and other Federal and State statues."[12] This statement creates greater urgency to undertake thorough assessment practices today because, as future requirements become more stringent, risks that today go unnoticed may be tomorrow's deal killers. Thus, current purchasers or lenders may be left holding the bag on problem properties unless they employ thorough assessment practices today.

---

[12] *Joint Explanatory Statement*, at H 9085.

CHAPTER SEVENTEEN

ENVIRONMENTAL ASSESSMENT AND CLEANUP AS CONDITIONS OF A TRANSACTION

17.1 Environmental Assessment as a Condition of Closing

17.2 Cleanup as a Condition of Closing

17.3 What if Cleanup Cannot or Will Not Be Completed Before Closing?

17.1 Environmental Assessment as a Condition of Closing

Assessment as a Condition of Closing. A purchaser of real estate should consider requiring the right to undertake an environmental assessment of the property during the escrow period. If a going business is to be acquired in addition to its physical location, the scope of the assessment should include the compliance of the business with applicable environmental laws (in addition to the physical condition of the real estate). The assessment right should be coupled with the condition that the results of the assessment must be satisfactory to the purchaser in its sole discretion. Without such a condition in the purchase agreement, the purchaser may be contractually bound to purchase the property regardless of its environmental condition, unless the seller has committed a fraud or there is a mutual mistake of fact providing a rescission right to the purchaser as a matter of common law. A contractual right of termination or cancellation for failure of condition is preferable.

Lenders typically condition their loan commitments in the same way. A lessee likewise may wish to enter into a lease which provides for a delayed commencement date during which time an environmental assessment can be performed. The lease should also provide that the lessee may terminate the lease if the results of the assessment are not satisfactory.

Assessment Before a Contract is Signed. Another possible approach for a prospective purchaser or lessee would be to review the environmental condition of the property before entering into any transaction agreements. This is sometimes preferred in order to retain the complete discretion as to whether to proceed with the transaction, unfettered by any contract language which might require the prospective purchaser or lessee to be "reasonable" in disapproving of the environmental condition of the property.

This approach also may be preferred where the negotiations on the basic deal are protracted and the parties wish to close the transaction quickly after it is entered into without waiting an additional period for a satisfactory assessment to be accomplished. The assessment can be undertaken concurrently with the negotiations. Indeed, the results of the assessment may answer some of the unknowns and focus the issues for the negotiations. In that way, the assessment will either facilitate the entry into an agreement on environmental issues or cause the termination of the negotiations before more time is wasted. Sellers sometimes prefer this approach particularly when the confidentiality of the transaction is important and the seller does not want to sign a contract and have escrow opened (increasing the risk of leaks of information that the property is being sold) until the transaction is unconditional.

Purchasers and lessees more often wish, however, to enter into a written purchase agreement or lease, or at least an option agreement, in order to tie up the property and prevent its sale or lease to someone else pending satisfaction of environmental or other conditions. Purchasers and lessees generally are unwilling to undertake the expense of an assessment unless a deal is otherwise in place. Moreover, if any assessment is to be conducted on behalf of a purchaser, lender or lessee, appropriate agreements should be in effect regarding access to the property, the conduct of the assessment and liability for any property damages or personal injuries which might arise out of the activities of consultants or agents on the property. Those arrangements are typically provided for in a purchase agreement or lease along with the environmental assessment condition. But it is possible to enter into an agreement covering those issues alone, before any purchase agreement, lease or option agreement is signed. Thus, either approach can be worked out as desired by the parties.

17.2 Cleanup as a Condition of Closing

If an assessment reveals, or a seller discloses, that the land is contaminated, the purchaser should consider requiring that the contamination be removed or remediated before the transaction is completed. That way, the purchaser would avoid becoming an owner of a known environmental problem with potential cleanup liability. The lender providing financing for the transaction should also consider such a requirement as a condition of the loan commitment. A prospective lessee would have a similar interest in avoiding CERCLA liability as an operator of contaminated real estate.

Naturally, the purchaser, lender or lessee would prefer that the seller or lessor perform the cleanup and make all the necessary arrangements for the treatment, transportation and disposal of the hazardous waste. This would avoid any potential CERCLA liability arising out of any cleanup activities on the part of the transferee. Those who arrange for the treatment, transportation or disposal of hazardous substances are commonly referred to as "generators" of the hazardous substances and may be strictly liable under CERCLA in the event of any release of such substances from the disposal site.[1]

Such a condition, if negotiated successfully, should be expressly stated in the transaction documents. A purchase agreement or loan commitment might contemplate remedial action by the seller during the escrow period before closing. A lease might provide for a delayed commencement date for the same purpose. The closing date of a sale or loan, or the commencement date of a lease, can be further deferred as necessary to allow completion of remedial action.

If that allocation of cleanup responsibility cannot be negotiated in advance, then the condition for a satisfactory assessment would at least give the purchaser, lender or lessee the right to terminate the transaction when the environmental assessment reveals the presence of contamination which is unacceptable. That termination right would set the stage for renegotiation if the parties wish to proceed with the transaction on modified terms. An important term which would be the subject of further negotiations would be the allocation of cleanup

---

[1]   42 U.S.C. § 9607(a)(3).

responsibility. The purchaser, lender or lessee would, as suggested above, prefer that the seller or lessor undertake that responsibility, especially if the seller or lessor wishes to preserve the previously agreed purchase price or rental amount. Presumably, that amount was originally established on the assumption that the property was clean. Whether an agreement can be reached will, of course, depend upon the specific facts, the scope of the risk involved and the relative business motivations of the parties.

17.3 What if Cleanup Cannot or Will Not Be Completed Before Closing?

Complete removal or remedial action before closing is the ideal for any purchaser, lender or lessee.[2] But that is not always possible in the real world. Sometimes contamination can take months or years to clean up, and the parties might not be able to wait that long. The seller may wish to sell the property even if some cleanup obligations remain. A purchaser or lessee may need the location to conduct business and might not be able to afford the luxury of waiting indefinitely until the property is completely cleaned up.

Under those circumstances, the prospective purchaser or lessee will have to decide whether the location and features of the property are desirable enough to warrant the assumption of the environmental risk of becoming an owner or operator of contaminated property. That risk may or may not be acceptable depending upon the nature and extent of the known contamination, whether at least part of it can be cleaned up before the transaction must be completed (hence reducing the risk), and whether satisfactory agreements can be reached regarding the allocation of cleanup responsibility and liability for environmental claims after the closing. Perhaps an arrangement can be made for holdback in escrow of a sufficient portion of seller's proceeds to cover the estimated cost of cleanup, or perhaps some other financial assurance can be given, in order to permit closing before the cleanup is completed. Another significant factor would be the amount of the purchase price or rent. The purchaser or lessee reasonably can be expected to request a price or

---

[2]   This, of course, does not apply to a transaction where the purchaser's objective is to buy contaminated property at a substantial discount, clean it up and sell it at a profit (see Chapter 9).

rental discount in view of any environment responsibility or risk which may be assumed. A substantial discount may induce a prospective purchaser or lessee to proceed with a transaction notwithstanding an element of risk. A lease might provide for a reduced rent during cleanup, with an increase (either to an agreed amount or to fair market rental value as determined by appraisal) to go into effect when the cleanup is certified to be complete.

Similarly, a lender who is requested to finance a purchase under such conditions will have to weigh the environmental risks and make an appropriate credit determination. Some lenders have firm policies against financing transactions where any contamination is known. Other lenders may consider making a loan on a contaminated property, especially if the risk can be narrowed by as much cleanup as is feasible before the transaction is completed. Such lenders often require more favorable loan terms in order to compensate for the degree of environmental risk, e.g., additional points or a higher interest rate. Thus, if financing is needed, the parties will have to find a willing lender, and the terms of the loan may have to be tailor made to the situation.

Assuming that cleanup cannot be completed before a transaction must be closed in order to satisfy the time requirements of the parties, and assuming that the parties nevertheless wish to proceed with the transaction, the parties will have to confront and allocate the environmental risks. They should do so even if no contamination is known or found during an assessment due to the possibility of its future discovery. Negotiations over allocation of environmental risks have thus become a feature of most real estate transactions, especially those involving commercial, industrial or undeveloped properties. In addition to the basic business points and conditions discussed in this chapter, the matters to be considered in such negotiations are the subject of Chapter 18.

CHAPTER EIGHTEEN

NEGOTIATED CONTRACTUAL PROTECTIONS

18.1   The Building Blocks

The preceding chapter discusses environmental assessments and cleanup as possible conditions of a real estate transaction. The parties also should consider a number of other contractual protections which would go into effect if the transaction closes, in order to allocate the risk of future environmental liability.

This chapter will discuss the basic methods or "building blocks" which are available to allocate environmental risks among the parties to a real estate transaction. There is no standard allocation. Whatever is mutually acceptable, given knowledge of the risks, is proper. The only wrong approach would be a failure to appreciate the potential environmental liabilities and a consequent failure to consider and allocate those risks by contract. Any party, corporate officer or legal counsel who handles a real estate transaction these days without considering potential environmental liabilities, the need for appropriate assessments and disclosures, and the possible methods for allocating environmental risks will be open for criticism by the persons who later incur unanticipated losses or liabilities.

The building blocks consist of the possible allocation strategies as well as the means of implementing and documenting the selected strategy. These include environmental representations, warranties, covenants, releases and indemnities. However, underlying all of those is the first building block, the significance of which is often not appreciated--the definition of the subject matter. This is really the heart and soul of any contractual protection.

18.2 What Hazardous Substances, Environmental Laws, Costs or Liabilities Will Be Covered by Contractual Protections?

It is important for the parties to have a meeting of the minds as to the scope of the contractual protection. They should understand the scope of the hazardous substances, environmental laws and potential costs or liabilities about which they are negotiating. These terms can be defined narrowly or broadly and the resulting contractual protection (through the applicable representation, warranty, covenant, release or indemnity) likewise will be narrow, broad or in between. Any hazardous substance, environmental law, cost or liability which is not covered within the scope of a contractual protection will be governed by applicable law.

For example, a buyer who obtains a contractual representation and warranty that no asbestos is contained in a building will have recourse against the seller should asbestos subsequently be discovered. But those provisions would not apply to PCBs or any other substance not included in the definition of the hazardous substances covered by the warranty. If such other substances are discovered in the future, the buyer may or may not have recourse depending upon whether the seller breached a disclosure obligation under statutory or common law principles, creating a cause of action for that reason. The buyer might also be able to pursue a contribution action for the cost of cleanup under CERCLA or the applicable state Superfund law, if the requirements of those laws are satisfied and the buyer has not waived such potential claims. Those possible causes of action will be subject to difficulties of proof which would not exist if the matter fell clearly within a contractual protection.

The party giving the protection ordinarily would prefer to have a narrow definition, or at least one that is specific enough so that the nature and scope of potential liability can be reasonably ascertained. Thus, a seller of contaminated property might wish to limit the scope of any indemnification to one or more specific hazardous substances which are known to be present on the property, with the buyer assuming the risk of all other hazardous substances which might be discovered in the future. On the other hand, the buyer who would receive the protection would generally prefer a broad definition which would cover any conceivable hazardous substance, hence allocating the risk to the seller.

The same conflicting interests apply with respect to the definition of which environmental laws, claims, costs and liabilities are covered by contractual protections. For instance, an indemnity clause might cover cleanup costs arising from a particular condition and exclude other cleanup costs and all third party toxic tort claims. The party giving an indemnity would prefer a narrow scope, and the party benefitted by the indemnity would prefer a broad definition.

Sample Long Form Definitions

On the theory that it is easier to cut back on a definition than to expand on it, the following are sample long form definitions of relevant terms which are fairly comprehensive[1]:

> (A)   "Hazardous Substance" as used herein shall mean any hazardous or toxic substance, pollutant, contaminant, material or waste which is or becomes identified, listed or regulated as such by the United States government, the State of California or any local governmental authority having jurisdiction over the

---

[1]   This form is based on federal and **California** law. The state law references should be changed for a transaction involving a property in another state.

Property,[2] including, without limitation, any material or substance which is (1) defined or classified as an "acutely hazardous waste," "extremely hazardous waste," "hazardous waste," "infectious waste," "etiologic agent," "non-RCRA hazardous waste," "restricted hazardous waste" or "volatile organic compound" under Section 25110.02, 25115, 25117, 25117.5, 25117.9, 25122.7 or 25123.6, or listed pursuant to Section 25140, of the California Health and Safety Code, Division 20, Chapter 6.5 (Hazardous Waste Control Law); (2) listed as known to cause cancer or reproductive toxicity under Section 25249.8 of the California Health and Safety Code, Division 20, Chapter 6.6 (Safe Drinking Water and Toxic Enforcement Act of 1986); (3) defined as a "hazardous substance" under Section 25316 of the California Health and Safety Code, Division 20, Chapter 6.8 (Carpenter-Presley-Tanner Hazardous Substance Account Act); (4) defined as a "hazardous material," "hazardous substance" or "hazardous waste" under Section 25501(j), (k), (l) or Section 25501.1 of the California Health and Safety Code, Division 20, Chapter 6.95 (Hazardous Materials Release Response Plans and Inventory); (5) defined as a "hazardous substance" under Section 25281 of the California Health and Safety Code, Division 20, Chapter 6.7 (Underground Storage of Hazardous Substances); (6) "used oil" as defined under Section 25250.1 of the California Health and Safety Code; (7) listed under Appendix X of Chapter 11, or defined as "hazardous or extremely hazardous" pursuant to Chapters 10 or 11, or which is "hazardous" under any criterion specified in Chapter 11, of Division 4.5, Title 22, California Code of Regulations; (8) listed in the Director's List of Hazardous Substances developed by the Director of

---

2   The term **"Property"** would be defined elsewhere in the purchase agreement, loan agreement, option agreement, lease or other transaction document and of course refers to the real estate which is the subject of the transaction.

the California Department of Industrial Relations pursuant to the Hazardous Substances Information and Training Act (California Labor Code § 6360 *et seq.*) and General Industry Safety Order 5194, Title 8, California Code of Regulations[3]; (9) defined or listed as a "toxic air pollutant" under Section 39665 or 39662 of the California Health and Safety Code, Division 26, Chapter 3.5 (Toxic Air Contaminants); (10) defined or classified as a "hazardous substance," "human carcinogen," "toxic" substance, "toxic substance causing chronic illness," "highly toxic" substance, "corrosive" substance, "irritant" substance, "strong sensitizer" substance, "flammable," "combustible" or "extremely flammable" substance, "radioactive substance," or "banned hazardous substance," under Section 28743, 28744.5, 28745, 28745.5, 28746, 28748, 28749, 28750, 28751, 28752 or 28756 of the California Health and Safety Code, Division 22, Chapter 13 (California Hazardous Substances Act); (11) defined as a "hazardous substance" under Section 2452 of the California Vehicle Code; (12) defined or regulated as a "waste," "contamination," "pollution," "nuisance" or "hazardous substance" under any Section of the Porter-Cologne Water Quality Control Act (California Water Code §§ 13000 et seq.); (13) defined as "hazardous waste," "leachate" or "pollution" under Section 25208.2 of the California Health and Safety Code, Division 20, Chapter 6.5 (Toxic Pits Cleanup Act of 1984); (14) defined as "water pollution" under Section 5650 of the California Fish and Game Code; (15) defined as a "pesticide," "pesticide chemical" or "economic poison," whether registered or unregistered, under Section 11404, 12503 or 12753 of the California Food and Agriculture Code; (16) defined or designated as a "toxic pollutant," "oil," "hazardous substance," "sewage," or "graywater" pursuant to the Federal Water Pollution Control Act, 33 U.S.C.

---

[3] The Directors List is updated every two years. Hearings are being held in early 1992 for that purpose.

§§ 1251 *et seq.* (33 U.S.C. §§ 1317, 1321 and 1322); (17) defined, identified or listed as a "hazardous waste," "used oil" or "solid waste," whether or not an "imminent hazard" pursuant to the federal Resource Conservation and Recovery Act ("RCRA"), 42 U.S.C. §§ 6901 *et seq.* (42 U.S.C. §§ 6903, 6921, 6973); (18) defined as a "hazardous substance" or "pollutant or contaminant" pursuant to the Comprehensive Environmental Response, Compensation and Liability Act of 1980, 42 U.S.C. §§ 9601, *et seq.* ("CERCLA") (42 U.S.C. §§ 9601(14) and 9601(33)); (19) defined or regulated as an "air pollutant" or "hazardous air pollutant" under any section of the Clean Air Act, 42 U.S.C. §§ 7401 *et seq.*; (20) a registered or unregistered "pesticide," whether or not posing an "imminent hazard," under the Federal Insecticide, Fungicide, and Rodenticide Act, 7 U.S.C. §§ 136 *et seq.* ("FIFRA") (7 U.S.C. §§ 136(l) and (u)); (21) regulated or prohibited under the Refuse Act of 1899, 33 U.S.C. §407; (22) defined as a "contaminant" in drinking water under the Safe Drinking Water Act, 42 U.S.C. §§ 300f *et seq.*; (23) listed as an "extremely hazardous substance" under the Emergency Planning and Community Right-To-Know Act of 1986 (42 U.S.C. §§ 11001 *et seq.*); (24) defined or listed as a "taxable substance" under Chapter 38 of the Internal Revenue Code of 1986 or the Superfund Revenue Act of 1986; (25) listed or regulated as a hazardous chemical substance or mixture under the Toxic Substances Control Act (15 U.S.C. §§ 2601 *et seq.*); (26) so defined or designated in any and all amendments to any of the foregoing laws or regulations or in any and all laws or regulations enacted pursuant to any of the foregoing laws or regulations or in replacement thereof or succession thereto; (27) so defined, designated or listed in or pursuant to any law, ordinance or regulation promulgated by any federal, state or local governmental unit with jurisdiction over the Property for the protection of human health, the environment or natural resources, whether similar or dissimilar to any of the foregoing laws or regulations and at any time in effect; (28) petroleum, including crude oil and/or any fraction thereof; (29) asbestos; (30) radon gas; or (31) _____ [fill in any specific known hazardous substances which are of concern in the particular transaction].

(B)   "Environmental Laws" as used herein shall mean any federal, state or local law, statute, ordinance, rule, regulation, order, consent decree, judgment, common law doctrine, requirement, limitation, restriction, administrative order or code, and provisions and conditions of permits, licenses and other operating authorizations, relating to (1) pollution or protection of human health or the environment or natural resources, (2) exposure of persons, including but not limited to employees, to Hazardous Substances or other products, raw materials, chemicals or other substances, (3) protection of the public health or welfare from the effects of by-products, wastes, emissions, discharges, disposal, releases or threatened releases of wastes, chemical substances or Hazardous Substances from industrial or commercial activities, (4) the regulation of the manufacture, use or introduction into commerce of chemical substances or Hazardous Substances, including, without limitation, their manufacture, formulation, labeling, distribution, transportation, handling, storage and disposal, (5) disclosure of the presence or suspected presence of any Hazardous Substances in connection with a real property transaction or otherwise, (6) use or development of real property in light of the presence of any release of Hazardous Substances, or (7) imposition of any liability on a present or past seller, owner or operator of real property with respect to any Hazardous Substances or other environmental conditions in, on, under, above or about such property, including but not limited to, the provisions of CERCLA; RCRA; the National Environmental Quality Act ("NEPA") (42 U.S.C. §§ 4321 *et seq.*); the Marine Protection, Research, and Sanctuaries

Act ("Ocean Dumping Act") (33 U.S.C. §§ 1401 *et seq.*); the Noise Control Act (42 U.S.C. §§ 4901 *et seq.*); the Occupational Safety and Health Act ("OSHA") (29 U.S.C. §§ 651 *et seq.*); the California Environmental Quality Act ("CEQA") (Public Resources Code §§ 21000 *et seq.*); the Hazardous Waste Disposal Land Use Law (California Health and Safety Code §§ 25220 *et seq.*); California Health and Safety Code §§ 25359.7, 25100 *et seq.* and 25300 *et seq.*; the California Occupational Safety and Health Act of 1973 (California Labor Code §§ 6300 *et seq.*); any other laws or regulations referred to in Paragraph (A) above (defining "Hazardous Substances"); _____ [fill in any other federal, state or local laws or regulations which are of concern in the particular transaction]; and any law or regulation implementing, preceding, succeeding or amending any of the foregoing, and any similar or dissimilar laws or regulations at any time in effect having any of the purposes designated above.

(C)   "Environmental Claim" as used herein shall mean any claim for personal injury or property damage made, asserted or prosecuted by or on behalf of any third party, including, without limitation, any governmental entity, any employee or former employee or invitee of any present, past or future owner or operator of the Property, any present, past or future owner or operator of neighboring land or any of their present, former or future employees or invitees, or the respective legal representatives, heirs, beneficiaries or estates, successors or assigns of any of the foregoing, relating to the Property or its operation and arising or alleged to arise under any of the Environmental Laws.

(D)   "Environmental Cleanup Liability" as used herein shall mean any cost or expense of any nature whatsoever voluntarily or involuntarily incurred to respond to, contain, remove, treat, remedy, clean up, abate or monitor any contamination, pollution or

374

Hazardous Substances located on, in, under, above or about the Property, to obtain site closure, or to restore the Property following such action, including, without limitation, (1) any direct costs or expenses for investigation, study, assessment, legal representation, cost recovery by governmental agencies or private persons, or on-going monitoring in connection therewith, or (2) any cost, expense, loss or damage incurred with respect to the Property or its operation as a result of actions or measures necessary to implement or effectuate any such response, containment, removal, remediation, treatment, cleanup, abatement, monitoring, closure or restoration.

(E) "Environmental Compliance Cost" as used herein shall mean any cost or expense of any nature whatsoever necessary to enable the Property to comply with all applicable Environmental Laws in effect at any time, including, but not limited to, all costs necessary to demonstrate that the Property is capable of such compliance.

Advantages of the Long Form Definitions

Checklist. The long form functions like a checklist and forces the parties to confront the potential scope and nature of the environmental concerns under negotiation. The definitions can be cut back or revised as appropriate for the transaction and the agreement of the parties.

Enforceability and Avoidance of Disputes. Use of a long form of definitions makes it clear that all of those definitions and the cited laws were considered by the parties and there was a meeting of the minds. That specificity enhances the enforceability of the contractual protection in view of the general rule of law that indemnities and releases are to be strictly construed.[4] The party receiving the contractual protection therefore has an interest in avoiding any ambiguity regarding which laws, regulations and hazardous substances are covered. The party giving the contractual protection also has an interest in the clarity of its obligations

---

[4]   *See, e.g., The Marmon Group, Inc., v. Rexnord, Inc.,* 822 F.2d 31 (7th Cir. 1987).

375

in order to avoid future disputes over the coverage of the protection, even though narrower coverage would be preferred by that party.

Streamlining of Allocation Provisions. The environmental terms, once defined to the satisfaction of the parties, would then be used in the various representations, warranties, indemnities, releases or covenants, streamlining those provisions.

These advantages usually are important to sophisticated parties, particularly in major transactions where environmental risks require careful analysis.

Disadvantages of the Long Form Definitions

Potential for "Blowing the Deal." The long form definitions may be intimidating to parties who are unfamiliar with environmental laws. A senior partner in the author's law firm once commented that proposing such definitions in a transaction (on behalf of a party seeking contractual protections) would be "worse than a waste of time" because it would frighten the other party, make the party proposing the definitions appear to be overreaching and unreasonable, and would, in sum, "blow the deal." A short form was used in that transaction.

Expensive Negotiations. The long form may invite protracted negotiations on the subject which might be uneconomic for the particular transaction.

Need to Update the Long Form. While the long form allows for amendments of the laws and other "similar" laws, it should be updated with each transaction, or at least periodically, to ensure that it reflects applicable laws as accurately as possible. This results in additional expense.

The Long Form Is Still Unclear. As comprehensive as it is, the sample long form includes mostly federal and state definitions. Thus, it may still be unclear to the parties exactly what "hazardous substances" are involved. The long form definitions cover hundreds and perhaps thousands of substances and mixtures. Extensive legal and factual due diligence would be required in order to determine the coverage of the definitions and their applicability to a given property. The cost of doing this might be prohibitive. The alternative would be to assume the risk of coverage without determining its scope, which might not be acceptable to a party giving the contractual protection.

However, some uncertainty is unavoidable when definitions are used rather than precise lists of named hazardous substances. Any specific listing of substances by name would likely be impractical. A detailed list would contain hundreds of scientific names which would not be understood by most parties. Such a list would itself be incomplete; the various lists of hazardous substances compiled by federal and state agencies are expanding as additional substances are identified as hazardous under applicable criteria. While a short list of named substances would be more precise and manageable, the scope of the protection would be reduced, which might not be acceptable to the party receiving the contractual protection. That party may want its protection to be as broad as the potential exposure to liability under the environmental laws, and, in that case, the statutory definitions must be used as a practical matter. Moreover, a contractual protection based on a statutory definition is no more unclear than the statute itself. Despite the risk of uncertain coverage, the parties to real estate transactions generally end up using statutory definitions, rather than long lists of chemical names, perhaps supplemented by specific mention of hazardous substances of particular concern to the parties.

Alternative Sample Short Form Definitions

At the other extreme, the definitions might be stated as follows:

(A) "Hazardous Substance" as used herein shall mean any hazardous or toxic substance, pollutant, material or waste which is or becomes identified, listed or regulated as such by or pursuant to any federal, state or local Environmental Law.

(B) "Environmental Law" as used herein shall mean any federal, state or local law or regulation for the protection of human health or the environment or natural resources at any time in effect.

(C) "Environmental Claim" as used herein shall mean any claim for personal injury or property damage arising under any Environmental Law.

377

(D) "Environmental Cleanup Liability" as used herein shall mean any cost or expense voluntarily or involuntarily incurred to respond to, remove, remediate, treat, clean up, abate or monitor any Hazardous Substances located on, in, under, above or about the Property, to obtain site closure or to restore the Property.

(E) "Environmental Compliance Cost" as used herein shall mean any cost or expense necessary to enable the Property to comply with all applicable Environmental Laws.

An even shorter and more likely alternative would be to dispense with the defined terms altogether. The operative short form language, brief as it is, may simply be worked directly into the appropriate release or indemnity clause or other contractual protection.

Advantages of the Short Form Definitions

Simplicity. The short form definitions appear to be relatively unimposing. They would be less likely to stimulate the kind of consternation which the long form definitions might trigger.

Less Expensive. It would be less expensive to prepare and negotiate the short form approach. In addition, the need for repeated updating of the definitions would be avoided.

Coverage. The short form retains the essence of the subjects covered by the long form, simply omitting the laundry list of laws. Thus, in concept, the coverage of the short form may be about the same as the long form. If that coverage can be obtained with less consternation and expense, the short form would seem to be more economic and practical.

Disadvantages of the Short Form Definitions

Potential for Disputes. The chief disadvantage of the short form approach is that it does not refer to any particular environmental laws or hazardous substances. The short form essentially avoids the complexity of the subject and may result in the party which gives the contractual protection failing to appreciate the actual scope of the protection the other party is expecting to receive. Thus, there is a much greater potential for dispute over the intended coverage of the contractual protection.

Enforceability. The general rule for strict construction of release and indemnity clauses calls into question whether the short form approach would be enforceable in the event of such a dispute. Short form provisions are used frequently because of the apparent advantages stated above, or because at least one of the parties is unsophisticated. Thus, the intent and enforceability of such provisions may provide fertile grounds for litigation in the future.

Expense Might Not Be Avoided. If the party who proposes to give the contractual protection is knowledgeable, the complexity of the subject will probably be appreciated notwithstanding the relatively benign appearance of the proposed short form provisions. Realizing the exposure involved, such a party may require more specificity, resulting in additional negotiations and expense.

Negotiated Application and Qualification of Both Long or Short Form Definitions

Both the sample long and short form definitions merely refer to hazardous substances or environmental laws without any particular application. How the definitions are used, applied or qualified is essential to the nature and scope of any contractual protection. For example, a representation and warranty that the real estate involved contains *no* "hazardous substances" would probably constitute a misrepresentation and an automatic breach of warranty because hazardous substances, as broadly defined, are all around us even in ordinary products (see § 1.2.2-1). Thus, the scope of the definition or its application ought to be qualified in some way. The representation, if it is to be absolute in nature, might be limited to one or more specifically identified hazardous substances which are of concern to the parties (e.g., asbestos or PCBs). Or the representation might be that there has been no "release" of a hazardous substance (or at least no release in reportable or harmful quantities). Such representations may require additional definitions to establish the parties' understanding of the term "release" as well as what quantity is "harmful" or "reportable" (perhaps using statutory definitions or regulatory standards).

Parties sometimes will agree to represent that any previous storage, use, handling or disposal of hazardous substances at the property has been in accordance with all applicable environmental laws, or that there

379

has been no *unlawful* disposal or release of hazardous substances at the property (at least to the best knowledge and belief of the representing party). This can be tricky; a disposal or release might have been perfectly lawful long ago, but cleanup liability may nevertheless apply under CERCLA, the state Superfund law or other environmental laws, or toxic tort liability might exist if the condition has become a nuisance or has injured anyone. Many other agreements are possible.

In sum, most transactions between sophisticated parties are likely to end up with defined terms somewhere in between the extremes set forth in the sample definitions. Greater specificity than the short form would enhance clarity and enforceability, yet the potential coverage of the long form probably will be narrowed to a scope which is mutually acceptable. Moreover, it would be appropriate to have some limitations or qualifications on how the definitions are applied. The point is that the parties should appreciate what protections are being given and received and that the subject is unavoidably complex. This requires careful consideration, which should be reflected in the contract documents. It would be prudent for the parties to obtain the assistance of qualified legal counsel, as well as environmental consultants as needed.

18.3   Risk Allocation Strategies

Any discussion of contractual allocation of environmental risks must proceed with the underlying assumption that such risks may be allocated by contract. Such an assumption has been challenged in a number of CERCLA cases, however.

The majority of decisions have upheld the right of the parties to allocate CERCLA liability as between themselves, without affecting the rights of third parties.[5] The chief issue in these cases has been whether

---

[5]   *See, e.g., Mardan Corp. v. C.G.C. Music, Ltd.*, 804 F.2d 1454, 1459 (9th Cir. 1986); *Harley-Davidson, Inc. v. Minstar, Inc.*, No. 90-C-1245 (E.D.Wis. bench ruling at hearing, Jan. 6, 1992) (reported at Toxics Law Reporter, pp. 1038-1039, 1-29-92); *Purolator Products Corp. v. Allied-Signal, Inc.*, 772 F. Supp. 124 (W.D.N.Y. 1991); *Niecko v. Emro Marketing Co.*, 769 F. Supp. 973 (E.D.Mich. 1991); *Central Ill. Pub. Serv. Co. v. Indus. Oil Tank*, 730 F.Supp. 1498, 1507 (W.D.Mo. 1990); *International Clinical Laboratory v. Stevens*, 710 F. Supp. 466 (E.D.N.Y 1989); *Southland Corp. v. Ashland Oil Inc.*, 696 F. Supp. 994 (D.N.J. 1988); *Channel Master v. JFD*, 702 F.Supp. 1229 (E.D.N.C. 1988);

a release, indemnity or other allocation clause must refer to
environmental liabilities with some degree of specificity in order to be
effective[6] or whether a general allocation is sufficient so that, for
example, a release or indemnity regarding "any and all claims" means
just what it says and releases or indemnifies against CERCLA and other
environmental claims as well as nonenvironmental claims.[7] That sort of

---

Versatile Metals, Inc. v. Union Corp., 693 F. Supp. 1563, 1573 (E.D.Pa.
1988); *Chemical Waste Mgt. v. Armstrong World Indus.*, 669 F. Supp. 1285,
1294-1295 (E.D.Pa. 1987); *FMC Corp. v. Northern Pump Co.*, 668 F.
Supp. 1285 (D.Minn. 1987), *appeal dismissed*, 871 F.2d 1091 (8th Cir.
1988). For a case to the same effect under state law, *see Griffith v. New
England Telephone & Telegraph Co.*, No. 90-P-1106 (Mass.App.Ct. Feb.
7, 1992) (ruling that contractual allocation of liability under the
Massachusetts Oil and Hazardous Material Release Prevention Act, the
state CERCLA analogue, is permissible in a commercial real estate
transaction).

[6] For cases ruling that an express allocation of CERCLA liability, or at
least environmental-type liabilities, is required, *see, e.g., Mobay Corp. v.
Allied-Signal, Inc.*, 761 F. Supp. 345 (D.N.J. 1991); *International Clinical
Laboratory v. Stevens*, 710 F. Supp. 466 (E.D.N.Y 1989); *Southland Corp.
v. Ashland Oil Inc.*, 696 F. Supp. 994 (D.N.J. 1988); *Channel Master v.
JFD*, 702 F.Supp. 1229 (E.D.N.C. 1988); *Chemical Waste Mgt. v.
Armstrong World Indus.*, 669 F. Supp. 1285, 1294-1295 (E.D.Pa. 1987).

[7] *See, e.g., Niecko v. Emro Marketing Co.*, 769 F. Supp. 973 (E.D.Mich.
1991) ("as is" sale where the contract stated that the buyer "assumes all
responsibility for any damages caused by the conditions on the property
upon transfer of title" was found to be more than a mere warranty
disclaimer and sufficient to release a statutory cleanup cost recovery
claim as a matter of contract law); *Jones-Hamilton Company v. Kop-Coat,
Inc.*, 750 F. Supp. 1022 (N.D.Cal. 1990) (a pre-CERCLA agreement "to
comply with all applicable Federal, State and local laws, ordinances,
codes, rules and regulations and to indemnify [defendants] against all
losses, damages and costs resulting from any failure of [plaintiff]..to do
so" was sufficient to include indemnification for liability under CERCLA
when subsequently enacted--as a matter of contract law, "when an
instrument specifically refers to the law, it refers not simply to the law at
the time at which the parties entered into the agreement, but also the law
at the time of enforcement") (this case is on appeal to the Ninth Circuit
on this issue, and oral argument took place on Jan. 16, 1992, Case No.
91-15054, as reported at Toxics Law Reporter, pp. 1036-1037 (1-29-92));
LTV Corp. v. Gulf States Steel Inc. of Alabama, 1991 U.S. Dist. LEXIS
12327 (D.D.C. July 1, 1991) (the words "any liability or obligation"

dispute normally arises out of agreements (especially pre-CERCLA agreements) which did not expressly contemplate or distinguish environmental liabilities from others. At this point, the cases are fairly evenly divided on the need for specificity, although the trend of the more recent cases appears to be toward allowing general, inclusive, language to be sufficient. As a prospective matter, however, parties who are aware of the potential for environmental liability may avoid such a dispute by allocating CERCLA or other environmental liability specifically.

Therefore, according to the majority of cases to consider the issue, it appears that a party may obtain an enforceable release of CERCLA claims from another party, which may be supplemented by an enforceable indemnity clause (if protection against third party claims is intended as well), using an appropriate degree of specificity. If this is the law, then a discussion of contractual allocation of potential CERCLA liability is useful.

However, a minority view has developed on this issue. One case noted that it is an "open question" whether a release of statutory rights under CERCLA can be effective in view of the fact that the exclusive list of defenses set forth in CERCLA does not include release of claims.[8] Another case has actually held that contractual allocations between private parties of potential CERCLA liability are *not* effective except where the party to whom the liability is allocated is not already liable as a PRP under CERCLA; in other words, insurance and indemnity arrangements are permissible whereby *additional* parties may become responsible by contract, but it is not possible for persons identified as PRPs under CERCLA to allocate and release CERCLA liability among themselves (although releases may still be effective as to

---

includes environmental liabilities); *In re Hemingway Transport, Inc.*, 126 Bankr. 650, 1991 U.S. U.S. Dist. LEXIS 4271 (D.Mass. 1991) (a general indemnity clause in a lease with "inclusive and unequivocal language" was sufficient to transfer CERCLA liability for cleanup costs); *Hays v. Mobil Oil Corp.*, 930 F.2d 96 (1st Cir. 1991) (an indemnity against property damage in a franchise contract precluded claims for contribution or indemnification for cleanup of gasoline-contaminated soil).

8   *International Clinical Laboratory v. Stevens*, 710 F. Supp. 466 (E.D.N.Y 1989).

other claims, such as state common law claims).[9] This ruling was followed in another case which found that PRPs may not enter into enforceable release or indemnity agreements regarding their CERCLA liability.[10] If this is the law, then a discussion of contractual allocation of potential CERCLA liability is largely moot.

In light of the divergent court rulings, the following discussion is for the benefit of those in the majority of jurisdictions where CERCLA liability may be allocated among the parties to a transaction, even if they are identified PRPs.

As noted previously, there is no standard or normal way to allocate environmental risks. Several basic allocation strategies do exist, however.

Sellers and Buyers

As noted in Chapter 9, sellers have traditionally expected to sell and walk away from a property without further involvement or liability. Buyers usually are not as familiar with a property and do not want to bear unknown environmental risks, especially those arising from past events. But the buyer will be in control of the property and the conduct of future cleanup efforts. If those efforts are not well designed and cost effective, the total cleanup cost will unnecessarily increase. The buyer's own business operations may contribute to any contamination. Sellers do not want to bear risks which a buyer will manage, or even aggravate, after a sale as this might affect the extent of potential liability. There are several possible ways of dealing with these conflicting concerns. The order of presentation of the allocation strategies does not imply any preference by the author. The determination of which strategy is best for a particular transaction will require the exercise of judgment based upon the circumstances, the applicable laws and the business motivations of the parties.

---

[9] *AM International v. International Forging Equipment*, 743 F. Supp. 525 (N.D.Ohio 1990). This case is on appeal to the Sixth Circuit, and has been specifically rejected in some of the more recent cases cited above.

[10] *CPC International Inc., v. Aerojet-General Corp.*, 759 F. Supp. 1269 (W.D.Mich. 1991).

Negotiated Contractual Protection

Silence. The parties may remain silent on the issue, with each party retaining or incurring any environmental risk or liability under applicable federal, state or local laws without the benefit of any contractual allocation or protection. This is the position of many parties in transactions which took place either before the environmental laws were enacted or afterwards without the knowledge or appreciation of the effect of those laws. While environmental liability is coming as a shock to many parties in such transactions, it may be reasonable to remain silent on the issue as a calculated risk in some situations. Negotiating the subject may be difficult or uneconomic. The parties might each be willing to assume that a particular property is not materially contaminated and to accept the risk of liability if hazardous waste or other preexisting environmental problems are discovered in the future. There is nothing necessarily wrong with this "let the chips fall where they may" approach as long as it is knowingly selected.

This position will not be acceptable to many parties who would prefer to have contractual protections; the potential risks may be too great to leave to chance. Moreover, if the transaction is being financed, the lender typically will require environmental provisions in the loan documents, which may in turn impact on what protections the buyer/borrower may require from the seller. Any corporate officer or legal counsel in a transaction utilizing the "silent" approach should take care to document that the issue was considered by the appropriate corporate superiors or the client and that silence was deliberately chosen.

Seller Assumes All Risk. A seller theoretically could assume and indemnify the buyer against all environmental risks arising from the property at any time. This allocation would in effect make the seller an insurer of the present and future condition of the property, which is not a likely choice as a practical matter. If this position is selected for some reason, the seller certainly ought to expect to receive a premium price for the property.

"AS IS" Sale; Buyer Assumes All Risk. This approach historically has been a common structure for real estate transactions. However, buyers knowledgeable of environmental risks are less willing these days to accept this approach without qualification. Even if a buyer will accept "as is" language, there is a trap for the unwary seller. A number

of courts have determined that an "as is" clause merely constitutes a warranty disclaimer and does not otherwise allocate or avoid potential liabilities under CERCLA.[11] One of those courts reviewed a pre-CERCLA exculpatory ("AS IS") clause in a purchase agreement and stated as follows:

> While a contract can, under appropriate circumstances, act to preclude recovery of response costs, there must be an express provision which allocates these risks to one of the parties .... Of course, Ashland cannot be expected to have presciently referred to CERCLA in an Agreement which was executed two years prior to the statute's enactment; however, some clear transfer or release of future "CERCLA-like" liabilities is required. The Agreement between Southland and Ashland is completely lacking in any language which expressly releases Ashland from future liabilities based on its hazardous waste disposal practices or imposes this liability on Southland.[12]

Based on those authorities, it is necessary not only to disclaim warranties but also to obtain a release from the buyer regarding CERCLA or other environmental claims which the buyer may now or in the future have against the seller. And if the seller expects to have protection against third party claims (e.g., by the government or toxic tort claimants), an indemnification clause from the buyer is also necessary. Thus, it would

---

[11]   *See, e.g., Southland Corp. v. Ashland Oil, Inc.,* 696 F.Supp. 994 (D.N.J. 1988); *Channel Master Satellite Systems v. JFD Electronics Corp.,* 702 F.Supp. 1229 (E.D.N.C. 1988); *Smith Land and Improvement Co. v. Celotex Corp.,* 851 F.2d 86 (3d Cir. 1988) *cert. den.* 109 S.Ct. 837 (1989); *Mardan Corp. v. C.G.C. Music, Ltd.,* 600 F.Supp. 1049, 1055 (D.Ariz. 1984), *affirmed,* 804 F.2d 1454 (9th Cir. 1986); *International Clinical Laboratories v. Stevens,* 710 F. Supp. 466 (E.D.N.Y. 1989); *Wiegmann & Rose International Corp. v. NL Industries,* 735 F. Supp. 957 (N.D. Cal. 1990). An "as is" clause is also insufficient to avoid liability for actual fraud in a transaction. *See, e.g., Gopher Oil Co. v. Union Oil Co.,* 1992 U.S. App. LEXIS 1076 (8th Cir. Jan. 28, 1992).

[12]   *Southland Corp. v. Ashland Oil, Inc.,* 696 F.Supp. 994, 1002 (D.N.J. 1988).

be prudent for a seller to obtain all of those provisions in order to allocate environmental risks fully to the buyer.

If this approach is selected in a situation where contamination is known to exist, the buyer would reasonably expect an appropriate price discount in most cases.

Seller Retains Risk of "Known" Problems, Buyer Assumes "Unknown" Risks. A compromise allocation would be for the seller to bear the cost of cleaning up contamination known at the time of the transaction such as a leaking UST. Such knowledge might have been disclosed by the seller or discovered by the buyer during an environmental assessment. The buyer typically would also want the seller to remain responsible for environmental conditions which the seller knew about but did not disclose. With those express exceptions, the buyer would assume the risk of other, unknown conditions. This allocation would be reflected in appropriate release and indemnification clauses from each party.

The seller in such a transaction should determine what it knows and therefore risks. If the seller is a large company, due diligence would be in order, including inquiry of appropriate corporate personnel and review of relevant corporate records. Depending on the law of the jurisdiction, disclosure obligations may apply to the extent the seller has knowledge of any hazardous waste condition or any other fact material to the transaction (see Chapter 3).

When the seller retains liability for known problems, the price ought to be at or near full fair market value (without regard to the known conditions).

Responsibility Divided as of Date of Sale. An allocation which is frequently considered is the division of responsibility as of the date of the transaction, with the seller remaining responsible for any environmental conditions existing at that time, known or unknown, and the buyer becoming responsible for any future condition which might be created. This allocation has the ring of fairness. A seller remaining responsible for existing conditions, known and unknown, would expect to receive full fair market value for the property.

It might be difficult, however, to determine whether a particular condition existed before the sale or was created afterwards. Therefore, the parties may wish to obtain an extensive environmental assessment in order to have a base line record of the condition of the property at the time of the sale. But there is always the possibility of unknown contamination or a misapprehension that future contamination preexisted the transaction. Thus, the chief drawback of this approach is the potential for disputes over the exact condition of the property at the time of sale. In addition, the seller may not want to have indefinite liability for either known or unknown conditions. The seller might prefer to sell at a discount and have the buyer take over any problem.

Sliding Scale and Monetary Caps. Another possible compromise is to develop a sliding scale mutual indemnity where the seller and buyer would share responsibility for conditions which might be discovered for a limited period after the sale, with the extent of the seller's share diminishing over time. At the end of the agreed period, the buyer would assume full responsibility. For example, the seller might remain responsible for 80 percent of the costs incurred in connection with cleanup of preexisting hazardous waste during the first year after the sale, with that liability decreasing to 60 percent in the second year, and so on until the fourth anniversary of the sale when the seller's share is reduced to 0 percent and the buyer becomes 100 percent responsible (the buyer's share having increased 20 percent each year from 20 percent in the first year). A variation of this approach would be to include a deductible amount which the buyer must pay, either annually or in the aggregate, before the sharing arrangement applies. Sellers sometimes require an aggregate cap on their monetary liability (perhaps based on a percentage of the purchase price).

The percentages, deductible amount, cap amount and time frame can be anything agreeable to the parties. One detail for negotiation would be whether the seller's percentage indemnity will apply only to expenses actually incurred in each year or to contamination discovered in each year even if the associated expenses are incurred later. Another point for discussion would be whether the sliding scale would apply to contamination which is known at the time of sale as well as unknown contamination. Other details also may be involved, such as appropriate controls on expenditures which will be shared.

The sliding scale approach can be a fruitful way to resolve the impasses which frequently occur in negotiations on other methods of allocation. It has the advantage of giving the buyer some assurance that it will not suffer full responsibility for preexisting conditions, while at the same time assuring the seller that its exposure will diminish and then cease at an agreed time or after an agreed maximum monetary amount. After all, the buyer will be managing the property and perhaps aggravating or creating problems, and the seller does not want to be exposed indefinitely to such risks.

The example sets the seller's first year share at 80 percent and the buyer's share at 20 percent for the practical reason that the seller would not want the buyer to go out and "gold plate" the property in the first year at the seller's expense. A significant sharing by the buyer, even in the first year, would help ensure that any assessment and cleanup measures undertaken by the buyer will be reasonable and cost effective. The deductible and cap variations serve the same purpose.

This approach does not avoid all problems. There still would be the potential for dispute as to whether contamination coming to light during the limited period existed beforehand or is the buyer's sole responsibility. That risk would be eliminated, however, upon the expiration of the agreed period.

A sliding scale mutual indemnity, particularly one which spans a period of years, might not be acceptable to a buyer who does not intend to own the property for a long-term or indefinite period. For example, a buyer may intend to acquire property for development and resale within a relatively short time frame. A developer may be wary of entering into any environmental covenants or indemnities (sliding scale or otherwise) which would survive the anticipated resale of the property. The developer might not be in a position to pass along that risk contractually to buyers in a residential development, for example.

The developer may reason that the property will be owned for a short while, that it will be improved rather than contaminated and that any subsequently discovered contamination is not likely to have originated during the developer's period of ownership and operation. Moreover, preexisting contamination may be identified and remediated as a part of the development (although a hazardous waste condition could be improperly handled or aggravated during construction). The developer may therefore prefer not to release potential environmental claims against the seller. If the seller will not indemnify the developer for preexisting conditions, the developer may prefer to omit contractual allocation provisions from the acquisition documents (other than environmental site assessment as a condition of the acquisition), relying on recourse against former owners and operators under applicable law should a hazardous substance condition be discovered during construction or afterwards. For these reasons, it may be particularly difficult for a seller to negotiate with a developer for a contractual allocation of environmental risks to the developer.

Environmental Review or Remediation Insurance. A new strategy for risk allocation arises from the recent availability of environmental review or remediation insurance. See §§ 21.5 and 21.6 in Chapter 21 for a discussion of these innovative insurance products. Some portion of the environmental risk arising in connection with a transaction may be allocated to an insurance company providing such coverages. In appropriate circumstances, the availability of insurance can make the difference between a deal and no deal.

Combination of Foregoing Approaches. The foregoing allocation strategies can be combined in many possible ways. For example, the parties might agree that the seller will be wholly responsible for certain known contamination, that environmental review insurance will be obtained, that the buyer will be wholly responsible for any conditions created after the sale, that a sliding scale mutual indemnity will apply to cleanup costs arising out of unknown preexisting contamination and exceeding the coverage of the environmental review insurance policy (with the seller's liability not to exceed 25 percent of the purchase price), that the indemnified party must give notice of a claim within three months of obtaining knowledge of the facts giving rise to the claim and in no event later than the expiration of the indemnity period, and that silence will allow the chips to fall where they may regarding any possible toxic tort claims by third parties. The permutations are limited only by the creativity of the parties and their counsel.

Regardless of whether a single approach or a combination is selected, a number of details would have to be negotiated, such as exactly which costs, expenses or liabilities will be covered by a party's indemnity or a mutual sliding scale indemnity, and which hazardous substances are included (see § 18.2). An indemnity clause may be crafted brilliantly, but if it does not cover very much it will be of limited benefit. Another detail might be the reservation or granting of a right of access for inspection and response to hazardous waste conditions by a party who will not be in possession of the land but has assumed a contractual responsibility in that regard. Whatever allocation is selected, and whatever its scope, the parties also should consider its impact on an appropriate purchase price for the property.

General economic conditions can have a significant impact on risk allocation negotiations. In time of recession, when there are fewer interested buyers, it may be difficult for a motivated seller to require significant contractual protections from a buyer. Indeed, the seller may have to retain environmental risk and even give certain protections to a buyer in order to make the sale. When the economy is stronger and there are more interested buyers, the seller may be in a better position to allocate environmental risk to a motivated buyer.

In sum, the parties should be aware that there are many ways to compromise environmental liability issues and that it ought to be possible to reach an agreeable allocation in most cases. Transactions fall apart over environmental issues when the parties or their counsel are not creative enough, when one or more of the parties is unwilling to compromise or when the party which would benefit from an important contractual protection does not believe that the other party is creditworthy enough to back up the protection and other assurances (e.g., insurance) are not available or sufficient.

Lenders and Borrowers

Lenders are in the business of loaning money and getting repaid without taking undue risk. As a result, many lenders are unwilling to finance transactions involving real estate which is known to be environmentally impaired or is at all suspect. Lenders typically require their borrowers to undertake environmental assessments as discussed in Chapter 16 to find out if an environmental problem exists. If the assessment reveals no problem, or if the lender can be persuaded to make the loan anyway, the lender normally will expect the borrower to bear the risk of any environmental costs or liability. In other words, the allocation of the risk is usually one-sided in favor of the lender. The lender might nevertheless incur environmental liability if it forecloses and becomes the owner of contaminated property or if it actively participates in the management of the borrower or the property sufficiently to lose the benefit of the secured party exemption to CERCLA liability (see Chapter 10). Lenders also may try to avoid environmental liability in other ways, such as by obtaining other clean collateral (see Chapter 19).

Lessors and Lessees

Lessors and lessees are in a different situation. Both continue to have interests in the property and both risk strict CERCLA liability as a result of the activities of the other (see Chapter 11). Nevertheless, many of the allocation strategies for sellers and buyers might be structured for a lessor and lessee. For example, the lessor could assume the entire risk, which would make more sense than a seller doing so. This might be appropriate when a lessee does not handle hazardous substances in its business and wishes the lessor to retain full responsibility for the underlying condition of the property.

Alternatively, the lessee could assume all environmental risks during the term of the lease and afterwards with respect to conditions created by the lessee. This might be appropriate especially if a property is believed to be clean at the beginning of the lease term. Or the liability might be shared, with the lessor retaining liability for any environmental condition existing upon commencement of the lease, known or unknown, and with the lessee assuming responsibility for any condition created during the term of the lease. That allocation would have the same difficulties of proof of condition at a particular time as would exist in a sales transaction using that allocation.

If there are other tenants, the lessee may require the lessor to bear the risk of conditions created by any of those tenants which might give rise to strict liability for the lessee. Presumably the lessor would in turn shift that risk onto the tenant causing the problem, pursuant to an environmental indemnity provision in the lease with that tenant. Moreover, in a multi-tenant project, the lessor typically retains responsibility for the common areas and the exterior of the property. Thus, the lessee may require the lessor to bear the risk of any hazardous waste conditions caused by third parties. This position would not be as compelling for a single-tenant property in the full possession and control of the lessee, who might reasonably be allocated the responsibility of taking appropriate precautions for the security of the property against third party contamination. Even then, the lessee may prefer that the lessor remain responsible for any third party contamination from sources which are beyond the control of the lessee, such as groundwater contamination migrating from neighboring lands.

In a long term lease situation, a sliding scale mutual indemnity approach might even work in some form. Indeed, many leases have long enough terms that they are for all practical purposes a change in ownership. Some are even treated that way for real property tax reassessment purposes.

Provision might be made for an environmental assessment of the leased property at or near the conclusion of the lease, with appropriate cleanup of any contamination caused by the lessee's operations, so that the property is returned to the lessor in the expected condition.

Thus, environmental provisions in leases are also subject to intense negotiation and creative approaches to allocating potential environmental liability, at the commencement of a lease, during its term and at its termination or expiration.

We now turn to how an agreed allocation is put into effect using the available methods of environmental representations, warranties, covenants, releases and indemnities.

18.4   Environmental Representations and Warranties

One of the methods of allocating risks is to have a party represent and warrant certain matters to the other. Typically, the party with superior knowledge or responsibility for a particular matter will make the relevant representations and warranties.

Representations and warranties can cover any number of subjects, but in this context, they relate to the environmental condition of a property. Representations and warranties are essentially retrospective in nature regarding present or past conditions. Those may be conditions known (in which case the representation functions as a formal disclosure) or unknown (in which case the warranty acts as a form of insurance that the facts are as represented).

If the representation is incorrect, then the other party will have a cause of action for breach of warranty under the contract without having to rely on statutory or common law claims which might or might not be available or may require additional elements of proof.

Sellers and Buyers

In a sale transaction, the seller is usually the one with a superior knowledge of the history and condition of the property. Sellers nevertheless prefer to disclaim any representations or warranties by selling the property "AS IS, WITH ALL FAULTS," leaving it to the buyer to conduct its own investigation and to satisfy itself as to the condition of the property. As noted in Chapter 3, however, sellers must make at least the minimum disclosures required in order to avoid liability for common law fraud or to comply with statutory disclosure requirements. In **California**, the seller has an obligation to disclose the existence of any release of a hazardous substance which has come to be located on or beneath the property.[13] That statutory duty probably is not waivable by the buyer. The legislature had the public policy objective of ensuring that buyers would be notified of such information so that a buyer would not have the benefit of the innocent landowner defense to Superfund liability if the transaction closes, and civil penalties may be assessed by the state in cases of knowing nondisclosure.

Buyers who are aware of the potential for environmental liability often are unwilling to rely on possible common law or statutory causes of action and will not accept an unqualified "AS IS" clause. Such buyers require specific disclosures or assurances with respect to environmental matters. Sellers might be asked to represent and warrant that no hazardous substances or wastes are located at the property, or there has been no release of any hazardous substance, or particular hazardous substances (e.g., asbestos, PCBs) are not present there; the seller's past use, storage, handling, treatment and disposal of any hazardous substances has been properly permitted and otherwise in accordance with all applicable federal, state and local laws; the seller has not received any notification from any governmental agency or private party regarding any known or suspected hazardous waste contamination at or near the subject property for which the seller may be a PRP; there

---

[13]   Cal. Health & Safety Code § 25359.7(a).

are no pending or threatened court or administrative proceedings, and no orders, judgments, settlements or consent decrees regarding or arising out of the environmental condition of the property; there is not and never has been a UST installed at the property, or there has been no past leakage from a UST, or any UST presently located at the property is not leaking and is in compliance with all regulatory standards and permit requirements; any friable asbestos has been properly removed and disposed of, enclosed or encapsulated, and any remaining asbestos has been and is being properly maintained in accordance with all applicable regulatory standards; the property is not subject to any use or development restriction arising out of any environmental law or regulation; all necessary operating permits are transferable to, or obtainable by, the buyer; the seller has made all disclosures required by law; and any other circumstances which may be of concern to the buyer.

A seller must review carefully each requested representation and warranty for accuracy. The language must be modified to include any qualification or exception necessary to ensure that each representation and warranty is not untrue or misleading in any way. It may be necessary for the seller to undertake a due diligence review, including inquiry of company personnel and records for relevant knowledge.

Buyers prefer that each representation and warranty be absolute. On the other hand, sellers most often do not wish to give unqualified representations and warranties and prefer to limit them to the seller's "best knowledge and belief." Where the seller is a large company or corporation, the seller's exposure can be managed by limiting the representation to the knowledge of a named officer or employee with responsibility for the subject in question. This can also limit the scope of the necessary due diligence. It is important to realize that a provision which is limited in this way is fundamentally changed from a factual representation of an environmental condition of the property into a statement about the status of knowledge of the seller or its named officer or employee. Thus, no warranty liability will exist even if the property was not in the expected condition as long as the representing party did not have knowledge of the truth and the representation about knowledge was accurate. This may limit the effectiveness of the contractual protection.

Sophisticated parties in major transactions often negotiate and include detailed provisions regarding what due diligence is expected of the seller, what records will be made available for the buyer's own review, and which representations and warranties are to be absolute in nature or may be qualified by knowledge (and, if so, whose knowledge).

The seller reasonably might refuse to give some of the requested representations and warranties. For example, the seller might prefer that the buyer satisfy itself with its own investigation regarding such matters as the presence of any particular hazardous substance (which is unknown to the seller) or what restrictions might impair the buyer's desired use or development of the property. The seller might wish to make various records available to the buyer for its own review, rather than representing what information may or may not be contained in those records. While the seller may agree to assign any transferrable permits, the buyer can investigate what permits are needed and whether they can be transferred or otherwise obtained. The seller might not want to become an "insurer" of such matters by making representations and warranties. It is not unusual for negotiations to end up with a few precise and limited representations and warranties, and the buyer otherwise accepting the property "AS IS."

The appropriate scope of representations and warranties may vary depending upon whether the transaction involves the acquisition of real estate alone or also of a going business. If only real estate is being acquired, the representations and warranties need only include matters relevant to its condition. However, if a business is also being acquired, the buyer's concerns will include more broadly the seller's past compliance with environmental laws and the potential for successor liability for monetary penalties or other third party claims which would not ordinarily be assumed with a mere purchase of assets. See Chapter 14 with regard to successor liability. The representations and warranties could cover those concerns as well. For example, the buyer may ask the seller to represent and warrant that there are no pending or threatened claims by any third party, governmental or private, and that there are no facts or events which, with notice or passage of time or both, would give rise to any third party claim or cause of action against the seller under any federal, state or local environmental law or regulation. This would force the seller to disclose knowledge along those lines or to provide the assurance of contractual recourse if such representations are not true.

Finally, in some states, representations and warranties in a purchase agreement are merged into the deed and do not survive its recordation unless the parties expressly have agreed to the contrary. Thus, if the buyer expects to have recourse after the closing, as opposed to merely an excuse for refusing to close, the purchase agreement should include a survival clause for the representations and warranties as well as other obligations which are intended to survive the closing. From its viewpoint, the seller may wish to include a time limit on liability, in effect a contractual statute of limitations. Otherwise, the potential liability under the representation and warranty or other contractual protection would continue indefinitely into the future. The seller would like to know that at some point the transaction really will be over, and that the buyer cannot appear with a liability claim.

Lenders and Borrowers

Lenders typically require borrowers to give representations and warranties covering many of the same matters which a buyer might request of a seller. After all, the lender may end up owning the property someday. The lender also will be more concerned about the nature of the borrower's business and may require relevant representations and warranties. The lender's concerns in this respect would be analogous to those of a purchaser of a business as well as real estate alone.

In addition, a lender might ask a borrower to represent and warrant that it conducted a sufficient environmental assessment before acquiring the real estate and thus is entitled to the benefit of the innocent landowner defense with respect to preexisting conditions; that the borrower's business operations or intended operations do not involve the use, storage, handling, treatment, transportation or disposal of hazardous substances in general, or specifically named hazardous substances; that the borrower's facilities are properly designed to prevent hazardous substance releases or discharges in violation of any environmental laws, such as **California's** Proposition 65; and any other matter arising from the particular circumstances.

If a sale transaction involves seller financing, then the documents may include appropriate representations and warranties from the buyer as a borrower. But a seller, not being a stranger to the property, might not be able to insist on representations and warranties which are as broad as a third party lender would require. Indeed, the buyer may be receiving some of those representations and warranties from the seller. The parties should consider appropriate provisions regarding the buyer/borrower's remedies in the event of any breach of warranty by the seller/lender. For instance, a right of offset against note payments may be provided, limited or prohibited.

Lessors and Lessees

The position of a lessee is analogous to that of a buyer. A lessee therefore may want many of the same kinds of representations and warranties from the lessor as a seller would be asked to give. The lessor would, in turn, like assurances that the lessee's business operations have been structured in accordance with applicable environmental laws. The lessor may also require the lessee to make an acceptable representation and warranty as to the nature of the business and the extent to which it involves the possession, use, storage, handling or disposal of hazardous substances. Such activities may or may not be appropriate depending upon the nature of the property, and the lessor will want to be satisfied that the property is being leased to the right kind of lessee.

In a sale/leaseback transaction, one would expect the representations and warranties to be from the seller/lessee for the benefit of the buyer/lessor whose position is analogous to that of a lender, especially in the case of a lease financing transaction. In the case of a true lease, the buyer/lessor might also incur direct environmental liability as an owner and would want the benefit of contractual protections for that reason as well.

18.5 Environmental Covenants

In contrast to representations and warranties, environmental covenants look forward to future conduct. That distinction is sometimes blurred. For example, a party may "represent and warrant" that it has obtained all required environmental permits and will continue to maintain such permits in full force and effect during the term of a lease or a loan. The latter warranty is really a covenant, a promise of future conduct.

A covenant can be either affirmative (promising to take certain action) or negative (promising to refrain from specified actions).

Sellers and Buyers

Most real estate sale transactions do not involve any ongoing relationship between the seller and buyer. Thus, environmental covenants regarding future conduct do not normally receive much attention in purchase agreements. The most significant environmental covenant in this context would be any cleanup obligations or environmental indemnities agreed to by the parties and which would survive the closing. Environmental indemnities are discussed separately in § 18.7.

An ongoing relationship would exist if the seller provides financing for the transaction. There are a number of business reasons why a seller might do so. From the environmental perspective, as noted in Chapter 4, some sellers wish to avoid triggering reporting requirements by limiting the scope of environmental assessments, e.g., no soil testing. Such sellers may have to provide financing in order to sell the property, as lenders can be expected to reject any deal which would constrain implementation of their standard environmental assessment protocols. Seller financing should be carefully considered in view of the risk that the buyer might be able to frustrate or delay the seller's exercise of remedies, in the event of the buyer's default, due to claims arising from the seller's prior ownership or from the transaction itself, claims which would not exist against a third party lender. The seller in such a case would want to have provisions in the purchase money note and security instruments minimizing this risk. See §§ 18.6 and 18.7 regarding environmental releases and indemnities.

If the seller, for whatever reason, provides financing for the transaction, it would be appropriate to include environmental covenants in the mortgage or deed of trust, much like those required by lenders (see below). However, the scope of those covenants may be affected by the agreed risk allocation between the parties as seller and buyer. The seller, not being a stranger to the property, should not expect to receive environmental covenants as broad as those which might be required by a hard money lender, particularly with respect to existing conditions which are the seller's responsibility.

In some cases, a seller may want to impose a restriction on the use of the property, a form of negative covenant. For example, the seller of a site which has been contaminated may wish to restrict future use to certain commercial or industrial purposes, in order to limit the number of potential plaintiffs who might be exposed to the contamination if the site were put to a more people intensive use (e.g., residential). Likewise, the seller may wish to prohibit the use of various chemicals, in order to avoid the risk of aggravation of a problem and the consequent increase in potential cleanup cost and liability.

How such negative covenants may or should be structured, and their enforceability, will depend upon the law of the applicable jurisdiction. For example, an available structure might be the recordation of covenants, conditions and restrictions (CC&Rs) imposing an equitable servitude benefitting and burdening neighboring lands. If that approach is not available, perhaps the seller can reserve in the deed a reversionary interest (or make the conveyance subject to condition subsequent) which would be triggered in the event of the breach of the negative covenant. Such forfeitures are strictly construed by the courts, however. Another approach might be to obtain the imposition of appropriate use restrictions by the applicable state health care agency under authority of state law, although the seller might not relish the implications of approaching the state agency with such a request. Of course, use restrictions have a negative impact on the value of land.

Lenders and Borrowers

Loan documents naturally include many covenants to be performed or observed by the borrower during the term of the loan. In the environmental context, borrowers are often required to covenant that they will comply with all applicable federal, state and local environmental laws and regulations respecting the possession, use, storage, handling, reporting, transportation and disposal of hazardous substances; provide the lender with copies of all reports made to, and business plans submitted to, any governmental agency; obtain and maintain all environmental permits required for equipment, hazardous materials and operations; design and maintain facilities and operations to avoid unlawful releases or discharges of any hazardous substances; promptly take all necessary and appropriate response, removal or remedial action in the event of an actual or threatened hazardous substance release or the discovery of preexisting contamination; remove, enclose or encapsulate any friable asbestos in accordance with all applicable procedures and precautions, and undertake a proper operation and maintenance program with respect to any asbestos which is not removed; promptly notify the lender in the event that any environmental notice is delivered or claim is asserted by any third party, whether governmental or private; promptly notify the lender of the introduction of any new activities which may increase the risk of environmental liability; comply with governmental orders; defend against third party toxic tort claims which affect the property; protect the lender's security interest in the property and its lien priority; make the property available for periodic environmental assessments by the lender during the term of the loan, at the borrower's expense, or undertake such assessments in accordance with the lender's standards; provide additional or substitute collateral if the lender believes that its security is impaired due to the presence or release of any hazardous substances; and reimburse the lender for any costs or expenses, including attorneys' and consultants' fees, which may be incurred by the lender in connection with environmental matters.

Depending upon the nature of the property and the borrower's business, the loan documents might include a negative covenant to the effect that the borrower will not possess, use, store, handle, transport or dispose of hazardous substances at the property (other than those contained in ordinary office supplies); or specifically identified hazardous substances may be prohibited. Additional matters which may be of concern to the lender based on the particular circumstances also may be included in the loan documents in the form of either affirmative or negative covenants.

A borrower should negotiate the specific language of the environmental covenants so that they are clear and within the borrower's reasonable ability to comply. The environmental covenants may be included in the loan agreement as well as the mortgage, deed of trust or other security instruments.

Lessors and Lessees

Environmental covenants similar to those noted previously may be included in a lease. The party providing each covenant may be either the lessor or lessee depending upon how potential environmental liabilities are allocated between them. Lessees may expect to be obligated to comply with environmental laws and regulations, and appropriate restrictions may be placed on the possession, use, storage, handling, transportation and disposal of hazardous substances in general or named hazardous substances in particular. The lessor may require a negative covenant from the lessee not to change the nature of its business as represented at the inception of the lease in any way which would increase the risk of environmental liability without the lessor's prior written consent. If the building has asbestos-containing construction materials, the lessor should have an appropriate operations and management program in place and the lease should include a covenant by the lessee to comply with that program. In some situations, it may be appropriate to allocate to the lessee the obligation to develop an asbestos operations and management program.

For a single-tenant property, the lessee may covenant to take all appropriate precautions to avoid hazardous waste contamination by third parties (at least from sources or avenues reasonably within the lessee's control). On the other hand, the lessor may be obligated to take reasonable measures to ensure the security of the leased property from hazardous substance invasions from external sources. This would probably be the case in a multi-tenant project. The lessor may also covenant to include hazardous substance restrictions in the leases of other tenants and to enforce those restrictions.

The lessor should consider including in the lease a covenant on the part of the lessee to disclose to the lessor the occurrence of any actual or threatened release of hazardous substance at the property. This might not be necessary in a state like **California** where such a disclosure duty is imposed on lessees by law.[14]

The lessor may want to pass through to the lessee various costs associated with environmental compliance as reimbursable operating expenses (if the form of the lease does not already require the lessee to bear all expenses of operation and maintenance of the premises). This could include such matters as asbestos abatement costs or other response to hazardous materials, if the lessee will agree to such an allocation.

---

[14]   Cal. Health & Safety Code § 25359.7(b).

Another anticipated cost may be the modification or replacement of the HVAC system when CFCs are banned. The lease may allocate that significant cost to one of the parties.

The lessor may wish to have the right to treat any breach of environmental covenants by the lessee as an event of default under the lease, or to require the lessee to cure the breach. Which alternative is better for the lessor will depend on the circumstances and the advisability of having the lessee remain in possession.

18.6   Environmental Releases

Once an allocation of environmental liability is agreed to by the parties, it would be appropriate to have each party expressly waive and release any statutory or common law right of action inconsistent with the allocation. As noted above, some courts have held that an "AS IS" clause in a purchase agreement merely disclaims any warranties by the seller but does not cut off any CERCLA right of action which may arise in favor of the buyer against the seller. Similarly, a disclosure by the seller that a hazardous substance condition exists, while perhaps adequate to preclude various common law and certain statutory claims, would appear to be insufficient alone to avoid a contribution action under CERCLA (except in the case of a disclosure by an intervening owner).

Thus, if the parties intend to shift environmental risks entirely to the buyer, then an "AS IS" clause should be supplemented with language which would be sufficient under applicable law to result in a waiver and release of environmental claims by the buyer.

Using the sample defined terms set forth in § 18.2, a broad form of release might look like this:

> *Releases.*   Except with respect to any representations, warranties and covenants expressly set forth in this Agreement, [*name of releasing party*], for itself and its legal representatives, successors and assigns (including successor business entities as well as successors-in-interest to, or assignees of any interest in, all or any portion of the Property) (the "Releasing Parties"), completely and unconditionally waives, releases, remises, acquits and forever discharges [*name of released party*]

and its agents and affiliates, as well as their officers, directors, shareholders, affiliates, employees, agents, attorneys and legal representatives, and their respective successors and assigns (the "Released Parties") from any and all actions, causes of action, suits, proceedings, costs, charges, damages, losses, contributions, liabilities and claims (including but not limited to, the fees and costs of experts, consultants and attorneys), whether known or unknown, suspected or unsuspected, of any kind or nature whatsoever which any of the Releasing Parties ever had, now has, or may, shall or can hereafter have or acquire arising out of, due to, or in respect of (1) the presence, release or threatened release of any Hazardous Substances in, on, under, above or about the Property, (2) the effect with respect to the Property of any Environmental Laws, (3) any Environmental Claim, (4) any Environmental Cleanup Liability, (5) any Environmental Compliance Cost, or (6) any defect, latent or patent, arising in connection with the Property.

The opening line of that provision allows for exceptions from the release with respect to any environmental risk which is to be allocated to the released party. Those matters should be set forth expressly in appropriate representations, warranties and covenants (including any agreed indemnities).

The laws of some states provide that a release will be ineffective against claims which were unknown when the release was given. However, a releasing party is generally permitted to waive that protection. A waiver of unknown environmental claims may be essential to an agreed allocation of risks. This would be accomplished in **California**, for example, by language such as the following:

[*Name of releasing party*] further agrees that all rights under Section 1542 of the California Civil Code and any similar law are hereby expressly waived with respect to the matters specifically released herein. Said Civil Code Section reads as follows:

> A general release does not extend to claims which
> the creditor does not know or suspect to exist in
> his favor at the time of executing the release, which
> if known by him must have materially affected his
> settlement with the debtor.

The party receiving the release may require further assurances such
as these:

> At the request of [*name of released party*], [*name
> of releasing party*] shall prepare, execute, acknowledge (if
> necessary), and deliver to [*name of released party*] such
> other documents as may be reasonably required by [*name
> of released party*] to evidence such release. The foregoing
> releases shall survive the closing of the transaction
> contemplated by this Agreement.

Two recent cases illustrate the need for releases in connection with
transactions. In these cases, the transaction itself created CERCLA
liability which did not otherwise exist. In the first case, the buyer of a
hotel was permitted to sue a seller for asbestos abatement costs incurred
during subsequent demolition. The court found that the seller knew that
the building itself was to be disposed of by the buyer, so that the sale of
the building with that knowledge constituted disposal of the asbestos in
the building. The seller was hence an owner at the time of disposal (i.e.,
the sale) and liable under CERCLA § 107(a)(2) when asbestos was later
released during demolition and response costs were incurred by the
buyer under state order.[15]

In the second case, the seller of a foundry was sued under CERCLA
on the ground that the sale constituted an arrangement for disposal of
transformers containing PCBs. The foundry was sold at a substantial
discount, a fraction of cost of disposal of the transformers, and the
evidence suggested that the seller's intent was to dispose of the

---

[15]   *CP Holdings, Inc. v. Goldberg-Zoino & Associates*, 769 F. Supp. 432
(D.N.H. 1991).

hazardous material by selling the property, resulting in liability under CERCLA § 107(a)(3) as an arranger or generator.[16]

The sellers in both of these cases apparently did not have the protection of adequate releases from their buyers. Especially in view of the second case, this concern could arise in any situation where risk is allocated to a buyer in return for a price discount. It seems unfair for the buyer to get both the discount and subsequent cost recovery, but that can happen if an adequate release is not obtained.[17]

18.7 Environmental Indemnities

The parties to a real estate transaction may use an indemnity clause to allocate the risk of environmental claims by third parties or expenses which might be incurred in connection with environmental laws. Such provisions may cover many of the same subjects mentioned in environmental covenants. The advantage of having an indemnity clause is that it would require proof only of an expenditure within the terms of the clause, without necessarily having to prove any breach of covenant or duty by the other party.

The need for an indemnity clause is illustrated by the Love Canal case. Nearly 40 years ago, Hooker Electrochemical Company sold real property for one dollar to the Niagara Falls Board of Education with language on the face of the recorded deed disclosing that the property was the site of chemical wastes and providing that the grantee and its successors and assigns assumed all risk and liability in connection therewith and would have no claims against Hooker or its successors or assigns. Hooker and its corporate successors nevertheless face multimillion dollar liability for cleanup costs incurred by the government and for damages to neighboring persons and property. The

---

[16] *Sanford Street Local Development Corp. v. Textron, Inc.*, 768 F. Supp. 1218 (W.D.Mich. 1991). Cf. *Jersey City Redevelopment Authority v. PPG Industries, Inc.*, 866 F.2d 1408 (3d Cir. 1988) (sale of real property did not constitute arranging for disposal).

[17] Another case suggests that the amount of a price discount may be considered by a court as a mitigating factor in order to avoid a double recovery by the buyer, but CERCLA liability nevertheless exists. *Smith Land & Improvement Corp. v. Celotex Corp.*, 851 F.2d 86, 90 (3d Cir. 1988).

exculpatory language in the deed was ineffective to avoid liability to third parties under subsequent environmental laws.[18]

Sellers and Buyers

Again using the sample defined terms set forth in § 18.2, a broad form of indemnity allocating risks to the buyer might read as follows:

> *Indemnification.* Except as otherwise expressly set forth in this Agreement, the Buyer, as Indemnitor, agrees to indemnify and hold the Seller and its agents and affiliates, as well as their officers, directors, shareholders, affiliates, employees, agents, attorneys, legal representatives, successors and assigns (the "Indemnified Parties") harmless from and to defend the Indemnified Parties, with counsel acceptable to the Indemnified Parties in their sole discretion, against any and all demands, allegations, threats, actions, causes of action, suits, proceedings, orders, decrees, judgments, settlements, costs, fees, charges, fines, penalties, damages, losses, liabilities, claims and expenses (including but not limited to any and all experts', consultants' and attorneys' fees and costs), whether known, unknown, liquidated, contingent, foreseeable, unforeseeable, voluntary or involuntary, which are suffered or incurred by, or assessed, levied or asserted by any person or entity (whether governmental or private) against, any of the Indemnified Parties with respect to any of the following:
>
> (1) Environmental Claims, Environmental Cleanup Liability and Environmental Compliance Costs arising at any time from or with respect to the existence, presence, release or threatened release of any Hazardous Substances at, on, in, from, onto, under or about the Property,

---

18 *U.S. v. Hooker Chemicals & Plastics Corp.*, 680 F.Supp. 546, 558 (W.D.N.Y. 1988) (Occidental Chemicals Corp., the corporate successor of Hooker, was found liable for cleanup costs under CERCLA); *U.S. v. Hooker Chemicals & Plastics Corp.*, 722 F.Supp. 960 (W.D.N.Y. 1989) (Occidental was found also liable for creating a public nuisance).

whether before, at or after the Closing, or the effect of any Environmental Laws applicable to the Property;

(2) Any claims or liabilities in respect of any mechanics' or materialmen's liens filed in connection with any work performed at, or material delivered to, the Property at the request of Indemnitor;

(3) Any claims or liabilities for personal injury or property damage occurring as a result of the entry, presence or activities of Indemnitor or any of its licensees, invitees, employees, agents or independent contractors at, in, on, under or about the Property; or

(4) Any and all other claims or liabilities arising at any time from or in connection with the physical or environmental condition of the Property or defects of any kind therein, latent or patent, whether before, at or after the Closing.

The foregoing indemnity obligations shall survive the Close of Escrow and the delivery of the Grant Deed to the Property.

Naturally, most buyers would prefer not to sign such a broad indemnity. The sample form would require revision to reflect the actual agreement of the parties. This form includes the basic elements or matters for which indemnity may be desired by any party. Additional matters can be included as the circumstances of an actual transaction dictate.

Lenders and Borrowers

Lenders typically require indemnification from borrowers covering many of the same items which are set forth above in the sample buyer's indemnity. This would protect the lender in the event that it incurs any expense or liability arising out of environmental matters. Of course, that protection is only as good as the ability of the borrower to back it up.

A borrower's obligation to indemnify a lender may be set forth in any of the loan documents. It usually is included as a covenant in the loan agreement and as a secured obligation in a mortgage, deed of trust or other security agreement. Lenders require security for the environmental indemnity as well as the loan because the buyer might not be able to repay the loan and discharge the environmental liability, and the collateral might provide the lender with its only practical source of recovery. If the collateral is contaminated, however, it might not have sufficient value, and the lender may incur strict CERCLA liability if it forecloses its security interest and becomes the owner of contaminated property. But those facts and their impact on the economics of the loan might not be known in advance, and the lender will want the security interest in the event that it may become useful.

Some states have debtor protection laws which govern the sequence and manner of enforcement of remedies by lenders whose loans are secured by a mortgage or deed of trust on real estate. **California**, for example, has an "anti-deficiency" law which, among other things, prohibits a lender who has conducted a nonjudicial foreclosure pursuant to a power of sale in a deed of trust from pursuing the debtor personally for the payment of any shortage or deficiency in the proceeds of the foreclosure sale as compared to the outstanding balance of the secured indebtedness.[19] A deficiency judgment is possible, however, if the lender instead uses the judicial foreclosure route. While this is a complex area of **California** real estate law which is beyond the scope of this book, it is easy to see how such debtor protection laws can have an impact on the effectiveness of any environmental indemnity which is secured by a mortgage or deed of trust on real estate. A nonjudicial foreclosure would extinguish the secured indemnity along with any deficiency in the underlying indebtedness on the loan. Moreover, the lender may not want to foreclose on contaminated property, either nonjudicially or judicially, for fear of becoming liable under CERCLA as an owner.

As a result, lenders frequently attempt to obtain both secured and unsecured environmental indemnities from borrowers on the theory that if it would be unwise to enforce the secured indemnity or if enforcement were precluded by a debtor protection law, then the debtor might be sued personally on the unsecured indemnity. The enforceability of an unsecured environmental indemnity has not yet been the subject of an authoritative court decision in **California**. Legal commentators have

---

[19]   Cal. Code of Civil Procedure § 580d.

raised doubts about the enforceability of an unsecured indemnity which covers the same obligations as a secured indemnity. The courts might not respect the attempt and might read the two pieces of paper as one secured indemnity subject to the debtor protections laws. It may be possible, however, to carve out obligations and place them in either the secured or the unsecured environmental indemnity but not both. In that case, the unsecured environmental indemnity should have independent validity. But it can be very difficult to distinguish the secured and unsecured obligations.

In recognition of the dilemma faced by lenders in light of the potential for environmental liability and the strictures of the debtor protection laws, **California** amended its debtor protection laws, effective January 1, 1992, to provide lenders with a greater degree of personal recourse against borrowers where the real property collateral is "environmentally impaired" as defined by the law. In general, the amendments clarify the lender's right of access to the property for inspection purposes, allow lenders under certain circumstances to waive the collateral and proceed against the borrower as if the debt had been unsecured, and allow lenders under certain circumstances to enforce environmental provisions in loan documents without running afoul of the debtor protection laws.[20] This legislation was the result of intense lobbying and ultimate compromise by lenders and real estate interests. Typical of compromise legislation, there are limitations and complexities. Any lender proposing to use an unsecured environmental indemnity, or to benefit from any available exceptions to debtor protection laws, should consult with qualified legal counsel to ensure that the provisions are properly structured within applicable law or available legal theories.

Lessors and Lessees

Leases may also contain environmental indemnities to implement the agreed allocation of environmental liabilities between the lessor and the lessee. Lessors typically require their lessees to provide indemnification with respect to any environmental liability arising from

---

[20] See Cal. 1991 Stats., c. 1167 (AB 1735), adding § 2929.5 to the Cal. Civil Code, and amending § 564 of, and adding §§ 726.5 and 736 to, the Cal. Code of Civil Procedure.

the lessee's activities during the term of the lease, and the lessee may in turn require indemnification from the lessor regarding other conditions which were not created by the lessee but which expose the lessee to environmental liability. Such clauses also may cover many of the other items which are set forth above in the sample buyer's indemnity, with appropriate modifications.

The default section of a lease should include breach of the lessee's environmental indemnity, as well as any of the lessee's environmental covenants or representations and warranties, as one of the events of default which would trigger the lessor's remedies, including possible eviction. The lessor would have a valid interest in avoiding further exposure to environmental liability by getting rid of a lessee who is violating the environmental provisions of the lease.

As with all other aspects of contractual protections for environmental liability, legal counsel should be consulted with respect to the structuring and enforcement of environmental provisions in leases.

18.8   Limitations of Contractual Protections

Contractual protections may or may not be effective when they are needed. Subsequent events may diminish or eliminate the creditworthiness of the obligated party and hence the practical availability of the negotiated protection. Further, the protection might not be binding on succeeding owners of the real estate.

18.8.1 Environmental Liability May Outlive Contractual Protections

One of the distinguishing characteristics of Superfund liability is that it is potentially unending, awaiting the discovery of contamination and subsequent cleanup action. As noted above, the passage of nearly 40 years after the sale of Love Canal did not protect Hooker Electrochemical Company and its successors. Moreover, agreements to allocate or transfer environmental liability, if enforceable at all as discussed in § 18.3 above, are only effective between the parties and are not binding on governmental agencies or third parties.[21] As a result, the party benefitted by a representation, warranty, release, indemnity or other contractual protection may still become involved in environmental

---

[21]   42 U.S.C. § 9607(e); Cal. Health & Safety Code § 25364.

proceedings brought by the government or a third party, e.g., a toxic tort claimant. When that occurs, the contractual protection will be only as good as the ability of the other party to perform its obligations at that time. Even if the contractual protection is unlimited as to time, there may be no practical recourse under the contract if the obligated party has become unable in the intervening years to perform its promise or to respond in damages by virtue of loss of assets, death, liquidation, dissolution or bankruptcy.[22]

Under **California** law, the shareholders of a liquidated and dissolved corporation (at least one dissolved prior to January 1, 1992 -- see below) may be sued only for predissolution, not postdissolution, claims, unless the dissolution constituted a fraudulent transfer.[23] The federal Court of Appeals for the Ninth Circuit has ruled that this corporate law generally precludes CERCLA contribution claims against the shareholders of a dissolved **California** corporation where the claims arose after the dissolution.[24] Other courts have declined to follow that ruling, however, and have determined that state laws regarding the capacity to be sued are preempted by CERCLA, so that a dissolved corporation could be sued, at least until all of its assets have been distributed.[25] Thus, the issue appears to be unsettled.

California has recently amended its corporate law with respect to corporations dissolved on or after January 1, 1992. Claims, whether arising before or after dissolution, may be stated against such

---

[22] The impact of bankruptcy is discussed separately in Chapter 23.

[23] Cal. Corporations Code § 2011(a); *Pacific Scene, Inc. v. Penasquitos, Inc.*, 46 Cal.3d 407, 250 Cal.Rptr. 651, 758 P.2d 1182 (1988).

[24] *Levin Metals Corp. v. Parr-Richmond Terminal Company*, 817 F.2d 1448 (9th Cir. 1987). See also *Columbia River Service Corp. v. Gilman*, 751 F. Supp. 1448 (W.D.Wash. 1990) (following the Ninth Circuit rule, but criticizing it).

[25] *U.S. v. Sharon Steel Corp.*, 681 F.Supp. 1492 (D. Utah 1987); *U.S. v. Distler*, 741 F. Supp. 643 (W.D.Ky. 1990); *U-Haul of Inland Northwest v. Yakima Rex Spray Co.*, No. 90-2-00155-4 (Wash. Superior Ct., Yakima County, Aug. 24, 1990) (reported at Toxics Law Reporter, pp. 534-535 (9-19-90)); *Traverse Bay Area Intermediate School District v. Hitco, Inc.*, 762 F. Supp. 1298 (W.D.Mich. 1991).

corporations to the extent of undistributed assets and against shareholders to the extent of their pro-rata share of the claim or the extent of corporate assets distributed to them, whichever is less. Such claims must be commenced prior to the expiration of the applicable statute of limitations or four years after the dissolution, whichever is earlier.[26] Thus, two different rules now apply in **California** based on the date of dissolution.

At any rate, depending upon the prevailing rule in the applicable jurisdiction, there might not be an available defendant in the event of any claims under a corporate representation, warranty or indemnity clause arising either before or after the dissolution of the corporation. Personal guaranties of shareholders could conceivably back up a corporate indemnity agreement, but such guaranties also may be of limited usefulness many years later after the death, dissolution or bankruptcy of the guarantor.

Thus, the identity, nature, creditworthiness and prospects for future longevity of the party to be obligated by a contractual protection will be of great importance to the party to be benefitted. If the latter party is not satisfied with the financial standing and prospects of the obligated party in relation to the potential environmental risk, the proposed transaction might not be feasible. The transaction might proceed, however, if the party receiving the contractual protection is persuaded to accept the risk of the eventual ineffectiveness of the protection. That persuasion might take the form of negotiated inducements in the economics of the transaction (e.g., an appropriate adjustment to the purchase price).

In a sense, environmental warranties, covenants and indemnities are no different than any other executory or contingent obligation which may be affected by subsequent events. The long-term nature of potential environmental liabilities makes this issue perhaps more poignant in this context than others. This is not to say that contractual protections should not be obtained. Rather, the benefitted party simply should realize that the potential liability may outlive the contractual protection, and that this is a risk factor which should be weighed appropriately in

---

26   Cal. 1991 Stats., c. 545 (SB 1188), amending Cal. Corporations Code
        § 2011(a).

the course of the negotiations and in the determination of whether to enter into the transaction at all, or on what terms.

18.8.2 Can Contractual Protections Be Made Binding on Succeeding Owners of the Real Estate?

Contractual protections typically purport to bind the "successors and assigns" of the obligated party. A seller obtaining a release from a buyer may expect it to bind future owners as well. Similarly, an environmental covenant or indemnity in a mortgage or deed of trust might be intended to bind not only the borrower, but all future owners who acquire the property while the security instrument remains in effect. Provisions such as these reflect the objective of the benefitted party to have the contractual protection survive future transfers of ownership and be binding on succeeding owners of the property. In legal parlance, the benefitted party would like to have the obligation "run with the land."

While such provisions may bind corporate successors (see Chapter 14), a substantial question exists as to whether they are effective to bind future owners or occupants of the real estate. In the first place, the term "successors and assigns" might or might not be construed broadly enough by any applicable case law to include successors-in-interest to the property as opposed to successor business entities. Even if the term does include successors-in-interest, it might be construed to encompass only those who succeed to the entire interest of the predecessor, not only some portion of the interest (for example, a buyer of the entire fee simple interest of the seller, but not a lessee). If the party receiving the contractual protection expects it to be binding on future owners and lessees of the property, it may be necessary to research the law of the applicable jurisdiction to determine whether that term is sufficient to accomplish that objective. Alternatively, more explicit language could be used (see, for example, the sample release set forth in § 18.6 which contains a broad definition of the term for purposes of identifying the Releasing Parties).

Assuming that the contractual protection is drafted in a matter which adequately includes succeeding owners or occupants of the real estate, as a matter of contract interpretation, the question remains whether the contractual provisions will be binding on and enforceable against them.

Environmental Releases. As indicated in Chapter 1, CERCLA and many state Superfund laws provide a statutory right of action for contribution among PRPs toward the cost of cleaning up hazardous waste. Those PRPs include, among others, the current owner of the contaminated real estate and the owner of the property at the time of the disposal. Assume that an owner, who owned a property when hazardous substances were disposed of there, sold the property and obtained a release of potential Superfund claims from the buyer, and that the release purported to bind the buyer and its successors and assigns. When the buyer subsequently assigns or sells the property, the question is whether the succeeding owner likewise is bound by the release and is precluded from pursuing a Superfund cost recovery action against the prior owner. Importantly, the succeeding owner would have a direct statutory cause of action which is independent of any rights assigned by the intervening owner. Not being a party to the release of its own statutory right, it is doubtful that the release would be binding on the succeeding owner unless it too agreed to release the former owners.

Environmental Warranties, Covenants and Indemnities. Similarly, the various promises of a property owner may provide recourse against that owner, but not necessarily against a future owner who has not assumed those obligations. Under **California** law, a purchaser of real estate subject to an earlier mortgage or deed of trust is not bound personally by any of the secured obligations unless those obligations are assumed by the purchaser.[27] This would include the obligation to repay the loan as well as any other obligations arising under the loan documents, such as environmental warranties, covenants and indemnities. Of course, the secured party may be in a position to foreclose on the real estate if the obligations are not performed, and this may compel the succeeding owner to perform the obligations in order to avoid losing the property. But that practical compulsion might be blunted upon the discovery of significant hazardous waste contamination. The new owner might not want to throw good money after bad, especially toward a loan on which he is not personally obligated; and it might not be wise for the secured party to foreclose on contaminated property. If a foreclosure is conducted or the lender

---

27 *Cornelison v. Kornbluth*, 15 Cal.3d 590, 125 Cal.Rptr. 557, 542 P.2d 981 (1975).

otherwise incurs cleanup costs, the lender would like to be able to obtain a personal judgment against someone, particularly if those costs exceed the value of the property. Recourse might exist under an unsecured environmental indemnity from the original borrower, if enforceable, or a deficiency judgment might be obtained against that borrower if proper procedures are followed. But the environmental indemnity in the mortgage or deed of trust simply is not going to be personally binding on the succeeding owner without an express assumption of that obligation.

A similar question involves the personal liability of a new owner of leased property, or an assignee of the lessee's interest, under the environmental provisions of an existing lease in the absence of an express assumption. Consideration should be given to whether the provisions of a lease, including environmental provisions, will "run with the land" to bind a new owner or a new lessee under applicable law.

Possible Techniques to Extend the Effectiveness of Contractual Protections. As suggested previously, possible techniques for extending the effectiveness of contractual protections would include (i) requiring a releasing party to indemnify the released party in the event of any environmental claim by a future owner who is not bound by the release, and (ii) a covenant by the obligated party not to sell or transfer the real estate without obtaining acceptable environmental releases, covenants and indemnities from the transferee.

While these approaches are sometimes utilized, they do not ensure protection. The indemnity may become worthless. The restriction on resale might be unenforceable as an unlawful restraint on alienation of real estate; and even if it is enforceable, it might only give rise to a breach of contract claim against the obligated party who sells without obtaining the required agreements from the new owner. That claim may be just as worthless as the indemnity clause. Moreover, future transfers might occur pursuant to foreclosure of voluntary liens (e.g., mortgages) or involuntary liens (e.g., tax liens, mechanics' liens, judgment liens, etc.). The purchasers at such foreclosure sales can hardly be expected to assume any contractual environmental liability.

These difficulties have led to the search for some other technique for making environmental releases, covenants and indemnities "run with the land." Whether any such technique exists will depend upon the law of each state.

The doctrine of "equitable servitudes" may be available in some states as a means of imposing an obligation which will "run with the land" under some circumstances. A major feature of that doctrine is that it normally requires at least two neighboring parcels of real estate which are benefitted or burdened, respectively, by the equitable servitude. This suggests that provisions could be included in the documents establishing a planned development of some kind whereby the separate parcels within the development would be benefitted and burdened by mutual environmental protection clauses. (Whether such provisions would be wise is another question.) But that feature of the doctrine renders it of doubtful applicability to most situations where only one parcel of real estate is involved and a party is attempting to obtain a personal right independent of any other real estate.

Another approach might be to reserve in the grant deed a reversionary interest, or to convey the property subject to condition subsequent, which would require future owners to accept the property subject to certain environmental provisions on peril of triggering the reversionary interest and losing the property upon failure to comply with the provisions involved. Such reversionary interests or conditions subsequent are deemed to be forfeitures and are strictly construed by the courts. Moreover, having such an interest in the chain of title would show up on title reports and may affect the marketability of the property as well as the availability of financing. In this context, a reversionary interest would achieve its objectives only if it encouraged compliance to avoid loss of the property. An owner of a contaminated property might be delighted to hand over the keys to a former owner. Thus, this approach is problematical.

Some parties are including environmental provisions, such as releases from the buyer, on the face of recorded grant deeds on the theory that doing so will establish actual or constructive notice of the provisions as to any party in the future who obtains an interest in the property. This may enhance the prospects of enforcing such a provision against the future owner or occupant, if the provision is otherwise enforceable.

Other techniques may be available under applicable law. These considerations are complex and subject to varied treatment in different jurisdictions. Thus, any party who wishes to obtain contractual protections which will "run with the land" and be binding on future owners of the real estate should obtain the advice of qualified legal counsel regarding the law of the applicable jurisdiction under the circumstances.

In sum, the parties to a real estate transaction involving environmental protection clauses should appreciate that those protections may become of limited utility and might not be binding on future owners of the real estate. Such an appreciation at the outset may assist the parties in appropriately weighing the merits of the transaction and would avoid undue surprise in the future when environmental claims arise and the protection turns out to be ineffective or insufficient.

CHAPTER NINETEEN

ADDITIONAL PROTECTIONS FOR LENDERS

Chapter 10 discusses the impact of environmental laws on the interests of lenders; Chapter 16 outlines the process of environmental due diligence; and Chapters 17 and 18 discuss contractual conditions and protections which may be considered by lenders and others. Those chapters quite rightly assume that a lender will wish to have a security interest in the real estate which is the subject of a loan transaction. There are, however, additional protections which might be considered by lenders.

Other Clean Collateral. In view of the risk that the real estate which is the subject of a transaction might be contaminated, lenders often seek additional *clean* collateral. Such collateral may consist of personal property belonging to the borrower. Thus, a lender may require a borrower to execute a security agreement and financing statement for filing under the Uniform Commercial Code in order to obtain and perfect a security interest in personal property collateral. The appropriate form of the security agreement and the manner of perfection (e.g., filing, taking possession) will depend upon the nature of the personal property and the law of the applicable jurisdiction. Personal property collateral may consist of any valuable asset other than real estate, including tangible items or intangible rights. A lender will want to consider essentially any personal property belonging to the borrower as possible collateral.

Lenders typically have standard form descriptions of personal property for use in security instruments. If a lender has not already had its forms updated from an environmental perspective, the lender should consider including in the collateral package an assignment of all statutory or common law claims which the borrower may have, now or in the future, against any other persons responsible for causing or contributing to hazardous substance releases in or about the borrower's real estate. This would permit the lender, in the event of a loan default, to acquire those rights upon foreclosure of the security interest and then to pursue such claims. This can be particularly important when the

419

lender also forecloses on the real estate; the lender will want to stand in the shoes of the borrower as owner of the real estate and to have the benefit of the borrower's environmental claims against others. In addition, for the same reason, lenders may wish to obtain an assignment of the borrower's rights in connection with any environmental consulting agreements or reports.

Intangible rights or claims of the kind discussed above constitute personal property and must be appropriately described in a security agreement or mortgage. The security interest also should be properly perfected in accordance with applicable law in order to gain lien priority.

Other clean collateral might also include other real estate owned by the borrower. Naturally, the lender should undertake an appropriate environmental assessment of any additional real estate offered as collateral.

Third Party Guaranties or Pledges. It may be possible for the lender to obtain a guaranty of the borrower's indebtedness from another person. If the guaranty is well drafted, the lender should have the option of exercising its remedies against the guarantor, in the event of the borrower's default, without first foreclosing on any collateral pledged by the borrower or otherwise pursuing remedies against the borrower. Such direct recourse against the guarantor might be particularly valuable if the borrower's property is contaminated. On the other hand, guarantors will not always agree to such a provision, preferring instead that the lender exhaust its remedies against the borrower before having recourse under the guaranty. This will be an important point for negotiation between the lender and the proposed guarantor.

A guarantor might, in addition, be asked to pledge personal property, or to grant a mortgage or deed of trust covering real estate owned by the guarantor, as security for the due and complete performance of the obligations under the guaranty. The lender should exercise due diligence regarding the environmental condition of such collateral. The same considerations apply regardless whether collateral is owned by the borrower or by a guarantor.

It is also possible for a lender to obtain a pledge or mortgage of assets from a third party as security for the borrower's indebtedness without obtaining a guaranty from the third party. Third parties who wish to facilitate financing for another are sometimes willing to risk loss of particular assets, but unwilling to assume personal liability on the debt. In such a case, the lender's only recourse, insofar as the third party is concerned, would be foreclosure of the security interest. This might be acceptable to a lender because the third party would normally have an incentive to make sure, if possible, that any default by the borrower is cured so that the property pledged by the third party will not be lost.

Letter of Credit. Another possible protection would be to have the borrower obtain the issuance of a letter of credit by another financial institution in favor of the lender. The terms of the letter of credit and the lender's ability to draw upon it would of course depend upon the situation and the negotiations of the parties. The issuing institution will need to be satisfied with the creditworthiness of the account party. The issuer may require collateral to secure the obligation of the account party to reimburse the issuer should the letter of credit be drawn upon. If the collateral includes real estate, the issuer will face the same environmental risks as any other lender. Thus, the issuer doubtless will require its own protections, including an appropriate environmental audit and other negotiated protections.

Additional protections for lenders are noted in Chapters 22 (Title Insurance) and 24 (Expert and Legal Opinions).

In sum, there are a number of approaches which can be considered by lenders in order to maximize the potential avenues of recourse in the event of a loan default by the borrower. If the lender has options, the best remedy, or an approach which minimizes environmental risks, can be chosen.

Enforcement of Remedies. Lenders face additional legal risks when it comes to enforcement of remedies, particularly in states like California with laws protecting debtors who have granted a mortgage or deed of trust encumbering real estate as security for a debt. If a lender makes a wrong move, a security interest or the balance of the debt itself can be extinguished under California's anti-deficiency law or one action rule. In 1991, California amended its debtor protection laws to give lenders more recourse against borrowers when property is environmentally impaired. But the amendments contain important qualifications.[1] This complex area of real estate law is beyond the scope of this book but is noted as a reminder that environmental risks must be kept in perspective along with the broader range of legal risks involved with any real estate financing transaction. Qualified legal counsel can assist the lender in understanding and weighing the various risks and selecting an appropriate enforcement strategy under the circumstances.

---

[1] See 1991 Stats., c. 1167 (AB 1735), adding § 2929.5 to the Cal. Civil Code, and amending § 564 of, and adding §§ 726.5 and 736 to, the Cal. Code of Civil Procedure.

CHAPTER TWENTY

DEAL STRUCTURE

How an acquisition is structured can affect the exposure of the acquiring party to successor environmental liability. Some commentators[1] have concluded that successor environmental liability can best be avoided by a cash-for-assets acquisition rather than a stock purchase, complemented by changes in the nature of the acquired business or its product lines. Such changes would be designed to interrupt the continuity of the business in order to avoid the impact of authorities imposing liability on a successor because it constitutes a mere continuation of the enterprise or product lines. Some environmental liabilities, of course, will be unaffected by deal structure, including RCRA and CERCLA liability arising automatically from ownership or operation of contaminated real property. However, other kinds of environmental claims, such as toxic tort or other common law claims and some statutory claims, can be affected by deal structure.

For additional discussion of this subject, see § 14.7 of Chapter 14.

However, the potential for successor environmental liability is only one of a number of matters which should be considered when determining the best structure for an acquisition. The risk of environmental liability may or may not be a controlling factor. For example, there may be tax or business reasons for structuring a transaction as a stock acquisition, and those reasons might be more palpable and compelling than contingent environmental risks. The relative weight to be given to environmental concerns will be a matter of judgment under the particular circumstances after consultation with corporate, tax, real estate and environmental counsel.

---

[1] *See, e.g.,* J. Russell/J. Richardson, *Avoiding Corporate Successor Environmental Liability*, 14 Chemical Waste Litigation Reporter 870 (Oct. 1987).

CHAPTER TWENTY-ONE

LIABILITY INSURANCE

21.1   Introduction

Parties to a real estate transaction should consider whether any insurance policies issued in the past may provide coverage for any existing environmental pollution of the property. The parties should also review the availability of new insurance coverage as a form of protection against future environmental liabilities or losses arising from hazardous substance contamination. In order to conduct some kinds of environmental-related activities, it is necessary to comply with financial responsibility laws which generally contemplate insurance as a means of compliance. Insurance coverage for environmental liabilities is very limited at this time, but the prospects for availability may improve in the future.

21.2   Comprehensive General Liability Insurance

Since 1970, most Comprehensive General Liability (CGL) insurance policies have contained a pollution exclusion which applies unless the "discharge, dispersal, release or escape is sudden and accidental." However, since January 1986, all CGL policies have absolutely excluded coverage for damage or loss resulting from environmental pollution. Whether coverage for such damage or loss was provided by pre-1986 CGL policies is the subject of numerous court cases with varying results. Coverage might be available under a pre-1986 CGL policy depending upon its provisions and the particular circumstances. Careful review of any such policy is warranted to determine whether it might provide coverage for any loss, damage, liability or cleanup cost arising from hazardous substance contamination. Even post-January 1986 policies should be reviewed in case an argument can be made that coverage exists for environmental-related damages of a kind which might not fall clearly within an exclusion. For example, coverage may exist for potential common law liability under doctrines such as negligence and nuisance which might be relevant to cases of environmental pollution (see Chapter 8). Thus, the existence of a pollution exclusion in a CGL policy should not be the end of the inquiry.

Coverage is more likely to exist if a policy is an "occurrence" rather than a "claims made" policy. An occurrence policy insures against any covered occurrence taking place during the policy period, even if claims arising out of the occurrence are made afterwards. In contrast, a claims made policy only insures against covered occurrences with respect to which a claim is made during the policy period. Thus, an occurrence policy issued many years ago may still provide coverage while a claims made policy would not.

Regardless of whether a CGL policy is an occurrence or a claims made policy, the incident or circumstances causing the damage or loss must be the kind of occurrence which is covered by the policy. It generally also is necessary for the occurrence to have taken place *during the policy period*. Environmental pollution frequently takes place over a lengthy period of time, and damages or injuries may result long after the hazardous substance release occurred. Thus, there has been much litigation over whether a covered event occurred during the period of an applicable policy. The courts have struggled to interpret policy language in such cases and have developed several different approaches.

Under the *exposure theory*, some courts have determined that the covered occurrence is the exposure of a pollutant to the environment, and that coverage therefore is triggered under an applicable CGL policy that is in effect when the release or exposure takes place. Other courts have applied the *injury-in-fact theory* which recognizes that injury or damage may or may not result immediately when the hazardous substance has been exposed to the environment. Those courts will determine when a person or property was in fact injured or damaged as a result of exposure to hazardous substances and coverage will be triggered under a CGL policy in effect at that time. Other courts apply the *manifestation theory* which looks farther down the time line, focusing on when the damage or injury was first discovered or manifested. This theory recognizes the long latency period which sometimes exists after exposure and initial injury before the damage is manifested by observable symptoms. Under that theory, coverage will be triggered under a CGL policy in effect when the manifestation occurs, even if the exposure and initial injury took place long before the inception of the policy period. Some courts have adopted the *continuous trigger theory* which finds coverage under all CGL policies with policy periods covering any portion of the time from the initial exposure until the manifestation of resulting injury or damage. Finally, in some jurisdictions, a different rule may be applied depending upon the nature of the claim. For example, California applies the manifestation theory for first-party progressive loss claims,[1] but the continuous trigger theory may apply to third-party pollution claims.[2]

Notwithstanding which trigger theory might be applied by the applicable court, some policies contain an exclusion regarding property damages to "property owned or occupied or rented to the insured," excluding first-party claims, so that coverage would not apply to governmentally mandated cleanup of hazardous substance contamination of the insured's own property.[3]

---

[1] *Prudential-LMI Commercial Insurance Co. v. Superior Court*, 51 Cal.3d 674, 274 Cal.Rptr. 387, 798 P.2d 1230 (1990).

[2] *Montrose Chemical Corp. v. Admiril Insurance Co.*, No. BO48757 (Cal.2d Dist.Ct.App. Feb. 27, 1992).

[3] *See*, e.g., *Western World Insurance Co. v. Dana*, 765 F.Supp. 1011 (E.D.Cal. 1991); *ACL Technologies Inc. v. Northbrook Property and Casualty Co.*, Cal. Orange County Superior Court, No. X-61-9576, ruling Aug. 6, 1991).

Thus, whether a particular CGL policy provides coverage will depend upon the facts, the nature of the claim, the exact policy language, and the theory which will be applied by the courts of the applicable jurisdiction in determining whether the covered occurrence took place during the policy period.

21.2.1　Insurance Archaeology

Some insurance experts provide a service called insurance archaeology. The object of that service is to locate old occurrence policies which might provide coverage for pollution or damage which occurred during the policy period under any of the coverage theories. It therefore may be well worth the effort of an investigation regarding the existence of insurance coverage. By some estimates, many millions of dollars of insurance coverage under old policies have been left unclaimed for lack of inquiry.

21.2.2　Insuring Clause: *Property Damage*

Assuming that a covered occurrence has taken place during a policy period, it must be determined whether the resulting damage is also covered by the policy. A typical CGL policy provides coverage for

> all sums which the insured shall become legally obligated
> to pay as damages because of injury to or loss, destruction
> or loss of use of property.

As one might expect, practically every word of this clause has been subjected to litigation because of the high stakes involved in environmental pollution cases.

One of the chief issues in such litigation is whether environmental damages and cleanup costs constitute covered "property damage." This issue is controversial and, as yet, unresolved. Some courts have ruled that cleanup costs are covered and other courts have reached the opposite conclusion.[4] For example, the federal Court of Appeals for

---

[4]　For a detailed examination of the divergent case precedents on this issue, *see* S. Mountainspring, *Insurance Coverage of CERCLA Response Costs: The Limits of "Damages" in Comprehensive General Liability Policies*, 16 Ecology Law Quarterly 755-801 (1989). *See also* O'Leary, *Current Trends in CGL Insurance Coverage for Environmental Claims: An*

the Eighth Circuit has held that the term "property damage" in a pre-1986 CGL policy does not include cleanup costs under CERCLA and RCRA.[5] On the other hand, the California Supreme Court has ruled recently that cleanup costs incurred to comply with government orders are covered damages, but that purely prophylactic costs incurred to prevent future release of hazardous substances are not incurred "because of property damage" and are not covered.[6] It has been reported that, at this point, a slight majority of the more than 44 courts which have ruled on the issue have held that hazardous waste cleanup costs are covered damages, and the battle on this issue between insurance companies and their insureds will continue in other courts.[7]

One might tentatively generalize from the divergent case authorities that pre-1986 CGL policies may cover actual loss or injury to property caused by hazardous substance releases, but not regulatory compliance costs in advance of releases. If this perception is borne out in future court decisions, then it would appear that CGL coverage may or may not apply depending upon what damages were caused by the hazardous waste, who was damaged and under what authority was responsive action required. Liability for damages suffered by a neighbor may be covered, but coverage might not apply if the government orders the removal of hazardous waste or other remedial action involving the insured's own property.

Introduction to Key Coverage Issues, Part I, Toxics Law Reporter, pp. 722 et seq. (10-31-90).

[5] *Continental Insurance Companies v. Northeastern Pharmaceutical & Chemical Co., Inc.*, 842 F.2d 977 (8th Cir. 1988), *cert. den., Missouri v. Continental Insurance Companies*, 109 S.Ct. 66, 102 L.Ed.2d 43 (1988).

[6] *AIU Insurance Co. v. Superior Court* (FMC Corporation, Real Party in Interest), 51 Cal.3d 807, 274 Cal.Rptr. 820, 799 P.2d 1253 (1990). The opinion did not indicate whether a cleanup order is a prerequisite to coverage. However, *Aerojet-General Corp. v. Superior Court*, 211 Cal.App.3d 216, 257 Cal.Rptr. 621 (1989), suggests that a cleanup order from the government is not essential.

[7] Gold and Arfmann, *The Insurance Industry and Superfund: Current Trends in Private Party and Government Cost Recovery Litigation*, Toxics Law Reporter, pp. 346 et seq. (8-14-91).

21.2.3   Insuring Clause: *Sudden and Accidental*

If hazardous substance cleanup costs are covered property damages, then the inquiry shifts to various policy exclusions. A chief line of defense for insurance companies has been the pollution exclusion contained in many pre-1986 CGL policies. However, those policies frequently contain a "sudden and accidental" exception to the pollution exclusion, or provide coverage for injury or damage "caused by accident." These terms have resulted in much hotly contested litigation over whether a release of hazardous substances was really sudden and accidental or was gradual and intended. So far, most courts to rule on these issues have determined that "sudden" is ambiguous and that a release of hazardous substances over a considerable period of time can be viewed as "sudden and accidental," and, hence, covered. But many courts have ruled that "sudden" is limited to events occurring in a very short amount of time, so that pollution occurring gradually or over a significant period of time is not covered.[8]

There is a similar potential for factual dispute over the general limitation of CGL coverage to occurrences which are "neither expected nor intended from the standpoint of the insured."[9] An example of such litigation involves the $1.8 billion insurance claim of Shell Oil Company for the cost of cleaning up pollution caused by a pesticide plant at the Rocky Mountain Arsenal in Denver, Colorado. The insurance companies argued that the pollution was well-known and deliberate and was not caused by a series of accidents or unexpected occurrences. That argument persuaded the superior court jury in California which found in favor of the insurers in 1989 after a 14-month long trial.[10] The same

---

[8]   *See*, e.g., the numerous cases cited in O'Leary, *Current Trends in CGL Coverage for Environmental Claims: An Introduction to Key Coverage Issues, Part II*, Toxics Law Reporter, pp. 748 et seq. (11-7-90); Jones, *Debate Rages Over Insurance Coverage*, The National Law Journal, p. 20 (2-24-92).

[9]   Indeed, many of the courts ruling that "sudden and accidental" is ambiguous (and, hence, to be construed against the insurer) believe that the term means "unexpected and unintended," removing the temporal aspect of the word "sudden" and expanding coverage.

[10]   *Shell Oil Company v. Accident and Casualty Insurance Co.*, San Mateo County Superior Court Case No. 278953.

line of argument recently resulted in another jury verdict for the defense in an insurance coverage dispute arising from the Aerojet-General multi-million dollar cleanup of a rocket manufacturing and testing plant.[11]

Thus, the manner in which the pollution occurred may be a critical factual matter to resolve in determining whether insurance coverage exists.

21.2.4   Assignment of Rights Under Insurance Policies

Whatever may be the merits of an insurance claim, the parties to a real estate transaction should consider including an assignment of rights under insurance policies as one of the assets to be transferred. This certainly would apply in a purchase and sale transaction where the buyer has assumed potential environmental risks arising from past events. Similarly, a lender should consider including the borrower's rights under insurance policies as one of the items of personal property to be assigned as security for the debt.

Under some policies, the term "insured" may be defined broadly to include transferees of the real estate, in which case an express assignment of rights would be unnecessary. Each policy therefore should be reviewed to determine whether an assignment is necessary, and, if so, permissible under the terms of the policy.

21.3   Environmental Impairment Liability Insurance

Environmental Impairment Liability (EIL) insurance is available to businesses such as hazardous waste treatment, storage and disposal facilities, hazardous waste transporters, hazardous waste cleanup or remedial action contractors, environmental consultants, chemical distributors, pollution equipment manufacturers and other companies with environmental exposure. EIL insurance normally covers cleanup costs which might not be covered by CGL policies. For example, in

---

[11]   *Aerojet-General Corp. v. Transport Indemnity Insurance Co.*, No. 262425 (Cal. San Mateo County Sup. Ct., verdict Jan. 13, 1992). For similar results where the disposal or release was intentional or known to the insured, and even part of deliberate waste dumping practices, *see Independent Petrochemical Corp. v. Aetna Casualty and Surety Co.*, No. 83-3347 (D.D.C. 12-6-91); *New York v. AMRO Realty Corp.*, 936 F.2d 1420 (2d Cir. 1991); *Broderick Investment Co. v. Hartford Accident & Indemnity Co.*, No. 90-1112 (10th Cir. 1-8-92).

Masonite Corp. v. Great American Surplus Lines Insurance Company,[12] the court reviewed a post-1980 EIL policy which excluded coverage for sudden and accidental events (the kind of event covered under the exception to the pollution clause in pre-1986 CGL policies as noted above). The court ruled, therefore, that the EIL policy covered environmental impairments only if the hazardous substance release was "gradual and fortuitous" (the kind of event excluded under CGL policies). Nevertheless, coverage applies only where the impairment is also "neither expected nor intended." Because the chemical discharges were intentional on the part of the insured, coverage was denied.

However, very few insurance companies are presently in the business of issuing EIL policies, and not all businesses desiring coverage will be approved for issuance of a policy. When available, EIL coverage is very expensive in relation to coverage limits. For example, typical policy limits might be $1,000,000/$2,000,000 with a deductible of $25,000 or more, for an annual premium of $10,000 to $25,000. Higher coverage limits (e.g., up to $5 million/$10 million) may be considered by a limited number of insurers. Such policies are usually issued on a claims made rather than an occurrence basis, and numerous exclusions apply.[13] Thus, as a practical matter, EIL insurance remains uneconomic and unavailable to most businesses who should have it.

The limited availability of EIL insurance has been the subject of great concern. For instance, in 1986 California's Governor George Deukmejian ordered the state Department of Insurance to hold investigative hearings to assess alternatives to EIL insurance. The Department considered possible alternatives including: (i) Captive

---

[12] 224 Cal.App.3d 912, 274 Cal.Rptr. 206 (1990).

[13] Most EIL policies exclude coverage for liabilities assumed under contract, unless the insured would be liable even in the absence of the contract. Thus, as parties to a real estate transaction negotiate the allocation of potential environmental liabilities (see Chapter 18), the party assuming liabilities may wish to consider whether that agreement would have the effect of triggering an exclusion to EIL or CGL insurance coverage upon which the party is placing reliance.

Insurance Companies, (ii) Risk Retention Groups,[14] (iii) State Assigned Risk Plan, (iv) State Reinsurance, (v) State Insurance Fund, and (vi) State Pooling Arrangements. The investigative hearings were held in October 1987. The Department of Insurance subsequently acknowledged that the lack of insurance coverage is a national and industry-wide problem, but nevertheless concluded that a private market for insurance exists and therefore did not propose anv legislation to solve the problem.

In recent years, there have been a number of conferences attended by insurance executives and other professionals for the specific purpose of considering the background, status and future prospects for EIL insurance coverage. The discussions and materials presented at those conferences have generally confirmed the limited availability of EIL coverage and have posited reasons for this situation including the following:

a. The difficulty of quantifying risk exposure;

b. The greater amount of losses than anticipated;

c. The increasing complexity of governmental regulations;

d. The frequent identification of new toxins under developing hazard criteria;

e. The perceived liberality of past court interpretations of policy coverage making it more difficult for insurers to delineate the scope of their insurance risk satisfactorily; and

f. Ultimately, the reluctance of insurance companies to provide insurance coverage under circumstances where the reliability of risk projections is doubtful and a reasonable chance to make a profit may not exist.

---

[14] The Federal Liability Risk Retention Act of 1981, 15 U.S.C. § 3901, authorizes the creation of risk retention groups and preempts certain state insurance laws in an attempt to facilitate the purchase of liability insurance.

Nevertheless, there is much pressure to find solutions to this problem and several companies are moving toward providing some kind of coverage or improving on current policy forms. The insurance industry anticipates that technologies for the management and control of hazardous materials will improve, so that exposure will be reduced and insurance coverage will become more feasible and affordable.

The California Attorney General filed a lawsuit in March 1988 against the leading insurance companies alleging the existence of a conspiracy in violation of the antitrust laws with respect to the unavailability of insurance for environmental pollution.[15] Ultimately, 19 states joined California in that federal court action, but the case was dismissed by the federal court in October 1989. Nevertheless, this case shows the serious concern which exists over the lack of EIL or CGL insurance for environmental pollution.

21.4   Financial Responsibility Standards

Federal laws and the laws of some states require certain businesses conducting environmental-related activities to comply with financial responsibility standards which generally contemplate insurance as a means of compliance. The limited availability of EIL coverage has a serious impact on the ability of regulated businesses to comply with such requirements. It therefore has been necessary to consider alternatives.

For example, the owners and operators of hazardous waste treatment, storage and disposal facilities (TSDF) must meet financial responsibility requirements imposed by federal law. In order to reduce the problem created by the constrained insurance market, on November 18, 1987, the EPA adopted a rule allowing use of a corporate guarantee as an additional financial responsibility mechanism. In addition, effective October 3, 1988, the EPA adopted other financial mechanisms, including letters of credit, surety bonds, trust funds, purchase of insurance by other firms on behalf of a TSDF, expanded provisions regarding corporate guarantees, and allowable combinations of such methods.[16]

---

[15]   *State of California v. Hartford Fire Insurance Company, et al.* (N.D. Cal. Case No. C 880981 WWS).

[16]   *See* 53 Federal Register 33938 (September 1, 1988).

Similarly, the EPA has expanded the allowable methods for satisfying the financial responsibility requirements applicable to owners and operators of USTs containing petroleum. For purposes of covering costs of corrective action and third-party liability, the EPA rules require all petroleum UST owners or operators with an average monthly throughput of more than 10,000 gallons to obtain financial assurance of at least $1 million per occurrence (or $500,000 per occurrence for an average monthly throughput of 10,000 gallons or less). All owners or operators must maintain an annual aggregate of $1 or $2 million depending on the number of USTs assured. These requirements may be satisfied by using any of the following mechanisms, alone or in combination, to cover the costs of taking corrective action and compensating third parties: insurance or risk retention group coverage, surety bond, guarantee, letter of credit, financial test of self-insurance, trust fund, a state required mechanism, or a state fund or other state assurance. The only combination of mechanisms not allowed is the financial test of self-insurance and a guarantee where the financial statements of the owner or operator and the guarantor are consolidated. The new rules were published on October 26, 1988, but were made retroactively effective as of January 24, 1988. However, *compliance* dates are scheduled in phases, anywhere from three to 24 months after the promulgation date depending upon the classification of the petroleum UST owner or operator.[17]

Financial responsibility standards such as those mentioned above will continue to supply pressure on the insurance industry to develop EIL and/or CGL policies which provide meaningful coverage at affordable rates. Naturally, the insurance industry will resist that pressure until exposures are reduced, risk projections can be made with greater accuracy and a profit can be made.

21.5 Environmental Review Insurance

The potential for environmental liability has become a serious impediment to the successful closing of real estate transactions. Potential buyers and lenders fear that hidden contamination lurks beneath the surface awaiting future discovery and loss. Environmental site assessments surely can help the parties identify potential problems,

---

[17]   *See* 53 Federal Register 43322 (October 26, 1988).

but no reasonable assessment can completely eliminate the risk. Not every square foot can be dug up and analyzed. Environmental indemnities from a party can help, but they too may provide limited protection.

Based on these considerations, some innovative people in the insurance business realized that there should be a market for insurance regarding the results of environmental site assessments, and it is now possible to obtain insurance coverage for the cost of cleanup of hidden contamination left undiscovered by an environmental site assessment.

To be insurable, an assessment must be conducted by an environmental consulting firm which has been approved by the insurer. In order to obtain approval, the consulting firm must utilize an assessment protocol acceptable to the insurer (and perhaps attend a training session covering the elements of the protocol). The assessment includes at least a Phase I Environmental Site Assessment, which involves an inspection of the site, review of various private and governmental records regarding the site, and review and consideration of other matters covered by the protocol.

After the assessment has been performed, the consultant renders a report to the parties and the insurance company. The insurer will, of course, exclude coverage for any hazardous substance contamination revealed by the report, but will insure against the existence of contamination which was not found by the assessment (like a title insurer excludes coverage for title defects identified by its title search and provides coverage for title defects which were missed by the search).

Naturally, environmental review insurance has conditions, policy limits and expires after an initial term unless extended. The premium cost varies depending upon the nature of the property and the range of risk factors identified by the consultant and the insurer. As a result, the insurance might not provide a significant degree of comfort in transactions which have a very large environmental risk potential (or where substantial contamination is found and excluded from coverage). But in appropriate situations, this kind of insurance can provide the insured parties with a measure of comfort against the fear of hidden contamination.

The ability of the parties to obtain environmental review insurance is an exciting development and is sure to add a new twist to negotiations regarding the allocation of environmental risk. To the extent that all or some portion of the risk can be insured against, this may provide a valuable supplement or alternative to contractual assurances by one of the parties. The insurance policy may be more comforting than an environmental covenant or indemnity by a party to the transaction. The availability of such insurance may indeed make it possible to complete some transactions which otherwise would have broken down over environmental considerations.

A pioneer of this innovative insurance product is First Environmental Review Insurance Company, Long Beach, California (underwritten by Lloyds of London). Another company offering such insurance is ERIC Underwriters Agency, Inc., Englewood, Colorado. There may be others entering this new market as well.

21.6 Environmental Remediation Insurance

Another new insurance product focuses on those situations which are excluded from environmental review insurance coverage because contamination is found. One program of this kind is merely an elaboration of environmental review insurance. If the consultant's report reveals hazardous substance contamination, the parties may elect to defer the closing of the transaction pending cleanup. Once the problem is cleaned up to the satisfaction of the insurer, the transaction is closed and the environmental review policy is issued without exception. This may be an acceptable approach where the contamination is relatively limited so that cleanup can be accomplished on a timely basis, before the deal falls apart due to delay.

A similar insurance program provides coverage for the results of environmental remediation. Where a qualified remediation contractor has completed the cleanup and "no further action" letters have been received from the applicable governmental agencies, the insurance policy provides coverage if previously undetected pollution is discovered and additional cleanup is required or if the pollution reoccurs from specified sources.

As with environmental review insurance, both the property owner and its lender can be insured by an environmental remediation policy.

437

Liability Insurance

This may encourage financing and development of properties which have been environmentally impaired but have been cleaned up. The availability of such insurance coverage (if adequate and affordable) may help overcome the residual stigma associated with formerly contaminated properties, so that they can be restored or redeveloped to productive use.

21.7 Effect on Real Estate Transactions

In sum, a purchaser or lender in a real estate transaction should include in the due diligence process a review of any insurance policies issued in the past which might be assigned by the seller or borrower or which otherwise might inure to the benefit of the transferee. The availability of new insurance coverages for the transferee's business, or for the results of site assessment or remediation, should also be considered as a means of protecting against financial loss. The existence of, or future prospects for, insurance coverage may be an important factor as the parties weigh the environmental risks of a particular transaction. It is anticipated that coverage will become more available and affordable in the future, but it may be a long time in coming.

CHAPTER TWENTY-TWO

TITLE INSURANCE

22.1   Introduction

Title insurance is a protection customarily obtained by parties to real estate transactions. Each party acquiring an interest in real estate, whether as a purchaser, lessee or lender, should consider requiring the issuance of an acceptable policy of title insurance as a condition of the transaction. In general, title insurance will give the insured party recourse under the insurance policy in the event that a person undisclosed in the policy has paramount title or senior lien rights resulting in loss or damage to the insured.

22.2   Exclusion of Environmental Protection Liens

In recent years, title insurance companies, like other parties to real estate transactions, have become concerned about environmental risks, and they have reviewed and updated their policy forms as a result.

22.2.1   1970 ALTA Title Insurance Policy Forms

Before 1987, the last major revision of title insurance policy forms took place in 1970. Hazardous waste issues were not in the forefront of thought at that time; many years would pass before the enactment of CERCLA with its lien provision, and several more years would pass before a number of states adopted superlien laws (see Chapter 2). In hindsight, representatives of the title insurance industry generally take the position that the 1970 policy forms do not provide coverage for environmental protection or cleanup cost recovery liens. This position can be disputed.

The 1970 American Land Title Association (ALTA) policy form provides coverage against any loss or damage sustained by the insured by reason of, among other things, any "defect in or lien or encumbrance on [the insured's] title," subject to the policy exclusions and those title exceptions disclosed in the policy. Thus, a cost recovery lien under federal or state environmental law which is not disclosed and excepted from coverage would appear to be covered unless such a lien falls under an express exclusion in the printed portion of the policy. The 1970 policy forms contain an exclusion for "governmental rights of police power *unless* notice of the exercise of such rights appears in the public records at Date of Policy" (emphasis added). Cleanup action by a governmental unit may well constitute exercise of the police power and a resulting lien may be excluded unless it appears in the public records on the policy date.

The term "public records" is defined in the 1970 forms as "those records which by law impart constructive notice of matters relating to said land." This definition apparently includes any law, federal, state or local, as long as it establishes that the records involved impart constructive notice regarding the land. In one case, for example, it was held that a public land order regarding a road right-of-way filed with the office of the Federal Register imparted constructive notice under federal (although not state) law and was therefore a public record within the meaning of the 1970 ALTA form; hence, the title policy provided coverage against loss or damage arising from that record.[1] This is significant from an environmental law perspective because federal response cost liens under CERCLA might be filed under federal law either with the clerk of the United States district court for the district in which the land is located or with the local office established under state

---

[1]   *Hahn v. Alaska Title Guaranty Co.*, 557 P.2d 143 (Alaska 1976).

law for the recordation of real estate documents.[2] It can therefore be concluded that both sets of records would be public records under the 1970 ALTA policy forms, and coverage would apply if a CERCLA lien was filed in either place when the policy was issued but was not expressly disclosed and excepted.

The title insurance industry would, of course, object to that conclusion. Countless 1970-form ALTA policies have been issued over the years without searches of records in the federal courthouse or in any government office other than the local office where real estate documents are normally recorded. If the definition of "public records" is as broad as suggested, this may well represent a substantial source of exposure for title insurance companies. The title insurance industry was evidently concerned about this in both environmental and nonenvironmental contexts, as demonstrated by the policy form revisions made in 1987.

22.2.2   1987 ALTA Title Insurance Policy Forms

The 1987 ALTA title policy forms explicitly exclude coverage for laws or regulations relating to

> environmental protection, or the effect of any violation of these laws, ordinances or governmental regulations, *except* to the extent that a notice of the enforcement thereof or a notice of a defect, lien or encumbrance resulting from a violation or alleged violation affecting the land has been recorded in the public records at Date of Policy [emphasis added].

The definition of "public records" has been revised to include, more narrowly,

> records established under state statutes at Date of Policy for the purpose of imparting constructive notice of matters relating to real property to purchasers for value and

---

2   See Chapter 2 for a detailed discussion of the proper place for the filing of CERCLA liens. As noted in that chapter, in some states the proper place for filing of CERCLA liens is in the local office established under state law for the recordation of real estate documents, and in other states the United States district court is the proper place for CERCLA liens to be filed.

without knowledge. [However, with respect to the exclusion noted above,] "public records" shall also include environmental protection liens filed in the records of the clerk of the United States district court for the district in which the land is located.

Representatives of the title insurance industry like to point out that expanded coverage, which did not exist under the 1970 ALTA forms, is provided by virtue of the exception from the exclusion for environmental protection laws and the explicit reference to environmental protection liens filed at the federal courthouse as constituting public records. Such public relations talk can be disputed for reasons discussed in the previous section. Moreover, it is significant to note that the exception which provides coverage for environmental protection liens may itself be limited to particular situations involving notices of enforcement action or liens "resulting from a violation or alleged violation" of environmental protection laws. Any other situation would fall within the general exclusion from coverage.

One of the lessons of Part I of this book is that cleanup cost recovery liens can arise out of circumstances which involved no violation of law at all. Hazardous waste disposal was not heavily regulated until RCRA was enacted in 1976 and stringent state waste disposal laws proliferated thereafter. Thus, the 1987 ALTA policy forms do not clearly cover all environmental protection liens which might be filed or recorded against a parcel of real estate, and room may exist for title insurance companies to deny coverage under some circumstances. It therefore can be argued that the 1987 forms provide more limited coverage for environmental protection liens than the 1970 forms. In any case, the 1987 forms restrict coverage to some extent. Otherwise, the title insurance industry would not have used exclusionary language in the first place.

22.3 Protective Endorsements

The title insurance industry has apparently anticipated that some parties will want more complete coverage on the subject of environmental liens than is provided by the standard 1987 ALTA form language. Lenders who make residential mortgage loans may obtain

ALTA Endorsement Forms 8 or 8.1 (California Land Title Association Forms 110.8 or 110.9) which insure, among other things,

> against loss or damage sustained by reason of lack of priority of the lien of the insured mortgage over . . . any environmental protection lien which, at Date of Policy, is recorded in those records established under state statutes at Date of Policy for the purpose of imparting constructive notice of matters relating to real property to purchasers for value and without knowledge, or filed in the records of the clerk of the United States district court for the district in which the land is located, except as set forth in Schedule B . . .[3]

This endorsement contains none of the limiting language that is set forth in the main policy form, confirming the observations discussed in section 22.2. Naturally, before a title company would issue an endorsement of this kind, it would search both the real estate records established under state law and the records at the appropriate United States district court and would exclude coverage for any CERCLA or other environmental protection lien which is revealed by the search. Such a search and endorsement would be desirable particularly in any state where the proper place for filing of CERCLA liens may be unclear (see Chapter 2).

Even though the standard endorsement forms apply only to lenders in residential loan transactions, it might be possible to negotiate with a title insurance company and obtain a special endorsement along the same lines for a purchaser in a residential transaction or for a lender, purchaser or lessee in a nonresidential transaction. Parties to real estate transactions should consider obtaining protective title insurance endorsements when available.

22.4 Use of Old Policy Forms

Another way to avoid an exclusion for environmental protection liens would be to use an old policy form which may provide broader

---

[3]   See § 22.5 regarding an additional aspect of the coverage provided by this form of endorsement.

443

coverage. Title insurance companies may issue an old policy form, if requested.

Real estate counsel frequently prefer the old forms for reasons aside from environmental concerns. The old forms have been subjected to years of scrutiny and court interpretations, and the scope of coverage has become fairly well established in most areas. One can safely assume that the 1987 revisions to the policy forms generally were not intended by the title insurance industry to expand the scope of coverage and to increase the exposure of the insurers. To the contrary, many of the revisions evidently were intended to clarify and narrow the scope of coverage in view of court rulings adverse to the title insurers. The narrowed definition of the term public records, as noted above, is but one example of the kinds of revisions made by the title insurance industry. The new forms, therefore, might provide less coverage in some respects than the old forms. Moreover, the revised forms may set the stage for litigation to obtain court interpretations of the new language or for renewed litigation over matters already resolved under the old forms.

Thus, parties to real estate transactions should give careful consideration to the desired coverage for environmental and other title matters and should determine whether a new form of policy, perhaps with one or more endorsements, would be sufficient or whether the issuance of an old form of policy should be requested.

22.5   The Problem of Superliens

Chapter 2 notes that several states have adopted laws which accord superpriority status to hazardous substance cleanup cost recovery liens, effective as of a date before the actual filing or recordation of the lien (see § 2.3 and Table 2-2). Such laws create the obvious prospect for liability on the part of a title insurance company under a policy issued before the filing of a superlien but after the retroactive effective date of the superlien. This potential for liability is avoided by the title insurance industry under the new policy forms which expressly exclude coverage for environmental protection liens unless they are *at Date of Policy* recorded in the appropriate public records (see § 22.2). Thus, a superlien which is not yet recorded when the policy is issued would be excluded.

444

At least two cases have considered the liability of insurers, with respect to superliens, under policies issued before the 1987 revisions. In *Chicago Title Insurance Company v. Kumar*,[4] Anil Kumar bought a 14-acre industrial site which was contaminated, but that condition was unknown at the time of the transaction. Kumar obtained a standard title insurance policy from Chicago Title without any endorsements extending coverage to claims relating to hazardous material. After the discovery of the contamination, Chicago Title and Kumar sought a court ruling whether Chicago Title was liable under the policy. Kumar contended that coverage existed because the contamination, which was present at the property when the policy was issued, constituted a defect in title. Kumar also argued that title was unmarketable by virtue of the power of the Commonwealth of Massachusetts to impose a lien under the Massachusetts Oil and Hazardous Material Release and Response Act. The court drew a distinction between the physical condition of the property and the status of record title and ruled in favor of Chicago Title:

> The mere possibility that the Commonwealth may attach a future lien ... as a result of the release of hazardous material (existing but unknown at the time a title insurance policy is issued) when the Commonwealth has neither expended moneys on the property requiring reimbursement nor recorded the necessary statement of claim, is insufficient to create a "defect in or lien or encumbrance on ... title." ... In the absence of further circumstances, we perceive a difference between the condition of the title to land and the physical state of the land. Protection as to the former is what the plaintiff's title insurance policy furnished when it provided coverage against defects in, or liens or encumbrances on, title. In this respect, the policy focused on liens actually in existence at the time it was written, not liens which might arise in the future. To hold otherwise on these facts would compel title insurance companies, when more specific coverage has not been requested, to perform a

---

[4]   506 N.E.2d 154, 24 Mass.App. 53 (1987).

physical inspection or survey of the land for buried hazardous material. [footnote omitted]

We also reject the defendant's arguments that the possibility . . . that a future lien might attach to the property, and the potential liability for the cleanup of hazardous material, renders the title unmarketable. Again, the defendant confuses economic lack of marketability, which relates to physical conditions affecting the use of the property, with title marketability, which relates to defects affecting legally recognized rights and incidents of ownership. "One can hold perfect title to land that is valueless; one can have marketable title to land while the land itself is unmarketable." [citation omitted] The presence of hazardous material may affect the market value of the defendant's land, but, on the present record, it does not affect the title to the land.[5]

While the *Kumar* case did not involve a superlien which had already been recorded, the language of the court's opinion would support the same conclusion even if the superlien has become an actuality rather than a mere possibility. As long as the lien does not exist of record when the policy is issued, coverage will not apply in the absence of a special endorsement. Thus, risk of loss in connection with a future cleanup cost recovery lien would normally rest on the property owner rather than the title insurance company.

In *South Shore Bank v. Stewart Title Guaranty Company*,[6] South Shore Bank sought a declaration that Stewart Title was liable for the expense of removal, cleanup and monitoring of hazardous waste on property covered by a lender's policy of title insurance. Unlike the *Kumar* case, the title policy in *South Shore* expressly contemplated the state superlien law and contained an endorsement which provided in part as follows:

The Company insures against loss or damage sustained by the insured by reason of a lien which attaches to the

---

5   *Id.*, 506 N.E.2d at 156-157.

6   688 F.Supp. 803 (D. Mass. 1988), *affirmed* 867 F.2d 607 (1st Cir. 1988).

insured premises pursuant to section 22a-452a of the Connecticut General statutes as a result of conditions existing on or at the insured premises as of the date of the policy if such lien claims priority over the lien of the insured mortgage.

In *South Shore*, the loan was made and the policy was issued *after* the effective date established by Connecticut law for superliens. Thus, a superlien would have priority over the insured mortgage. The borrower defaulted on the loan and a subsequent environmental assessment revealed the presence of hazardous waste. The bank, apparently believing that it had coverage under the endorsement, notified Stewart Title of the discovery and that a claim would probably be made under the title policy following foreclosure. The bank in fact became the purchaser at the foreclosure sale, and the action for declaratory relief was later commenced by the bank.

Stewart Title filed a successful motion for summary judgment in that case. The court noted that a lien under the code section cited in the endorsement would arise only when environmental costs had been incurred and appropriate lien filing procedures had been followed by the state. The bank had failed to allege the existence of a commissioner's lien, and, in fact, the state had not yet expended any funds. The court therefore determined that the statutory lien did not apply. The court also ruled, as a matter of law, that "the possibility that the commissioner may file a lien does not trigger insurance coverage under the endorsement."[7] Such a possibility is not a title defect covered by the insurance policy.

It is not clear from the opinion of the *South Shore* court whether the result would have been the same if a commissioner's lien had in fact been filed before the summary judgment motion was decided. The lien would have had superpriority under the Connecticut law, and, assuming that the hazardous waste condition existed at the date of the policy, the endorsement might have provided insurance against it. The language of the endorsement does not appear to be limited to commissioner's liens actually in existence but undisclosed in the policy at the time of its issuance. Indeed, the endorsement appears to refer to any

---

[7]   *Id.*, at 805.

commissioner's lien claiming priority over the lien of the insured mortgage where the hazardous waste condition existed at the date of policy. In that regard, the bank had argued that the policy of the law for prompt response to hazardous waste conditions would be frustrated if the property owner must wait for a lien to be filed by the commissioner. However, the court concluded that the purpose of the reference to the statute in the endorsement was "not to ensure immediate response to environmental pollution but rather to protect the insured from a challenge to its title by reason of a commissioner's lien that has priority over South Shore's legal rights in the Property."[8] Under the facts, no commissioner's lien or title defect yet existed.

The *Kumar* and *South Shore* cases have comforted title insurance companies on the issue of their potential liability for hazardous waste cleanup costs in superlien states. *Kumar* demonstrates that standard coverage says nothing about the physical condition of a property and only provides coverage with respect to the status of record title when the policy is issued. Even when a special endorsement provides coverage for losses resulting from a superlien which attaches due to physical conditions existing at the date of the policy, *South Shore* establishes that coverage will not exist until such a superlien actually has been filed and loss or damage has been sustained as a result. An insured party who must expend funds to clean up a property, perhaps under compulsion of a governmental order, will have no recourse under such an endorsement unless and until the state itself expends funds and files a superlien. Even if the state files its lien, the coverage probably would be limited to the amount of the lien, not including any additional cleanup costs incurred by the insured.

In *Lick Mill Creek Apartments v. Chicago Title Insurance Co.,*[9] the plaintiff obtained an ALTA policy and later incurred hazardous waste cleanup costs. The plaintiff sued under the title insurance policy, contending that coverage should extend beyond defects in title to the condition of the property itself by virtue of the fact that a physical inspection and survey is performed in connection with an ALTA form of

---

8 *Id.,* at 805-806.

9 231 Cal. App. 3d 1654, 283 Cal. Rptr. 231 (1991). This case did not involve a superlien. California does not have a superlien law at this time.

policy. The court had no difficulty rejecting that contention and ruling that the policy did not provide coverage for hazardous substance contamination. Even though a site inspection is done for such policies, the purpose and scope of that inspection is only to identify exceptions to title. The condition of the property for any other purpose is not the subject of such an inspection. The court cited the *Kumar* and *South Shore* cases with approval.

These cases show that parties who receive title insurance coverage should not expect to be able to shift the cost of environmental cleanup to the title insurance company unless very specific coverage is provided to that effect, in either regular lien or superlien states. After all, title insurers are in the business of insuring *title* at the time of a transaction, not the physical condition of the property. Title insurers normally become involved with physical conditions only when extended coverage is requested with respect to such matters as possible encroachments affecting *title* as shown by a survey. It is indeed surprising that the endorsement considered in the *South Shore* case was even issued by Stewart Title; that endorsement appears to provide coverage for future superliens, at least once they are filed, which goes beyond the traditional role of title insurance. Thus, any party to a real estate transaction who wishes cleanup cost coverage under a title insurance policy will have to negotiate a special endorsement to that effect. The likelihood of obtaining such an endorsement would not appear to be very great.

On the other hand, ALTA Endorsement Forms 8 and 8.1 provide coverage for

> . . . any environmental protection lien provided for by any state statute in effect at Date of Policy, except environmental protection liens provided for by the following state status: [list of any applicable state laws.]

A title insurance company issuing this endorsement would research and list any state environmental protection lien laws, especially those authorizing superliens which might gain priority over the insured mortgage. The liability of the title insurance company would be limited to any such law which is in effect when the policy is issued but is not listed. The insured would obtain no coverage regarding statutes disclosed in the endorsement or those which are enacted after the issuance of the policy. At least the title insurance company would be providing a useful assurance that all existing applicable state environmental protection lien laws have been brought to the attention of the insured party. It would be wise for that party to obtain a proforma copy of the endorsement in advance of the closing so that the information can be weighed along with the other environmental risks of the transaction. As suggested in § 22.3, parties other than lenders may wish to seek special endorsements along similar lines.

22.6 Mechanics' Liens and the Discovery of Contamination During Construction

Construction lenders face a special risk in that the construction project itself may uncover previously unknown hazardous waste. Thus, construction loan documents might include a provision allowing the lender to stop further funding if the borrower does not clean up the property in a timely manner. However, if the construction lender exercises its rights under such a clause, an interesting problem might arise regarding the lien priority of the construction deed of trust in relation to the mechanics' liens of contractors on the project.

The lien priority of mechanics' liens under state law normally relates back to the commencement of the project. Construction lenders therefore typically require that the construction deed of trust be recorded *before* the project is commenced, ensuring that it will have priority over any mechanics' liens. The construction loan documents might include appropriate representations and warranties from the borrower to the effect that the project has not yet been commenced. But in some cases the deed of trust is recorded after construction has begun. Construction lenders customarily obtain mechanics' lien coverage from a title insurance company in order to insure against loss of lien priority if that is the case.

Assume that a project commenced before the construction deed of trust was recorded, that the construction lender has obtained mechanics' lien coverage and that the construction loan agreement contains a provision entitling the lender to cease further funding if hazardous waste is discovered. If the construction lender exercises that right and stops funding, the lender would surely risk loss of lien priority of its construction deed of trust to the mechanics' liens. In addition, the lender may risk loss of the mechanics' lien coverage under the title insurance policy. The reason is that additional disbursements could be made by the construction lender to pay the sums due to the contractors, up to the full amount of committed loan funds, and, thus, the existence of the mechanics' liens is within the control of the lender. Title insurance coverage in such a case would be precluded under the standard exclusion for defects, liens or encumbrances "created, suffered, assumed or agreed to" by the insured lender.[10]

Accordingly, in any case where construction has commenced before the recordation of the construction deed of trust, the lender should carefully consider how to exercise its remedies in the event of the discovery of hazardous waste and the failure of the borrower to clean up the condition. The lender might consider advancing more committed loan funds to pay the contractors and remove the mechanics' liens, and then stop further funding. Whether it is wise to cease funding and have an incompleted project will be another business decision for the lender to make.

---

[10] The loss of mechanics' lien coverage when a lender ceases funding on a loan which is not fully advanced is established by a line of cases including: *American Savings & Loan Association v. Lawyers Title Insurance Corporation*, 793 F.2d 780 (6th Cir. 1986); *Brown v. St. Paul Title Insurance Company*, 634 F.2d 1103 (8th Cir. 1980); *Bankers Trust Company v. Transamerica Title Insurance Company*, 594 F.2d 231 (10th Cir. 1979).

CHAPTER TWENTY-THREE

BANKRUPTCY

Dean G. Rallis, Jr. Esq.
Janet S. Hoffman, Esq.
BAKER & HOSTETLER, McCUTCHEN BLACK

23.1 Introduction

23.2 Automatic Stay

23.3 Priority of Claims for Cleanup Costs

23.4 Discharge of Claims

23.5 Abandonment of Property

23.6 Indemnity and Contribution Claims of Other PRPs

23.7 Conclusion

23.1   Introduction

The parties to any real estate transaction should be aware of the potential impact of the federal bankruptcy laws on state and federal environmental laws. Just as the Bankruptcy Code is designed to provide a "fresh start," the environmental laws are intended to provide fresh air, water and soil. However, the policies of these statutes often conflict in various cases. This chapter will not discuss the substance of the bankruptcy laws in any detail, but will point out the most important interactions between the bankruptcy laws and the environmental laws. In essence, bankruptcy is both a risk of, and a means of protection against, environmental laws. Environmental liabilities may be great enough to force a party into bankruptcy where some relief may be available.

Bankruptcy has been used in the past, and will undoubtedly continue to be used in the future, as a method to avoid environmental liabilities in whole or in part. Even when the impetus for the filing of a voluntary petition in bankruptcy is not the desire to escape liability for environmental problems, a party's bankruptcy may affect its liabilities under the environmental laws. The bankruptcy of a party to a real estate transaction may result in the shifting of costs for the cleanup of contaminated property to the parties not protected by the bankruptcy laws. Bankruptcy also may result in a reduction in the assets of the bankrupt party's estate to the detriment of unsecured and secured creditors when some or all of the assets are used to pay the cleanup costs that are determined by the bankruptcy court as administrative expenses of the bankruptcy estate. The bankruptcy of a lessor or lessee of contaminated property, a borrower whose loan is secured by contaminated property, a party which has given an environmental indemnity with respect to a contaminated site, a fellow PRP with respect to a site, or a seller of contaminated property, will create potential problems for the other parties to the transaction.

This chapter highlights several ways in which bankruptcy can affect a real estate transaction. The following summaries are not intended to be comprehensive, and counsel should be consulted in each case regarding the effect of the bankruptcy of a party to a real estate transaction.

23.2 Automatic Stay

One of the fundamental protections which the bankruptcy laws afford a debtor is the protection of the automatic stay,[1] the purpose of which is to give the debtor some time to get its affairs in order without having to deal with creditor actions and to provide for an orderly administration of the debtor's estate. Once a petition for bankruptcy has been filed (e.g., either Chapter 7 or Chapter 11),[2] the automatic stay precludes various creditor actions. For example, a creditor may not commence or continue a lawsuit against the debtor based upon prepetition activities or claims, nor enforce against the debtor, property of the debtor, or property of the estate, a judgment obtained prior to the commencement of the bankruptcy case.[3] The automatic stay continues until the case is dismissed or closed, a discharge is granted or denied, or

---

[1]   11 U.S.C. § 362(a).

[2]   11 U.S.C. §§ 301, 302, or 303.

[3]   *Id.*, § 362(a)(1) and (2).

when property is no longer "property of the estate."[4] The automatic stay may terminate earlier upon request of a party in interest and the bankruptcy court granting such request.[5]

However, there are instances when the automatic stay does not apply.[6] For example, the automatic stay does not apply to the commencement or continuation of an action or proceeding by a governmental unit to enforce its police or regulatory power,[7] nor does it apply to the enforcement of judgments other than money judgments obtained by governmental units in such actions.[8] Thus, while a private party who seeks contribution from the debtor for environmental cleanup costs must file a claim with the bankruptcy court, a governmental unit such as the EPA may maintain a separate action to enforce the environmental laws. However, any money judgment resulting from such a suit cannot be enforced outside the confines of the bankruptcy case without prior bankruptcy court approval.[9]

The courts have determined under the governmental unit exception to the automatic stay provisions that the following actions were not subject to the automatic stay: a CERCLA action brought by the federal government to recover the costs incurred in cleaning up two hazardous waste sites (once the amount of the debtor's liability was determined in that action, however, the government would have to file a claim with the bankruptcy court for the amount of the money judgment)[10]. a state action to compel compliance by the debtor with a consent order requiring corrective actions where the purpose of the suit was to prevent

---

[4] 11 U.S.C. § 362(c).

[5] 11 U.S.C. § 362(d), (e) or (f).

[6] 11 U.S.C. § 362(b).

[7] 11 U.S.C. § 362(b)(4).

[8] *Id.*, § 362(b)(5).

[9] *Id.* Generally speaking, however, any such monetary claim will be treated in the bankruptcy case.

[10] *U.S. v. Nicolet, Inc.*, 857 F.2d 202 (3rd Cir. 1988); *In re Commerce Oil Co.*, 847 F.2d 291 (6th Cir. 1988); *City of New York v. Exxon Corp.*, 932 F.2d 1020 (2nd Cir. 1991).

future harm[11]; an action to determine civil fines and penalties for violation of state water pollution laws[12]; an EPA action to compel compliance by the debtor with RCRA and state environmental laws regarding permits.[13]

Any party to a transaction which has obtained but not yet enforced a judgment against the debtor may file a claim with the bankruptcy court. That claim, if it is unsecured, is not likely to be paid in full.[14] Generally, it will also not be paid until the liquidation or reorganization of the debtor has been completed.

The following example illustrates a situation in which the bankruptcy of a lessee will affect the lessor. Suppose that a lessor has leased property to the debtor whose business operations resulted in contamination of the property. The lessor as owner of the property has been required to remove the hazardous waste from the property at considerable expense. The owner has gone to court and obtained a judgment against the lessee/debtor for its fair share of the cleanup costs. If the lessee subsequently files for bankruptcy, that judgment, if uncollected at the time of the filing of the petition in bankruptcy, is stayed from enforcement. The lessor will be left with an unsecured claim against the debtor or its bankruptcy estate. The assets in that estate, furthermore, may be reduced if the debtor while in bankruptcy must also defend governmental or third party actions in connection with its contamination of that or other property; the administrative expenses incurred will reduce the assets available for distribution to creditors.

The assets of the estate available for general unsecured creditors also would be reduced if the automatic stay does not apply to injunctions obtained by governmental agencies which require the expenditure of

---

11 *Penn Terra Ltd. v. Dept. of Environmental Resources*, 733 F.2d 267 (3rd Cir. 1984).

12 *In re Commerce Oil Co.*, 847 F.2d 291 (6th Cir. 1988).

13 *In re Commonwealth Oil Refining Co., Inc.*, 805 F.2d 1175 (5th Cir. 1986), *cert. den.*, 483 U.S. 1005 (1987).

14 *See* Chapter 2 for a discussion of Superfund and other liens which protect certain governmental lienholders in bankruptcy proceedings because they are secured creditors rather than general unsecured creditors.

funds. The argument has been made that to require the expenditure of funds by the debtor's estate in order to comply with governmental orders is no different than requiring the debtor to pay any money judgments obtained by a governmental agency. The courts which have faced this issue have reached different conclusions. One court determined that the expenditure of funds needed to comply with the injunction would prevent future harm, rather than provide monetary compensation from past harm, and that the injunction therefore was not subject to the automatic stay.[15] Another court has expressed the view that the expenditure of funds required by an injunction constitutes a money judgment subject to the automatic stay.[16]

Thus, the automatic stay may provide a respite from environmental claims, but that respite might not apply to certain governmental actions. Future cases may clarify further the extent of the protection provided by the automatic stay in environmental cases.

23.3 Priority of Claims for Cleanup Costs

As noted previously, it is unlikely that all of the unsecured creditors (and in some cases, even secured creditors and administrative claimants) will receive full payment through a bankruptcy case. Thus, the order or priority in which claims are paid from the available assets is very important. For example, secured claims have priority over the claims of the general unsecured creditors relative to the secured creditor's collateral. Other claims, called administrative claims, also have priority over general unsecured claims. In some instances, the court may determine that certain administrative claims have, in effect, higher priority over secured claims relative to the secured creditor's collateral.[17] Administrative expenses are the "actual, necessary costs and expenses of preserving the estate" incurred after the filing of the bankruptcy petition.[18] The Bankruptcy Code provides that administrative expenses are payable from the assets of the estate prior to

---

[15]   *Penn Terra Ltd. v. Dept. of Environmental Resources*, 733 F.2d 267 (3rd Cir. 1984).

[16]   *Illinois v. Electrical Utilities*, 41 Bankr. 874 (N.D. Ill. 1984).

[17]   11 U.S.C. § 506(c).

[18]   11 U.S.C. § 503(b)(1)(A).

the payment of the claims of general unsecured creditors.[19] To the extent that cleanup costs can be considered administrative expenses, the entity seeking payment for such costs will benefit. The courts have not agreed thus far on whether cleanup costs can be characterized as administrative expenses, nor has the United States Supreme Court resolved the issue.[20]

Those courts which have considered the issue and have treated cleanup costs as administrative expenses have done so for the following kinds of costs: cleanup costs incurred on account of pollution resulting from activities of the debtor during the pendency of the bankruptcy case[21]; CERCLA response costs to clean up hazardous wastes on the debtor's property[22]; costs incurred to address CERCLA liability[23]; costs incurred by a state agency in removing hazardous waste[24]; post-petition cleanup costs incurred by the EPA[25]; costs to remove the immediate threat to public health caused by buried pesticides[26]; costs necessary to render the property marketable.[27] The rationale behind these decisions is typically the requirement that state laws be complied with in the management and operation of the property of the estate.[28]

---

[19]   *Id.*, §§ 503(b)(1)(A) and 507.

[20]   The Supreme Court did not have the question before it in *Midlantic National Bank v. New Jersey Dept. of Environmental Protection*, 474 U.S. 494 (1986), *reh. denied*, 475 U.S. 1091 (1986). New York State, which had expended funds on the cleanup of a parcel of property owned by the debtor during the course of the bankruptcy proceedings, sought in the lower court proceeding to have its claim for reimbursement of those monies treated as an administrative expense.

[21]   *In re Chateaugay Corp.*, 944 F.2d 997 (2nd Cir. 1991).

[22]   *In re Wall Tube and Metal Products Co.*, 831 F.2d 118 (6th Cir. 1987).

[23]   *In re T.P. Long Chemical, Inc.*, 45 Bankr. 278 (Bankr. N.D. Ohio 1985).

[24]   *In re Stevens*, 68 Bankr. 774 (D. Me. 1987).

[25]   *In re Peerless Plating Co.*, 70 Bankr. 943 (Bankr. W.D. Mich. 1987).

[26]   *In re FCX, Inc.*, 96 Bankr. 49 (Bankr. E.D.N.C. 1989), *cert. den.*, 109 S.Ct. 1118 (1989).

[27]   *In re Mowbray Engineering Co., Inc.*, 67 Bankr. 34 (Bankr. M.D. Ala. 1986).

[28]   28 U.S.C. § 959(b).

Cases in which cleanup costs have not been treated as administrative expenses include the following: a claim for reimbursement from the lessee's estate of cleanup costs incurred by a lessor of property[29]; a claim for cleanup costs based on an indemnity contract[30]; costs to repair pre-petition environmental damage.[31] The courts in these cases have based their decisions on the view that the claims were based on pre-petition activity of the debtor and that in these instances the cleanup costs would not benefit the estate (for instance where the value of the property after cleanup would be lower than the amount of debt it secures). Furthermore, at least one court, while recognizing that cleanup costs were administrative expenses with priority over general unsecured creditors, refused to grant the cleanup costs priority over secured creditors.[32]

The *Dant & Russell*[33] case illustrates the treatment which may be accorded cleanup costs when the debtor is a lessee of the contaminated property rather than its owner. In this case, the lessor incurred cleanup costs and sought administrative priority of its claim in the lessee's bankruptcy case. In declining to adopt the lessor's position, the court emphasized its view that administrative costs are to be incurred to preserve the estate for the benefit of the unsecured creditors. The cleanup costs incurred by the lessor were much greater than the assets of the lessee's estate available for distribution to unsecured creditors. Thus, treating the lessor's claim as an administrative expense would have benefitted the lessor rather than the unsecured creditors and would have eliminated any recovery by the unsecured creditors. The court also found that the administrative expenses incurred by a lessor could not exceed the fair and reasonable rental value of the property. Finally, the court focused on the fact that the majority of the contamination occurred prepetition, and therefore the cleanup costs should also be viewed as prepetition costs not entitled to be treated as administrative

---

[29] *In re Dant & Russell, Inc.*, 853 F.2d 700 (9th Cir. 1988).

[30] *In re Southern Railway Co.*, 758 F.2d 137 (3rd Cir. 1985).

[31] *In re Pierce Coal and Construction, Inc.*, 65 Bankr. 521 (Bankr. N.D.W.Va. 1986).

[32] *In re T.P. Long Chemical, Inc.*, 45 Bankr. 278 (Bankr. N.D. Ohio 1985).

[33] *In re Dant & Russell, Inc.*, 853 F.2d 700 (9th Cir. 1988).

expenses. (The court reached its conclusions notwithstanding the indemnification provisions of the lease.)

In sum, environmental cleanup costs may or may not have priority in a bankruptcy proceeding depending upon the circumstances and the applicable case authorities.

23.4 Discharge of Claims

As noted above, monetary claims against the debtor are generally discharged to the extent that they are not satisfied through the bankruptcy proceeding.

One issue which arises in both Chapter 7 and Chapter 11 cases is whether injunctions are dischargeable debts or claims. The Bankruptcy Code permits the discharge of prepetition claims, releasing the debtor from any future obligations with respect to those claims. In determining whether an injunction is dischargeable, the courts have focused on whether the injunction has essentially become a monetary obligation. In the leading United States Supreme Court case, it was held that an individual debtor's cleanup obligations under an injunction could be discharged because the debtor was no longer in possession of the contaminated property, which had been taken over by the state, and no longer had control of his other assets, which were in the hands of a receiver.[34] Under the circumstances, the debtor's cleanup obligation under the injunction had been converted into a monetary obligation to the state which if not discharged would have to be satisfied from the debtor's postpetition earnings. The Supreme Court also noted that any subsequent owner of the property would continue to be subject to the state environmental laws which led to the injunction. The Supreme Court expressly did not hold that an injunction against bringing further hazardous substances onto the property or against disposal of hazardous substances into the state's waters were dischargeable.

In a more recent case, the Second Circuit decided that the issue of dischargeability of an injunction is determined on whether such injunction is a "claim." If the injunction does no more than impose an obligation as an alternative to a payment right, such is a claim and accordingly discharged. On the other hand, if the injunction requires a

---

[34]   *Ohio v. Kovacs*, 469 U.S. 274 (1985).

debtor "to take any action that ends or ameliorates current pollution, such [injunction] is not a claim."[35]

Other claims which have been held to be dischargeable include the following: an order requiring restoration of marshland which required the debtor to spend money was a monetary obligation dischargeable under Chapter 7[36]; an injunction requiring reclamation of an abandoned coal mine was dischargeable to the extent that it required the expenditure of funds.[37]

The dischargeability of claims is also somewhat difficult to define. Several recent court decisions do not provide clear guidance on this issue. One court suggests a very broad definition of "claim" to include obligations that arise under CERCLA that relate to prepetition releases or threatened releases by the debtor which, accordingly, are susceptible to being discharged.[38] This court went further to suggest that a claim is no limited by what the EPA or anyone else knew or could have known about the debtor's prepetition conduct at the time of the bankruptcy.[39] Another court applied an "injury standard," i.e., that for a claim to be discharged, the claimant must have suffered identifiable, compensable injuries prepetition (or pre-confirmation in a Chapter 11 case).[40] Finally, a lower court ruled that prepetition obligations for response costs are "claims" only to the extent they were "fairly contemplated by the parties" at the time of the bankruptcy filing.[41]

23.5 Abandonment of Property

The Bankruptcy Code permits a bankruptcy trustee to "abandon any property of the estate that is burdensome to the estate or that is of

---

35   *In re Chateaugay Corp.*, 944 F.2d 997 (2nd Cir. 1991).

36   *In re Robinson*, 46 Bankr. 136 (Bankr. M.D. Fla. 1985), *rev'd on procedural grounds*, 55 Bankr. 355 (1985).

37   *United States v. Whizco, Inc.*, 841 F.2d 147 (6th Cir. 1988).

38   *In re Chateaugay Corp.*, 944 F.2d 997 (2nd Cir. 1991); *see also In re Jensen*, 127 Bankr. 27 (Bankr. 9th Cir. 1991).

39   *Id.*, 944 F.2d at 1005.

40   *In the Matter of Penn Central Transportation Co.*, 944 F.2d 164 (3rd Cir. 1991), *cert. den.*, 112 S.Ct. 1262.

41   *In re National Gypsum*, 134 Bankr. 188 (N.D.Tx. 1991).

inconsequential value and benefit to the estate."[42]   Bankruptcy trustees have attempted to use this provision of the Bankruptcy Code to abandon contaminated real property.   However, the United States Supreme Court has placed limits on the ability of a trustee to abandon contaminated property.[43]   The Supreme Court held that "a trustee may not abandon property in contravention of a state statute or regulation that is reasonably designed to protect the public health or safety from identified hazards."[44]   In that case, the trustee had attempted to abandon a site contaminated by PCBs.   The mortgages encumbering the property exceeded its value.   In addition, the trustee abandoned waste oil stored at a separate site.

The *Midlantic* decision has been followed by a bankruptcy court holding that the site of a former pesticide plant could be abandoned only after buried pesticides had been removed at the expense of the estate, based on the court's determination that the buried pesticides presented an imminent danger to the health of area residents.[45]   The court rejected the argument of the EPA that the release of a CERCLA hazardous substance was sufficient to meet the imminent and substantial endangerment standard of *Midlantic* prohibiting abandonment until the violation had been corrected, finding instead that it was the responsibility of the bankruptcy court to make that determination.   The court also required only that action be taken to remove the immediate threat of harm, even though it recognized the possibility of additional harm which would not become apparent until some time in the future.

Another bankruptcy court formulated a list of the factors which should be considered in determining whether to permit the abandonment of a contaminated site.[46]   The court considered the following factors: the imminence of danger to the public health and safety, the extent of probable harm, the amount and type of hazardous

---

[42]   11 U.S.C. §554(a).

[43]   *Midlantic National Bank v. New Jersey Dept. of Environmental Protection*, 474 U.S. 494 (1986), *reh. denied* 475 U.S. 1091, 106 S.Ct. 1482 (1986).

[44]   *Id.*, 106 S.Ct. at 762 (1986).

[45]   *In re FCX, Inc.*, 96 Bankr. 49 (Bankr. E.D.N.C. 1989), *cert. den.*, 109 S.Ct. 1118 (1989).

[46]   *In re Franklin Signal Corporation*, 65 Bankr. 268 (Bankr. D.Minn. 1986).

waste, the cost of bringing the property into compliance with environmental laws, and the amount and type of funds available for cleanup. That court interpreted the *Midlantic* decision as requiring only minimal steps before abandonment would be authorized, such as conducting an environmental assessment of the site, ceasing further toxic discharges, and fencing off the site to prevent public entry.

In other cases abandonment has been permitted when the court found no immediate threat to the public health and safety.[47] If the bankruptcy court permits contaminated property to be abandoned because there is no immediate threat to the public health and safety, even though there is the potential of a future threat, the cleanup costs for the property will be the responsibility of the person to which the property has been abandoned.

23.6 Indemnity and Contribution Claims of Other PRPs

If a PRP in a CERCLA action files a petition in bankruptcy, the remaining PRPs in that action typically file indemnity and contribution claims against the debtor. Those claims may be disallowed by the bankruptcy court if they are found to be contingent,[48] which is the case when the liability of each PRP has yet to be fixed. One bankruptcy court found that the indemnity and contribution claims of codefendants in a hazardous waste site suit were contingent and would be allowed only when they had been made certain by completion of the CERCLA action and payment by the other PRPs to the government.[49]

23.7 Conclusion

As this chapter makes clear, a filing in bankruptcy by any party to a real estate transaction can significantly complicate both the cleanup of contaminated property and the allocation of the costs associated with the

---

[47]   *In re Oklahoma Refining Co.*, 63 Bankr. 562 (Bankr. W.D. Okla. 1986); *In re Smith-Douglass, Inc.*, 75 Bankr. 994 (E.D. N.C. 1987), *aff'd*, 856 F.2d 12 (4th Cir. 1988); *State of New Jersey Dept. of Environmental Protection v. North American Products Acquisition Corp.*, 1992 WL 29222 (D.C.N.J. 1992).

[48]   11 U.S.C. §502(e)(1)(B).

[49]   *In re Charter Co.*, 862 F.2d 1500 (11th Cir. 1989). *See also In re Hemingway Transport Inc.*, 105 Bankr. 171 (Bankr.D.Mass. 1989); *In re Dant & Russell, Inc.*, 951 F.2d 246 (9th Cir. 1991).

cleanup, perhaps frustrating a negotiated contractual allocation of environmental liability. It is important that each party to a real estate transaction focus on the financial stability of the other parties and take all possible steps to protect its position in the event of the bankruptcy of any other party.

CHAPTER TWENTY-FOUR

EXPERT AND LEGAL OPINIONS

24.1   Expert Opinions

24.2   Legal Opinions

Opinions of experts and legal counsel can provide protection for parties to real estate transactions. The most important element of that protection is the knowledge such experts can supply. It is essential to have knowledge of the environmental risks involved with a transaction, both factual and legal, in order to avoid, minimize or allocate them. Secondarily, recourse might be available against an expert, or the expert's errors and omissions insurance carrier, in the event of professional negligence causing loss or damage to a party relying upon the expert's advice.

24.1   Expert Opinions

Parties to a real estate transaction can seek the expert assistance of environmental consultants for a number of important purposes. For example, consultants can be used to assess the environmental condition of real estate, as discussed in Chapter 16. Consultants can also be used, perhaps in conjunction with legal counsel, to determine whether the past business operations on a property have been conducted in compliance with environmental laws and regulations. Similarly, environmental consultants can review plans for future business operations to assess the risk of hazardous substance releases and to design appropriate precautions. Information supplied by environmental consultants can be critical to the accurate appraisal and valuation of real estate which is contaminated or borders on other contaminated property (see Chapter 15).

However, the parties to a real estate transaction should not expect to receive a *guaranty* from the consultant, for instance, that the property is free of hazardous substance contamination. Such a guaranty is not feasible short of an extremely intrusive and costly assessment. The chance of locating hazardous waste has been likened to the chance of biting into a chocolate chip in a cookie. One may or may not hit a chocolate chip. Similarly, while a consultant can exercise judgment as to where to drill holes and take soil samples, a large measure of luck will determine whether any hazardous waste is found even if it is present under the surface of the property. The degree of luck involved will diminish as more bites or samples are taken. One would expect ultimately to consume an entire cookie and to enjoy all of the chocolate chips. But it is not likely that a consultant will be asked or allowed to dig up an entire parcel of real estate in order to find hidden hazardous waste or to prove its nonexistence with absolute certainty. There will be an economic limitation on the extent of the sampling and some measure of luck will always remain as a practical matter. The consultant's opinion or report therefore will be qualified by the nature of the property and the nature and scope of the investigation for which the party was willing to pay.

Many consultants attempt to include exculpatory language in their consulting agreements limiting or excluding liability for their professional negligence. Some consultants go even further and seek indemnification from the client with respect to any potential liability arising from the consultant's activities. Such provisions would diminish the effectiveness of the protection sought by hiring the consultant in the first place, and most consultants will agree to delete such language from their consulting agreements if pressed.

24.2   Legal Opinions

Attorneys are occasionally asked to render legal opinions regarding environmental matters, usually in connection with real property transfers, business acquisitions or lending transactions.

Compliance with Environmental Laws and Permit Requirements. Buyers and lenders sometimes desire the comfort of a legal opinion to the effect that the seller's or borrower's business has been conducted in compliance with all environmental laws and regulations, that all required environmental permits have been obtained and are in full force and effect, and that such permits are either transferrable or can be replaced. A similar opinion may be sought regarding nonenvironmental permits applicable to a business. In order to give such an opinion, counsel must conduct a wide ranging review of all laws, regulations and permitting requirements applicable to the business and must determine the status of compliance. This will involve various avenues of inquiry, including pure legal research as well as interviews with (i) persons representing the business involved, (ii) other experts or consultants, and (iii) representatives of governmental agencies having jurisdiction over the property or the business.

Such efforts are expensive and fraught with peril that some obscure regulation might be overlooked. Moreover, even if the business is being conducted in compliance with all laws now in effect regarding such matters as the disposal of hazardous wastes, that is no assurance that there will be no environmental liability in the future under strict liability principles, perhaps as a result of accidental releases or the accumulation of lawful releases. Thus, law firms requested to give compliance opinions should carefully consider their experience and ability to do so, and should qualify their opinions as appropriate. As noted, the main reason for having a law firm undertake such a review is to obtain the knowledge which will be revealed, even if there is a chance of something being missed.

Enforceability. The parties to a real estate transaction also may be comforted by legal opinions to the effect that all the covenants and indemnification clauses which they won after hard fought negotiations on environmental and other matters will be enforceable. Such legal opinions are most often required of the borrower's counsel by lenders in major transactions. As noted in § 18.7 (Environmental Indemnities), the question of enforceability is complex under the laws of some states, particularly when contractual obligations are to be secured by interests in real estate and perhaps unsecured as well. The enforceability of the provisions may depend upon the steps which are taken by the benefitted party. In other words, a provision which may be enforceable in the abstract may become unenforceable by virtue of a mistaken or improvident pursuit of remedies. As a result, enforceability opinions are usually qualified in a number of ways, and legal opinions should be given only with great care by law firms after appropriate, and possibly expensive, legal research. Thus, not every transaction will warrant a legal opinion, and not all law firms should be accepted as qualified to render a desired opinion.

Expert and Legal Opinions

Attorneys are just as loathe as environmental consultants to give guaranties. Qualifications and limitations typically are included in legal opinions by competent law firms. Sometimes the qualifications are so broad that it is difficult to discern whether any opinion has been given at all. But a party requesting an enforceability opinion should expect the attorneys giving the opinion to protect themselves in a reasonable way. Indeed, it has been said that the main value of an enforceability opinion is not the recourse which might exist against the attorneys in the future, but the effect the opinion has in establishing the good faith intent of the party who is represented by the attorneys to be bound by the agreement. If that party really does not intend to be bound as a result of a substantive legal principle or even a technicality, the attorneys, in order to protect themselves, would have to reveal that principle or technicality as a qualification in the opinion. This should come to the attention of the parties before the closing of the transaction, as it is good practice for the legal opinion to be circulated in draft form for review beforehand. The knowledge set forth in the draft opinion can be a great source of protection for the party requesting the opinion, as the risk associated with an unacceptable qualification can be avoided either by opting out of the transaction or by clarifying and eliminating the problem and proceeding with the transaction with an acceptable form of legal opinion.

Environmental Due Diligence. As noted in Chapter 16, legal counsel may be asked to advise whether sufficient environmental due diligence has been conducted in order to satisfy the requirements of the innocent landowner defense.

CONCLUSION

The rapid development of environmental laws and consciousness in the last decade has created a whole new layer of complexity for the parties to real estate transactions. Transfer-triggered and other disclosure obligations have become more detailed and significant. Land use restrictions for environmental purposes may affect the value of real estate and the prospects for development. The risk of successor liability and even personal liability of innocent parties for environmental cleanup costs has increased dramatically. Potential environmental liability, which can exceed the value of a property or the balance of a loan has become a frequent and critical issue for negotiations and can be a deal breaker. Many properties are becoming unmarketable or less valuable as environmental problems or fears come to light. Lenders are becoming more cautious when considering real estate as security or how best to exercise remedies in the event of default. Involvement of environmental counsel and consultants is becoming an increasing necessity in many transactions.

It is prudent for the parties to real estate transactions to consider the impact of environmental risks and to consider possible protections such as environmental assessments and audits, deal structure, negotiated conditions and allocation of potential liability, expert opinions, and the existence or availability of insurance coverage. Bankruptcy implications and protections may also be important.

Despite the range of risks, it should be possible to negotiate and accomplish most real estate transactions if the parties and counsel are creative enough. Finally, some entrepreneurs are developing novel approaches in an effort to turn the environmental losses of others into profit opportunities.

This book will have served its purpose if the reader has gained an appreciation for the broad range of concerns and how environmental risks might be handled in real estate transactions as a practical matter. Sensitivity to these concerns is important, and the assistance of experts should be obtained when needed.

APPENDIX A

FannieMae

Multifamily

Conventional Selling
Environmental Hazards
Management Procedures

Section 501

Chapter 5. Environmental Hazards Management Procedures

There is increasing concern nationwide that properties involved in real estate transactions might contain unknown environmental problems that could present major liabilities to the purchaser and its lenders. As a consequence, we require that lenders take responsible actions to manage the risk of loss from environmental damage and liability. This chapter outlines those requirements.

The lender's primary responsibilities are 1) an environmental assessment of the property, which must be completed before we will issue an Offer to Commit (or a Commitment), and 2) ongoing confirmation after purchase that the borrower is maintaining the property in an environmentally sound manner.

We expect lenders to perform these functions diligently. Lenders are expected to educate themselves in the areas of environmental regulation and management and to have available qualified experts in order to make sound and appropriate judgments. They must take responsibility also for assessing a borrower's ability to maintain the property and impressing upon them of the need to protect the property asset from environmental liability and value loss.

We do not approve environmental consultants. Therefore, lenders must not give any consideration to a consultant's representation that he or she is approved or qualified by us. Lenders are responsible for the selection of environmental consultants and will be solely accountable for their performance. Lenders must take appropriate steps to ensure that a consultant is qualified to perform the required work.

**Section 501
The Environmental
Assessment**

We require an environmental assessment of all properties submitted for a Commitment.

In order to use resources effectively the assessments are to be conducted in two phases. The Phase I assessment is principally a screening exercise, which focuses on (1) a review of available documents, (2) interviews with people aware of site operations, and (3) an inspection of the site. In cases where Phase I is inconclusive, a Phase II assessment is required. Phase II assessments generally involve a more detailed review of the site, including specialized physical sampling. An environmental consultant qualified to perform the work must do the Phase II assessment on the lender's behalf.

A property must be acceptable under either the Phase I or Phase II assessment for each of the specific hazards listed. If it is not acceptable as measured by any one of the hazard assessments, the property is ineligible and can not be the subject of a Commitment.

473

Multifamily

The Phase I and II assessments represent our current standards. However, lenders must use diligence when evaluating the property and should make appropriate inspections to learn its true condition. Lenders should disclose their knowledge of actual or suspected environmental problems. Properties with obvious environmental impairments should not be the subject of a Commitment.

The lender must submit a completed Phase I assessment as part of the loan application package, and is encouraged to submit any required Phase II assessment as part of the loan application package. However, the lender may wait until later in the application review process before submitting any required Phase II assessment.

Upon review of the completed Phase I and/or Phase II assessments we may, at our discretion, impose additional assessments and/or environmental actions as a requirement for, or condition of, the Commitment.

**Section 501.01
Phase I Assessment**

The purpose of the Phase I screening assessment is to quickly determine whether information currently exists to clearly evaluate a property's environmental status. The assessment involves a review of records, interviews with people knowledgeable about the property, and an inspection of the property, the building, its fenceline and adjoining properties.

The lender must complete the Phase I assessment, see Exhibit I, including the Phase I information checklist. While it is not expected that a lender use every information source when performing the assessment, enough information should be gathered to document each assessment decision.

If clear documentation exists that a property is environmentally sound in regards to a particular hazard, then no Phase II assessment is required for that hazard. If there are obvious problems or if the status of the property is uncertain, then either the property fails the test or a Phase II assessment for that hazard is required.

The lender must submit a completed Phase I assessment as part of the loan application package.

**Section 501.02
Phase II Assessment**

Phase II assessments are required for each of those hazards for which the property was not acceptable under the Phase I assessment. The lender may submit a Phase II assessment as part of the loan application package. Alternatively, the lender may wait for the preliminary results of our review of the application before performing a Phase II assessment. However, we will not consider issuing an Offer to Commit (or a Commitment) until after we have received and reviewed any required Phase II assessment.

474

The Phase II assessment will involve a more detailed physical site inspection and review of historical records. The purpose of Phase II is typically to determine the presence or absence of an uncertain liability (e.g., asbestos, or leaking underground storage tanks) or to quantify the extent of an observed or suspected liability (e.g., soils or ground water contamination). Because of the specialized nature of the investigations under Phase II, these assessments must be conducted by a consultant qualified to perform the work.

Examples of the kind of work to be performed in a Phase II assessment would include:

(1) Bulk asbestos sampling and analysis, and, if required, development of abatement and maintenance programs.

(2) Underground storage tank leak testing.

(3) Soil sampling and analysis.

(4) Groundwater sampling and analysis.

(5) Testing of suspected PCB contaminated soil and/or facilities.

(6) Investigation of status of Superfund or RCRA enforcement actions related to neighboring properties.

Lenders should complete and submit the Phase II assessment, see Exhibit 2, with consultant's report attached. No specific protocol is mandatory for the Phase II assessment consultant report. However, it should include a full description of the sampling procedures, the laboratory results and recommendations. The consultant must certify in the report that the assessment was performed diligently and in accordance with all regulatory and good management standards, and that, to the best of its knowledge, the results are complete and accurate. The report must be signed by an officer of the consulting firm that performed the work.

It is essential that all regulatory standards and good management practices be followed at all times and especially where physical sampling and laboratory analysis is involved.

**Section 501.03
Consultant's
Qualifications**

Lenders must use care in choosing firms to perform environmental functions. The lender should confirm, for example, that firm personnel have adequate and appropriate education and training to carry out consulting duties. Membership in relevant professional associations is also encouraged.

Beyond training and education, we believe consultants should be able to demonstrate successful prior experience in their areas of expertise. Lenders are therefore required to have available in the property file copies of 3 (three) letters of reference and endorsement

475

attesting to the consultant's prior work. The letters should clearly
state the scope of the work performed for the previous clients and
the nature of the business purpose the work was intended to support. At least one of the references should be from a real estate firm
that used the consultant to support a residential property transaction. Documentation of previous experience with the current
lender may be substituted for one of the reference letters.

It is of utmost importance that the documented experience be relevant to the current duties both in terms of functions (e.g., physical
sampling, operating and maintenance monitoring, underground tank
testing) and media (e.g., air, water and specific chemicals). For example, previous experience removing asbestos does not qualify a
firm to perform groundwater tests. Lenders must demonstrate that
the consultant has successfully completed work of a substantially
similar nature to that currently being performed on the subject
property.

We reserve the right at any time to refuse to accept any future en-
environmental assessment, report, warranty or certification from individual consultants, consulting firms or branch offices of consulting
firms. We will notify a lender that a particular consultant is no
longer acceptable to us. In addition, lenders may not use people or
firms to perform assessments that are excluded from participation in
EPA-assisted programs. The list of such people and firms is maintained by the regional offices of the EPA and is published from time
to time in the Federal Register.

The consultant shall not be affiliated with the buyer or seller of the
property, nor by a firm engaged in a business that might present a
conflict of interest.

Section 501.04
Unacceptable
Environmental
Conditions

The existence of one or more of the following situations or similar
conditions make the property ineligible for the Prior Approval product line:

(1) Structure built over a sanitary landfill or other solid, hazardous
or municipal waste disposal site.

(2) Presence of friable asbestos containing materials; or substantial
amounts of non-friable asbestos containing material that can
not be safely incapsulated and/or removed or will not be
routinely inspected and maintained by the borrower.

(3) Presence of high-risk neighbors with evidence of spills or soil or
groundwater contamination on or around their properties.

476

FannieMae

Conventional Selling
Environmental Hazards
Management Procedures

Multifamily

Section 501.04

(4) Documented soils or groundwater contamination on the subject property and/or a documented tank leak greater than 0.05 gal/hr (National Fire Protection Association standard) and any of the following three situations:

- Physical constraints posed by the site-specific geology, geohydrology or subsurface structure that render corrective actions technically impossible;

- Constraints that render treatment processes or disposal options prohibitively expensive, i.e., beyond the financial capabilities of the current owner; or

- Potentially responsible parties unwilling or financially incapable of instituting corrective actions on neighboring properties.

(5) Soil sampling values above the following limits:

PARAMETER	CONCENTRATION (ppm)
Metals	
Chromium	100
Zinc	350
Lead	100
Copper	170
Arsenic	20
Cadmium	3
Selenium	20
Nickel	100

PARAMETER	CONCENTRATION (ppm)
Organics	
Total Volatile Organics	1
Total Hydrocarbons	100
Total Petroleum Hydrocarbons	100

477

Multifamily

(6) Groundwater sampling values above the following limits:

PARAMETER	CONCENTRATION (ppm)
Arsenic	.05
Boron	1
Cadmium	.01
Chromium	.05
Lead	.05
Mercury	.002
Selenium	.01
Silver	.05
Total organics (volatiles and base neutrals)	.1
Total petroleum hydrocarbons	1

(7) PCB contamination where:

- Physical constraints posed by the site-specific geology, geohydrology or subsurface structure that render corrective actions technically impossible.

- Constraints that render treatment processes or disposal options prohibitively expensive (i.e., beyond the financial capabilities of the current owner).

(8) High radon levels (i.e., above 4 pCi/l) that can only be corrected through large capital improvements and/or extensive ongoing maintenance programs that are beyond the financial or technical capability of the borrower.

(9) Conditions which represent material violations of applicable local, state or federal environmental or public health statutes and laws.

(10) Properties that are currently the subject of environmental or public health litigation or administrative action from private parties or public officials.

Section 501.05
Remedial Actions

Properties that fail to meet a particular standard may in some cases be corrected through remedial actions and retested. This should only be done with the advice and written endorsement of a qualified consultant. In general, remedial actions should be completed and their effectiveness confirmed by the lender before we issue an Offer to Commit (or a Commitment). All actions must be taken in accordance with all regulatory and good management standards.

In addition, we may require additional remedial actions.

478

FannieMae

Conventional Selling
Environmental Hazards
Management Procedures

Multifamily

Section 501.06

We will consider issuing an Offer to Commit (or a Commitment) prior to the completion of remedial work only when the following conditions are met:

1) A qualified environmental consultant must state in writing that a) the work can be completed within 90 days after loan delivery (or a period not to exceed the time allowed for any repair or moderate rehabilitation work connected with the loan), and b) the work will make the property eligible under the environmental standards;

2) Prior to loan delivery, the borrower must have a signed contract with a qualified firm to perform remediation services within the time frame mentioned above in sub-paragraph 1. The lender must secure a performance escrow (included in any repair, completion or rehabilitation escrow) from the borrower for 150% of the gross contract amount;

3) When the work is finished, a qualified consultant must state in writing that the job has been satisfactorily completed and that the property meets the environmental eligibility standards.

**Section 501.06
Ongoing
Operations and
Maintenance**

Some properties may have conditions that are currently acceptable but must be confirmed through the life of the loan with ongoing operations and maintenance (O&M) actions. It is the lender's responsibility to recognize when regulatory standards and/or good management practices require O&M programs to maintain the environmental integrity of the property. It is also the lender's responsibility to assess the borrower's ability to carry out any such program. The loan is not eligible for the Prior Approval product line if the borrower and/or its agent is clearly not financially or organizationally capable of performing necessary O&M functions.

A written O&M plan must be developed by the borrower no later than the completion of remedial work. A qualified consultant, retained either by the borrower or the lender, must endorse the plan in writing, stating that the provisions, if carried out with diligence, are sufficient to maintain the property in accordance with applicable regulatory standards and sound business practice. The consultant must also confirm in writing that the borrower has the organizational and financial capacity to carry out the actions as prescribed.

In addition we may require additional O&M provisions.

479

Multifamily

**Section 501.07
Environmental
Superlien States**

We face increased risks from properties located in states with environmental superlien laws that may be applied to multifamily residential properties eligible for the Prior Approval product line. These laws give environmental authorities the ability to place a first priority lien on subject properties. This lien takes precedence over our mortgage and clearly threatens the value of our security collateral.

Currently several states have superlien statutes and other states are considering such legislation. It is the lender's responsibility to know whether the property state has an applicable law, or will have one as of the anticipated Commitment date.

In order to guard against the risks that these laws present, we require that a qualified environmental consultant confirm in writing that, to the best of its knowledge, the Phase I assessment was performed with diligence and is complete and accurate. This is in addition to any endorsements and certifications required for any Phase II assessment, remedial action plans or O&M plans.

**Section 502
nder Responsibilities
After Loan
Commitment**

The loan administration functions involved in servicing multifamily mortgages and the accounting policies and procedures are discussed in Parts III and IV, respectively. In addition to those servicing and accounting responsibilties, the lender must take the additional steps discussed in this section to manage the risk of loss from environmental damage and liability.

**Section 502.01
Provisions for
Operations and
Maintenance
Activities**

The lender must make sure that the borrower has available all required resources and personnel to effectively carry out on-going operations and maintenance activities identified during the environmental assessments and application review.

**Section 502.02
Property
Photographs**

At or just prior to purchase of the loan by us (or no later than the completion of any remedial work) the lender must take a series of photographs to visually document the condition of the property. The photographs should be taken both inside the building and around the grounds (including adjacent sites). The photos should be clearly dated and labeled with a site description of the view presented. The photos become part of the loan file.

**Section 502.03
Ongoing Compliance
with Environmental
Standards**

The lender must confirm in writing from time to time that, after we purchase the loan, the borrower is maintaining the property according to any applicable O&M programs, environmental law or regulation. It is not expected that the lender perform a formal Phase I or

480

FannieMae

Multifamily

Conventional Selling
Environmental Hazards
Management Procedures

Section 502.04

II assessment. However, the lender must make an on-site inspection and inquiry in preparing the certification. The scope of the certification should include both the buildings and grounds and cover the activities of the borrower, tenants, sub-lessors, their agents and any other third parties. These confirmations must specifically address the ongoing effectiveness and adequacy of all current remedial and maintenance actions.

For performing loans, this confirmation should normally be included as part of the annual physical inspection and report on the property. In addition, an inspection and confirmation must be made immediately following the occurrence of events which might reasonably be expected to impact the environmental condition of the property or the efficacy of prescribed remedial or maintenance actions. Such events would include fire, flood, building construction or rehabilitation, spills or leaks of hazardous wastes or materials, unusual or intense use of property facilities or significant changes in custodial or management personnel.

If the lender is unable to affirmatively confirm the property's environmental status, it must prepare a report which describes the property's current condition and the actions required to return it to, and maintain it in, its condition at the time we purchased the loan. The lender must submit this report to us. Further, upon notice by us, the lender must request of the borrower that he take all prescribed actions.

The lender must promptly confirm the environmental status of the property as soon as possible after implementation of any remedial actions.

**Section 502.04
Reporting Environmental
Incidents and
Correcting Violations**

The lender must notify us of any known or suspected environmental incidents that violate any environmental laws, regulations or statutes.

At our direction, the lender must require that the borrower report all known violations of applicable environmental statutes to the appropriate local, state or federal authority in full compliance with all provisions of the law.

In addition, at our direction, the lender must require that the borrower take all necessary actions to ensure that all violations are promptly corrected and that the property is bought back to and maintained in full compliance with appropriate environmental statutes and good management practices.

481

Section 502.05
Non-Performing
Loans

A full description of the actions to be taken during the period of default is included in Part III of this guide.

The lender must prepare an environmental evaluation of the property for the asset audit. The evaluation should be in the form of a written declaration that the property has been maintained according to sound environmental practice and any prescribed O&M plans, and is therefore still acceptable according to the standards of the assessment that was performed prior to our purchase of the loan.

If the lender cannot affirmatively declare that the property is still in the original acceptable condition, it must state the nature of the new conditions, their cause and an estimate of the actions and resources required to bring the property back to its original acceptable condition.

We may require a Phase I, and, if appropriate, Phase II assessment for properties in default. The emphasis of such assessments should be to quantify the scope and degree of any hazards present and to estimate the cost of bringing the property into compliance with applicable regulations and sound business practice.

Lenders should take all reasonable actions to protect the environmental integrity of the property during borrower delinquency or default. The lender should determine whether the borrower or property manager has adequate knowledge and resources to perform required remedial and maintenance activities. The lender must continue to confirm ongoing compliance with environmental requirements through the entire period of delinquency. If the lender cannot gain access to the property, it must inquire of state and local health and environmental authorities on at least an annual basis regarding compliance of the subject property with applicable environmental laws and regulations.

Section 502.06
Liquidation

Upon final loan payment (either as scheduled or as a prepayment in full), the lender should take a series of photographs to visually document the condition of the property. The photographs should be taken both inside the building and around the grounds (including adjacent sites) and should, to the degree possible, replicate the pictures taken at loan purchase (see section 502.02 above). The photos should be clearly dated and labeled with a site description of the view presented. The photos become part of the loan file.

482

Multifamily

Exhibit 1 Phase I Environmental Assessment

– PROPERTY LOG –

Fannie Mae Loan # _____

Property Address _____

_____

_____

Borrower Address _____

_____

_____

Borrower Phone _____

Lender Company Name _____

Individual Lender
Environmental Underwriter _____

Individual Environmental
Consultant _____

Firm Name and Address _____

_____

Consultant Phone _____

Date Assessment Completed _____

Assessment Results _____

483

Exhibit 1 Phase I Environmental Assessment (Cont....)

– SUMMARY OF RESULTS AND RECOMMENDATION –

1. Phase I Assessment Results (check applicable result for each hazard)

Hazard	Acceptable	Acceptable Requires O & M	Fail	Possible Remedy	Phase II Required
Asbestos	___	___	___	___	___
PCB	___	___	___	___	___
Radon	___	___	___	___	___
UST	___	___	___	___	___
Waste Sites	___	___	___	___	___
Other ___	___	___	___	___	___
___	___	___	___	___	___

2. Attach a brief explanation for each hazard requiring a Phase II assessment. List data deficiencies, test results etc., requiring further assessment.

3. Attach a brief explanation for each hazard that is acceptable but requires Operations and Maintenance (O & M) actions. What actions are required and how should they be performed?

4. Attach a brief explanation for each failed hazard that could be corrected with remedial actions. What actions are required and how should they be performed?

5. Underwriter's Comments.

Signature: _____ Date: _____

484

FannieMae

Multifamily

Conventional Selling
Environmental Hazards
Management Procedures

Exhibit 1

Exhibit 1 Phase I Environmental Assessment (Cont...)

– INFORMATION CHECKLIST –

Check the information sources used to perform the Phase I assessment.

1. *Overall Property Description*

_____ Building Specifications	_____ Neighborhood Zoning Maps
_____ Historical Aerial Photos	_____ Neighborhood Land Use Maps
_____ Current Aerial Photos	_____ List of Commercial Tenants
_____ Title History	On-site
_____ Site Survey	_____ Verification of Public Water and
_____ Interviews with Local	Sewer
Fire, Health, Land	_____ Interviews with Builder, and/or
Use or Environmental	Property Manager
Enforcement Officials	_____ Other _____

2. *Asbestos*

_____ Dated Building Construction or Rehabilitation Specifications
_____ Engineer's/Consultant's Asbestos Report
_____ Other _____

3. *Polychlorinated Biphenyls*

_____ Utility Transformer Records
_____ Site Survey of Transformers
_____ Site Soil and Groundwater PCB Test Results
_____ Other _____

4. *Radon*

_____ Water Utility Records
_____ Gas Utility Records
_____ On-Site Radon Test Results
_____ Other _____

5. *Underground Storage Tanks*

_____ Oil, Motor Fuel and Waste Oil Systems Reports
_____ CERCLIS/HWDMS Results on Neighborhood (within radius of one mile)
_____ Site Soil and Groundwater Tests
_____ Site Tank Survey
_____ Other _____

485

Exhibit 1 Phase I Environmental Assessment (Cont...)

6. *Waste Sites*
   _____ CERCLIS/HWDMS Results on neighborhoods (within radius of one mile)
   _____ State EPA site lists for neighborhoods (within radius of one mile)
   _____ Site Soil and Groundwater Test Results
   _____ Other _____

7. *Additional Hazards*
   _____ Urea Formaldehyde Foam Insulation Survey
   _____ Interior Air Test Results
   _____ Lead Paint Survey
   _____ Lead in Drinking Water Test Results
   _____ Other _____

486

FannieMae

Multifamily

Conventional Selling
Environmental Hazards
Management Procedures

Exhibit 1

Exhibit 1 Phase I Environmental Assessment (Cont...)

Answer all applicable questions by checking the appropriate box.
(Y — Yes, N — No, DK — Don't Know)

A. Asbestos   Y N DK

Note: All asbestos related assessments, testing, remedial action and
maintenance programs must be in compliance with EPA document
"Guidance for Controlling Asbestos — Containing Materials in
Buildings" (EPA 560/5-85-024, 1985).

1. Was the building constructed prior to 1979?   ☐ ☐ ☐

2. Does a site walk through reveal any visible evidence of asbestos?   ☐ ☐ ☐

3. Is there any documented evidence of asbestos?   ☐ ☐ ☐

   Note: If the answer to all three of the above questions is "no", then stop,
   the property is acceptable for asbestos. If the answer to any of the
   questions is "yes" or "don't know", answer the questions below.

4. Is there an asbestos survey by a certified, independent firm performed
   since 1979?   ☐ ☐ ☐

   Note: If the answer to question 4 is "yes", answer the question below.
   Otherwise, stop, a Phase II assessment is required.

5. Did the survey find the building to be free of treated or untreated ACM? ☐ ☐ ☐

   Note: If the answer to question 5 is "yes", then stop, the property is
   acceptable for asbestos. Otherwise, either the building fails or a
   Phase II assessment is required.

6. Underwriter's Comments:

487

Multifamily

Exhibit 1 Phase I Environmental Assessment (Cont....)

7. Phase I Assessment Results (circle one)

Acceptable	Acceptable Requires O & M	Fail	Fail, Possible Remedy	Phase II Required

8. Underwriter's Signature: _____

   Date: _____

B. Polychlorinated Biphenyls (PCBs)   Y N DK

1. Are there any florescent light ballasts containing PCBs in the building?   ☐ ☐ ☐

2. Are there any transformers or capacitors containing PCBs anywhere on the property?   ☐ ☐ ☐

3. Is there any visible or documented evidence of soil or groundwater contamination from PCBs on the property?   ☐ ☐ ☐

   Note: If the answer to all three questions is "no", then stop, the property is acceptable for PCBs. If the answer to any question is "don't know", then stop, a Phase II assessment is required. Otherwise, answer the questions below.

4. (If question 1 above is "yes") Are any of the lights damaged or leaking?   ☐ ☐ ☐

5. (If question 2 above is "yes") Are any of the capacitors or transformers inside residential buildings?   ☐ ☐ ☐

6. (If question 2 above is "yes") Are any of the transformers or capacitors not clearly marked, well maintained or secure?   ☐ ☐ ☐

7. (If question 2 above is "yes") Is there any evidence of leakage on or around the transformers or capacitors?   ☐ ☐ ☐

8. (If question 3 above is "yes") Have PCB concentrations of 50ppm or greater been found in contaminated soils or groundwater?   ☐ ☐ ☐

   Note: If the answers to questions 4, 5, 6, 7, and 8 are all "no", then the property is acceptable for PCBs. Otherwise, the property either fails or requires a Phase II assessment.

488

FannieMae

Multifamily

Conventional Selling
Environmental Hazards
Management Procedures

Exhibit 1

Exhibit 1 Phase I Environmental Assessment (Cont....)

9. Underwriter's Comments:

10. Phase I Assessment Results (circle one)

Acceptable	Acceptable Requires O & M	Fail	Fail, Possible Remedy	Phase II Required

11. Underwriter's Signature: _____

   Date: _____

C. Radon

Y N DK

1. Were the results of an EPA approved short-term radon test, performed in the basement within the last six months, at/or below 4 pCi/l or 0.02 WL?   ☐ ☐ ☐

   Note: If the answer is "no" or. "don't know", then stop, a Phase II assessment is required. If the answer is "yes", answer the questions below.

2. Is there any evidence that nearby structures have elevated indoor levels of radon or radon progeny?   ☐ ☐ ☐

3. Have local water supplies been found to have elevated levels of radon or radium?   ☐ ☐ ☐

4. Is the property located on or near sites that currently are or formerly were used for uranium, thorium, or radium extraction or for phosphate processing?   ☐ ☐ ☐

   Note: If the answer to questions 2, 3 or 4 is "yes", then a Phase II assessment is required. If the answer to questions 2, 3 and 4 is "no", then the property is acceptable for radon. A property may be acceptable for radon with a "don't know" answer for questions 2, 3 or 4 but the underwriter must justify the decision.

5. Underwriter's Comments:

489

Exhibit 1 Phase I Environmental Assessment (Cont....)

6. Phase I Assessment Results (circle one)

| Acceptable | Acceptable Requires O & M | Fail | Fail, Possible Remedy | Phase II Required |

7. Underwriter's Signature: _____

   Date: _____

D. Underground Storage Tanks (USTs)   Y N DK

   Note: In the questions below, "API" stands for "American Petroleum
         Institute" and NFPA stands for "National Fire Protection Association"

   1. Is there a current site survey performed by a qualified engineer which indi-
      cates that the property is free of any USTs?   ☐ ☐ ☐

   2. Is there any visible or documented evidence of soil or groundwater contami-
      nation on the property?   ☐ ☐ ☐

   3. Are there any petroleum storage and/or delivery facilities (including gas
      stations) or chemical manufacturing plants located on adjacent properties? ☐ ☐ ☐

      Note: If the answer to question 1 is "yes", and the answers to questions 2
            and 3 are "no", then stop, the property is acceptable for USTs. If the
            answer to question 2 or 3 is "yes" or "don't know", then stop, either
            the property fails or a Phase II assessment is required. Else, answer
            the questions below.

   4. Are there any active underground tank facilities on-site for such activities
      as motor fuel, waste oil or fuel oil storage?   ☐ ☐ ☐

   5. (If "yes" to question 4) Have these facilities been maintained in accordance
      with sound industry standards (e.g. API Bulletins 1621 and 1623; NFPA
      Bulletins 329, 70, 77 etc.)?   ☐ ☐ ☐

      Note: If the answer to 4 is "no", skip to question 8 below. If the answer to
            4 is "don't know" then stop, either the property fails or a Phase II
            assessment is required. If the answer to 5 is "no" or "don't know"
            then stop, either the property fails or a Phase II assessment is
            required. If the answer to both questions 4 and 5 is "yes", answer
            the questions below.

490

FannieMae

Multifamily

Conventional Selling
Environmental Hazards
Management Procedures

Exhibit 1

Exhibit 1 Phase I Environmental Assessment (Cont...)

6. (If "yes" to question 4) Are any of the tanks more than 10 years old? □ □ □

7. (If "yes" to question 6) Have any of the tanks that are more than 10 years old *not* been successfully tested for leaks within the last year using an API approved test? □ □ □

   Note: If the answer to question 6 is "no", answer the questions below. If the answer to question 6 is "don't know", then stop, either the property fails or a Phase II assessment is required. If the answer to question 7 is "no", then answer the questions below. Otherwise, stop, either the property fails or a Phase II assessment is required.

8. Are there any deactivated USTs on the property? □ □ □

9. (If "yes" to question 8). Were all of the tanks deactivated in accordance with sound industry practices (e.g. API Bulletins #1604 and #2202 or NFPA Bulletin #30)? □ □ □

   Note: If the answer to question 8 is "no", or if the answer to question 9 is "yes" then the property is acceptable for USTs. If the answer to question 8 is "don't know" or if the answer to question 9 is "no" or "don't know" then either the property fails or a Phase II assessment is required.

10. Underwriter's Comments:

11. Phase I Assessment Results (circle one)

Acceptable	Acceptable Requires O & M	Fail	Fail, Possible Remedy	Phase II Required

12. Underwriter's Signature: _____

    Date: _____

491

Exhibit 1 Phase I Environmental Assessment (Cont....)

E. Waste Disposal Facilities   Y N DK

1. Are there results of physical testing (including on-site sampling of soil and groundwater meeting all regulatory standards and sound industry practice) indicating that the property is free of waste contamination and is being operated in an environmentally safe manner?   ☐ ☐ ☐

2. Are there any obvious high risk neighbors in adjacent properties engaged in producing, storing or transporting hazardous waste, chemicals or substances?   ☐ ☐ ☐

   Note: If the answer to question 1 is "yes" and the answer to question 2 is "no", then stop, the property is acceptable for waste disposal facilities. Otherwise, answer questions below.

3. Was the site ever used for research, industrial or military purposes during the last 30 years?   ☐ ☐ ☐

4. Has any of the site space ever been leased to commercial tenants who are likely to have used, transported or disposed of toxic chemicals (e.g. dry cleaner, print shop, service station, etc.)?   ☐ ☐ ☐

5. Is water for the building provided either by a private company or directly from a well on the property?   ☐ ☐ ☐

6. Does the property or any site within 1 mile, appear on any state or federal list of hazardous waste sites (e.g. CERCLIS, HWDMS etc.)?   ☐ ☐ ☐

7. Is there any documented or visible evidence of dangerous waste handling on the subject property or neighboring sites (e.g. stressed vegetation, stained soil, open or leaking containers, foul fumes or smells, oily ponds etc.)?   ☐ ☐ ☐

   Note: If the answer to any of questions 2 through 6 are "yes" or "don't know", then either the property fails or a Phase II assessment is required. If the answer to all questions 2 through 6 are "no", then the property is acceptable for waste disposal facilities.

8. Underwriter's Comments:

492

FannieMae

Multifamily

Conventional Selling
Environmental Hazards
Management Procedures

Exhibit 1

Exhibit 1 Phase I Environmental Assessment (Cont...)

9. Phase I Assessment Results (circle one)

Acceptable	Acceptable Requires O & M	Fail	Fail, Possible Remedy	Phase II Required

10. Underwriter's Signature: _____

    Date: _____

F. Additional Hazards

                Y N DK

1. Is there any visible or documented evidence of peeling lead paint on the floors, walls or ceilings of tenant or common areas? ☐ ☐ ☐

   Note: If the answer to question 1 is "no", the property is acceptable for lead paint. Answer the questions below. If the answer is "yes" or "don't know", the property fails. The application may continue, but remedial actions to remove or cover all peeling lead paint must be taken prior to Commitment by Fannie Mae. Answer the questions below.

2. Do the tenant areas contain Urea Formaldehyde Foam Insulation that was installed less than a year ago? ☐ ☐ ☐

3. (If the answer to question 2 is "yes" or "don't know") Did the current HVAC system meet ASHRAE standards when it was installed? ☐ ☐ ☐

   Note: If the answer to question 2 is "no", or if the answer to question 3 is "yes", then the property is acceptable for UFFI. Answer the question below. If the answer to question 3 is "no" or "don't know", then the property fails. The application may continue, but the Lender must demonstrate prior to Commitment by Fannie Mae that the ventilation system currently meets ASHRAE standards.

4. Does the drinking water in the project contain lead at levels above 50 ppb? ☐ ☐ ☐

   Note: If the answer to question 4 is "yes" or "don't know", the property fails. Action must be taken prior to Commitment by Fannie Mae to reduce the lead content of the drinking water. Otherwise, the property is acceptable for lead in drinking water.

5. Underwriter's Comments:

Multifamily

Exhibit 1 Phase I Environmental Assessment (Cont....)

6. Phase I Assessment Results (circle one)

Acceptable	Acceptable Requires O & M	Fail	Fail, Possible Remedy	Phase II Required

7. Underwriter's Signature: _____

   Date: _____

494

Multifamily

Exhibit 2 Phase II Environmental Assessment

– PROPERTY LOG –

Fannie Mae Loan # _____

Property Address _____

_____

_____

Borrower Address _____

_____

_____

Borrower Phone _____

Lender Company Name _____

Individual Lender
Environmental Underwriter _____

Individual Environmental
Consultant _____

Firm Name and Address _____

_____

Consultant Phone _____

Date Assessment Completed _____

Assessment Results _____

495

Multifamily

Exhibit 2 Phase II Environmental Assessment (Cont...)

– SUMMARY OF RESULTS AND RECOMMENDATIONS –

1. Phase II Assessment Results: (Check results for each applicable hazard. Put "N/A" for those hazards not requiring a Phase II assessment.)

Hazard	Acceptable	Acceptable Requires O & M	Fail	Possible Remedy
Asbestos	_____	_____	___	_____
PCB	_____	_____	___	_____
Radon	_____	_____	___	_____
UST	_____	_____	___	_____
Waste Sites	_____	_____	___	_____
Other _____	_____	_____	___	_____
_____	_____	_____	___	_____
_____	_____	_____	___	_____

2. Attach a brief explanation for each hazard that is acceptable but requires O & M actions. What actions are required and how should they be performed?

3. Attach a brief explanation for each hazard that failed but could be corrected with remedial actions. What actions are required and how should they be performed?

4. Underwriter's Comments.

Signature: _____   Date: _____

5. Consultant's Comments.

Signature: _____   Date: _____

Name: _____

Title: _____

Company: _____

496

APPENDIX B

Thrift Bulletin

Handbook: Thrift Activities	Section: 210
Subjects: Lending Risk Assessment	TB 16

February 6, 1989

Environmental Risk and Liability

Summary: This Bulletin addresses the potential risks and liabilities that thrift institutions can incur as a result of adverse environmental factors. It also contains guidelines for the development of policies of reasonable due diligence to protect institutions against financial risks created by such factors.

For Further Information Contact:
The FHLBank District in which you are located or the Policy Analysis Division of the Office of Regulatory Activities, Washington, DC.

Thrift Bulletin 16

Introduction

Environmentally related hazards can be a source of high risk and potential liability to an insured institution or service corporation in connection with its mortgage or commercial loans and real estate investments. Potential environmental problems may exist in a myriad of forms such as asbestos insulation, underground storage tanks, surface impoundments, septic tank systems or oil and gas wells.

Thrift problems with pollution and hazardous waste contamination have grown as Federal, state and local governments have passed comprehensive environmental regulations and laws imposing liabilities on landowners and others for cleaning up the environment. Thrifts must be aware of and concerned with regulations that impose cleanup liability on an absolute or strict liability basis, particularly when governments have the right to assign liability to persons or entities no longer holding title to the property.

Potential Risks And Liabilities To Institutions

There are at least eight basic categories of risk that an association can face as a result of environmentally contaminated property. These include:

1. The risk that the collateral for a real estate loan or property to be acquired may be drastically reduced in value after discovery of the existence of hazardous waste contamination.

2. The risk that the borrower cannot repay the loan if the borrower must also pay for the cost of cleaning up the contaminated property. The cost for cleanup in many cases can be significant and may exceed the institution's encumbrance on the property.

3. The risk that a mortgage loan may lose priority to a cleanup lien imposed under the laws of those states that require super priority liens for the cost of cleanup. In each of these super lien states, a lien granted to the state securing the cost of cleaning up hazardous waste contamination may have priority over a lender's mortgage.

4. The risk that a lender may be liable to the extent of any credit extended to any debtor who has operated property containing hazardous wastes, has generated such waste, or has transported it in an improper manner. This risk extends to all creditors, not just those who hold as collateral the property containing the hazardous waste.

5. The risk that the thrift may become directly liable for the cost of cleaning up a site if it forecloses on a contaminated property or becomes involved in the management of a company that owns or operates a contaminated facility, or is involved in decisions pertaining to the disposal of toxic or hazardous waste.

6. The risk that a lender may not be able to pursue its foreclosure remedies and may have no practical alternative but to give up its loan security, and the right to recover on the loan itself. This could lead to charging off the loan balance.

7. The risk that the borrower does not maintain collateral or property with an environmental risk potential in an environmentally sound manner.

8. The risk that, aside from the statutory liabilities that can be imposed for toxic waste contamination, there is also potential liability for personal injury or property damage.

499

To address these potential risks and liabilities, thrifts should develop internal underwriting and risk management procedures and revise their mortgages, guarantees, indemnities, contracts, and other loan documents to protect themselves against potential environmental hazards and to maintain the value of their loans and real estate investments.

Purpose Of Environmental Risk Policy

The most expeditious means by which a thrift institution may commence protective action against potential environmental risks and liabilities is to develop and implement a written environmental risk policy. Such a policy will serve several critical purposes. It will:

1. establish a level of due diligence in all real estate transactions;

2. establish a means of identifying excessive environmental risk in properties being considered as collateral or for acquisition, or in properties being analyzed prior to foreclosure, or to meet standards set by buyers in the secondary market;

3. minimize environmental contamination of the borrower's property through the life of the loan by alerting institution staff to a potential problem property and providing for collateral monitoring and periodic property inspections throughout the loan term.

4. establish guidelines for a satisfactory inquiry into the uses of property and for other protective actions as needed to qualify for the "innocent landowner"[1] defense in the event that it acquires, through foreclosure or otherwise, a contaminated property that it could not have reasonably known to be contaminated; and

5. support the institution's adherence to the principles of safety and soundness.

Environmental Risk Policy Components

The following are essential components in an institution's environmental risk policy:

1. A stated assessment of potential environmental problems and liabilities. (i.e., an acknowledgement of the risks cited under "Potential Risks and Liabilities to Institutions" (pgs. 1 & 2)) and a declaration that a policy of due diligence is adopted to protect the institution from such risks.

2. A requirement that loan applicants provide information on environmental matters pertaining to their business and facilities. Institutions should develop a form covering specific questions to which applicants respond. The questions should request information concerning past, present or proposed uses of the proposed collateral, potential hazards, insurance availability for the property as it pertains to environmental matters, and contacts by any Federal, state or local government agencies concerning environmental matters that must be resolved in order to obtain business and environmental permits.

3. A requirement that an acquiring institution, in a purchase or participation loan, ensure that adequate due diligence regarding environmental risk matters has been met by the lead lender and a requirement that all loans sold to Freddie Mac or Fannie Mae meet with the environmental due diligence standards imposed by those agencies.

4. A requirement that all loan requests, in which the proposed real property collateral has a higher environmental risk potential than other types of real property, have a Phase I Environmental Risk Report (See Appendix) prepared for the institution prior to approval of the loan.

Most one-to-four family residential properties will not need a Phase I Environmental Risk Report. If cursory property inspections or records research, however, disclose a high potential for environmental risk, then Phase I reports are likely necessary.

Examples of properties that should have a Phase I Environmental Risk Report include:

a. Proposed construction properties (other than a proposed individual one-to-four family residential property).

b. Industrial properties and properties on industrially zoned land.

c. Properties located close to industrial areas.

d. Properties that include or are close to an existing or former gas station site.

e. Commercial properties that include an automotive repair facility or a dry cleaning establishment where the work is done on the premises.

f. Properties adjacent to railroad tracks or underground pipelines (excluding one-to-four family residential properties).

---

[1] an exemption from liability for an innocent landowner who acquires property unaware of the presence of hazardous material. The landowner must not have conducted, permitted or contributed to the release of hazardous substances and must have had, after appropriate inquiry, no knowledge of the pollution at the time the property was acquired.

500

g. Properties that have served as or are close to a refuse or waste disposal site.

h. Properties where the past uses or the surrounding uses include the storage of or usage of hazardous or toxic substances (e.g., pesticides).

i. Properties suspected of containing asbestos material that is or may be friable (easily crumbled or crushed into powder and capable of being absorbed into the environment).

j. Properties where the emanation of radon gas from the soil may result in detrimental health effects to building occupants. (Institutions may need to consult with qualified environmental firms regarding the seriousness of radon problems in specific areas.)

k. Residential properties where there are known hazardous conditions on or in the property's immediate vicinity: where Superfund sites[2] exist within a one mile radius; where the site is in close proximity to oil and gas production; where there is asbestos within the building structure; where the site is a corner lot property (and is known to have been previously used as a gas station locale); or where the historic use of the property prior to its residential zoning is cause for concern.

[2] Sites identified by the Environmental Protection Agency (EPA) from which hazardous substance releases occurred or from which releases could occur (e.g., abandoned hazardous waste dumps and chemical spills). The EPA is authorized to undertake removal or remedial actions at such sites.

5. The designation by the institution's board of directors or senior management of one or more qualified staff persons as the association's "designated environmental risk analyst(s)". These staff members should receive special training through courses or seminars in reviewing and interpreting environmental risk reports for the institution, and should assist in the development of the institution's environmental risk policy.

6. Criteria for the selection and retention of a roster of qualified environmental experts retained for risk analysis reports. The association should confirm that the organization or individual has appropriate education, training and experience. The consultant should not be affiliated with the buyer or seller of the property nor with a firm engaged in any business that might present a conflict of interest.

7. A requirement that it will be the loan officer's responsibility (after consultation with the designated environmental risk analyst) to order the Phase I Environmental Risk Report on the subject property as needed. Guidelines regarding environmental risk reports follow:

a. The association must be the client on the environmental risk report. This provision will maximize the likelihood that the institution will receive an objective report that discloses all of the pertinent facts.

b. The institution should only use environmental risk auditors from its approved roster.

c. The loan officer, with assistance from the institution's designated environmental risk analyst, should have the

responsibility to review the outside environmental audit reports and judge the conclusions of the report after consulting with any environmental risk resources considered necessary. Final acceptance of environmental risk reports and decisions concerning the information in the report should be made by the institution's senior management.

8. A requirement that appraisal reports fully disclose the findings and take into consideration any environmental risk factors and related costs identified in environmental risk reports.

9. A requirement that any potential environmental problems noted in an environmental risk report be considered by the institution's required approval authority and senior management before the loan is approved or the property is purchased.

10. Criteria for determining the circumstances in which loan requests may be declined due to environmental factors. Some reasons for declining loans based on environmental factors are:

a. The structure is built over a sanitary landfill or other solid, hazardous or municipal waste disposal site.

b. There are materials containing friable asbestos or substantial amounts of non-friable asbestos that cannot be safely encapsulated or removed or will not be routinely inspected and maintained by the borrower.

c. There is evidence of spills or soil or groundwater contamination on or around the loan applicant's properties.

501

d. There is documented soil or groundwater contamination on the subject property and:

i. physical constraints posed by the site specific geology, geohydrology or subsurface structure render corrective actions technically impossible; or

ii. constraints render treatment processes or disposal options prohibitively expensive, i.e., beyond the financial capabilities of the current owner; or

iii. environmental hazards or potential hazards exceed the value of the land or the requested loan amount; or

iv. potentially responsible parties are unwilling or financially incapable of instituting corrective actions on neighboring properties.

e. There is laboratory analysis of soil and groundwater samples that indicates they exceed action levels established by government agencies.

f. There is polychlorinated biphenyls (PCB) contamination where:

i. physical constraints posed by the site specific geology, geohydrology or subsurface structure render corrective actions technically impossible; or

ii. constraints render treatment processes or disposal options prohibitively expensive (i.e., beyond the financial capabilities of the current owner).

g. There are radon levels above acceptable limits that can only be remedied through large capital improvements or extensive ongoing maintenance programs that are beyond the financial or technical capability of the borrower.

h. There are conditions that represent violations of applicable local, state or Federal environmental or public health statutes and laws.

i. The properties are currently the subject of environmental or public health litigation or administrative action from private parties or public officials.

11. Procedures for reviewing collateral before completion of foreclosure procedures or acceptance of a deed in lieu of foreclosure. The procedures may include, but should not be limited to:

a. A review of the existing loan file (including site inspection, leases, reports and completion of an environmental checklist).

b. A review of the loan documents and any subsequent modifications.

c. A determination as to whether any guarantees or indemnities were obtained on the loan.

d. A determination as to whether the borrower has any environmental impairment insurance or other applicable insurance that could be utilized for an environmental hazard claim.

e. A review of the current tenants and real property uses.

f. Procurement of a Phase I Environmental Risk Report if conditions suggest it is necessary.

12. An acknowledgement of the importance of coordination and cooperation among the institution's loan origination department, its loan servicing department, its designated environmental risk analyst, its legal counsel, and its appraisers, to carry out the environmental risk policy and to enlist the help of environmental specialists and applicable government agencies in this endeavor.

— Darrel W. Dochow, Executive Director

502

The following is a brief description of the various types of environmental risk reports that institutions may need to employ.

1. A Phase I Environmental Risk Report is a qualitative assessment of the property. A typical Phase I Report includes, but is not limited to:

a. A historical review of the use and improvements made to the subject site.

b. A review of building, zoning, planning, sewer, water, fire, environmental and other department records that would have information on or have an interest in the property and neighboring sites.

c. A review of the Department of Health Services, Solid Waste Management Board, Regional Water Quality Control Board, Air Quality Management District, and other Boards or Agencies records and files whose actions may affect the subject property and neighboring properties.

d. An investigation of the subject property and neighboring properties with regard to the Environmental Protection Agency's National Priority List or Comprehensive Environmental Response Compensation and Liability Information System (CERCLIS) list and similar state lists.

e. An inspection of the site and all improvements with particular attention to the use of hazardous materials in the structures or operating equipment.

f. A verification as to whether present or past owners or tenants have stored, created or discharged hazardous materials or waste, and review of whether appropriate procedures, safeguards, permits and notices are in place.

g. An analysis of old aerial photographs to determine the construction or destruction of buildings and the existence of ponds and disposal areas on the property over time.

h. Interviews with neighbors to determine prior uses of the subject property (if appropriate and only if deemed acceptable by the parties involved in the transaction). Confidentiality must be recognized.

i. A review of building records and a visual inspection of the building(s) to determine if asbestos-containing building materials may be present.

j. A review of scientific literature to determine the potential existence of radon in the soil.

k. A written report summarizing the findings.

2. Phase II Environmental Risk Report

A Phase II Report is performed if "red flags" are apparent to the lender or if they are disclosed during the Phase I investigation. This report consists of all Phase I activities plus combinations of the following field tests and activities.

a. Testing of underground storage tanks for content and integrity.

b. Soil gas analysis to identify the potential for petroleum hydrocarbons and volatile organic compounds such as industrial solvents and dry cleaning chemicals.

c. Bulk soil sampling.

d. Groundwater sampling if groundwater may be impacted by land activities.

e. Limited surface water sampling if there is a pond, lagoon or stream on the property.

f. A comprehensive review of the regional and local geology to determine the pathways leaked chemicals would follow in the event of a spill or leak.

g. A list of individual groundwater wells or subsurface water bodies that may be affected by a spill or leak.

h. A comprehensive inspection of the building for asbestos-containing building materials. This should include collecting and analyzing samples of the building material for friable asbestos. It is strongly recommended that inspections be performed by EPA-certified inspectors and analyses be completed according to EPA guidelines.

i. If no listed hazardous materials or waste are found, an appropriate verification should be provided.

j. A written report summarizing the finding.

3. Phase III Environmental Risk Report

A Phase III Environmental Risk Report is much more detailed and consists of all of the Phase I and Phase II activities in addition to involved soils, water and air quality analyses. As in a Phase I and Phase II Report, a Phase III Report also includes a written report summarizing the findings of the investigation.

Based upon the Phase I, Phase II or Phase III report results, subsequent steps regarding further assessment, corrective action or preventative programs should be submitted. This should include gross cost estimates for correcting any discovered contamination

Institutions should not hesitate to contact environmental firms and question the principal investigator for the project regarding observations, conclusions and recommendations made in the environmental assessment reports.

503

APPENDIX C

102D CONGRESS
1ST SESSION

H. R. 1643

To clarify the liability of lending institutions under the Comprehensive Environmental Response, Compensation, and Liability Act of 1980, and for other purposes.

IN THE HOUSE OF REPRESENTATIVES

MARCH 22, 1991

Mr. OWENS of Utah (for himself, Mr. WELDON, Mrs. MEYERS of Kansas, and Mr. DELLUMS) introduced the following bill; which was referred to the Committee on Energy and Commerce

---

A BILL

To clarify the liability of lending institutions under the Comprehensive Environmental Response, Compensation, and Liability Act of 1980, and for other purposes.

1   *Be it enacted by the Senate and House of Representa-*

2   *tives of the United States of America in Congress assembled,*

3   **SECTION 1. SHORT TITLE.**

4   This Act may be cited as the "Superfund Liability

5   Clarification Act".

1 SEC. 2. CLARIFICATION OF LIABILITY OF LENDERS UNDER

2   COMPREHENSIVE   ENVIRONMENTAL   RE-

3   SPONSE,   COMPENSATION,   AND   LIABILITY

4   ACT OF 1980.

5   (a) CLARIFICATION OF SECURITY INTEREST EXEMP-

6 TION.—Paragraph (20) of section 101 of the Com-

7 prehensive Environmental Response, Compensation, and

8 Liability Act of 1980 (42 U.S.C. 9601(20)) is amended—

9   (1) by striking out the last sentence of subpara-

10   graph (A); and

11   (2) by adding at the end the following new sub-

12   paragraph:

13   "(E)(i) The term 'owner or operator' does not

14   include a person, who, without participating in the

15   management of a vessel or facility, holds indicia of

16   ownership primarily to protect his security interest

17   in the vessel or facility. The exclusion of the preced-

18   ing sentence shall apply to any mortgage lender, in-

19   sured depository institution, or Federal lending in-

20   stitution who acquires the vessel or facility through

21   foreclosure or who conducts a restructuring of a loan

22   or other extension of credit with the owner of the

23   vessel or facility, if such mortgage lender, insured

24   depository institution, or Federal lending institution

25   complies with procedures or guidelines imposed pur-

26   suant to clause (iii). For purposes of the exclusion

1   in the first sentence of this subparagraph, the

2   phrase 'participation in the management of a vessel

3   or facility' does not include—

4   "(I) selling collateral;

5   "(II) actions taken by a mortgage lender,

6   insured depository institution, or Federal lend-

7   ing institution to comply with procedures or

8   guidelines imposed pursuant to clause (iii), in-

9   cluding the conduct of a Phase I Environmental

10   Audit of the vessel or facility (as such term is

11   used in paragraph (35)(C) of this section);

12   "(III) actions taken by a mortgage lender,

13   insured depository institution, or Federal lend-

14   ing institution to responsibly manage the vessel

15   or facility upon learning of any contamination

16   so as not to cause a release of a hazardous sub-

17   stance from or at the vessel or facility or to

18   harm the public health and safety or the envi-

19   ronment, during any period while the lender or

20   institution is acting to administer or wind down

21   the affairs of the owner of the vessel or facility

22   or while diligently proceeding to pass title of the

23   vessel or facility;

1   "(IV) the status of having the capacity or

2   ability to affect hazardous waste disposal man-

3   agement decisions of the vessel or facility; or

4   "(V) engaging in so-called 'work-out' ac-

5   tivities, including restructuring or renegotiation

6   of the terms of a loan or other obligation, pay-

7   ment of additional interest, extension of a pay-

8   ment period, specific or general financial advice,

9   suggestions, counseling, guidance, or other ac-

10   tions reasonably necessary to protect a security

11   interest.".

12   (b) DEFINITIONS.—Subparagraph (E) of section

13 101(20) of the Comprehensive Environmental Response,

14 Compensation, and Liability Act of 1980 (42 U.S.C.

15 9601(20)), as added by subsection (a), is amended by add-

16 ing after clause (i) the following:

17   "(ii) For purposes of this subparagraph:

18   "(I) The term 'indicia of ownership' means

19   evidence of interests in real or personal prop-

20   erty held as security for a loan or other obliga-

21   tion.

22   "(II) The term 'primarily to protect a se-

23   curity interest' means, with respect to indicia of

24   ownership in a vessel or facility, that the indicia

25   of ownership are held for the purpose of secur-

1 ing payment or performance of an obligation

2 and not for protecting an investment.

3 "(III) The term 'acquires the vessel or fa-

4 cility through foreclosure' means that the vessel

5 or facility is acquired through conveyance pur-

6 suant to the terms of an extension of credit pre-

7 viously contracted, or through purchase at sales

8 under judgment or decree, power of sale, or

9 from a trustee, if such property was security for

10 an extension of credit previously contracted.

11 "(IV) The term 'extension of credit' in-

12 cludes lease transactions that are functionally

13 equivalent to a secured loan and that are au-

14 thorized by and comply with regulations issued

15 by the appropriate Federal banking agency or

16 State banking authority.

17 "(V) The term 'insured depository institu-

18 tion' has the meaning given such term by sec-

19 tion 3 of the Federal Deposit Insurance Act

20 and includes an insured credit union and a leas-

21 ing company that is an affiliate of an insured

22 depository institution. The term also includes

23 the Federal Deposit Insurance Corporation, the

24 National Credit Union Administrator Board,

25 and the Resolution Trust Corporation, in such

1 corporations' or Board's capacity as con-

2 servator, receiver, or liquidating agency for any

3 insured depository institution described in the

4 preceding sentence.

5 "(VI) The term 'mortgage lender' means a

6 person who is regularly engaged in the business

7 of making extensions of credit secured, in whole

8 or in part, by real property to nonaffiliated par-

9 ties.

10 "(VII) The term 'Federal lending institu-

11 tion' includes any agency, department, or other

12 unit of the United States Government not oth-

13 erwise described in this clause which makes

14 loans on the security of any vessel or facility,

15 including economic and industrial development

16 agencies.".

17 (c) ENVIRONMENTAL RESPONSIBILITIES.—Subpara-

18 graph (E) of section 101(20) of the Comprehensive Envi-

19 ronmental Response, Compensation, and Liability Act of

20 1980 (42 U.S.C. 9601(20)) is further amended by adding

21 after clause (ii) the following:

22 "(iii) For purposes of this subparagraph, the

23 Administrator, in consultation with each appropriate

24 Federal banking agency, the National Credit Union

25 Administration Board, and each Federal lending in-

1   stitution, shall take necessary actions to assure that

2   depository and lending institutions develop and im-

3   plement adequate procedures to evaluate potential

4   environmental risks that may arise from or at ves-

5   sels or facilities subject to their lending activities.

6   The Administrator, in consultation with the Sec-

7   retary of the Department of Housing and Urban De-

8   velopment, shall promulgate guidelines to assure

9   that mortgage lenders develop and implement equiv-

10   alent procedures to evaluate potential environmental

11   risks that may arise from or at vessels or facilities

12   subject to their lending activities.".

13   (d) LIABILITY NOTWITHSTANDING EXCLUSION.—

14 Subparagraph (E) of section 101(20) of the Com-

15 prehensive Environmental Response, Compensation, and

16 Liability Act of 1980 (42 U.S.C. 9601(20)) is further

17 amended by adding after clause (iii) the following:

18   "(iv) Nothing in this subparagraph shall affect

19   the liability under this Act of a person who, by any

20   act or omission, causes or contributes to a release or

21   threatened release of a hazardous substance from or

22   at a vessel or facility.".

23   (e) REGULATIONS.—The Administrator of the Envi-

24 ronmental Protection Agency shall promulgate regulations

25 to carry out the amendments made by this section.

1   (f) EFFECTIVE DATE.—The amendments made by
2 this section shall take effect on the date of the enactment
3 of this Act.

4 SEC. 3. CLARIFICATION OF INNOCENT LANDOWNER DE-
5   FENSE UNDER COMPREHENSIVE ENVIRON-
6   MENTAL RESPONSE, COMPENSATION, AND LI-
7   ABILITY ACT OF 1980.

8   (a) CLARIFICATION.—Section 101(35) of the Com-
9 prehensive Environmental Response, Compensation, and
10 Liability Act of 1980 (42 U.S.C. 9601(35)) is amended
11 by redesignating subparagraphs (C) and (D) as sub-
12 paragraphs (D) and (E), respectively, and inserting after
13 subparagraph (B), the following:

14   "(C)(i) A defendant who has acquired real property
15 establishes a rebuttable presumption that he has made all
16 appropriate inquiry within the meaning of subparagraph
17 (B) if he establishes that, immediately prior to or at the
18 time of acquisition, he obtained or conducted a Phase I
19 Environmental Audit of the real property which meets the
20 requirements of this subparagraph.

21   "(ii) For purposes of this subparagraph, the term
22 'certified environmental professional' means an individual
23 (or an entity managed or controlled by such individual)
24 who is certified under a State certification program that
25 complies with criteria promulgated in regulations by the

1 Administrator as being qualified to conduct one or more
2 aspects of a Phase I Environmental Audit. Such term may
3 include engineers, environmental consultants, and attor-
4 neys. For purposes of this subparagraph, the term 'Phase
5 I Environmental Audit' means an investigation of the real
6 property, conducted by a certified environmental profes-
7 sional, to determine or discover any indications of the
8 presence or likely presence of a release or threatened re-
9 lease of hazardous substances on the real property and
10 which complies with standards for environmental audits
11 established by the American Society for Testing and Mate-
12 rials (hereinafter referred to as 'ASTM') and contained
13 in regulations promulgated by the Administrator.

14   "(iii) Notwithstanding any other provision of this
15 paragraph, if the Phase I Environmental Audit reveals the
16 presence or likely presence of a release or threatened re-
17 lease of hazardous substances on the real property to be
18 acquired, no presumption shall arise under clause (i) with
19 respect to such release or threatened release unless the
20 defendant has taken reasonable steps, in accordance with
21 current technology available, existing regulations, and gen-
22 erally acceptable engineering practices, as may be nec-
23 essary to confirm the absence of such release or threat-
24 ened release.".

1   (b) REGULATIONS.—The Administrator of the Envi-

2 ronmental Protection Agency shall promulgate regulations

3 to carry out the amendment made by this section. The

4 regulations shall include standards for environmental au-

5 dits as recommended by the ASTM.

6   (c) INTERIM ENVIRONMENTAL AUDIT STANDARDS.—

7 (1) During the period beginning on the date of the enact-

8 ment of this Act and ending on the effective date of the

9 regulations relating to standards for environmental audits

10 promulgated under this section, the definition of the term

11 "Phase I Environmental Audit" and related provisions

12 contained in paragraphs (2), (3) and (4) of this subsection

13 shall apply for purposes of section 101(35)(20)(C) of the

14 Comprehensive Environmental Response, Compensation,

15 and Liability Act of 1980 (as added by subsection (a)).

16   (2) During the period referred to in paragraph (1),

17 the term "Phase I Environmental Audit" means an inves-

18 tigation of the real property, conducted by a certified envi-

19 ronmental professional, to determine or discover any indi-

20 cations of the presence or likely presence of a release or

21 threatened release of hazardous substances on the real

22 property and which consists of a review of each of the fol-

23 lowing sources of information concerning the previous

24 ownership and uses of the real property:

1   (A) Recorded chain of title documents regard-
2   ing the real property, including all deeds, easements,
3   leases, restrictions, and covenants for a period of 50
4   years.

5   (B) Aerial photographs, maps, and other appro-
6   priate historical information which may reflect prior
7   uses of the real property and which are reasonably
8   obtainable through State or local government agen-
9   cies.

10   (C) Recorded environmental cleanup liens
11   against the real property which have arisen pursuant
12   to Federal, State, and local statutes.

13   (D) Reasonably obtainable Federal, State, and
14   local government records of sites or facilities where
15   there has been a release of hazardous substances
16   and which are likely to cause or contribute to a re-
17   lease or threatened release of hazardous substances
18   on the real property, including investigation reports
19   for such sites or facilities; Federal, State, and local
20   environmental reports required by law; reasonably
21   obtainable Federal, State, and local government en-
22   vironmental records of activities likely to cause or
23   contribute to a release or a threatened release of
24   hazardous substances on the real property, including
25   landfill and other disposal location records, under-

1   ground storage tank records, hazardous waste han-

2   dler and generator records and spill reporting

3   records; and such other reasonably obtainable Fed-

4   eral, State, and local government environmental

5   records which report incidents or activities which are

6   likely to cause or contribute to a release or threat-

7   ened release of hazardous substances on the real

8   property.

9   (E) A visual site inspection of the real property

10   and all facilities and improvements on the real prop-

11   erty, and a visual inspection of immediately adjacent

12   properties from the real property, including an in-

13   vestigation of any chemical use, storage, treatment

14   and disposal practices on the property. Such visual

15   inspection shall include notation of discolored soil,

16   stressed or discolored vegetation, any sheen on

17   water, dead or sick animals, strange smells, and the

18   presence of any barrel, tank, container, or sump.

19   (F) A visual site inspection of adjacent prop-

20   erty, to the extent permitted by the owners or opera-

21   tors of such property.

22   (3) For purposes of paragraph (2), a record shall be

23 considered to be reasonably obtainable if the record, a

24 copy of the record, or a reasonable facsimile of the record

1 is obtainable from a government agency by request within

2 30 days after submission of a request.

3 (4) During the period referred to in paragraph (1),

4 no presumption shall arise under clause (i) of section 101

5 (35)(20)(C) of the Comprehensive Environmental Re-

6 sponse, Compensation, and Liability Act of 1980 (as

7 added by subsection (a)) unless the defendant has main-

8 tained a compilation of the information reviewed in the

9 course of the Phase I Environmental Audit.

10 (d) EFFECTIVE DATE.—The amendment made by

11 this section shall take effect on the date of the enactment

12 of this Act.

O